THE GOTHS IN SPAIN

THE GOTHS IN SPAIN

BY

E. A. THOMPSON

OXFORD
AT THE CLARENDON PRESS

1969

Oxford University Press, Ely House, London W. 1

GLASGOW NEW YORK TORONTO MELBOURNE WELLINGTON
CAPE TOWN SALISBURY IBADAN NAIROBI LUSAKA ADDIS ABABA
BOMBAY CALCUTTA MADRAS KARACHI LAHORE DACCA
KUALA LUMPUR SINGAPORE HONG KONG TOKYO

PRINTED IN GREAT BRITAIN

PREFACE

THERE is a difference between writing a history of the Goths in Spain and composing a history of Spain in the Gothic period. The writer of a general history of Spain in the sixth and seventh centuries would centre his work on the towering figure of St. Isidore of Seville. Indeed, the development of Latin literature in this period would fill a large part of his book. He would write at length on the sources of the Visigothic laws. He would not neglect the Treasure of Guarrazar and those strangely attractive little churches of the seventh century which survive here and there in remote parts of the Spanish countryside as well as in the crypt of the Cathedral of Palencia. The direct and indirect influence of Byzantine art on the art of Visigothic Spain is a problem that has been studied in recent years with some positive results.

Such are the subjects, some may think, that give interest to the history of Spain in the centuries that elapsed between the fall of Roman power there and the landing of the Saracens at Gibraltar. On not one of them shall I have a word to say.

My concern is with the Goths, who ruled Spain for two centuries. What were the political and military achievements of their kings? How did they govern their subjects, Roman as well as Gothic? How much of the administrative machine of the Roman Emperors did they preserve? What manner of civil service of their own did they evolve? What changes, if any, can be traced in their system of government during these two hundred years? What can be learned of their armed forces? Did the Arian kings persecute their Catholic subjects? If not, what limits did they set to the freedom of the Catholic Church? What was the character of the Councils of Toledo? To what extent did Goths rise to high office in the seventh-century Church? These are some of the questions that I have tried to answer.

But even here there are lamentable omissions. Thus, it is at present all but impossible to analyse the reasons for the dramatic collapse of Visigothic power before the Arab assault; and so it will remain until far more work has been done on the period as a whole. The first Englishman to discuss the fall of the kingdom and to try

to account for it was St. Boniface. Writing to King Ethelbald of
Mercia (*Ep.* 73, Tangl) in 746–7, he put it down to the Goths'
moral degeneracy and their homosexual practices. It is not clear
that modern research, such as it is, has gone very much deeper. The
fact is that, in comparison with England and France in these two
centuries, Spain has aroused extraordinarily little interest among
students of history outside Spain—and what has been written in
Spanish has not always been illuminating. True, valuable works
have appeared : some of them are listed on p. xiii below. But their
number is minute; and no comprehensive history of the Goths
in Spain has been published in the twentieth century except by
Spaniards. This is a pity. We cannot afford to be ignorant of so long
and so fruitful a period of Spanish history. Part of the reason for
our neglect may perhaps lie in the fact that our sources hardly ever
give us a glimpse of the personality of the kings or bishops of that
day. We grievously miss the work of some Spanish Procopius or of
a Gregory of some Spanish Tours. And so the impression has
gained ground that the history of Spain in these centuries is 'dry',
that it is concerned not with men and women but simply with
columns of Mansi and Migne, pages of Zeumer and Mommsen.
Perhaps it is so; but, whatever the reason, the neglect is regrettable.

   The result is that a number of questions are raised in the following pages which, so far as I can discover, have not been asked
before. Here are two examples. We know—though some Spanish
scholars have unwisely denied it—that King Reccesuinth abolished
the use of Roman law in his kingdom. But the evidence seems to
suggest further that he carried through at the same time a most
far-reaching and striking reform of the administration. What was
its nature? What were his motives? Again, the minutes of the
Councils of Toledo supply us with magnificent lists of the Spanish
bishops. What was the numerical relation of Gothic bishops to
Roman bishops? The answer can be found by counting names, but
it gives rise to a question of baffling obscurity. Was there some
tension, which our other sources conceal from us, between Goths
and Romans in the higher reaches of the Catholic Church? I hope
that scholars will tackle these and other questions; for the purpose
of this book is to incite others to fill some of the numberless gaps
in our knowledge of that dark period of history.

   Some of my omissions, then, and the narrow view which I
appear to take of history, have been forced upon me by the lack of

preliminary studies of Visigothic Spain. Others are self-imposed. I am not competent to discuss those creeds which the seventh-century bishops set out at the beginning of several of their councils, or the mysterious appearance of the *Filioque* clause in the acts of the Third Council of Toledo, or the heresy of the Monotheletes and the Spanish bishops' reaction to it in the reigns of Erwig and Egica. These are matters for theologians, whose powers of concentration are superior to mine. Still further omissions are forced upon us all by the nature of our evidence. Political history scarcely figures in it at all; and, if we leave aside our knowledge of the kings' attitude to usurpers and to the Jews, very little is left. And, finally, I disregard the Sueves of Galicia so far as possible. Most of our evidence about them relates to the fifth century; and I hope to discuss it elsewhere.

Unless otherwise stated, I accept the chronology proposed by K. Zeumer, 'Die Chronologie der Westgothenkönige des Reiches von Toledo', *NA* xxvii (1902), pp. 409–44. For the acts of the Church councils I cite the text of Mansi but have checked it, often with much profit, against that published by J. Vives, *Concilios visigóticos e Hispano-Romanos* (Barcelona–Madrid, 1963). The card-index on which I base my figures in Chapter Twelve was drawn up on Vives's text. No use has been made of the so-called *Fragmenta Gaudenziana*, of which a text is conveniently printed by Zeumer in his edition of the laws; for we still do not know when or where that document was written or for what purpose it was designed. With one exception I have rigorously adhered to the rule of using no sources except those that were written in the sixth or seventh century. Chronicles and other documents composed between the ninth and the thirteenth centuries have been ruthlessly ignored. They contain much lively information, which is open to no criticism except that of being fictional. The one exception is the Chronicle of 754, which, however untrustworthy its narrative may be, can certainly not be ignored.

I have used modern place-names throughout and have added the old Roman name in brackets after each of them. Thus, even a small atlas will enable the reader to identify the various places. I owe much to having been awarded a Leverhulme Research Fellowship in 1966, which made it possible to visit many of the most important sites.

CONTENTS

ABBREVIATIONS

AFTER citations of the chronicles I add in brackets a reference to the volume and page of Mommsen, *Chronica Minora*.

Barlow Claude W. Barlow, *Martini Episcopi Bracarensis Opera Omnia* (Yale, 1950).

CTh *Codex Theodosianus*, ed. T. Mommsen and P. M. Meyer.

Epist. Wisig. *Epistolae Wisigoticae*, ed. W. Gundlach, in *Epistolae Merowingici et Karolini Aevi*, i, MGH (Berlin, 1892).

Fiebiger–Schmidt Otto Fiebiger and Ludwig Schmidt, *Inschriftensammlung zur Geschichte der Ostgermanen*, Kais. Akademie d. Wissenschaften in Wien: phil.-hist. Klasse, Denkschriften, 60. Band, 3. Abhandlung (Vienna, 1917).

Fontaine Jacques Fontaine, *Isidore de Séville et la culture classique dans l'Espagne wisigothique* (Paris, 1959).

Garvin see *VPE*.

Grosse R. Grosse, *Las fuentes de la época visigoda y bizantina*, fasc. ix of A. Schulten and L. Pericot, *Fontes Hispaniae Antiquae* (Barcelona, 1947).

HF *Historia Francorum*.

HG *Historia Gothorum*.

Hillgarth J. N. Hillgarth, 'La conversión de los visigodos: notas críticas', *Analecta Sacra Tarraconensia*, xxxiv (1961), pp. 21–46.

Jones A. H. M. Jones, *The Later Roman Empire, 284–602* (Blackwell, Oxford, 1964).

Juster J. Juster, 'La condition légale des Juifs sous les rois visigoths', *Études d'histoire juridique offertes à P. F. Girard*, ii (Paris, 1913), pp. 275–335.

Katz S. Katz, *The Jews in the Visigothic and Frankish Kingdoms of Spain and Gaul* (Cambridge, Mass., 1937).

LV *Leges Visigothorum*, ed. K. Zeumer, MGH, *Legum Sectio i* (Hannover and Leipzig, 1902).

Lynch C. H. Lynch, *St. Braulio, Bishop of Saragossa (631–651), His Life and Writings* (Washington, 1938).

Magnin E. Magnin, *L'Église wisigothique au VIIe siècle*, i (Paris, 1912).

Mansi J. Mansi, *Sacrorum Conciliorum nova et amplissima Collectio*.

Martinez Diez   Gonzalo Martinez Diez, *La colección canónica Hispana,* i (Madrid–Barcelona, 1966).

McKenna   S. McKenna, *Paganism and Pagan Survivals in Spain up to the Fall of the Visigothic Kingdom* (Washington, 1938).

Menendez Pidal   R. Menendez Pidal (ed.), *Historia de España,* iii (Madrid, 1940).

MGH   Monumenta Germaniae Historica.

Miles   George C. Miles, *The Coinage of the Visigoths of Spain: Leovigild to Achila II* (New York, 1952).

Mommsen   T. Mommsen, *Chronica Minora,* 3 vols. in the MGH.

Mullins   Sister P. J. Mullins, *The Spiritual Life According to St. Isidore of Seville* (Washington, 1940).

NA   *Neues Archiv der Gesellschaft für ältere deutsche Geschichtskunde.*

PL   J. P. Migne, *Patrologia Latina.*

REB   *Revue des études byzantines.*

Scott   C. A. A. Scott, *Ulfilas, Apostle of the Goths* (Cambridge, 1885).

Séjourné   P. Séjourné, *Le Dernier Père de l'Église: St. Isidore de Séville* (Paris, 1929).

Settimane   *Settimane di Studio del centro italiano di studi sull'alto medioevo,* esp. vol. iii (Spoleto, 1956).

Stein   E. Stein, *Histoire du Bas-empire* (Paris, 1949-59).

Stroheker   K. F. Stroheker, *Germanentum und Spätantike* (Zürich and Stuttgart, 1965).

Thompson   E. A. Thompson, *The Visigoths in the Time of Ulfila* (Oxford, 1966).

Tomasini   Wallace J. Tomasini, *The Barbaric Tremissis in Spain and Southern France: Anastasius to Leovigild* (New York, 1964).

Vives   J. Vives, *Inscripciones cristianas de la España romana y visigoda* (Barcelona, 1942).

VPE   *Vitas Sanctorum Patrum Emeretensium,* ed. J. N. Garvin (Washington, 1946).

Wallace-Hadrill   J. M. Wallace-Hadrill, *The Long-haired Kings* (Methuen, London, 1962).

Zeiss   Hans Zeiss, *Die Grabfunde aus dem spanischen Westgotenreich,* (Berlin, 1934).

Zeumer   This name unqualified means Zeumer's edn. of the *LV.*

Ziegler   A. K. Ziegler, *Church and State in Visigothic Spain* (Washington, 1930).

fact, however, a similar history, language, and religion counted for little, and the three peoples faced the sixth century in isolation from one another. We can study them separately, and a narrative of Visigothic history in the sixth and seventh centuries need contain few references to Italy or Africa.

In 418 the Roman government had settled the Visigoths in the province of Aquitanica Secunda on the western seaboard of Gaul between the mouth of the Garonne and that of the Loire. The barbarians were to be the Federates of the Imperial authorities, owing them military service and having no control over the Aquitanian population in whose midst they had been planted. They lived under their own laws and leaders, and they preserved their own customs, religion, and language.

In 475 King Euric (466–84), who published a code of Gothic laws, declared his independence of Rome and expanded his king-dom eastwards to the Rhone and southwards to the Mediterranean and the Pyrenees. By the end of the century the Visigoths had crossed the mountains into Spain and numbers of them had begun to live in the Spanish provinces. They eventually won control of the entire peninsula apart from the kingdom of the Germanic Sueves in Galicia and the formidable mountains of the Basques north of Pamplona. And so Euric's son, Alaric II (484–507), ruled over the largest political unit in western Europe: apart from Galicia and the Basque mountains his kingdom stretched unbroken from the south bank of the Loire to the Pillars of Hercules.

In 506 he produced a code of laws—the *Breviarium Alaricianum*—for his Roman subjects, since Euric's code applied only to Goths; and he permitted the Catholic bishops of his Gallic realm to meet in the Council of Agde (Dép. Hérault). There was peace and order within his kingdom. But throughout his reign the menace of the Franks, his north-eastern neighbours, grew continuously more alarming; and in 507 Alaric and the flower of his army were destroyed by Clovis and the Franks on the gently undulating plains around Vouillé, some 18 kilometres west of Poitiers. The Visigoths lost the bulk of their Gallic possessions, and thenceforth, apart from the province of Narbonensis (p. 11 below), they were confined to four provinces of Spain—Tarraconensis, Carthagini-ensis, Lusitania, and Baetica.

Visigothic kingdom of Toulouse, see the literature cited in Elfriede Stutz, *Gotische Literaturdenkmäler* (Stuttgart, 1966), p. 21.

INTRODUCTION

B Y the year 500 the Western Roman Empire had disappe
as a political entity. Romulus Augustulus, the last of
Western Emperors, had been deposed in 476, and
Western provinces were now ruled by barbarian kings. In A
the Vandals had passed the summit of their power. Gone wer
days when their fleets swept the western Mediterranean and
interfered with the grain route from Egypt to Constantinopl
Italy Theodoric and the Ostrogoths had ousted the mixed for
barbarians led by King Odoacer, who had taken the plac
Romulus Augustulus. The Ostrogothic administration of Italy
now setting the world an example of tolerant and peaceful gov
ment. Three great Germanic peoples had settled in what is
France. The Burgundians in the Rhone valley still admitted
overlordship of the Roman Emperor at Constantinople and
few years would exchange their Arianism for the Catholic
of Nicaea. But their influence on events was slight, and witl
generation they were to be engulfed by the Franks, who ir
north-east of the country were gathering their strength to pla
remarkable role on which Clovis had already launched them. I
was the Visigoths in south-western France and in Spain
controlled the largest and seemingly the most powerful king
in western Europe.

Of all these peoples it might seem that the Visigoths,
Vandals, and the Ostrogoths were likely to stand or fall toge
for strong ties bound them one to another. They had had a si
history. They spoke a common language, though presumably
local variations. They shared a common religion, Arian Ch
anity, which had now been all but stamped out among the R
populations of West and East alike. It was the Visigothic Bi
Ulfila who had translated the Bible into Gothic in the fc
century; but most of our knowledge of the Gothic Bible is
vided by an Ostrogothic manuscript of the sixth century, and
is evidence that another text went back to a Vandal origina

[1] G. W. S. Friedrichsen, *New Testament Studies*, xi (1964–5), pp. 281–9
the view that the Ambrosian palimpsests were written, not in Italy, but

B

They formed only a small minority of the population there. We have no statistics, but their Hispano-Roman subjects may have outnumbered them by ten to one, perhaps by far more. Their civilization was much less developed than that of the Roman provincials. Some of them lived in cities, but there was no such thing as a Visigothic city: they lived in the old Roman cities. They brought with them into Spain Euric's code of laws; but that code was written in Latin and had been drafted by Roman lawyers. They worshipped the Christian God; but their religion was a Roman heresy and its theology had been developed by Romans, not by Goths. They had smiths and potters of their own, but they possessed neither architects nor sculptors nor painters nor glass-workers nor miners. They were familiar with the use of coined money, but their moneyers were Romans and their coins were the Roman *tremisses* (one-third of a solidus). Following the Roman practice they sometimes set up grave-stones over their dead, but these stones were inscribed not in Gothic but in Latin.

How, then, did these barbarians, who had so much to learn from the Romans, govern their civilized provinces, in each of which a Roman governor and his staff still survived, still administered Roman law, and still collected the Roman taxes?

PART ONE

THE ARIAN KINGDOM

I · FROM GESALIC TO LIUVA

OUR only continuous source of information for the reigns of the Spanish kings from Gesalic to Liuva (507–68) is the *History of the Goths* by St. Isidore of Seville. As a eulogy of the Goths it may have served some purpose. As a history it is unworthy of the famous savant who wrote it. He could hardly have told us less, except by not writing at all. A few lines on each reign record a few events without cause or consequence. The king has neither personality nor policy. Having learned his name, the dates of his accession and his murder, and a few actions of his with no chronology within the reign, no context, and little comment, we pass on to his shadowy successor. We know more of King Chindasuinth (642–53), whose reign nobody chronicled, than of King Athanagild, whose history was written by St. Isidore. Of the long series of Late Roman chronicles, which was founded and inspired by St. Jerome, this is almost the last and almost the least.

Gregory of Tours was well informed about Spain. He disliked Goths, not only because they were heretics. He delighted to tell of how the Franks defeated and humiliated them. He is proud to record the proofs that he himself put forward to refute their blasphemous heresy. But a detailed history of them lay outside the scope of his work.

Whenever Spain impinged on Byzantine affairs in the first half of the century—and it rarely did so—Procopius and Jordanes mention it. But they finished writing before Justinian's generals developed their campaign in Spain. Their works, with a couple of letters by Cassiodorus, a fragmentary law of King Theudis, and some scattered information in the seventh-century *Lives of the Holy Fathers of Merida*, practically complete the list of our sources.

The political history of Spain from Gesalic to Liuva can hardly be said to be known.

1. *The Kings*

When Alaric II fell at Vouillé in 507 his son Amalaric was still a child. The defeated Visigoths, therefore, after falling back on

Narbonne, chose the dead king's illegitimate son Gesalic to succeed him; and since they never recognized hereditary succession to the throne, Gesalic was no usurper. He continued the war, but Toulouse, his capital, went up in flames, and he could not even hold Narbonne against the Franks' allies, the Burgundians. His army had suffered severe losses, and he was forced to fall back into Spain.[1] Utter disaster was prevented by Theodoric, the Ostrogothic King of Italy, who intervened in France in 508 to stop the Frankish advance. His general Ibbas recovered Narbonne and in 510 compelled the Franks and Burgundians to raise the siege of Arles, where a Visigothic garrison held out bravely in conditions of cruel hardship and famine.[2] But practically all of the Visigothic kingdom in Gaul was lost for ever.

After a honeymoon period with the Ostrogoths, Gesalic is said to have sided with their enemies, though the identity of these enemies is uncertain (p. 10 below);[3] and in 511 Ibbas drove him out of Spain. His reign had been turbulent: apart from the murder of Goiaric in the palace at Barcelona (p. 115 below), a count named Veila is also known to have been killed there.[4] With neither men nor money Gesalic fled to Africa, hoping that the Vandals would assist him back to his throne. But although the Vandals gave him money, for fear of Theodoric they provided no men and sent the exile off to France.[5] The Franks were no more willing than the Vandals to help him. But they did not interfere with his efforts to help himself, and at the end of a year's hiding in Aquitaine he returned at last to Spain with an army, was defeated twelve miles from Barcelona by Ibbas, and fled to the Burgundian kingdom beyond the river Durance, where he was caught and killed.[6] Such was the inglorious career of the first monarch of Spain.

[1] Chron. Gall. 689, 690 (i. 665), 'et Barcinona [a slip for Narbona] a Gundefade rege Burgundionum capta'; 691 (i. 666), 'et Geseleicus rex cum maxima suorum clade ad Hispanias regressus est'; Isidore, HG 37 (ii. 282).

[2] Cassiodorus, Var. iii. 32 (cf. iv. 7); Vita S. Caesarii, i. 28 ff.; Caesarius, Sermo 70 (ed. Morin, i. 297); Jordanes, Get. lviii. 302. The account given in the Vita Caesarii is suspect when it deals with the attitude of the Jews: see Katz, pp. 114 f. For brevity's sake I have oversimplified the events which took place north of the Pyrenees after Vouillé: see the important study of E. Ewig, Die fränkischen Teilungen und Teilreiche (511–613), Akademie der Wissenschaften und der Literatur in Mainz, Abh. 9 (1952), not all of whose arguments convince me.

[3] Cassiodorus, Var. v. 43, 'qui nostris inimicis, dum a nobis foveretur, adiunctus est'.   [4] Chron. Caesaraug., s.a. 511 (ii. 223).

[5] Ibid., s.aa. 510, 513 (ii. 223); Isidore, HG 38 (ii. 282); Cassiodorus, loc. cit.

[6] Isidore, loc. cit.

Theodoric acted as regent for Amalaric, who was his grandson, from 511 until his own death in 526;[1] and the period of the regency was marked by few domestic or foreign wars, though the Visigoths managed to recover some places that Clovis had overrun, including Rodez (which was lost again in 531) and Béziers.[2] The Basques may have taken advantage of their weakened condition. The Catholic bishops of the province of Tarraconensis, when they met at the Council of Lerida in 524, found it necessary to declare that clergy who served at the altar in besieged cities must not shed blood, not even the blood of the enemy; and they laid down severe penalties. Perhaps some city of their province had been beleaguered by the Basque mountaineers, as happened often enough later on.[3]

Religious tolerance was characteristic of the Ostrogoths; but the general recovery from the disaster of 507 was slow. Two documents of the years 523–6 throw some light on the difficulties of the period. Theodoric entrusted the administration of Spain to two chief officials, one Roman, one Ostrogothic; and they had many administrative and other abuses to remedy. Spanish corn went to feed the city of Rome; for Theodoric received the tribute of Spain and in return paid the Visigoths their annual donative.[4] But the tax-collectors were raising more in taxes than ever reached Theodoric's treasury; and the King demanded that his revenues should be restored to the amount which they had reached under Euric and Alaric II. The tax-collectors (*exactores*) and the collectors of the arrears of taxes (*compulsores*) were extortionate. Officials followed the age-old practice of using false weights in collecting revenues in grain. The staff of the mints that now existed in Spain—there had been no mint there in Roman times—were working in some cases not for the government but for private persons. Excessive rents were being wrung from the lessees of the royal estates. Customs dues had been raised to a fraudulent height. Homicide was rife. And much besides. Theodoric tried to remedy it all, though with what effect we do not know. It seems to have been he who soon after 510 initiated a new type of *tremissis* (p. 3 above) which began to be minted about this time and was quickly imitated by the

[1] Chron. Caesaraug., *s.a.* 513 (ii. 223); Procopius, *BG* v. 12. 43–8; Mommsen, *Chron. Min.* iii. p. xxxvi; idem, *Ges. Schr.* vi. 354 n. 2.
[2] Greg. Tur., *HF* iii. 21.   [3] Conc. Ilerd. 1.
[4] Procopius, *BG* v. 12. 48; Cassiodorus, *Var.* v. 35.

Burgundians and the Franks. On its reverse the coin shows Victory striding right, holding out a wreath or crown before her in one hand and carrying a palm-branch in the other. The coin was designed so as to be easily distinguishable from Byzantine coins of the period. It was struck in great quantities, was of excellent weight and quality, and was perhaps designed to pay the Visigoths their donative. Its reverse type continued to be used until Leovigild abolished it.[1]

Late in his reign Theodoric appointed an Ostrogoth called Theudis as military commander in Spain. This Theudis, who was afterwards to become king there, married a Hispano-Roman lady of such wealth that he was able to maintain a private army of 2,000 men and so to make himself all but independent of the aged Theodoric, far away in Italy. The King was afraid to attack him in case an outbreak of war would invite a renewed Frankish invasion or a revolt against Ostrogothic rule by the Visigoths themselves. This second possibility suggests that the Ostrogothic ascendancy was unpopular among at least the Visigothic nobility, who may have resented a situation in which the highest offices in the land were held by foreigners. It is not out of the question, then, that the 'enemies' of the Ostrogoths with whom Gesalic had sided (p. 8 above) were a 'home rule' party among the Visigoths themselves, aiming to rid Spain of Ostrogothic overlordship. And, indeed, a few years after the relief of Arles by the Ostrogoths, some Visigoths stabbed and nearly killed no less a person than Theodoric's Praetorian Prefect of Gaul, a man named Liberius, who lived to play a formidable role in Spain forty years later.[2] In the end, Theodoric left Theudis in command, and Theudis tactfully sent the annual tribute to Italy without fail.

With the death of Theodoric in 526 Amalaric became king in his own right and signed an exceedingly favourable treaty with Athalaric, Theodoric's grandson and successor in Italy. By the terms of this treaty he freed Spain from the duty of sending tribute to Italy. He recovered the Visigothic royal treasure, which had fallen into Ostrogothic hands at Carcassonne after the flight from Vouillé. He won the right for those many Visigoths and

---

[1] Cassiodorus, *Var.* v. 39. On this coinage see Tomasini, esp. pp. 45–63, 153, who supposes this coinage to have been issued by Theodoric for commercial use. The mints may have been in Narbonne rather than in Spain.

[2] *Vita S. Caesarii*, ii. 10; Procopius, *BG* v. 12. 50–4.

Ostrogoths who had intermarried during the regency to choose their nationality freely.[1] Most important of all, he fixed finally the Visigothic frontier in France. The western arm of the Rhone delta became the boundary between the Ostrogoths and the Visigoths, and it remained the Visigothic frontier for the rest of their history: Beaucaire (Ugernum) was a Frankish, not a Visigothic, fortress when the Franks replaced the Ostrogoths in that region.[2] So was Uzès. Arles itself, in spite of its courageous defence in 508–10, was lost to the Visigothic kingdom. A strip of land, then, stretching from the western arm of the Rhone to the Pyrenees, with its capital at Narbonne, formed a separate province of the kingdom, the province known as Septimania or Gallia Narbonensis or simply Gallia. The first of these terms was derived from the old Roman name of Béziers, Colonia Iulia Septimanorum Baeterrae, where *Septimanorum* refers to the veteran soldiers of the Seventh Legion whom Octavian had planted there centuries ago. The name does not imply that there were seven cities in the province; and in fact the province included the eight Catholic bishoprics of Narbonne, Nîmes, Agde, Béziers, Elne, Lodève, Maguelonne, and the exposed Carcassonne (often the first objective of Frankish invaders), as well as the valley of the Tet, down which one of King Wamba's columns marched in 673 on its way from Spain to crush the revolt of Nîmes and Narbonne. Septimania, then, was held by the Visigoths until the destruction of their kingdom by the Muslims early in the eighth century; and the Franks, who eyed it greedily, were never able to tear it from their grasp.

Of Amalaric's internal administration we hear only that *c.* 529 he appointed a Roman called Stephanus to act as Prefect of the Spanish provinces (*Hispaniarum praefectus*), perhaps in order to perform some of the functions of the old Roman Praetorian Prefect. But the experiment came to nothing, and Stephanus was discharged from his post at Gerona a couple of years later.[3] Otherwise, there is information only about Amalaric's marriage and his death.

He married the Frankish princess, Clothild, a daughter of Clovis, and tried to convert her to Arianism. His motives in requesting the

---

[1] Procopius, *BG* v. 13. 4–8; cf. Jordanes, *Get.* lviii. 302. See R. de Abadal, *Del Reino de Tolosa al Reino de Toledo* (Madrid, 1960), p. 60.

[2] Jo. Biclar., *s.a.* 585 (ii. 217); Greg. Tur., *HF* viii. 30 (p. 396. 12), 'Ugernum Arelatense castrum'; cf. ix. 7.

[3] Chron. Caesaraug., *s.a.* 529 (ii. 223), where I do not understand *in concilio*. For a different account see de Abadal, op. cit., pp. 61 f.

marriage are not clear. If she were to become an Arian she could not act as intermediary between her husband and her brothers, the Frankish kings. If she remained a Catholic her position in Amalaric's court would be untenable, as in fact it became. For she resisted her husband's arguments in favour of Arianism. He maltreated her. He ordered dung to be poured over her on her way to church; and in the end, it was said, she sent her brother a napkin stained with her blood to prove the misery of her life. So Gregory of Tours says, and, although he gives part of his narrative only as a rumour, his tale is not altogether a mere atrocity story; for Procopius confirms that Clothild was dishonoured by Amalaric because of her unyielding Catholicism. But there is another tradition, which has nothing to say of the Queen's maltreatment. According to this account, Childebert set out on his expedition to Spain because he had decided to subjugate the country, or at any rate, we may suppose, the Visigothic province in Gaul; and we hear of Amalaric being 'ensnared by the frauds of the Franks'.[1]

Be that as it may, Clothild's marriage was an unhappy one; and in 531 Childebert of Paris felt bound to help his kinswoman in her difficulties.[2] Although he was severely harassed by an energetic Visigothic defence, he marched south into Septimania and managed to defeat Amalaric in a stubborn battle at Narbonne. The King fled to Barcelona and while trying to take refuge in a *Catholic* church was killed in the forum either by his own troops or by a Frank named Besso. After their victory Childebert and his sister retired to France without trying an invasion of Spain: either the Franks had won their objective in rescuing the ill-used Queen, or the vigour of the Visigothic defence had daunted them. But they did take some territory in Aquitanica Prima from the Visigoths; and its Visigothic inhabitants emigrated to Spain with their wives and children.[3]

---

[1] *Vita Aviti Conf. Aurel.* 12 (MGH, *SS. rer. Merov.* iii. 385). Note Jordanes, loc. cit., 'qui Amalaricus in ipsa aduliscentia Francorum fraudibus inretitus regnum cum vita amisit'. That the initiative in arranging the marriage came from Amalaric is shown by Greg. Tur., *HF* iii. 1.

[2] Wallace-Hadrill, pp. 132, 190.

[3] Procopius, *BG* v. 13. 13; de Abadal, op. cit., p. 60; but Zeiss, p. 135 n. 2, would refer the passage to 507 rather than to 531. On Amalaric's last war see Chron. Caesaraug., *s.a.* 531 (ii. 223); Isidore, *HG* 40 (ii. 283); Procopius, *BG* v. 13. 9–13 (who stresses the stubborn character of the battle); Greg. Tur., *HF* iii. 10 (where note *dicitur*); *Vita Aviti Conf. Aurel.*, loc. cit., 'ab adversariis in itinere multas perpessus insidias', etc.; Jordanes, loc. cit.

Amalaric died hated and despised by all.[1] He was the last descendant of the great Theodoric I who had reigned in Toulouse from 418 until he fell fighting Attila and the Huns on the Catalaunian Plains in 451. His line had lasted for 113 years. No other dynasty succeeded in establishing itself on the Visigothic throne for so much as one third of that period.

The King's death seems to have been instigated by Theudis, the old commander of Theodoric the Ostrogoth.[2] What part he had played during the reign as a whole we do not know; but during the final campaign he appears to have been in open revolt against Amalaric,[3] and his activities probably undermined the Visigoths' sturdy resistance to the Franks. But he now succeeded Amalaric and managed to hold Arles momentarily. In spite of a Frankish invasion in the early years of his reign, which led to the loss of a couple of places near Béziers,[4] he kept his throne until he was murdered for unknown reasons in 548. Of his internal rule we know that he continued the liberal Ostrogothic policy towards the Catholic Church (p. 32 below)—he was an Ostrogoth himself—and that towards the end of his reign, on 24 November 546, he published a law at Toledo on the costs and expenses of litigants.

There is no reason for thinking that this law applied to the Visigoths: it was directed solely at the Roman courts of the kingdom and was apparently addressed to the Roman provincial governors, not to the Visigothic *duces* (p. 143 below). The courts that the King has in mind have Roman executive officers (the *executores* or *compulsores*), not the *saiones* who enforced the decisions of the Visigothic judges. The legislator directs that his law should be included in the *Breviarium* of Alaric II; but no such law of Theudis was ever included in Leovigild's code, which applied to Goths only; for when King Chindasuinth refers to a 'previous law' relating to legal costs, the law which he has in mind was not that of

---

[1] Isidore, loc. cit.

[2] Ibid. 43 *fin.* (ii. 285). For an interesting theory about Theudis's accession see de Abadal, op. cit., pp. 62 f. But I am not convinced by his view, which is accepted by J. N. Hillgarth, *Historia*, xv (1966), pp. 495 f., that the Visigoths conquered Baetica only towards the middle of the century; and he overlooks the fact that Toledo appears to have been the capital in 546, when Theudis published his law on costs there.

[3] Procopius, *BG* v. 13. 13.

[4] Greg. Tur., *HF* iii. 21, 23, with Dalton ad loc. Presumably he recovered Lodève, which had been represented at the Frankish Council of Clermont in 535.

Theudis, though he was familiar with the wording of Theudis's enactment.[1]

In his law the king lays down a maximum for the payments that litigants made voluntarily to the judge so as to have their cases heard. If the payments were kept within this maximum there could be no question of bribery. The judge was considered to have been bribed only if the payments exceeded the maximum, or if, as a result of receiving them, he gave a crooked judgement. Now, the Ostrogoths in Italy also legalized bribery in a similar way, though in the Burgundian kingdom in the Rhone valley it had been a capital offence for a judge to accept payment of any kind from the litigants even if he went on to give a just judgement.[2] What is surprising in Theudis's law is the enormous size of the costs which he legalizes. The payments alone, he says, are not to amount to more than the value of the article that had given rise to the dispute in the first place; and in addition to the payments the losing party had also to pay the expenses and fees of the court officer (*executor*) together with witnesses' expenses—and perhaps the judge could also order him to reimburse the winning party to the amount of *his* payments to the judge.[3] The Roman judges had little cause to complain of this arrangement.

Theudis, then, was responsible for the only piece of Visigothic legislation known from the period between Gesalic and Liuva. Two military events of consequence are also recorded. In 541 the Franks went further than they had ever gone before: they crossed the Pyrenees and invaded Spain itself. The motives of Kings Childebert and Chlotar for launching this attack are unknown; and since Gregory of Tours on this occasion cannot supply them with an excuse it may seem that their aggression was unprovoked and was

---

[1] On the *lex prior* mentioned by Chindasuinth in *LV* ii. 1. 26 see Zeumer, *NA* xxiii (1898), pp. 88 ff. But Zeumer's arguments (ibid., pp. 80–91) that the law applied universally in the kingdom, to Romans, to Goths as well as to Romans, are unconvincing. He believes that soon after the time of Alaric II the administration of justice in Spain was unified, and the Roman provincial governors became judges of first instance for Goths and Romans alike. But who then were the *comes civitatis* and the *iudex territorii* who appear *passim* in Leovigild's code? Zeumer's pp. 82–3 are misconceived.

[2] Zeumer, art. cit., pp. 94 f. There is a reference to the *munera* of judges in Conc. Tarracon. 10, where clergy are forbidden to accept them. In Theudis's law the payments are called *suffragia* or *commoda*: the Romans had called them *sportulae*.

[3] Zeumer, art. cit., p. 95, though I do not see that *all* the costs taken together are to be equal to, or less than, the value of the disputed article: the *suffragia* alone are thus limited.

due to their desire to collect treasure and fame. They penetrated past Pamplona, ravaged much of the province of Tarraconensis, and reached Saragossa, which they besieged for forty-nine days. According to Gregory, they retired from the city in awe of the tunic of St. Vincent the Martyr, which the devout inhabitants paraded around the walls.[1] But Spanish and Byzantine writers give a more solid reason for the withdrawal: the Franks left Spain because Theudis's general, Theudigisel, blocked the Pyrenean passes in their rear and soundly defeated them. True, he allowed some of them to escape into France in return for a huge bribe; but the rest he massacred.[2] This was the last Frankish attack on the Visigoths for more than half a century; and it was the first, but not the last, occasion on which the Visigoths defeated a Frankish army.

But they were less successful against the Byzantines. The destruction of the Vandal kingdom in Africa in 534 had brought the Byzantines into direct contact with the Visigoths for the first time since the days of Alaric I early in the fifth century. Just before Belisarius's army landed in Africa in 533 the doomed Vandal King, Gelimer, had tried in vain to negotiate an alliance with Theudis, and indeed at one time he planned to take refuge with Theudis in Spain if he should lose the war against Belisarius.[3] Now, early in 534 the Byzantines went on to occupy Ceuta (Septem) on the Straits of Gibraltar; and before seizing the town they were obliged to expel a Visigothic garrison.[4] When had the Visigoths crossed the Straits and taken Ceuta? We do not know. It may be that Theudis had done so in 533 when he saw that Belisarius was on the point of overthrowing the Vandals.[5] At any rate, the Byzantines rebuilt the fortifications of the town, which had been neglected by the Vandals, and left a garrison there. This garrison was commanded by a tribune, who also controlled a squadron of ships (*dromones*). His duties were not only to keep a constant watch on the Straits but also to send full reports on events in Spain and France to his

---

[1] *HF* iii. 29.

[2] Isidore, *HG* 41 (ii. 284); Chron. Caesaraug., *s.a.* 541 (ii. 223), where for *reges numero v* read *reges numero ii*; Jordanes, *Get.* lviii. 302, 'Thiudis . . . Francorum insidiosam calumniam de Spaniis pepulit'.

[3] Procopius, *BV* iii. 24. 7–17; iv. 4. 34.

[4] Idem, *BG* iv. 5. 6, who does not mention the Visigoths; but cf. Isidore, *HG* 41 (ii. 284), 'milites qui Septem oppidum pulsis Gothis invaderant' (*sic*). For *milites* in this sense see p. 320 n. 4 below.

[5] This date is accepted by Stein, ii. 560, though L. Schmidt, *Geschichte der Wandalen*[2] (Munich, 1942), p. 140 n. 3, rather arbitrarily dates the event to 544.

immediate superior, the *dux* of Mauretania, who would forward them to higher authorities.[1] If the Visigothic occupation is correctly dated to 533, Theudis's action should be seen, not as a move to divert the Byzantine forces from their attack on the Vandals, but as an effort to safeguard Spain against invasion by the new rulers of Africa.

Later, in 540, the Ostrogoths in Italy, now under severe pressure from the Byzantines, chose a certain Ildibad as their king; and one reason for electing him was that he was Theudis's nephew and so might have some hope of receiving help from the Visigoths.[2] But it was not until shortly before Theudis's death that the Visigoths went into action; and once again it is more likely that their aim was to protect themselves rather than to help the Ostrogoths. Crossing the Straits of Gibraltar in force they stormed Ceuta; but then one Sunday they innocently laid down their arms so as not to defile the Sabbath with warfare. The Byzantines saw their opportunity, attacked the Visigothic army by land and sea, and destroyed it.[3] The Visigoths never regained a footing in Africa.

Theudis was murdered in his palace in 548; and after the ephemeral reign of Theudigisel—he had led Theudis's army against the Franks in 541 and was murdered when 'very merry' at a banquet in Seville[4]—Agila ascended the throne in December 549. He was the first pure-blooded Visigoth to do so since the death of Alaric II. The chief event of his reign was the landing of the Byzantines in southern Spain, an event of such interest that we must notice carefully the King's actions and their chronology. In 550 he marched against the city of Cordoba, which was in revolt against him (pp. 321 f. below). It was the first armed rebellion against the Gothic kings of Spain, and for many years it was successful. Whether the citizens of Cordoba rebelled against the central government because it was Visigothic or because it was Arian or simply because it was the central government, is not recorded. True, the chronicle describes them as rebelling against

---

[1] Cod. Justin. i. 27. 2 § 2; Procopius, *Aed.* vi. 7. 14–16.

[2] Idem, *BG* vi. 30. 15.

[3] Isidore, *HG* 42 (ii. 284). Procopius says nothing of the incident. On the date and campaign see F. Fita, 'Ceuta visigoda y bizantina durante el reinado de Teudis', *Boletín de la Real Academia de la Historia*, lxviii (1916), pp. 622–8, corrected by H. Messmer, *Hispania-Idee und Gotenmythos* (Zürich, 1960), pp. 116 f.; Stein, ii. 561 n. 1.

[4] On him see Isidore, *HG* 44 (ii. 285); Chron. Caesaraug., *s.a.* 544 (ii. 223); Jordanes, *Get.* lviii. 302; Greg. Tur., *HF* iii. 30, 'valde laetus'; idem, *Glor. Martyr.* 24 (p. 502).

'the Goths' and not simply against Agila or Athanagild or Leovigild; but the phrase is too vague to prove that this was a revolt against Gothic rule as such. And there is no reason at all for supposing that the Cordobans rebelled in order to exchange their Visigothic masters for Byzantine masters. Be that as it may, Agila was defeated by the citizens and lost his son, the royal treasure, and the bulk of his army. He was obliged to retreat to Merida, the capital of the province of Lusitania.[1]

When he was thus weakened, a nobleman called Athanagild also rebelled. He established himself in Seville, capital of the province of Baetica, and tried to dethrone Agila,[2] though there is no reason to think that he was acting in collusion with the rebels at Cordoba. In 551–2 he appealed to the Emperor Justinian for help; and at the moment when Jordanes completed his history, Justinian was preparing to send an expedition to Spain under the command of an 80-year-old civil servant, that same Liberius whom some Visigoths had almost stabbed to death forty years earlier (p. 10 above).[3] In June or July 552 the Byzantines landed in Spain, joined forces with Athanagild, and helped him to defeat Agila's army, which had marched southwards from Merida towards Seville. But after three years of indecisive campaigning the Visigoths realized that they were destroying themselves under the very eyes of the Byzantines. Accordingly, the King's supporters assassinated him at Merida in March 555 and placed Athanagild on the throne,[4] though Athanagild himself dated the beginning of his reign from the outbreak of his revolt in 551.[5] Now that the Byzantines had served his purpose he tried to force them out of Spain, but this he could not do. He fought many battles against them, often beat them, and took some towns that they had occupied, but expel them he could not. Nor could his successors for nearly three quarters of a century.[6]

[1] Isidore, *HG* 45 (ii. 285). I cannot follow R. Gibert, *Settimane*, iii (Spoleto, 1956), pp. 573–5, who supposes that there was a separatist movement in Baetica throughout the whole period from Agila to Hermenegild.

[2] Isidore, *HG* 47 (ii. 286), 'cum iam dudum sumpta tyrannide Agilanem regno privare conaretur'. On Athanagild's noble birth see Venantius Fortunatus, *carm.* vi. 1. 124–7.

[3] Jordanes, loc. cit., who alone mentions Liberius in this connection. Hence, it is not entirely certain that Liberius actually landed in Spain, though there is no reason to doubt that he did so. On the chronology see Stein, ii. 562 n. 2, 820.

[4] Isidore, *HG* 46 (ii. 286); Chron. Caesaraug., *s.a.* 552 (ii. 223); Greg. Tur., *HF* iv. 8, who says nothing of Athanagild's invitation to the Byzantines.

[5] Fiebiger–Schmidt, 256–7.

[6] Isidore, *HG* 47 (ii. 286); Greg. Tur., loc. cit.

That is what our sources tell us directly about the Byzantine landing in Spain. But the establishment of so remote a Byzantine province is of such interest that in an Appendix we shall look again at these events and try to find out whether this is in fact all that can be known about the winning of Justinian's most westerly dominions.

Before he died in 568 Athanagild married his two daughters Brunhild and Galsuintha to the Frankish kings Sigibert of Austrasia and Chilperic of Neustria respectively. It was not that Athanagild arranged dynastic marriages so as to safeguard his northern frontier. The initiative in the two marriages came not from him but from the Franks. The King sent his daughters to France with vast treasures, and in the usual manner of Visigothic princesses who were married off to the Frankish kings they listened meekly to the teachings of the priests and of their husbands and obligingly joined the Catholic Church.[1] The Frankish princesses who went to Spain, on the other hand, were by no means so amenable. Amalaric's bride, Clothild, had been intractable in 531; and the refusal of Ingundis to become an Arian in 579 led to disaster for Arians and Catholics alike.

Athanagild left the kingdom in ruins. There is numismatic evidence of a financial crisis.[2] A number of revolts apart from that at Cordoba had broken out, and he was not able to put them down. The kingdom probably looked in 568 as though it would break up into a number of independent fragments. In 550–60 Catholicism scored a victory in Spain by winning the Sueves of Galicia from Arianism, though this event is not known to have altered the relationship of the two kingdoms.

Athanagild was the first Visigothic king since Euric to die in his bed, and he was survived by his widow, Goisuintha, who was to play so strange a role later on. We do not know why the throne lay vacant for five months after his death; but the interregnum must have helped to weaken the monarchy as such and to further the cause of the various rebels who had established themselves as independent rulers during his reign, and must have enabled them to consolidate their power. But at length he was succeeded by one Liuva, who in his second year as king associated his brother Leovigild with him on the throne. Liuva took Gallia Narbonensis

---

[1] Greg. Tur., *HF* iv. 27 f.
[2] Tomasini, p. 149.

as his province and left his brother to govern Spain. It does not follow that he chose a small and peaceful province for himself while leaving to his brother the dangerous task of restoring the Spanish kingdom. On the contrary, Septimania may have appeared in 569 to be as acutely threatened as any province of the realm. It seems to have been in that year that the Frankish kings, Sigibert and Guntramn, had armies in and around Arles. After a siege and a battle Guntramn's army succeeded in routing its opponents and in capturing Arles; and in the general confusion Liuva may have thought that the eastern frontier of Septimania needed as careful a watch as any region south of the Pyrenees.[1] But he died in 572 leaving as sole ruler of the kingdom the greatest of its kings.

That is practically all that has been recorded about Visigothic political history from Gesalic to Liuva. We have some superficial information about their relations with the Franks. We know of a few purely external events relating to the Byzantine landing. There is a list of the administrative abuses that were rife in the last years of Theodoric the Ostrogoth; and a fragmentary law about judicial costs still survives. It all amounts to little. One point, however, is clear. The assassination of Visigothic rulers by their subjects was almost a matter of course. Between 531 and 555 no fewer than four successive kings were murdered—Amalaric, Theudis, Theudigisel, and Agila. It was too much even by the standards of the sixth century. After telling of the murder of Theudigisel, Gregory of Tours turns aside to observe that 'the Goths had adopted this detestable custom of killing with the sword any of their kings who did not please them, and of appointing as king whomsoever their fancy lighted upon'.[2] Isidore of Seville appears even to frown on the murderers of Agila (p. 77 below). In fact, the principle of hereditary succession to the throne never took root among them, though some of the kings tried hard to establish it; and the method of succession was still an unsolved problem when the kingdom was destroyed. Throughout the entire history of Visigothic Spain only two kings were followed on the throne for more than a couple of years by their sons. These were Leovigild and Chindasuinth; and at least in the case of Leovigild contemporaries thought it worthy of remark that his son was able to succeed him in peace (p. 92 below).

---

[1] Greg. Tur., HF iv. 30. For the interregnum see Isidore, HG 47 (ii. 286).
[2] Greg. Tur., HF iii. 30.

2. *Spain and the Mediterranean*

The history of the sixth-century kings shows that, although Spain was distant from the great centres of power, the country was watched with interest from time to time by the other Mediterranean states. The Ostrogoths were glad to govern it during Amalaric's minority, and they probably derived some profit from doing so. Justinian thought it worth his while to try to incorporate it in his restored Roman Empire. Both the Ostrogoths and the Vandals would have welcomed help from it during their desperate wars with Byzantium.

But they received none. The Spanish monarchs showed little interest in foreign states. Evidently they were determined that their country should not become embroiled in the quarrels of others. They appear to have felt no special ties with the Germanic states, not even with the Ostrogoths, over against the Byzantines. Indeed, there is reason to think that they resented the overlordship of Theodoric in 511–26. Although they were obliged by geography to have comparatively close dealings with France, they left the initiative wholly to the Franks. In spite of their increasing military superiority over their northern neighbours, the Visigothic kings always acted on the defensive against them. Even the French campaigns of Reccared later on were defensive (p. 75 below). The kings never once aimed at conquest in France: they clung to Septimania, but they never tried to extend its frontiers. That they had at one time ruled from the Pyrenees to the Loire and that Toulouse had once been their capital city were facts that they might almost seem to have forgotten. In this total failure to expand their kingdom they were strangely unlike the Franks and the Lombards and the Byzantines. Part at least of the reason was probably the extreme insecurity of the kings at home. Too many rivals were ready to strike them down.

And yet Spain was in close touch with the outside world in non-political ways. There is no parallel now to the tumultuous years of the mid-fifth century when the Western Empire was falling and Vandal fleets swept the Mediterranean. In those days the Galician chronicler, Hydatius, could learn nothing of Eastern events for years on end, and he was glad to set down in his chronicle even the remotest piece of information which reached him from the Orient. (Indeed, it is not certain that he knew much at times about events in Spain itself outside his native Galicia.) True, there were one or two exceptional periods in the sixth century. Thus, although John of Biclarum, who returned from Constantinople to Spain *c.* 576 (p. 81 below), is well informed on Eastern events for a year or two after his return, he knows very little—though his ignorance is not total—about the East during the rebellion of Hermenegild, when relations between Byzantium and Toledo were strained.[1] Even so, towards the end of the sixth century, Spain was probably in closer contact with the Eastern Roman Empire than was France.[2]

Throughout the existence of the Byzantine province (552–624) there must have been a great deal of movement both of officials and of correspondence between southern Spain and Constantinople; and indeed in the letters written by the Patrician Caesarius and King Sisebut *c.* 614–15 we catch a glimpse of East Roman officials travelling to Byzantium in company with a Visigothic diplomat and returning safely.[3] There were also semi-official visitors to the East, like Leander of Seville, who travelled to Byzantium *c.* 580, apparently in order to persuade the East Roman government to give active help to the rebel prince, Hermenegild (p. 66 below). There were private visitors, like the chronicler John of Biclarum, who went to Constantinople about the year 560 (perhaps at the very time when Athanagild was trying to expel the Byzantines from Spain), was instructed in both Greek and Latin scholarship there, and returned to his native land sixteen years later. Towards the end of the century Licinianus, Bishop of Cartagena, died at Constantinople.[4] Visits of 'Greek' clergy to Spain were sufficiently numerous in 518 to cause Pope Hormisdas to write 'to all the bishops of Spain' to explain what they ought to do if such Oriental clerics as had not dissociated themselves from the heretical Acacius should ask to be admitted to their communion.[5] Again, a certain Paul, a physician, arrived from the East in Merida, the capital city of Lusitania, and became bishop there in the middle of the century.[6]

[1] I have modified Mommsen, *Chron. Min.* ii. 207 f., but see J. N. Hillgarth, *Historia*, xv (1966), p. 488, for a somewhat different view.
[2] This may be inferred from Norman H. Baynes, *Byzantine Studies and Other Essays* (London, 1955), pp. 309 ff.
[3] *Epist. Wisig.* 3 ff. (pp. 663 ff.)
[4] Isidore, *De Vir. Illustr.* 60 (PL 83. 1104); Gregory I, *Dial.* iii. 31.
[5] *Ep.* 26 (A. Thiel). On the dispute in question between Rome and the East see A. A. Vasiliev, *Justin the First* (Cambridge, Mass., 1950), pp. 132 ff., with extensive bibliography. [6] *VPE* iv. 1. 1.

Some years later, when a company of traders from the East reached Spain and visited Merida—they may have sailed up the Guadiana— a boy called Fidelis was among their number; and he turned out to be Paul's sister's son. He eventually succeeded his uncle as bishop of Merida in disreputable circumstances (pp. 43 f. below). Silk garments from the East were in use in the church there; and of the ten Christian inscriptions written in Greek which have been found in Spain, four were discovered in or around Merida.[1] The bishops of the province of Gallia speak in 589 of Syrians and Greeks in Septimania as well as of Goths, Romans, and Jews; and most of these Syrians and Greeks, like the crew of the ship that had carried Fidelis to Spain, were doubtless traders.[2] We hear incidentally of an Oriental trader in Nîmes.[3] It is not surprising that the second half of the sixth century saw the beginning of a profound Byzantine influence on objects of daily use among the Visigoths (p. 152 below).

The Popes were in frequent contact with Spain, and in 514 Pope Symmachus anticipated no difficulties if clergy from Gaul or Spain should wish to visit him. In 518 Pope Hormisdas wrote the letter which we have already mentioned. At the end of the century Gregory the Great treats journeys from Spain to Rome as nothing out of the ordinary; and there is no need to emphasize his own close relations with Leander of Seville, and their unimpeded correspondence. Moreover, in the first half of the century a number of art styles and even specific objects of daily wear found their way from Italy to Spain (pp. 149 f. below). It does not follow that all such articles appeared in Spain as a result of trade with Italy: some of them may have been worn by Ostrogothic officials and soldiers stationed in Spain, where they were copied by Visigothic craftsmen. But this artistic association of Italy and Spain vanished after the overthrow of the Ostrogothic kingdom and cannot be traced in the late sixth and seventh century: there seems to be no contact, for example, between the art of the Visigoths and that of the Lombards.[4]

---

[1] *VPE* iv. 3. 2 ff.; v. 3. 12; Vives, 418–19, 425–6. Only two such Greek inscriptions have been found in the Byzantine province—both at Cartagena: Vives, 422–3. The others come from Mertola, Carteia, Solana de los Barros (near Seville), and Ecija, all of them places easily accessible to travellers coming from the sea. I do not know why Fontaine, ii. 846, says that the arrival of Fidelis and his merchants is regarded by the author of the *VPE* as something exceptional.

[2] Conc. Narbon. 4, 14.

[3] Greg. Tur., *Glor. Martyr.* 77 (p. 539).

[4] *Epist. Arel. Gen.* 28 (MGH, *Epistolae Merow. et Karolini Aevi*, i. 41);

Traders also sailed between Spain and Africa. In the closing years of Theodoric the Ostrogoth, shippers who had been instructed to convey Spanish grain to Italy were found to be selling it in Africa.[1] In 533 merchants sailing direct from Carthage were able to outstrip Vandal ambassadors who had coasted from Carthage to the Straits of Gibraltar.[2] The monk Nanctus moved from Africa to Lusitania in the reign of King Leovigild.[3] Nor was he an isolated example, for at about the same time a monk called Donatus, foreseeing trouble from the Moorish barbarians in Byzantine Africa, sailed to Spain with about seventy other monks and an extensive library; and after his arrival he founded the famous monastry of Servitanum, of which the site is unknown.[4]

On the other hand, there was little cultural exchange between Spain and France in the sixth century, for the civilization of France had sunk so low that it had little to offer to the Spaniards; and when Isidore of Seville wrote his *De Viris Illustribus* he found occasion to mention no Gaul later than Avitus of Vienne, who had died in 518.[5] But it does not follow that traders and other travellers between the two countries were few. Little is known specifically of trade with the Franks, but the archaeological evidence makes it clear that there was much commerce across the frontier of Septimania. Frankish goods and art styles reached Narbonensis in abundance and northern Spain in some degree, as is shown by the Visigothic cemetery that has been excavated at Pamplona. But between France and Spain as a whole there was but little commercial contact.[6] It is known, however, that trade was carried on by sea between France and the Suevic kingdom in Galicia late in the

Gregory I, *Ep.* xiii. 47 (pp. 410. 24; 411. 30). On Gregory and Leander see Fontaine, ii. 842–6, with references. Zeiss, pp. 102 f., 105, 108 f., *et saepe.*

[1] Cassiodorus, *Var.* v. 35. On relations with Africa see esp. Fontaine, pp. 854 ff.

[2] Procopius, *BV* iii. 24. 11. There is no evidence for the view of Fontaine, ii. 855, that Theudis was at Seville at the time. Procopius's expressions would equally well suit Toledo: Zeiss, p. 75 n. 2.

[3] *VPE* iii. 2.

[4] Ildefonsus, *De Vir. Illustr.* 4 (*PL* 96. 200); Jo. Biclar., *s.a.* 571 (ii. 212), cf. *s.a.* 584 (ii. 217). Ildefonsus seems to indicate *c.* 570 as the date. When he adds 'iste prior in Hispaniam monasticae observantiae usum et regulam dicitur adduxisse', he illustrates how little an educated seventh-century Goth knew about the early history of monasticism in Spain. There were severe Byzantine reverses in Africa in 569–70: Jo. Biclar., *s.a.* (ii. 212).

[5] Fontaine, ii. 835 ff.

[6] Zeiss, pp. 118, 123. Imports from France: ibid. 32, 68, 112, etc. For Pamplona see ibid. 79 f., 111 f. For Goths in France see Greg. Tur., *HF* iv. 26 (p. 159. 12), 51 (p. 188. 16).

sixth century (p. 88 below); and in the middle of the century communications between Galicia and Tours were open and easy, while in the sixth and seventh centuries seaborne traffic went northwards from Spain and seems even to have reached Ireland.[1] We hear incidentally of a saint who sailed from the East to Galicia and of a Spanish merchantman which put in at Marseilles in 588 'with the usual merchandise'[2]—and there is no reason to think that either voyage was anything exceptional. In the time of Liuva and Leovigild, Catholic clergy from France sometimes settled in the Visigothic kingdom and indeed were welcomed there by the Arian sovereigns (pp. 81 f. below).

Slaves from Spain and kidnapped children were sometimes sold abroad.[3] Indeed, the position of overseas traders in sixth-century Spain was sufficiently important for Leovigild to include a title on them in his law code (and this title was not omitted in the seventh-century revisions of the code). One law refers to them as selling gold, silver, clothing, and ornaments in Spain, which suggests that they were chiefly concerned with trade in luxuries; and they were not above selling stolen goods.[4] The legislator was obliged to impose severe penalties on foreign traders who hired labourers in Spain and then transported them to their own country.[5]

Although Spain kept foreign political entanglements at a distance and indeed avoided them altogether when possible and resisted outsiders stubbornly when they forced themselves upon her, she was closely bound in the sixth century to France, Italy, Africa, and the Byzantine Empire by trade and the interchange of clergy and letters. It appears that the Roman population, or at any rate the educated section of it, was very conscious of nationality. As we have seen, the bishops of Narbonensis in 589 distinguished the Roman, Greek, Gothic, Syrian, and Jewish inhabitants of their province. The author of the *Lives* of the bishops of Merida is careful to point out that Bishops Paul and Fidelis were natives of the Greek East whereas Masona and Renovatus were Goths.

---

[1] J. N. Hillgarth, 'The East, Visigothic Spain, and the Irish', *Studia Patristica*, iv (Berlin, 1961), pp. 442–56, with bibliography in the footnotes; idem, 'Visigothic Spain and Early Christian Ireland', *Proceedings of the Royal Irish Academy*, lxii (Dublin, 1962), Section C, no. 6, pp. 167–94. For communications with Tours see Greg. Tur., *De Virtut. Martini*, i. 11. On the relations of Suevic Galicia with France see Fontaine, ii. 836 n. 2.

[2] Isidore, *De Vir. Illustr.* 35 (PL 83. 1100); Greg. Tur., *HF* ix. 22.

[3] *LV* vii. 3. 3; ix. 1. 10; Valentinian, *Nov.* 33.

[4] *LV* xi. 3. 1.   [5] *LV* xi. 3. 3.

Isidore draws attention to the fact that the chronicler, John of Biclarum, was a Goth, and in his eyes a Gothic writer seems to have been something of a rarity. (In fact, John is the only sixth-century Goth in Spain who is known to have published books.) The author of the *Lives* revealingly observes that Masona 'was indeed a Goth but was wholly devoted to God with very ready heart' (v. 2. 1). And yet John of Biclarum, Goth though he was, is the only ecclesiastic, Arian or Catholic, of the sixth-century kingdom of whom it can be said with certainty that he was educated in Greek as well as in Latin. Even though Leander of Seville and Licinianus of Cartagena spent a considerable time in Constantinople, it by no means follows that they knew Greek;[1] and John's education in the two languages was thought worthy of note and perhaps of envy by St. Isidore, who, polymath though he was, knew little or no Greek.[2] As for the Goths, they always felt themselves to be distinct from the Roman population of Spain. Catholic Goths, like Renovatus, might call themselves by Roman names, but they never called themselves Romans.

[1] Fontaine, ii. 853 n. 2. St. Martin of Braga in the Suevic kingdom, of course, certainly knew Greek and taught it to the monk, Paschasius of Dumium: Barlow, p. 9 n. 14.
[2] Fontaine, ii. 849 ff.

II · RELIGION

THE political history of sixth-century Spain, then, is known only in barest outline. Not so the history of the Catholic Church in this period; for there still survive the minutes of several provincial synods, together with some papal letters and a number of references in the law code of Alaric. Of the Arian Church we know far less. The literature produced by it is not known to have been extensive—indeed, we do not know even the name of a single Arian author or whether men still continued to write in Gothic—and King Reccared after his conversion to Catholicism systematically destroyed such Arian documents as existed.

1. *Religion and Foreign Policy*

When the Catholic Franks attacked the Visigothic kingdom in 507, the general population of Alaric's territory can hardly be said to have rallied to his support. Indeed, Gregory of Tours says that 'many' of the Gauls were anxious to have the Franks as their rulers, and he gives three specific examples—Quintianus, Bishop of Rodez, and Volusianus and Verus, Bishops of Tours, though he admits that tension arose between Quintianus and his fellow-citizens when the Bishop was suspected of hoping for a Frankish victory.[1] (As Quintianus was an African, he may have held a more jaundiced view of Arian Germans than many other Romans held.) But from the attitude of these three bishops we cannot generalize about that of the entire Catholic hierarchy of the kingdom. And even if the entire hierarchy favoured the Franks it would by no means follow that all the Catholics in the realm were pro-Frankish. On the contrary, Catholic Roman aristocrats fought and died for the Arian Visigoths in the battle

---

[1] *HF* ii. 35, cf. 36; *Vit. Patr.* iv. 1 (p. 674) for Quintianus; *HF* ii. 26; x. 31 § 7–8. In *HF* ii. 23 *fin.* Gregory says that 'everyone' in the Burgundian kingdom wished to be ruled by the Franks; but he specifies only Abrunculus, Bishop of Langres, who, he says, became suspect to the Burgundians, 'cumque odium de die in diem cresceret' he fled to Clermont-Ferrand. For a criticism of my point of view on the Gallo-Roman attitude to the Franks see Wallace-Hadrill, p. 173.

of Vouillé in 507,[1] and Arles held out even after the defeat and withstood a long siege. There is, in fact, no convincing evidence that the Catholics in the Visigothic kingdom tended in general to side with the Catholic Clovis, though some of the higher clergy were undoubtedly inclined to do so. It might be truer to say that the Roman landowners, who as a class had not been dissatisfied with the rule of the barbarian kings, gave considerable support to Alaric in 507, whereas the poorer classes had now lost their earlier enthusiasm for the conditions of life under Visigothic rule and stayed neutral. Conversely, the Arian Burgundians helped the Catholic Franks against the Arian Visigoths in the years following 507.[2] And when Catholicism became the official religion of the Visigothic kingdom in 589, Catholic Franks sided violently with the Spanish Arians who, sooner than accept the new faith, rebelled against King Reccared—and it is actually reported that many Catholics in Spain itself joined them![3]

The Catholic Byzantines were invited to Spain in 552 by the Arian Athanagild to help him dethrone his Arian sovereign, Agila. But there is no evidence that Athanagild based his revolt on the Catholic Roman population of the south, or that any Catholic welcomed the Byzantines as liberators. Moreover, Catholic Romans living in Visigothic Spain are not known to have co-operated politically or militarily with the Byzantines after their landing. The revolt of Cordoba, for instance, is not said to have been assisted by the Byzantines, and there is no evidence that as a result of it Cordoba was ever occupied by the armies of East Rome (p. 322 below). Indeed, so eminent a Catholic as Leander of Seville, whose parents had fled from Cartagena to the Visigothic kingdom as a result of the Byzantine landing there, was intensely critical of conditions in the Byzantine province.[4] His brother, Isidore of Seville, clearly regards the

---

[1] *HF* ii. 37 (p. 88).

[2] *Vita S. Caesarii*, i. 28; cf. Chron. Gall. a. DXI. 688 (i. 665), 'Tolosa a Francis et Burgundionibus incensa'; ibid. 690, quoted on p. 8 n. 1 above; Greg. Tur., *HF* ii. 37. But there is no valid evidence that the Catholics in the Burgundian kingdom betrayed their Catholic king to the Catholic Franks: the *Passio S. Sigismundi*, 8 (MGH, *SS. rer. Merov.* ii. 337) carries no weight, as Krusch shows in his introduction to the text, ibid. 329 f.   [3] *VPE* v. 10. 2.

[4] *Regula*, 21 (PL 72. 892), esp. 'ego tamen expertus loquor, sic perdidisse statum et speciem illam patriam, ut nec liber quisquam in ea supersit, nec terra ipsa solita sit ubertate fecunda, et non sine Dei iudicio. terra enim cui cives erepti sunt, et concessi extraneo, mox ut dignitatem perdidit, caruit et fecunditate', etc.

Byzantines as unwelcome foreigners in Spain, whose expulsion was brought about by Gothic courage. When the Visigoths became Catholic in 589 the hostility that existed between Toledo and Byzantium is not known to have diminished: later Visigothic kings—Witteric, Gundemar, Sisebut, and Suinthila, as well as Reccared himself—attacked the Byzantine province as energetically as their Arian predecessors had done. (Only the ephemeral kings, Liuva II (601–3) and Reccared II, who ruled for a few days in 621, failed to do so.)

True, our sources are few and brief, and the absence of reference to such co-operation hardly proves that it never took place. But we must argue on the basis of such evidence as exists, and what that evidence shows is that there was a great deal of co-operation on the part of Catholic Spaniards, including clergy, with foreign peoples *after* 589, that is, when the kingdom was Catholic, but not before that date, when the kingdom was Arian. It is difficult, then, to accept the view that the conversion of the Visigoths to Catholicism was a political defeat for the Byzantines in that it lost them multitudes of potential allies inside the Visigothic kingdom. There is no evidence that they ever had any allies there before 589 apart from the Arian Athanagild, who first invited them to Spain, and Hermenegild, whom we shall meet later on. The idea of a community of interests of the Germanic kingdoms over against the Romans, or of Arian Germanic kingdoms over against the Franks, did not occur to the fifth- and sixth-century Germans.[1] (It does not follow, however, that the Arian kings were always indifferent to the sufferings of Arians living beyond their frontiers.)[2] Nor were the Visigoths after 589, the Franks, and the Byzantines drawn closer together by the fact that they were now, all three of them, Catholics. The Byzantines might profess to feel that a common Catholicism formed a political bond between two states;[3] but in 589–90, at the very moment of the conversion, the Byzantine Governor-General in Spain dismissed the Visigoths as mere 'barbarian enemies'.[4]

[1] A. Boretius, 'Ueber Gesetz und Geschichte der Burgunder', *Historische Zeitschrift*, xxi (1869), pp. 1–27, at p. 19.

[2] Avitus of Vienne, *Ep.* 7 (ed. Peiper, 36. 12 ff.); Victor Vitensis, *Hist. Persec.* i. 24; cf. Procopius, *BV* iv. 1. 4.   [3] Idem, *BG* v. 5. 9.

[4] Vives, 362. From this inscription Goubert, *REB* iii (1945), pp. 136 f., rightly argues that Comenciolus was sent to Spain not later than 1 September 589. In any

Clovis may or may not have used sectarian differences as a political weapon; but it still remains the case that religious or sectarian differences were not a decisive factor in the foreign policy of the barbarian kingdoms at some of the most important crises of their sixth-century history. The barbarian kings followed their political interests and made alliances with foreign countries or fought foreign armies irrespective of the sectarian allegiance of their allies or their enemies. The populations of the various kingdoms are never known to have protested against their rulers' attacks on co-religionaries, or to have given an especial welcome to attacks on those whom they regarded as heretics. Heresy did not make another nation an enemy, just as orthodoxy did not make it a friend.

2. *The Arian Kings and the Catholic Church*

Alaric II changed remarkably little in the day-to-day life of the Catholic Church. He deprived the Catholic clergy of some of their fiscal privileges.[1] They were forbidden by the King as well as by canon law to engage in trade; and in 516 the bishops of the province of Tarraconensis found it advisable to reaffirm the ban on the clergy engaging in commerce or usury.[2] Clergy were still free from serving on the city councils; and, as in Roman times, city councillors (*curiales*), members of the city guilds (*collegiati*), coloni, and slaves were forbidden to take orders. It was only in 633 that suitable slaves of the Church were declared eligible for the diaconate and the priesthood, though they had to be manumitted before being ordained.[3]

Catholic bishops had previously had the right of trying civil cases between laymen when both parties agreed. Under Alaric they lost their jurisdiction in such cases.[4] They also lost their exemption from being called as witnesses in the secular courts;[5]

event, he used the term *hostes barbaros* when he knew that the Visigothic king was already Catholic.

[1] *CTh* xvi. 2. 8, 10, 14, 24, all disappear from the *Breviarium*. I quote the *Breviarium* from Mommsen's edn. of the Theodosian Code. Unless otherwise stated the reference in each case is to the *interpretatio*, not to the original Roman law.

[2] Valentinian, *Nov.* 35 (p. 149. 133); Conc. Tarrac. 2 f.

[3] *CTh* xvi. 2. 2; Valentinian, loc. cit. (p. 148. 129 ff.); IV Tolet. 74; cf. IX Tolet. 11; Conc. Emerit. 18.

[4] *CTh* i. 27. 1 f. disappear from the *Breviarium*. But the clergy have this right except in criminal cases in Conc. Tarrac. 4.

[5] *CTh* xi. 39. 8 was omitted by Alaric.

but Alaric confirmed to priests (but not to lower clergy) their immunity from torture when summoned as witnesses, though they could still be punished for perjury.[1] The King continued to give the Catholic bishops the right to appear in a court formed by other Catholic bishops: no one could sue them in the public courts, at any rate in civil cases.[2] But a bishop condemned in an episcopal court could still appeal to a secular judge.[3] If a layman brought either a civil or a criminal action against a cleric in the public courts, the cleric was obliged to appear there—even bishops had to do so in serious cases.[4] Moreover, the rule that actions must be heard in the court of the defendant continued to apply to the clergy in cases where they took action against laymen, unless the defendants agreed to appear in an ecclesiastical court.[5] But even in criminal cases bishops and priests did not need to appear personally in the courts: they could send a representative instead,[6] and it was only in the time of King Reccesuinth (649–72) that they were prohibited from appearing at all—they must not become involved in the rough-and-tumble of the public courts.[7]

Church courts dealt with purely ecclesiastical affairs;[8] and a cleric who had recourse to a public court in order to avoid ecclesiastical punishment was to be excommunicated, according to the Council of Agde, along with the judge who heard his case. According to the same Council, no cleric could sue a man in the public courts without his bishop's permission.[9] But when Reccared was converted to Catholicism the Catholic hierarchy remarked that clerics often disregarded their bishops and sued one another in the public courts: the practice was sternly prohibited at the Third Council of Toledo.[10] The Council of Agde declared further that if a layman took action against a cleric or the Church and lost it, he was to be excommunicated.[11] Bishops were to try to reconcile those who had long been at law with one another, and if their efforts were unsuccessful the litigants were liable to excommunication.[12]

---

[1] *CTh* xi. 39. 10.   [2] Ibid. xvi. 2. 12.
[3] Ibid. xi. 36. 20, with Jones, iii. 139 n. 48.
[4] Valentinian, *Nov.* 35 *init.*; *CTh* xvi. 2. 23; Conc. Agath. 32.
[5] Valentinian, *Nov.* 35 (p. 148. 126 f.)   [6] Ibid., p. 148. 121 f.
[7] *LV* ii. 3. 1; cf. 1. 19.   [8] *CTh* xvi. 2. 23; cf. 11. 1.
[9] Conc. Agath. 8, 32.   [10] III Tolet. 13.   [11] Conc. Agath. 32.
[12] Ibid. 31.

Alaric urged his judges to deal expeditiously with cases involving a Catholic church so that the law officers (*defensores*) of the church should not be kept waiting unduly for a decision.[1] He retained the Roman law that gave the property of bishops and other clergy as well as of monks and nuns, who died intestate without heirs, to the church or monastery to which they had belonged.[2] Criminals could still seek asylum in the Catholic churches provided that they did not carry arms with them; and it was still a capital offence to drag them out.[3] (Indeed, the Council of Lerida in 524 or 546 found it necessary to forbid Catholic clergy to drag out their slaves or pupils or to whip them when they had taken refuge in a Catholic church.)[4] It continued to be illegal to ordain a man against his will; and it is noteworthy that bishops who took part in this type of offence were still liable to be sent to Rome to be judged by the Pope. But if a man were consecrated as bishop against his will, he was obliged to continue in his unwanted office.[5]

Not one of Alaric's laws relating to the Catholic Church is known to have been altered by Reccared when he became a Catholic in 589. The outlook of Alaric's successors, too, was remarkably tolerant as compared with the attitude shown later on by the Catholic kings towards the Arians. Throughout the eighty-four years that separated the death of Euric from the accession of Leovigild (484–568) no major clash between Arianism and Catholicism is reported from Spain.[6] In 514 Pope Symmachus (498–514) instructed Caesarius of Arles, a city which at that time lay outside the Visigothic kingdom altogether (though it was part of the Ostrogothic dominions), to keep an eye on questions of religion which might arise not only in Gaul but also in Spain; and less tolerant kings than Theodoric the Ostrogoth might not have sanctioned this breach of the state frontier (p. 34

---

[1] *CTh* ii. 4. 7.

[2] Ibid. v. 3. 1. Cf., on the testamentary rights of nuns, deaconesses, etc., Marcian, *Nov.* 5.

[3] *CTh* ix. 45. 4. For the manumission of slaves in Catholic churches see ibid. iv. 7. 1; cf. 9. 1.

[4] Conc. Ilerd. 8.   [5] Majorian, *Nov.* 11.

[6] F. Görres, 'Kirche und Staat im Westgotenreich von Eurich bis auf Leovigild', *Theologische Studien und Kritiken*, lxvi (1893), pp. 708–34. The view put forward by Jo. Biclar., *s.a.* 590 (ii. 219), that the conversion of the Visigoths to Catholicism took place 'post longas Catholicorum neces atque innocentium strages', is unsupported by any other evidence.

below).[1] Isidore of Seville stresses the tolerance of King Theudis in granting peace to the Church and in allowing the Catholic bishops to meet at a council in Toledo (of which we hear nothing elsewhere) and arrange freely what they thought necessary for the discipline of their Church.[2] His only word of criticism is for King Agila, who profaned the tomb of the martyr Acisclus in the course of his campaign against the rebels of Cordoba. Of Athanagild's attitude we know nothing.

In the Arian period the Catholics could build and repair churches,[3] and found and endow monasteries in freedom: they continued to do so even in the early years of Leovigild.[4] They could accept Jewish converts into the Church, though it cannot be said that they welcomed them very warmly—Jewish converts had to remain as catechumens for eight months before they were baptized[5]—and all Catholic clergy and laymen were forbidden by the Council of Agde in 506 to eat with Jews.[6] Catholics could write and circulate their books without hindrance;[7] Masona of Merida, even when he had been exiled by Leovigild, was able to correspond freely.[8] They could correspond with the Pope in Rome: Pope Hormisdas addressed two extant letters to 'all the bishops of Spain' and two others to Baetica and Tarragona. They could visit Italy.[9] Caesarius in Ostrogothic Arles was able to have his books circulated in Spain.[10] The Catholic bishops could travel freely to their synods provided that they were not occupied on the king's business, which had priority;[11] and they

---

[1] *Epist. Arel. Gen.* 28 (MGH, *Epist. Merow. et Karol. Aevi,* i. 41).

[2] *HG* 41 (ii. 283 f.) There is no need to ascribe a mistake to Isidore here, with Messmer, op. cit. (p. 16 n. 3 above) p. 120 n. 155, who thinks that Isidore's reference is to the Second Council of Toledo.

[3] Vives, 279, 301, 356 (if the restoration is on ther ight lines); *VPE* v. 3. 3; Conc. Tarrac. 8.

[4] *VPE,* loc. cit.; Conc. Agath. 27, 28; Vives, 278. John was founder as well as abbot of Biclarum: Mommsen. *Chron. Min.* ii. 208.

[5] Conc. Agath. 34, 'Iudaei, quorum perfidia frequenter ad vomitum redit', etc. The phrase is based on 2 Pet. 2: 22.

[6] Conc. Agath. 40.

[7] Numerous authors of the period are mentioned by Isidore, *De Vir. Illustr.* 30, 33, 45, etc. (PL 83. 1098 ff.). See also Vives, 279, the tombstone of Justinian, Bishop of Valencia in the middle of the sixth century (p. 43 below), who 'scripsit plura posteris profutura ⟨seclis⟩', which confirms Isidore, op. cit. 33.

[8] *VPE* v. 7. 10.

[9] Mansi, viii. 429 ff. (where John of Tarragona visits Italy in 517); cf. ibid. 467 f., 478 f.

[10] *Vita S. Caesarii,* i. 55.   [11] Conc. Agath. 35; cf. Conc. Tarrac. 5 f.

were instructed by their councils to visit the churches of their dioceses annually without any suggestion that their right to travel might be impeded by the kings.[1] Not only bishops and priests from the cathedral churches but also parish priests and some laymen were invited to the synods; and no fear was expressed that these might be forbidden to travel.[2] (We do not hear again of laymen being present at the sixth-century provincial synods.) And we have seen that at least two groups of African monks settled in Spain and preferred to live in the Visigothic kingdom rather than in the Byzantine province (p. 23 above).

Catholics were free to combat Priscillianism;[3] but the two learned books in which Leander of Seville castigated Arianism 'in a vehement style' were written when he was living out of the country.[4] A Roman of high rank called Turribius not only combated paganism and Priscillianism, but even dared to win over some Visigoths to Catholicism.[5] At the Council of Valencia in 549 it was stated as a well-known fact that some persons were converted to Catholicism as a result of hearing sermons preached in the churches; but whether these persons were won from paganism or from Arianism is not clear.[6] In 582, at a critical time during the revolt of Hermenegild, Masona, Bishop of Merida, preached vigorously against Arianism, and although King Leovigild shortly afterwards exiled him, he did so for other reasons and not because of his anti-Arian sermons (p. 78 f. below).

The Catholics held many synods—at Agde (Agatha) in 506, at Toledo in 507,[7] at Tarragona and Gerona in 516 and 517, at Lerida and Valencia in 524 (though these may have met in 546 and 549 respectively). They held the Second Council of Toledo in 527, and another at Toledo which only Isidore mentions (p. 32 above), and finally a council at Barcelona c. 540. At Agde the bishops directed that a synod should meet every year. They

---

[1] Conc. Tarrac. 8.   [2] Ibid. 13.

[3] See Montanus's two letters appended to the acts of the Second Council of Toledo in Mansi, viii. 788 ff.

[4] Isidore, op. cit. 57 (PL 83. 1103). We do not know where Leander published his *Responsiones*, which are also mentioned there.

[5] Montanus, *Ep. ad Theoribium* (Mansi, viii. 790), 'nam de terrenorum dominorum fide quid loquar? cui ita tuum impendisti laborem, ut feroces cohabitantium tibi animos ad salubrem regulam et normam regularis disciplinae duceres'. The phrase *feroces animos* suggests barbarians, that is, Visigoths, the *terreni domini*. The words *cohabitantium tibi* may indicate the *hospites* living on Turribius's estate. Despite the commentators on this letter, Turribius was a bishop, not a monk.

[6] Conc. Valent. 1.

[7] Mansi, viii. 347, with the letter of Caesarius of Arles printed ibid. 343.

noted in their record of the meeting that they had assembled
with the permission of King Alaric II, and they prayed for his
kingdom and his long life. At the Second Council of Toledo they
thanked Amalaric and prayed to God that the King might
throughout his reign grant them freedom.[1]

In spite of all this, signs of tension and even isolated cases of
oppression are not wanting. Although the bishops thanked the
kings at Agde and at the Second Council of Toledo, their words
were formal and showed no warmth. At Toledo they found it
necessary to pray that the King's tolerance might continue. At
the councils held under Ostrogothic rule they did not think fit
to refer to the King at all: Theodoric's liberal spirit was notorious.
Moreover, a hint dropped in one of the canons of the Council
of Lerida could be taken to suggest that some Catholics were
forced, even tortured, to join the Arians.[2] At Toledo one of the
signatories was a bishop called Martianus, whose see is not
named. The reason why he was present at the Council was that
he had been exiled to Toledo 'because of the Catholic faith'.[3]
This implies at least one instance of persecution of which we
have no other information, though that is not certain; for the King
might have given a different reason for having banished Martianus.

Again, the two surviving letters of Montanus of Toledo
show that at least Amalaric kept careful watch on the activities
of the Catholic bishops. Montanus points out to the faithful of
Palencia that they had invited bishops from another province
than their own to consecrate certain of their churches—those of
Segovia, Buitrago (Britablum), and Coca (Cauca). This blurring
of the provincial boundaries was contrary to the interests of the
King, who had heard of the matter. In future, when a church is
to be consecrated, the metropolitan must be informed by letter
so that the consecration may be performed either by himself or
by a fellow-bishop appointed by him.[4] Montanus wrote at the

---

[1] Mansi, viii. 323, 787.

[2] Conc. Ilerd. 9, 'de his qui in praevaricatione rebaptizati, sine aliqua necessitate
vel tormento delapsi sunt', etc. There is a reference in *VPE* iv. 1. 3 to *conturbationum
procellas* which troubled the Church in Merida towards the middle of the sixth
century; but the passage, which is discussed by Garvin, pp. 358 f., seems to suggest
internal conflicts rather than Arian persecution.

[3] Mansi, viii. 787, who prints the name 'Maracinus'.

[4] Ibid. 789c–d, 'nec provinciae privilegiis nec rerum domini noscuntur utilitatibus
convenire; quia iam ad ipsum huiuscemodi fama perlata est'. Can it be that Montanus
has the national boundary in mind and that bishops from the Suevian kingdom had

same time to Turribius (p.33 above) emphasizing that the old
custom must be restored: and if Turribius ignores this warning
Montanus will be obliged to report him to the King and also
'to our son Erganis' (perhaps the Gothic *dux* of the province).[1]
Evidently the King thought it important that the provincial
boundaries should in some ways be rigid barriers; and indeed,
during the Catholic period, too, the provincial frontiers had a
very real significance.[2]

Further, all the councils held in Spain in the first half of the sixth
century were provincial synods. Although a couple of bishops from
other provinces attended the Council of Tarragona in 516, no
national assembly met throughout the period of the Arian kingdom.
(In the seventh century, provincial synods met only when the king
commanded them to do so.)[3] A more serious matter is that after
the synod held at Barcelona about 540, or that of Valencia, if 549 is
its correct date, the Catholic bishops did not assemble again, even at
a provincial synod, until the reign of Reccared. That is to say, while
nine Catholic synods are known to have met in the forty-three
years from 506 to 549 (assuming that to be the date of the Council
of Valencia), not a single one is known to have met in the thirty-
seven years between 549 and 586, when Reccared came to the
throne. Now, a council was held in the neighbouring kingdom of
the Sueves in 561, in the reign of the Catholic King Ariamir. The
opening address of Lucretius, Metropolitan of Braga, makes it
clear that a long time had elapsed since a council had met in that
kingdom; and Lucretius implies that this was due to the inter-
ference of the Arian kings of Galicia.[4] The prohibition of councils
was a weapon, then, that Arian kings could and did use against
their Catholic subjects. The Visigothic kings followed the same
policy; for some words spoken by Reccared in his preliminary
address to the Third Council of Toledo in 589 show that in the preceding decades Catholic synods had been banned in his kingdom.[5]

Reccared lifted the ban. Who had imposed it? In view of
Isidore's praise of the tolerance of Theudis, and the fact that

---

been invited to Palencia? On this Montanus see Ildefonsus, *De Vir. Illustr.* 3 (*PL* 96.
199 f.), with Sister Athanasius Braegelmann, *The Life and Writings of St. Ildefonsus of
Toledo*, Diss. Washington, 1942, pp. 47 ff.

[1] Mansi, viii. 791.   [2] IV Tolet. 34 *fin.*   [3] See p. 280 below.
[4] Barlow, p. 105.
[5] Mansi, ix. 997, 'et quia decursis retro temporis haeresis imminens in tota
ecclesia catholica agere synodica negotia denegavit', etc.

councils are known to have met in Theudis's reign, it cannot have been he who prohibited Catholic councils. We never hear that Athanagild oppressed the Catholics of Spain, though he never allowed them to hold a synod. There is no evidence that he took steps either to conciliate or to persecute his Catholic subjects when he was surrounded by the three Catholic powers, France, Suevia, and Byzantium. The most likely candidate, then, is Agila, whose reign is twice described as oppressive by our Catholic authorities (p. 328 below). His motives are unknown; but if it was he who originally imposed the ban, Athanagild, Liuva, and Leovigild maintained it.

Perhaps the ban was a less severe hardship for the Church than it might at first sight appear. Pope Hormisdas, writing in 517 to all the bishops of Spain, had stressed that two provincial synods, or, if that were impossible, at least one synod, should be held in each year. The Third Council of Toledo declared that two synods should be summoned annually but that, in view of the great distances involved and the poverty of the churches of Spain, one synod at least ought to assemble in whatever place the metropolitan of the province should choose. At the end of the Second Council of Toledo the bishops had instructed Montanus to send out invitations to a synod at the appropriate time 'according to the decrees of earlier canons'; but the Third Council ruled that the bishops should decide the place and time of their next meeting before each synod ended so that the metropolitan might be spared the trouble of sending out the letters of invitation. But even though the provinces held only one synod at most in each year, the bishops' attendance left something to be desired. At Tarragona in 516 the synod laid down a severe penalty for bishops who, when summoned by their metropolitan to a synod, failed without good reason to attend. Now, even longer distances and heavier expenses were involved for bishops when they attended national councils than when they attended provincial ones; and in fact after the Third Council of Toledo the Catholic kings did not summon another national council for forty-four years.[1]

But in spite of this ban the general tolerance of the Arian kings

---

[1] Hormisdas, *Ep.* 25 (A. Thicl. p. 792); III Tolet. 18; II Tolet. 5; Conc. Tarrac. 6. The Catholic Church in Galicia, too, evidently had difficulty in making its bishops attend synods: see Martin of Braga, *Canones ex Orientalium Patrum Synodis*, 19 (Barlow).

is impressive and contrasts sharply with the attitude of the Catholics after the conversion of 589. Arian tolerance was not confined to the kings: it appears to have run right through the Arian population. An Arian who visited Tours in 584 declared that he believed what the Catholics believed; and he even attended mass in a Catholic church there, though he refused to partake of communion and he found fault with the Catholic form of the benediction (p. 84 below). Another Visigoth, whose name was Agila, had talked with Gregory of Tours four years earlier and said these remarkable words: 'Speak not evil of the law which thou thyself observest not; as for us, though we believe not the things which ye believe, yet we do not speak evil of them, for the holding of this or that belief may not be imputed as a crime. And indeed we have a common saying that no harm is done when one passing between the altars of the Gentiles and the church of God, payeth respect to both.'[1] Shortly after making this statement, which was not characteristic of sixth-century Catholics, Agila himself was forcibly 'converted' to Catholicism.

To what extent had Catholicism made headway among the Visigoths themselves? Few of them are known to have been Catholic in the fourth and fifth centuries. In the sixth century a Visigothic woman called Hilduarens, who died at Arahal near Ecija on 15 March 504, was probably a Catholic, for her sarcophagus was re-used for the Catholic monk, Fulgentius, and this would hardly have been done if the sarcophagus had had Arian associations.[2] But from 504 until the accession of King Leovigild in 568 we hear of no Visigoth who was a Catholic apart from the alleged converts of Turribius (p. 33 above); and among the signatories of the numerous Catholic synods that met in the first half of the century not a single one bears a Germanic name. In the early years of Leovigild we hear of only two Visigothic Catholics—the chronicler, John of Biclarum, who was then abbot of a monastery, and Masona, who was Bishop of Merida.

---

[1] Greg. Tur., *HF* v. 43; vi. 40, transl. O. M. Dalton. See F. J. Dölger, *Antike und Christentum*, vi (Münster, 1950), pp. 69 f.

[2] Vives, 149–50. See also ibid. 214, the tombstone of Ringilio, which was found in a Catholic Roman cemetery at Tarragona and cannot be dated. Was the Immafrita of ibid. 69, who died on 8 November 579 and was buried at Toledo, a Catholic or an Arian? Some believe that even the *dux* Zerezindo, who died on 30 July 578 (ibid. 153), was a Catholic, which in view of his high rank would be interesting, if true.

If this were all, we might conclude that only a small fraction of the barbarians had individually been converted to Catholicism before the general conversion of 589. But the names of the bishops who signed the minutes of the Third Council of Toledo give rise to a puzzle. Some of these were converts from Arianism, and these, of course, have Germanic names. But the vast majority of the bishops who signed had never been Arians. They had been Catholic throughout, and the curious fact is that some of these, too, bear Germanic names. The question is, how many? Masona of Merida and Theodoric of Cazlona (Castulo) were certainly Visigoths. But what of Mutto, or Motto,[1] of Jativa (Saetabis)? Is his name Roman or Gothic? It is probably Gothic.[2] And what of Ermaric, certainly a German, who describes himself as *Laniobrensis*? How is that term to be interpreted? Where was the see situated? Did it lie in Galicia (in which case the Bishop was a Sueve and so is irrelevant to our argument) or did it lie in the Visigothic kingdom, in which case Ermaric was a Visigothic Catholic? We are particularly well informed about the dioceses of Galicia, which have been carefully studied. Nowhere among them is there an *ecclesia Laniobrensis*.[3] The probability would seem to be, therefore, that Ermaric was a Visigoth. Hence, certainly two, probably three, and possibly four Visigoths had become Catholic bishops by the year 589. It might be argued that, while Masona was certainly a Catholic bishop in Leovigild's reign, the others may not have been appointed until after the accession of Reccared. But that hardly alters the position; for, to have been appointed to bishoprics in the period 586–8, they must already have been high dignitaries in the Catholic Church for some years previously, that is to say, when Leovigild was on the throne. Now, if, in fact, as many as three or four Catholic sees, that is, some five per cent of the total number, were occupied by Visigoths in the years immediately preceding the general conversion, the swing towards Catholicism may well have been substantial. In that case the conversion of 589 would seem to have been the culmination of a process that had been gathering momentum during the previous decades. It may be, therefore, that the kings banned conciliar meetings at a time when increasing

---

[1] Mansi, ix. 1001; x. 478.

[2] See E. Förstemann, *Altdeutsches Namenbuch²*, i (Bonn, 1900), pp. 1128 ff.

[3] *Laniobrensis* does not recur in the lists of the signatories until that attached to XIII Toledo in 683. There is no mention of it in P. David, *Études historiques sur la Galice et le Portugal du VIᵉ au XIIᵉ siècle* (Lisbon and Paris, 1947), pp. 19 ff.

numbers of their own followers were deserting the traditional faith.

On the other hand, it was not unknown for Catholics to go over to Arianism, even though the Arians insisted on rebaptism, which had been a criminal offence in the Roman law of the Late Empire, though under Alaric it ceased to be so.[1] Yet at the Council of Lerida the Catholic bishops dealt with persons who had been rebaptized, and forbade the faithful even to eat with them. Those who had been voluntarily rebaptized were to pray for no less than seven years among the catechumens, two further years among the faithful, and then, if the bishop should show mercy, they might be admitted to communion. In the reign of King Theudis, Justinian, Bishop of Valencia, devoted part of his *Responsiones* to the question of rebaptism, which he showed to be impermissible. The problem was one of importance under an Arian government.[2] Some Catholics avoided it by remaining Catholic themselves while having their children baptized as Arians.[3] There is no means of saying whether these amounted to a significant number of the Catholic population; but it cannot be doubted that the drift towards Catholicism among the Goths was historically more significant than the drift towards Arianism among the Hispano-Romans.

3. *The Two Churches*

There is no evidence that between the death of Ulfila in 381–3 and the accession of Leovigild in 568 any doctrinal change or development of note had been officially accepted by the Arian Visigoths. The action of the Third Council of Toledo in explicitly condemning the teachings of the Council of Rimini, which had met in 359, shows that Rimini was still fundamentally the official doctrine in Spain, as it had been for Ulfila himself long ago. Until the last decade of its life Gothic Arianism was a static doctrine, unchanged and apparently incapable of change. But in 580 Leovigild conceded the correctness of the Catholic teaching relating to the Son, the central point at issue between Catholicism and Arianism. The King's aim in making this dramatic concession will be

---

[1] *CTh* xvi. 6.

[2] Conc. Ilerd. 9, 14; Isidore, *De Vir. Illustr.* 33 (PL 83. 1099).

[3] Conc. Ilerd. 13. Those who believed in rebaptism were anathematized by III Tolet. 15. Rebaptism was also a problem in the Suevic kingdom of Galicia: see Pope Vigilius's letter printed in Barlow, p. 292.

discussed later on. But he did not achieve his aim. In fact, he must have gone far towards undermining his followers' belief in Arianism as such. The concession was a radical one. If this could be conceded practically the entire Arian position fell to the ground. It is not out of the question that Leovigild's action in 580, although designed to save Arianism, contributed to its utter destruction nine years later.

The Arians of Spain commonly referred to Catholicism as 'the Roman religion', while Arianism was considered by them to be 'the Catholic faith'.[1] To become a Nicaean was, so to speak, to become a Roman, to cease to be a Goth. But they cannot seriously have regarded Arianism as 'catholic': that would have been in contradiction with the use of Gothic as the liturgical language and with the requirement of rebaptism of converts from Catholicism. It is hard to believe that any Gothic king saw Arianism as a truly catholic faith, a potential national religion in which all the peoples of Spain might one day unite. It was the religion of the Goths, and of the Goths only; and that is what it was intended to be. True, there is some evidence that an occasional Catholic joined the Arians voluntarily or otherwise; but such conversions were spasmodic and unofficial. Officially rebaptism was obligatory until 580.

No list has survived of the Arian bishoprics of Spain. The Visigothic bishops who renounced Arianism in 589 were Ugnus of Barcelona, Fruisclus of Tortosa (Dertosa), and two bishops from Valencia, Murila and Ubiligisclus.[2] (We do not know why the city required two Arian bishops.) In addition to these, we hear of a bishop of Narbonne called Athaloc (p. 103 below), of a bishop called Uldila whose see is unnamed, and of Sunna of Merida, whom we shall meet later. But presumably there were several others: it is unthinkable, for instance, that there was no Arian bishop of Toledo.

Nothing is known of their method of appointment in normal conditions. Leovigild himself appointed Sunna to Merida in 582, but the circumstances were exceptional, and it would be unsafe to conclude that all Arian bishops were appointed by the Crown. Only one Arian synod is known to have met in Spain during the

---

[1] Greg. Tur., *In Glor. Martyr.* 24 (p. 502), 'Romanos enim vocitant nostrae homines relegionis'; cf. 78, 79 (p. 541); Jo. Biclar., *s.a.* 580 (ii. 216), 'de Romana religione ad nostram Catholicam fidem venientes' (so the MSS.).

[2] Mansi, ix. 988.

sixth century. This was Leovigild's synod of 580, but it is hard to believe that it was unique: even if doctrinal changes and definitions were thought superfluous, it is scarcely credible that the bishops managed their affairs and defined their attitude to new problems and new situations without once meeting together in the course of eighty years. The synod of 580 certainly reached the decisions which Leovigild wished it to reach—whether with or without opposition is unknown—, but again it would be unwise to generalize from the case of a synod held at the height of a civil war and to suppose that the Arian hierarchy was normally abject before the king.

The Gothic services were held in the Gothic language,[1] and they took place before daybreak.[2] It was a custom of the Goths, or at any rate of the Ostrogoths, to provide a special communion cup for the royal family distinct from that served to the people in general—a practice which, in the opinion of Gregory of Tours, made it possible for an assassin to poison an Ostrogothic queen without massacring the entire congregation as well.[3] In Visigothic Spain—where a Catholic was tonsured when beginning his training for the clerical life—the Arian tonsure differed from the Catholic: only a small *circulum* was shaved on the head, and the hair was otherwise worn long like that of laymen.[4] (Catholic clergy who wore their hair long had it cut forcibly, if necessary, by the archdeacon;[5] and the Council of Barcelona instructed all clergy to cut their hair but not to shave their beards.)[6] The triple as well as the simple immersion at baptism was recognized by the Catholic Church until it was noticed that the Arians of Spain immersed thrice. In a letter to Leander of Seville, Gregory the Great then recommended the Catholics to immerse once only so as to distinguish themselves from the heretics.[7] (His letter was written in April 591 when Arianism had been smashed, and the need to distinguish Catholic baptismal rites from Arian ones might seem to have been less pressing than it had formerly been.) The problem was a puzzling one: it had already been raised among the Catholics of the Suevic kingdom of Galicia. It had been discussed by Pope Vigilius in 538 in a letter to Profuturus, Metropolitan of Braga,

[1] Thompson, p. xiv n. 2.
[2] Socrates, *HE* vi. 8. 1 f.; Sidonius, *Ep.* i. 2. 4.
[3] Greg. Tur., *HF* iii. 31, but his story is apocryphal.
[4] IV Tolet. 41; cf. II Tolet. 1; Séjourné, pp. 191 f. [5] Conc. Agath. 20.
[6] Conc. Barcinon. 3. [7] Gregory I, *Ep.* i. 41.

who had asked Rome for a ruling on this and other matters; and
Vigilius, unlike his great successor, had declared in favour of the
triple immersion.[1] St. Martin of Braga later confirmed the Pope's
ruling: if the Catholics immersed only once, so as to distinguish
themselves from the Arians, might they not then be confused with
the Sabellians, who also practised the simple immersion?[2] In
spite of Gregory's authority, the position in the Visigothic kingdom remained confused: his ruling had to be re-enacted as late as
633, when the Fourth Council of Toledo found that the triple
immersion was still widespread.[3] Thus, on this issue, as on the
problem of the date of Easter in 577,[4] the Catholics of Galicia were
not wholly in step with the Catholics of the Visigothic kingdom.

Little is known about Catholic ordinands. Some became candidates after marriage. Turribius had had a distinguished secular
career before becoming a bishop (p. 33 above). The Second
Council of Toledo laid down the procedure for dealing with boys
whose parents had dedicated them to the Church in early childhood.
After being tonsured, they were educated by a prefect in the
bishop's palace (*domus ecclesiae*) under the eye of the bishop. When
they had completed their eighteenth year the bishop questioned
them before the whole clergy and people on their attitude towards
marriage. If they undertook to preserve their chastity, they were
appointed subdeacons from their twentieth year; and if they lived
blamelessly to the end of their twenty-fifth year, they were appointed deacons, provided that the bishop was satisfied that they could
carry out their duties. But if they then married or committed
fornication, they were held guilty of sacrilege and were expelled
from the Church. If at the time of their interrogation by the bishop
they expressed a wish to marry, they were allowed to do so freely;
and if later on, when they were of mature age, they and their
wives took a vow of continence, they might aspire to Holy
Orders.[5]

The Council of Narbonne pointed out in 589 that no bishop was
allowed to appoint an illiterate man as deacon or priest. If any such
had already been appointed, he must be forced to learn to read; and

[1] Text in Barlow, pp. 291 f. See David, op. cit., pp. 83 ff.
[2] Martin, *De Trina Mersione*, with Barlow, pp. 251–8.
[3] IV Tolet. 6; cf. Isidore, *De Vir. Illustr.* 40 (*PL* 83. 1102 f.); Ildefonsus, *De Cognit. Bapt.* 117 (*PL* 96. 160).
[4] Greg. Tur., *HF* v. 17, with Barlow, p. 261.
[5] II Tolet. 1. For a modification see IV Tolet. 55.

if he was slow in doing so, he must forfeit his salary until he succeeded in learning.[1]

Apart from a vague reference at the Third Council of Toledo (canon 1), the method of appointing bishops is not mentioned in the conciliar documents until the bishops of Tarraconensis met in the Church of the Holy Cross at Barcelona in 599, ten years after the conversion to Catholicism. The bishops enacted there that no layman could be appointed to a see without going through the regular grades, even if the king ordered it—for Reccared had high-handedly and not always wisely made appointments to bishoprics (p. 110 below). He could not be enthroned even if the clergy and people of the city assented or if he had been chosen by the bishops. The procedure was to be that two or three names, which the clergy and people of the city had agreed upon, should be submitted to the metropolitan and his suffragans; and these after a period of fasting should make the choice by casting lots.[2] But we shall see that neither this nor the ruling of the Fourth Council of Toledo in 633 stopped the kings from appointing both clergy and laymen to the sees.

Leander of Seville was succeeded as bishop of that great city by his brother Isidore; and their third brother, Florentius, became bishop of Ecija. In the time of King Theudis four brothers— Justinian of Valencia, Justus of Urgello, Nebridius of Egara, and Elpidius of Huesca—all obtained sees.[3] There is no reason to doubt that both groups of brothers succeeded through merit rather than through corrupt influence. In fact, the Catholic bishops are not known to have dealt at their synods in this period with the questions of nepotism and simony. Yet a glaring case arose soon after the middle of the century at Merida, the metropolitan see of Lusitania. The Metropolitan Paul, who had been a physician before coming from the East to Spain, performed a successful operation on the wife of a very rich Roman 'senator' of his diocese. In gratitude the senator at once made over to the Bishop one half of his property and in his will bequeathed him the other half. Now, this man was richer than any other senator in Lusitania; and when he and his wife died, Paul became so rich that 'all the means of the

---

[1] Conc. Narbon. 11. For the Byzantine province see the letter of Licinianus of Cartagena to Gregory the Great: Gregory I, *Ep.* i. 41 (p. 60. 13 ff.)

[2] Conc. Barcinon. 3, where note *per sacra regalia.*

[3] Isidore, op. cit. 33, 35, with D. H. Quentin, 'Elpidius, évêque de Huesca', *Revue bénédictine*, xxiii (1906), pp. 257–60, 487 f.

Church were reckoned as nothing in comparison with his goods'.[1] This wealth ought to have been given by Paul to his church (p. 50 below), but the Bishop regarded it as his private property. After many years he actually consecrated his nephew Fidelis as his successor and stated in his will that if the clergy of Merida accepted Fidelis as their new bishop he would bequeath all his riches to Fidelis in the first instance and after Fidelis's death to their church; but otherwise he would dispose of his property elsewhere.[2] After Paul's death there was an outcry in Merida against the wholly irregular consecration of Fidelis. But when Fidelis threatened to remove both himself and his riches from the church, the opposition reluctantly agreed to acquiesce in Paul's wishes: Fidelis would be bishop, and at his death he would leave all his possessions to the church in Merida. The result was that no church in Spain was richer than that of Merida, which in Leovigild's reign actually established a lending bank with a capital of 2,000 solidi.[3]

These events took place when the meetings of synods and councils in Spain had been banned by the kings (p. 35 f. above). Yet the clergy of Merida might well have remembered the letter that Pope Hormisdas (514–23) had addressed to all the bishops of Spain on 2 April 517. The Pope had been disturbed by reports which reached him from that country. In his letter he urged the Hispano-Romans to take care when appointing bishops. They must appoint only men of upright character. They must not consecrate laymen or penitents. Nobody must pay money in return for a bishopric: popular consent attests the judgement of God.[4]

At this time there was evidently contention among the bishops of southern Spain; and the Pope took the unusual step of sending one Sallustius to be papal vicar of the two provinces of Baetica and Lusitania simultaneously, instructing him to see that the decrees of the holy councils were enforced, to resolve disputes, and to hold synods when necessary. Hormisdas lived to see the end of the strife, for Sallustius was successful in restoring peace to the Church in Baetica. We still possess the letter in which the Pope expresses his joy that the dissensions have at last come to an end.[5] But he gives no hint of the nature of the points at issue. The Catholic

---

[1] *VPE* iv. 2. 18.
[2] Ibid. iv. 4. 4, discussed by Garvin, pp. 385 ff.
[3] *VPE* iv. 5. 1–3. On the incident see Garvin, pp. 385–7. The bank: *VPE* v. 3. 9.
[4] Mansi, viii. 432.   [5] Ibid. 433 f., 479 f.

Church, it seems, did not always present a united front to its Arian rulers; and Paul and Fidelis did little to increase its credit.

The general rule in Late Roman times was that the revenues of a church should be divided into four equal parts, the bishop taking one, the local clergy another, a third being devoted to the repair and lighting of the church, while the fourth quarter was given to the poor. But in Spain the arrangement was different. Here the offerings of the faithful were divided into three equal parts among the bishop, the clergy, and a fund for the maintenance and lighting of the church, while the poor were left to charity. As early as 516 the bishops of Tarraconensis speak of an 'ancient custom' whereby the bishop takes one third of the whole income of a parish church, though they imply that if on his annual visitation the bishop found the church to be in bad repair he was himself to have it repaired.[1]

But their legitimate income by no means satisfied some of the bishops. In 589 a number of them were found to be cruelly oppressive and extortionate to the parish priests in their dioceses. Transport duties and 'taxes' were imposed on the local clergy, who were urged by the Third Council to take their complaints to the metropolitans.[2] Even before that date many men who had founded and endowed churches had asked that the endowment should not pass under the bishop's control. It appears that some bishops would divert the endowment to their own uses, leaving the church to fall into ruin and the clergy to survive without an income.[3] Such bishops were in future to be reported to their synod, but both in 589 and again in 633 it was repeated that the bishop had full control over the endowments.

Apart from questions of liturgical usage the sixth-century Catholic synods were particularly occupied with two problems: (i) the celibacy of the clergy, and (ii) the misappropriation of church property by the clergy. So many enactments were passed on these two subjects that offences would seem to have been widespread.

The celibacy of the clergy was in theory universal among the Catholics of the West by the time the battle of Vouillé was fought and lost. But the Spanish councils were frequently obliged to

[1] Conc. Tarrac. 8, 'quia tertia ex omnibus per antiquam traditionem, ut accipiatur ab episcopis, novimus statutum'. The same rule held in the Suevic kingdom: I Bracar. 7 (Barlow, p. 112); II Bracar. 2. For donations 'pro luminaria ecclesiae vestrae atque stipendia pauperum vel qui in aula beatitudinis vestrae quotidianis diebus deservire videntur', see *Formulae Visigothicae*, 8 f.
[2] III Tolet. 20.   [3] Ibid. 19; IV Tolet. 33.

discuss it, and Spanish clergy (presumably below the rank of subdeacon) were condemned if they married without consulting with their bishop or if they married a widow, a divorcee, or a prostitute.[1] The question of celibacy arose at Agde in 506, at Tarragona in 516, at Gerona in the following year, and at the Second Council of Toledo in 527. At Agde the bishops referred to 'priests, deacons, subdeacons, and so on, who are not free to marry'.[2] They cited a decretal of Pope Innocent to show that married priests or deacons must not return to the bed of their wives on pain of being unfrocked.[3] At Tarragona they declared that readers and doorkeepers who wished to live with or marry an adulterous woman had either to leave her or be dismissed from their posts.[4] If ordained after marriage all clergy in that same province of Tarraconensis, from the bishop to the subdeacon, had to live separately from their wives. If one did not wish to do so, he must have a brother cleric to live with him so as to sustain him and to testify to his upright life.[5] No widower could be ordained at all if he were known to have associated with another woman, slave or free, after his wife's death.[6] If it were found that a priest or deacon had been twice married before his ordination, he was allowed to continue in his office in name only. Such a priest could not celebrate mass, and such a deacon could not serve at the altar.[7] In 619 it was found that some men had been consecrated as deacons at Ecija (Astigi) although they were married to widows: they were dismissed from their appointments.[8]

The bishops, supported by Alaric II, repeatedly enacted that a priest must not keep any woman in his house except his mother or sister or (in Gallia) his daughter or niece.[9] Slave- and freed-women must be removed from his home.[10] At Gerona in 517 it was laid down that those who were unmarried when ordained might have either a slave or a friend or their mother or sister in their home to look after them.[11] At Toledo the bishops declared that no cleric, from the rank of subdeacon up, could live with a woman, whether she was free, freed, or slave: his female slaves must be handed over to his mother, sister, or other close relative.

---

[1] IV Tolet. 44. [2] Conc. Agath. 39. [3] Ibid. 9.
[4] Conc. Tarrac. 9. [5] Conc. Gerund. 6.
[6] Ibid. 8. For the Byzantine province see Gregory I, *Ep.* i. 41 (p. 60. 13 ff.), Licinianus to Gregory. [7] Conc. Agath. 1.
[8] II Hispal. 4. [9] Conc. Agath. 10; *CTh* xvi. 2. 44.
[10] Conc. Agath. 11. [11] Conc. Gerund. 7.

A guilty cleric was not only to be unfrocked—and he then became
liable for service on his city council[1]—and driven from the doors
of his church, but was also to be deprived of the company of his
fellow-clergy and laymen and might not even converse with
them.[2] The Third Council of Toledo dealt with the matter more
drastically (pp. 100 below).

The Arians, too, were served partly by a married clergy, and
presented an acute problem in 589, when numbers of married Arian
clergy joined the Catholic Church. What was to be done with their
wives? The Third Council of Toledo declared that all bishops,
priests, and deacons who had abandoned Arianism should be
forbidden to cohabit with their wives; that is to say, the Council
applied to them the same rules as applied to Catholics who had been
ordained after marriage. Any who disregarded this ruling should be
reduced to the status of reader.[3] The converted Arian priests and
deacons were mentioned again at the provincial Council of
Tarraconensis that met at Saragossa in 592: those who lived a
chaste life should continue to function as priests in the Catholic
Church, but others were to be reduced in rank.[4]

The problems of defending Church property against misappropriation by the clergy puzzled both the Catholic and the Arian
churches for decades. The Council of Agde in 506 laid down the
rule that if a bishop was compelled by the interests of his church to
sell any of its property, he had first to state the reasons for the
projected sale to two or three of his comprovincials; and if they
approved, they had to sign the deed of sale. Any other form of
transaction was invalid. If a bishop manumitted any of the church's
slaves, he was allowed to present him with property worth not
more than 20 solidi. (Money or property was often given to the
freed slave in confirmation of his being set free.)[5] If in fact he gave
him more, the excess was to be recovered by the church when the
bishop died.[6] After the conversion in 589 this was one of the first
matters to which the bishops attended. They once again enacted
that bishops could not legally alienate the property of the Church
except to assist monks, other churches in the diocese, strangers,
clergy, or the poor. But even these could be helped only provided

[1] *CTh* xvi. 2. 39.   [2] II Tolet. 3.
[3] III Tolet. 5; cf. Conc. Hispal. 3.   [4] Conc. Caesaraug. 1.
[5] *VPE* v. 13. 4; *LV* v. 7. 1; *Formulae Visigothicae*, 6, etc.
[6] Conc. Agath. 7; cf. 45.

that the interests of the cathedral church were left unimpaired. If the bishop wished to dedicate one of his diocesan churches as a monastic church he had first to obtain the permission of his provincial synod. Moreover, church slaves could only be freed in accordance with the manner laid down by the canons.[1] A specific case was discussed by the First Council of Seville in 590. The bishops there addressed a letter to Pegasius, Bishop of Ecija (Astigi). The deacons of the latter had supplied them with an inventory not only of the church's slaves who had been set free by Pegasius's predecessor, Gaudentius, but also of those whom the late bishop had given as gifts to his relatives. The Council pointed out that those transferred from the Church's ownership by Gaudentius were not legally free, and the others were not legally the property of Gaudentius's relatives unless the Church had been adequately compensated from Gaudentius's property.[2] When Masona of Merida lay on what he thought was his death-bed, he manumitted some of his church's slaves and gave them a little property, and he did not compensate his church. But his officious archdeacon, Eleutherius, would probably have cancelled the Bishop's action had he not suddenly died while Masona was still alive.[3]

Priests, too, could be a problem in this respect. If they sold Church property or gave it away as a gift, the sale or gift was invalid; and the loss to the church in question had to be made good out of the priest's own property, if he had any.[4] Priests had also to make good the loss, and they were liable to excommunication, if they falsified, suppressed, or handed over to the Church's adversaries any document showing the Church's title to any of its possessions.[5] In 589, when the State became Catholic, the bishops of Septimania enacted that any priest, deacon, or subdeacon who made away with property belonging to his church or to his bishop's palace without the bishop's permission had not only to restore what he had taken, but had also to leave his church and spend two years in penance, after which he might return to his duties.[6]

---

[1] III Tolet. 3, 4, 6.   [2] Conc. Hispal. 1 f.   [3] *VPE* v. 13. 1 f.

[4] Conc. Agath. 22. See also II Tolet. 4. St. Aemilianus was relieved of his duties as priest at Vergegium by the Bishop of Tirassona for reducing the revenues of his church. We have no details about his offence, but his fellow-clerics informed on him to his bishop: see Braulio, *Vita S. Aemiliani*, 5 f. (PL 80. 706).

[5] Conc. Agath. 26.   [6] Conc. Narbon. 8.

The most fruitful opportunity for priests arose when a bishop died, or even when he still lay dying. When Masona of Merida thought that he was dying, he was careful to instruct his archdeacon to look after the church.[1] The Council of Tarragona in 516 declared that when a bishop died intestate an inventory of all his property should be carefully drawn up by his priests and deacons after he had been buried; and if any of them purloined anything he was to be subject to the law of theft.[2] But this was an inadequate precaution, and the Council of Lerida also dealt with the matter. When a bishop died, his goods were not to be indiscriminately plundered by the clergy, as had often happened. The bishop who came to bury him was to protect all his belongings. It was strictly forbidden for any cleric of whatever rank or office to remove or to conceal anything at all from the palace of a dead or dying bishop. A guardian must be appointed who with one or two reliable assistants would preserve everything until the new bishop arrived.[3] This, too, was not enough. The matter was raised yet again at the Council of Valencia. The clergy were the usual culprits, stealing all the bishop's effects and those of his church, from books to crops and flocks of sheep. When a bishop lay dying, therefore, his neighbouring bishop was to go to him, and after conducting the burial service was at once to keep careful watch over the goods of the church so that the clergy might have no opportunity for theft before a successor was appointed. An inventory was to be drawn up and sent to the metropolitan, who would appoint a visitor to pay the clergy their salaries, and, if there was some delay in consecrating a new bishop, to give the metropolitan from time to time an account of the property entrusted to him.[4] The same Council forbade the late bishop's relatives to take away any of his property without informing the metropolitan or his comprovincials; otherwise they might well take not only his personal effects but some of his church's property as well.[5]

But the clergy might steal the goods of a church on other occasions than on the death of a bishop;[6] or they and their bishops (like Paul of Merida) might regard as their own private property gifts that members of their congregations had given them

[1] VPE v. 13. 2.   [2] Conc. Tarrac. 12.   [3] Conc. Ilerd. 16.
[4] Conc. Valent. 2; VII Tolet. 3; IX Tolet. 9.   [5] Conc. Valent. 3.
[6] Conc. Agath. 5.

—all such gifts in fact belonged to their respective churches.[1] This unedifying matter was still being debated in the seventh century when the bishops who met at the Seventh Council of Toledo in 646 referred to the decisions of the Council of Valencia and added to them the ruling that any bishop who was summoned to bury a fellow-bishop and delayed to do so was to be barred by his provincial council or by his metropolitan from celebrating mass or partaking of communion for the space of one year; and if the senior clergy of the church of the dead or dying bishop delayed to summon him, they, too, were to be punished. But in 655 in the province of Carthaginiensis the visiting bishop was awarded a fee of 72 solidi if the see of the late bishop was a rich one, and of 36 solidi if it was poor.[2]

Even in the fifth century the Arian Church, too, had had to concern itself with the problem of bishops and priests who privately sold church property or gave it away as a gift without the consent of their colleagues. Such sales and gifts were declared invalid by King Euric, but no punishment was prescribed in the civil code;[3] doubtless the Arian authorities dealt with wrong-doers. Moreover, as soon as a bishop was consecrated, he was obliged at once to draw up an inventory of his church's property, and this inventory was to be signed by five witnesses. When he died his successor was required to compare this inventory with the existing property of the church; and if anything were found to be missing, the late bishop's heirs had to make good the loss from their own property. If the late bishop (or priest or deacon) were found to have sold anything, his successor was required to restore the purchase-money to the purchasers and so to recover the article in question.[4] A further law was framed so as to prevent ecclesiastical property from passing into private hands. The heirs of bishops and other clerics whose sons had entered the service of a church, and who had been presented with land or other property by the church, were obliged at once to return the property if the sons became laymen or if they entered the service of another Arian church.[5]

One or two of Leovigild's laws illustrate the influence of the Arian clergy over their congregations, even the property-owners among them. It became a widespread practice to persuade another

---

[1] Conc. Agath. 6; cf. 4.   [2] VII Tolet. 3.   [3] Cod. Euric. 306; *LV* v. 1. 3.
[4] *LV* v. 1. 2.   [5] Cod. Euric. loc. cit.; *LV* v. 1. 4.

man's slaves, whether male or female, to flee to a church and complain to the clergy there of their master's ill-usage of them. The priests could be induced to compel the owner to sell the slave in question. (How they compelled him is not recorded, but it is clear that their authority was great.) The priest or a third party would then buy the slave on behalf of those who had instigated the mischief, and the latter would gain possession of their neighbour's slave even when he had originally had no intention whatever of selling him. The law now directed that the clergy should restore such a slave to his original owner, who was entitled to keep the money that he had been paid for the slave. The cleric who had connived at the fraudulent sale had to provide the owner with a second slave of equal value with the first.[1] Again, if a local judge were unable to lay hands on an accused man because some powerful person protected him, he was to inform the king if he were near at hand, or, if the king were not easily accessible, the local bishop.[2] Evidently, even a powerful landowner would hesitate to disobey the bishop. This is the only case recorded by the laws of the Arian kings where the Arian bishop took any part in the civil administration. But Leovigild's code, of course, is only a fragment, and the parts of it which Reccesuinth discarded may have had more to say on this matter.

We hear little else about the Arian Church. A criminal could run for asylum to an Arian as well as to a Catholic church,[3] and slaves could be manumitted there.[4] The inventory of those goods that a guardian was to hold on trust for his ward might also be given for safekeeping to the Arian clergy.[5]

The evidence is very slight; but what little there is does not suggest that the Arian clergy played a very different role among their flocks from that taken by the Catholic bishops among the Hispano-Romans. There is no evidence whatever that they had any influence on the secular legislation of the kings or on their political policies.

4. Heretics, Jews, and Pagans

The numerous Roman laws against heresy were in many cases directed against Arianism itself and were naturally discarded by

---

[1] Ibid. v. 4. 17. [2] Ibid. vii. 1. 1, where *dux* may not be the right reading.
[3] Ibid. iii. 2. 2; 3. 2; vi. 5. 18; ix. 2. 3; 3. 1–4. [4] Ibid. v. 7. 2; cf. 9.
[5] Ibid. iv. 3. 3.

Alaric II. But he included in his code a law of Theodosius II which condemned a number of minor sects together with three which are of some interest.[1] One of these three sects was the Eunomians, the followers of the fourth-century bishop, Eunomius, who had once signed the minutes of the Council of Rimini, the basis of the beliefs of Ulfila himself. But afterwards he had gone on to work out an extreme theory of the Trinity, which is not known to have had followers in Spain. The second of these condemned heresies was Priscillianism, the only heresy of consequence to emerge from Roman Spain. During the sixth century its stronghold was the Suevic kingdom in Galicia, though it also had its adherents in the Visigothic kingdom. Turribius in Palencia was able to combat Priscillianism openly under the Arian kings (p. 33 above); but the letter of Montanus, Bishop of Toledo, to the brethren of Palencia expresses his concern that Priscillianism was honoured both in name and in fact among the faithful of that area. Montanus reminds them that this heresy had been condemned by the secular law as well as by the holy bishops; but in fact it was still causing concern to the holy bishops in the middle of the seventh century.[2] Thirdly, Alaric condemned Manichaeism. He took over into his code a harsh Roman law which forbade the Manichees to hold public office and to live in the cities—his hope was to prevent proselytism —and to enter into contracts and to receive or bequeath legacies: their property went to the Treasury. It was an offence to conceal Manichees or to connive at their activities.[3] None of these heresies is known to have won Visigothic adherents, and Leovigild's code is silent about them.

Alaric discarded most of the Roman laws relating to the Jews, but he retained the ban on intermarriage between Romans and Jews, which Jewish law also prohibited and which the Council of Elvira had frowned upon at the beginning of the fourth century.[4] But cases of intermarriage still occurred in the seventh century and

[1] Theodosius, *Nov.* 3.

[2] Mansi, viii. 789E. In this letter (as in his letter to Turribius) Montanus reproves the priests of Palencia for consecrating chrism when they must have known that only bishops were entitled to do so. For Priscillianism in the seventh century see Braulio, *Ep.* 44 (*PL* 80. 693D).

[3] Valentinian, *Nov.* 18; cf. *CTh* xvi. 7. 3 interpretatio. Justinian, Bishop of Valencia in the reign of Theudis, wrote against the Bonosians: Isidore, *De Vir. Illustr.* 33 (*PL* 83. 1099). But that hardly proves that there were Bonosians in Spain in his time.

[4] *CTh* iii. 7. 2 = ix. 7. 5; Mansi, ii. 8.

were still regarded as a problem.[1] Jews and Samaritans were forbidden to hold any public appointment, civil or military, or to be *defensor* (p. 125 below) of a city, or a prison guard; for they might use these posts to inflict harm on Christians, even on Christian priests. They were allowed to repair their synagogues, but not to build new ones: if they did so, the building was to be converted into a *Catholic* church, and the builders were to pay the ruinous fine of 50 lb. gold to the Treasury.[2] On the other hand, civil suits between Jews, if both parties agreed, might be heard by their own clergy rather than in the public courts; and in such cases the decisions of their clergy were as binding as if they had been imposed by a royal judge.[3] Jews could not be dunned for debts to the Treasury or on any other account on the Jewish Sabbath.[4] But whereas Roman law had allowed baptized Jews to revert to Judaism without penalty, Alaric withdrew this concession, and such persons now became liable to the penalty laid down for converts to Judaism.[5]

A Jew who converted either a Christian slave or a Christian freeman to Judaism was punished by death and the confiscation of his property,[6] while the proselyte, if a freeman, lost his property to the Treasury and forfeited his testamentary rights.[7] The converted slave was set free. Jews were forbidden to molest any of their number who had been converted to Christianity.[8] Alaric also took over into his code a somewhat vague Roman law that appeared to forbid Jews to own Christian slaves; but the law laid down no penalty and was clearly a dead letter.[9]

In all, the king was interested mainly in preventing proselytizing by the Jews. They ranked, of course, as Roman citizens and were liable to tax. But in religious matters in general he left them to live their lives in peace. His attitude was one of astonishing liberality in

---

[1] IV Tolet. 63, etc.

[2] Theodosius, *Nov.* 3. The remains of a synagogue have been excavated at Elche near Cartagena; Vives, 431–2. It is described as a Christian church by J. Puig y Catafalch, *Byzantion*, i (1924), p. 525.

[3] *CTh* ii. 1. 10. [4] Ibid. ii. 8. 26. [5] Ibid. xvi. 8. 23.

[6] Ibid. xvi. 9. 1 (which also applies in the case of non-Christian slaves); Theodosius, *Nov.* 3, with Katz, p. 43 n. 4; cf. *CTh* iii. 1. 5, with Katz, p. 98. But see Paul, *Sentent.* v. 22. 4.

[7] *CTh* xvi. 7. 3, 8. 7. But Paul, *Sentent.* v. 22. 3, adopted by Alaric, states that Roman citizens who allow themselves or their slaves to be converted to Judaism are not only to lose their property but to be banished to an island for life, and physicians who perform circumcisions are to be punished capitally.

[8] *CTh* xvi. 8. 5. [9] See the interpretation, ibid. iii. 1. 5.

comparison with what was to come under some of the Catholic kings of the seventh century. Such documents as we possess suggest that this tolerance was shared by the Gothic population at large. At any rate Masona, the Catholic Visigoth who became bishop of Merida in the reign of King Leovigild, showed great kindness to Jews and pagans alike, and when he founded a hospital he opened it to Jews as well as to Christians; and our authority for his action is in no way critical of him for his attitude.[1] But at the Council of Agde in 506 the bishops had forbidden Catholic priests and even laymen to eat with Jews.[2]

Under Alaric's laws Christians who lapsed into Judaism or into paganism were denied the right of testifying in the courts.[3] Although the King discarded the twenty-five laws 'de paganis' of the Theodosian Code (xvi. 10) and did not interfere with pagan belief as such, he was by no means uninterested in certain pagan practices. Magicians, makers of spells, men who invoked storms to damage the grape harvest, those who made men mad by invoking demons, those who inquired into the future (especially the king's future), diviners known as *harioli*, those who offered sacrifices by night to demons, were all alike guilty of a capital crime.[4] For while Arians and Catholics watched each other suspiciously and defended their positions, and disputed and debated in the cities, outside the city walls pagan practices survived on a scale which exasperated the bishops, who were more interested in paganism than were the kings. At the Council of Agde in 506 the Catholic hierarchy found it necessary to forbid on pain of excommunication both their clergy and their laity to pay attention to augury and divination or the foretelling of the future by inspecting the Scriptures; and these practices appear to have been widespread.[5] At the Third Council of Toledo the bishops admitted that 'the sacrilege of idolatry is firmly implanted throughout almost the whole of Spain and Septimania'. Hence, every bishop along with the local judge was to inquire into paganism in his district and to crush it. Landowners, too, were to extirpate it from their estates and households, but the death penalty was explicitly ruled out. Excommunication was the penalty for bishops, judges, and land-

---

[1] *VPE* v. 2. 7, 3. 5.   [2] Conc. Agath. 40.   [3] *CTh* xvi. 7. 3.
[4] Ibid. ix. 16. 3, 4, 7. Observe that Theodosius, *Nov.* 3 § 8, is not noticed in the interpretation of that Novel. See further Paul, *Sentent.* v. 21; 23. 15 ff.
[5] Conc. Agath. 42.

owners who neglected this duty.[1] Psalms alone should be sung at the funerals of clerics, and not the baneful song that was usually sung by the people over the dead; nor should men slash their own breasts or those of their kinsmen or members of their family. The bishops tried to stamp out the dances and foul songs which the people used to arrange on saints' days when they ought to have been at church and which interrupted the divine service with their noise.[2] At the synod of Narbonne held in that same year the bishops were aghast to hear that many Catholics considered Thursday, Jupiter's day, to be a holy day and would do no work on it. They enacted that free persons who refused to work on Thursdays should be excluded from the Church and should spend a year in penance, while slaves should be beaten.[3] The synod also gave its attention to diviners called *caragii* and *sorticularii*. Those who consulted them were to be excluded from church and were to pay a fine of six ounces of gold to the *comes civitatis* (p. 139 below), while the diviners themselves, when found, were to be beaten and sold as slaves and their price given to the poor.[4] (King Reccared is not known to have confirmed the decisions of this synod.) Some landowners had already been in action along these lines even under the Arian kings; for Montanus, writing *c.* 531, was able to congratulate Turribius on wiping out paganism in his area (p. 33 above).[5]

What we should very much like to know is whether these practices were confined to the Hispano-Romans or whether they could also be found among the Visigoths themselves. The fact that a number of them were banned in the legislation of King Chindasuinth (642–53)[6] does not prove that they could be found among the Goths, for Chindasuinth intended his laws to apply to the Romans as well as to the Goths. But the fact that both the Third Council of Toledo and the synod of Narbonne instructed Gothic officials (the *iudex territorii* and the *comes civitatis*) to inquire into pagan practices shows that some at least of these practices could be

---

[1] III Tolet. 16.

[2] Ibid. 22–3, with Fontaine, i. 439, on the *ballematiae*. Note the co-operation of the bishop and the *iudex*, p. 100 below. They are required to co-operate again in the fight against paganism in 681: XII Tolet. 11.

[3] Conc. Narbon. 15. Some women in Arles, too, would not work on Thursdays: Caesarius, *Sermo* 52 (p. 230, Morin); cf. 13 (p. 68), etc.

[4] Conc. Narbon. 14.

[5] Mansi, viii. 790, 'idololatriae error abscessit'.

[6] *LV* vi. 2. 4 f., and the whole title; cf. xi. 2. 2.

found among the Goths, for these officials had no jurisdiction over Romans at that date. Moreover, a Gothic cemetery dating from the early sixth century has been excavated at Estagel (Dép. Pyrénées-orientales). A child buried in it seems to have had a great iron stake driven through its breast, and, though there is no parallel to this elsewhere in the cemetery, it appears to have a significance which could hardly be thought Christian. [1]

But in general we know nothing of the pagan survivals that could still be found among the Visigoths when they were nominally Arians, nor do we know whether their paganism had been affected as a result of entering the Roman Empire, or whether any specifically Roman practices had been adopted by them. But the attitude of the Arian kings is clear. Although they frowned on certain pagan practices that were thought to injure life or property, just as they frowned upon proselytism by the Jews, yet pagans and Jews, like Catholics and the Arians themselves, were allowed to practise their devotions and observe their rites without fearing the interference of the State.

---

[1] R. Lantier, 'Le cimetière wisigothique d'Estagel', *Gallia*, i (1943), pp. 153–88, at pp. 173, 183; J. M. Santa-Olalla, 'El cementerio hispano-visigodo de Estagel', *Archivo español de Arqueología*, xiv (1940–1), pp. 128–31. But the practice of nailing corpses, which has been particularly remarked in the provinces of Soria and Guadalajara, appears to be of Hispano-Roman origin: H. Obermaier, 'Leichennagelung im spanischen Mittelalter', *Forschungen und Fortschritte*, ix (1933), pp. 169–71; Zeiss, pp. 90 f. For a pagan practice which was condemned in Leovigild's code and was therefore presumably Gothic see *LV* xi. 2. 2 'si quis mortui sarcofacum abstulerit, dum sibi vult habere remedium', etc.

III · LEOVIGILD

ISIDORE's chronicle is of less importance for the reign of Leovigild than for earlier Visigothic history, for we still possess the chief source of his information about this formidable king. His source is the superb chronicle written by a Catholic Goth of Santarem (Scallabis) in Lusitania, John by name, founder and abbot of an unidentified monastery called Biclarum, a man educated in both Greek and Latin, who ended his career as Bishop of Gerona. He was exiled by Leovigild, as we shall see, but that did not dim his admiration for the energetic and heretical monarch. The chronicle covers the period 567–90 and can stand comparison with the great chronicles of fifth-century Gaul. It is rare indeed that we can detect in it an error of fact or of judgement (p. 31 n. 6 above, p. 104 n. 4 below).

Leovigild was the most remarkable of the Arian kings of Spain. He restored the power of the monarchy, he re-established Visigothic control over the huge areas of the country which Athanagild had lost, and at the end of his reign he incorporated the Suevic kingdom of Galicia in his realm. He reformed the coinage, restored order after the financial chaos of Athanagild's later years, and produced coins that were wholly independent of the Byzantine coinage: they showed the King's bust and his name together with the name of the mint that issued them. He dressed himself 'in royal raiment and seated himself upon a throne'. Hitherto the kings had worn much the same dress as their subjects and had been accessible to all, like the old Germanic chieftains. But Leovigild surrounded the throne with something of Byzantine pomp, though the details of what he did are not recorded.[1]

We do not know at what date he carried through his revision of Euric's code of laws and published a revised code which remained in force among the Gothic population for about three quarters of a century. (The Romans were still subject to Alaric's *Breviarium*.)

---

[1] Isidore, *HG* 51 (ii. 288), 'primusque inter suos regali veste opertus solio resedit; nam ante eum et habitus et consessus communis ut populo, ita et regibus erat'. For possible numismatic confirmation of this see Miles, p. 48; P. Grierson, *Numismatic Chronicle* (1953), p. 81 n. 12.

Isidore remarks that what the King did was to amend those of Euric's laws which were inadequate, to omit those which were obsolete, and to add a large number of new ones of his own.[1] His code has not survived: even its title is lost. But 324 of its enactments were included without change by King Reccesuinth (649–72) in the code which he published about 654. There they are entitled *antiquae* so that a large fraction of Leovigild's legislation can be identified. It is admirable law, lucid, reasonable by the standards of its day, and to the point. Except in a law that he took over from Euric[2] he never quotes the text of the Scriptures to justify his legislation and never invokes a religious sanction for it.

He carefully reproduced the distinction between the Gothic and the Roman inhabitants of his kingdom in a few laws which concerned the division of the land.[3] Here the distinction was of importance to him: some of his revenues depended on the preservation of Roman-owned land, while it was politically important to prevent the Romans from encroaching on land owned by noble Goths. Otherwise he rarely refers to the distinction between the two nationalities over which he ruled. But that does not mean that he wished to obliterate it: he was legislating for Goths only. True, the most important single enactment that has been ascribed to him is that by which the ban on the intermarriage of Goths and Romans was annulled. In Alaric's code mixed marriages had been punished capitally. The Catholic Church in Spain also frowned on them: at the Council of Elvira, which met at the beginning of the fourth century, the bishops had forbidden Catholic girls to be given in marriage to heretics who refused to join the Catholic Church. Now, it has often been thought that Leovigild's purpose in removing the ban was to break down one of the strongest barriers to the fusion of the two nationalities and that his ultimate aim was to merge Goths and Romans into one united people. That is not the case. The King

---

[1] Isidore, loc. cit. The view that it was Leovigild, not Reccesuinth, who abrogated in Spain the *Breviarium* of Alaric II is perverse: the arguments in favour of it, such as they are, are set out by A. Larraona and A. Tabera, 'El derecho Justinianeo en España', *Atti del congresso internazionale di diritto romana, Bologna e Roma, 1933* (Pavia, 1935), ii. 85–182, at 88–97, who themselves reject the theory and give a bibliography in their footnotes. The further theory, associated with the name of Garcia Gallo, that Leovigild's code as well as those of Euric and Alaric applied successively to all the inhabitants of the kingdom, Romans as well as Goths, is argued with bibliography by Alvaro d'Ors, 'La territorialidad del derecho de los Visigodos', *Settimane*, iii (Spoleto, 1956), pp. 363–408. The theory is misconceived.

[2] *LV* iv. 2. 15.   [3] Ibid. x. 1. 8 f., 16.

gives his reason in the text of the law, and he says nothing of any far-reaching change of policy on the relations of Goths and Romans. According to his words, the old law had lost its strength; and he repealed it because it could not be enforced. His action was not part of a systematic attempt to unite the two peoples of his kingdom: there is no evidence that such a scheme ever entered his head. In fact, several examples of inter-marriage are known from the sixth century, when it was illegal,[1] whereas, curiously enough, very few are recorded from the seventh century, when it was permitted. Some seventh-century cases may be concealed by the fact that, although no Hispano-Roman is known to have taken on a Gothic name, Catholic Goths like John of Biclarum did sometimes call themselves by Latin names. In the seventh century a Gothic name denotes a Goth; a Latin name denotes either a Hispano-Roman or a Goth. Nor is there any evidence that Leovigild withdrew in some respects the favoured position that the Goths enjoyed over their Roman neighbours (p. 124 below).[2]

He made an attempt to solve the old problem of the succession to the throne. In 573, perhaps taking a hint from his brother Liuva, he associated his two sons with himself on the throne, with a view to their succeeding him when he died (p. 64 below). Whether he expected them to be joint rulers after his death, as he and Liuva had been joint rulers after Athanagild's death, is unknown. If so, his

---

[1] Ibid. iii. 1. 1; cf. *CTh* iii. 14. 1; Mansi, ii 8. See K. Zeumer, *NA* xxiii (1898), pp. 477 ff.; ibid. xxiv (1899), pp. 573 ff. Specific cases of intermarriage, like those of Fravitta and Athaulf in an earlier day, are rarely recorded, but one is apparently indicated in Vives, 86, 'Sinticio ... cognomento Dindomum paterno traens linea Getarum', a tombstone dated to 632 found at Salacia; but Sinticio was born in 572 (not 562, as Zeumer, *NA* xxiv (1899), pp. 575) so that it is just possible, though perhaps unlikely, that his parents were married after Leovigild had changed the law. See also Vives, 360, 371. Another possible case is that of Diusvirus and Wiliesinda, who lived in Narbo late in the fifth century: Fiebiger–Schmidt, *Inschriftensammlung*, 99, who make the couple Burgundian; but Narbo was never in Burgundian hands. Theudis, who married a rich Hispano-Roman woman (p. 10 above), was of course an Ostrogoth. For the old view that the first wife of Leovigild himself was a Roman see p. 64 n. 2 below. For the marriage of a Roman with a Suevic woman of Galicia see Vives, 502–3 (A.D. 634), and long ago Wallia's daughter had married a Sueve: Sidonius, *carm.* ii. 361 f. It was against the custom of the Rugi to marry a foreign woman: Procopius, *BG* vii. 2. 3. The position in Vandal Africa is obscure: C. Courtois, *Les Vandales et l'Afrique* (Paris, 1955), p. 220 n. 3. In Ostrogothic Italy intermarriage continued to be banned by Roman law (Mommsen, *Ges. Schr.* vi. 475), but seems to have been permitted in the Burgundian kingdom (*Legg. Burg.* xii. 5) and among the Franks.

[2] Cf. Cod. Euric. 312, with *LV* v. 4. 20; and see Zeumer, *NA* xxiii (1898), pp. 434 f.

plan is not precisely paralleled in the whole of Visigothic history. But his action had only a limited measure of success, and in the year 603 his last known descendant, his grandson Liuva II, was dethroned and murdered.

1. *The Restoration of the Kingdom*

John of Biclarum says that the kingdom, which had been diminished by various rebellions, was wonderfully restored to its old limits by the King.[1] The rebellious areas lay in the south and the north-west. Yet Leovigild began his operations with an attack on the Byzantine province. Whether he had inherited a war from Athanagild or whether this was an act of aggression on his part, is unknown. At all events, he had chosen his time well, when the Byzantines were distracted by enemies in Europe, Asia, and Africa.[2] He ravaged the regions of Bastetania (around the city of Baza) and of Malaga, and repulsed the Byzantine troops; but in the course of two campaigning seasons he is reported explicitly to have taken no more than the town of Medina Sidonia (Asidona), which was betrayed to him by one Framidaneus, whose nationality is unknown; and he slew the Byzantine soldiers there.[3] There is some reason for thinking that Baza itself fell at this time (p. 321 below), but there is no evidence that he was able to break right through the Byzantine province and reach the sea at a point between Malaga and Cartagena.[4] In none of his later campaigns did Leovigild fight to such little effect. The Byzantines were the most powerful of his opponents, and he never fought them again.

He was more successful when he turned to the revolt at Cordoba, which had never been put down since its outbreak in Agila's time despite the attack upon it by Athanagild (p. 322 below); but the city fell to Leovigild. Now for the first time we hear of a peasant revolt in Visigothic Spain. Such revolts had been common enough in the mid-fifth century under the rule of the Emperors; but nothing is heard of them under earlier kings. Leovigild, however,

---

[1] Jo. Biclar., *s.a.* 569 (ii. 212), 'provinciam Gothorum, quae iam pro rebellione diversorum fuerat diminuta, mirabiliter ad pristinos revocat terminos'; cf. Isidore, *Chron.* 403 (ii. 477).

[2] Stroheker, pp. 147 f.   [3] Jo. Biclar., *s.aa.* 570, 571 (ii. 212).

[4] *Contra*, Stroheker, p. 147; but in that case Jo. Biclar. has written a misleading entry in his chronicle. It is not his purpose to understate the achievements of Leovigild.

faced an extensive peasant rebellion which involved him in the reduction of 'many cities and forts'.[1] Our authority seems to imply that the field of the peasants' operations lay somewhere in the vicinity of Cordoba, and the second peasant revolt of the reign broke out in 577 in Orospeda (the eastern part of the Sierra Morena). But whether the citizens of Cordoba were in alliance with the 'rustics' outside their walls is very doubtful. It is more likely that the country-folk took advantage of the revolt of the great city in their neighbourhood to throw off the domination of Cordoba and of the central government alike. But Leovigild crushed them, at any rate for the time being.

These southern events occupied the period when he and his brother Liuva were joint rulers. But at the end of the southern campaigns Liuva died, and Leovigild henceforth reigned alone. For the next three years he appears to have been active in the north-west of his kingdom. In 573 he is reported to have entered Sabaria, laid waste the Sappi, and subjugated 'the province itself'. Unhappily, Sabaria and the Sappi are not otherwise known, so that the direction of the King's vigorous attacks in this year cannot be traced. But it is not improbable that the Sappi were an Asturian people, and possibly Sabaria takes its name from the Sabor, a tributary of the Douro.[2] In 574 Leovigild was in Cantabria. He slew those who were overrunning the region—their identity is not stated—and he took the town of Amaia, seized the citizens' wealth, and brought the province under his sway.[3] St. Braulio of Saragossa refers to this campaign in his *Life of St. Aemilianus*. He mentions the slaughter of the 'senate' of Cantabria, one of whose members was called Abundantius. It would be interesting to know more of this senate, the members of which were presumably Romans, and of their aims and organization. There is certainly no reason for thinking that they were 'rustics' like the rebels of the south whom the King had crushed two years earlier. On the contrary, they included men of some wealth; and since there is no question of

[1] Jo. Biclar., *s.a.* 572 (ii. 213), 'multasque urbes et castella interfecta rusticorum multitudine in Gothorum dominium revocat'.

[2] Idem, *s.a.* 573 (ii. 213); cf. Grosse, p. 154. Sabaria is 'probably on the Suevic frontier south of the middle Douro', Stroheker, p. 149.

[3] Jo. Biclar., *s.a.* 574. For an attempt to reconstruct Leovigild's activities in this area see F. Mateu y Llopis, 'Sobre los límites de la conquista visigoda en Vasconia y Cantabria', *Ampurias*, vi (1944), pp. 222–5. Miles, p. 100, suggests that he also took Saldania during this campaign.

their having collaborated with any foreign power, their aim was presumably to set up an independent state in their neighbourhood, ruled by the local Hispano-Roman landowners. But the free state of Cantabria did not please St. Aemilianus, now in the hundredth year of his age. The austere hermit believed it to be characterized by murders, thefts, incest, violence, and a variety of other vices.[1]

In 575 Leovigild entered the mountains of Orense, took prisoner a certain Aspidius, a leading man of the district (*loci senior*), together with his wife and sons, and subjugated the region.[2] In 576 he disturbed the frontier of the Sueves in Galicia, but at the request of King Miro (570–82) he agreed to peace, at any rate for the moment. Already in 574, when Leovigild was in Cantabria, Miro had sent envoys to the Frankish king, Guntramn, but they had been intercepted by King Chilperic.[3] The weakness of the Sueves is illustrated by the fact that in the time of Visigothic chaos in Athanagild's reign they seem to have made no move to occupy Orense, Asturia, or Cantabria, all of which had freed themselves from the control of the central government.[4] Perhaps it was news of events in the south that had obliged Leovigild to break off his operations against the Sueves; at all events, in 577 he left the north. He entered the eastern part of the Sierra Morena (Orospeda), took the towns and forts of the area, but evidently left the region too soon, for the country-folk (*rustici*) rebelled again and were reduced by Gothic forces, which are not said to have been led by the King in person. Thereafter the whole of Orospeda was under Gothic control.[5]

When Leovigild came to the throne, according to a contemporary, the kingdom had been reduced by numerous rebellions.[6] Clearly, considerable areas of Spain had detached themselves altogether from the sway of Toledo. There was no move in Septimania (which Leovigild is not known ever to have visited); but a

---

[1] Braulio, *Vita S. Aemiliani*, 26 (PL 80. 712), who mentions Amaia in cap. 9. The city's name is thought to be preserved in that of Peña de Amaya, north-west of Burgos: Stroheker, p. 149 n. 3.

[2] Jo. Biclar., *s.a.* 575 (ii. 214).   [3] Greg. Tur., *HF* v. 41.

[4] But it is not clear whether the Runcones, whom Miro attacked in 572, lived in Galicia or in what was nominally Visigothic territory: Jo. Biclar., *s.a.* 572 (ii. 213). They are doubtless identical with the Roccones who were defeated by Suinthila in Sisebut's reign (p. 161 below).

[5] Jo. Biclar., *s.a.* 577 (ii. 215). On the site of Orospeda see A. Schulten, P.-W. xviii. 1. 1196.

[6] Jo. Biclar., *s.a.* 569 (ii. 212).

huge strip of territory on the Visigothic side of the Suevic frontier, consisting of Oronse, Asturia, and Cantabria, had won its independence. There was no one central authority directing the entire rebel area. A number of separate, local revolts had broken out independently of one another. It would be of interest to know something about the character of these rebellions, whether the same motives inspired them all and whether they had all broken out during the reign of Athanagild, or whether some, like that at Cordoba, dated from as far back as Agila's time. The rebellions as a whole were of two kinds—those of the peasantry in the south and those led by comparatively rich Romans in the north. In each case the aim of the rebels was not simply to replace Leovigild as ruler in Toledo: their purpose was to break free from Toledo altogether and to live in independence. They made no approaches, so far as we know, to any foreign power. There is nothing to suggest that these were revolts of Catholics against an Arian government. We do not hear that they were revolts of Romans as such against the rule of barbarians, although the rebels certainly belonged in the main to the old Catholic Roman population. The revolts indicate a tendency towards fragmentation in the kingdom. Had it not been for the energy and skill of Leovigild, the end of the sixth century might have seen Spain divided into a number of small, independent, and (if St. Aemilianus's impressions were correct) incompetent kingdoms.

But when Leovigild had been on the throne for ten years all the revolts had been decisively crushed, and all of what had once been Visigothic territory was again governed from Toledo. The King had fought not without success against the Byzantines. He had struck fear into the Sueves. The Frankish border was untroubled. In 578, then, he had solved his most pressing military problems, and no campaign is recorded from that year. Not only rebels but also potential usurpers had been eliminated; for he was ruthless in dealing with his opponents at home. According to Isidore of Seville he killed or exiled the most powerful and noble men of his kingdom,[1] though it is not certain whether these were Goths or Romans or both. According to Gregory of Tours, he slew all those who had been accustomed to murdering the kings.[2] He ruled the entire Iberian peninsula apart from the Byzantine province and the Suevic kingdom (both of which he had

---

[1] Isidore, *HG* 51 (ii. 288).   [2] Greg. Tur., *HF* iv. 38.

threatened) and the Basque country in the north, which the Gothic kings never managed to subjugate. He celebrated the end of his campaigns by founding in Celtiberia the city of Recopolis, named (curiously enough in Greek) after his younger son Reccared. He is the first Germanic king to have founded a new city. Its ruins still survive on the hill of Cerro de la Oliva overlooking the Tagus south of the village of Zorita de los Canes in the extreme south of the modern province of Guadalajara (some fifty kilometres southeast of the town of Guadalajara). There seems to have been a settlement with a church there before Leovigild's time, so that what the King did was to develop and fortify an already existing site of considerable military strength.[1] We do not know whether he moved Gothic settlers into it. It was still in existence at the beginning of the eighth century, for coins of King Wittiza were minted there; but it never became a bishopric.

2. The Rebellion of Hermenegild

As soon as Liuva elevated him to the throne, Leovigild had strengthened his position by marrying Goisuintha, the widow of his predecessor, Athanagild. It was his second marriage and remained without issue; but his first wife, of whom nothing is known,[2] had borne him two sons, of whom the elder was called Hermenegild and the younger Reccared. When Liuva died, he associated these two sons with himself as rulers of the kingdom. We do not know what powers he gave them, but he did not partition the kingdom. His aim was simply to secure the succession, as Liuva had done in a different way before him; but it was not until 579 that he took a further step in this matter, a step that led him into the one disaster of his life.[3]

In 579 he married the elder son, Hermenegild, to a Catholic Frankish princess called Ingundis, the daughter of King Sigibert I

[1] See K. Raddatz, 'Studien zu Reccopolis, I', *Madrider Mitteilungen*, v (1964), pp. 213-33.

[2] Jo. Biclar., *s.a.* 573 (ii. 213). The old view that she was a Roman was wisely rejected long ago by F. Görres, 'Ueber die Anfänge des Westgothenkönigs Leovigild', *Forschungen zur deutschen Geschichte*, xii (1872), pp. 597-9, and in other papers; cf. Scott, p. 196; Stroheker, p. 140 n. 2. But it has unexpectedly reappeared in H. Giesecke, *Die Ostgermanen und der Arianismus* (Berlin and Leipzig, 1959), p. 105; Miles, p. 22; and many others.

[3] Görres, art. cit. 609 n. 1; Stroheker, p. 142. See also R. Gibert, *Settimane*, iii (Spoleto, 1956), p. 575. But Greg. Tur., *HF* iv. 38, is wrongly thinking of the partitions of Merovingian France when he ascribes a partition to Leovigild.

and Brunhild (p. 18 above), Athanagild's daughter: hence Ingundis was the granddaughter of his own second wife, Goisuintha. As the girl made her way from France to Toledo she passed through the Visigothic town of Agde in Gallia Narbonensis, where the local bishop, Phronimius, warned her not to accept the 'poison' of Arianism, an action which Leovigild did not fail to notice (p. 81 below). Goisuintha warmly welcomed the girl to Spain and at once set about trying to convert her to Arianism and to induce her to submit to rebaptism. But Ingundis, who was not much more than twelve years of age, was as obstinate a Catholic as Amalaric's Frankish wife had been long ago (p. 12 above); and unfortunate scenes followed. Her grandmother pulled her hair and dashed her to the ground, kicked her until she bled, and then ordered her to be stripped and ducked in a fish-pond. But even this style of argument did not convince Ingundis of the Son's inequality with the Father.[1]

What Leovigild and Hermenegild thought of this fracas is unknown. The King himself in no way molested his son's wife, nor did he see any reason to distrust Hermenegild; for he now gave the prince part of his kingdom to rule over—presumably the province of Baetica—and Hermenegild and his wife went to Seville, where they were to live.[2] That Leovigild gave his son a province bordering on the Byzantine possessions is an indication of his complete confidence in him. But his confidence was misplaced.

In Seville Ingundis and a local monk called Leander, the elder brother of St. Isidore and future bishop of that city (if indeed he was not bishop there already), began to try to convert the prince to Catholicism. If the conversion of the Visigoths to Catholicism could be ascribed to any one man, that man was Leander.[3] At first Hermenegild showed some reluctance to change his faith, but in the end he took the fateful step of joining the Catholic Church and assumed the name John, a name which he did not use on his coins or in his one surviving inscription. It has been said that 'in the political situation of the kingdom the transference of the allegiance of the heir apparent from the Arian to the Catholic confession both

---

[1] Greg. Tur., *HF* v. 38. Is Gregory quite certain that Ingundis never wavered from her Catholicism? Note *ut adserunt quidam*, p. 244. 13 f.

[2] Ibid. iv. 38.

[3] So Isidore, *De Vir. Illustr.* 41 (PL 83. 1103). On Leander see F. Görres, 'Leander von Sevilla', *Zeitschrift für wissenschaftliche Theologie*, xxix (1886), pp. 36–50, who supposes that Leander was not consecrated as bishop until 584. Isidore suppresses the fact that his brother had converted Hermenegild.

involved and proclaimed a withdrawal of his allegiance to the king. This ecclesiastical defection was necessarily accompanied by a political rebellion.'[1] But Leovigild did not immediately regard it as such. He tried to save the situation by opening negotiations with Hermenegild. He asked for a meeting, which was refused. Threats and promises had no effect; and the prince entered into an alliance with the Byzantines.[2] In spite of Leander's antipathy to the Byzantine province and the conditions of life there (p. 27 n. 4 above), he now went to Constantinople to try to further the rebel's interests in the Eastern Empire.[3] We do not know what the prince gave in return for his alliance with the Byzantine commanders in Spain, but there is no reason to think that he allowed them to occupy any of the cities subject to him (p. 72 below). And Leander's efforts resulted in little gain; for the resources of Byzantium were too strained at this time by commitments on various frontiers to allow of the Emperor's sending reinforcements to Baetica at the other end of the world.[4] The subsequent course of events suggests that the Byzantines undertook no more than to aid the prince in the field if he should be brought to battle and should appeal to them for help.

Leovigild had gone to extraordinary lengths to avoid war. But his efforts failed. Hermenegild began a rebellion against his father which, as a contemporary Catholic writer says, caused greater destruction both to the Romans and to the Goths of Spain than did the attacks of their foreign enemies.[5] In his propaganda, however, he portrayed himself as a victim of his father's religious persecution.[6] A curious fact is that the revolt is said by a contemporary

---

[1] Scott, 199; cf. F. Görres, *Zeitschrift für die historische Theologie*, xliii (1873), p. 19; Stroheker, pp. 152 f.

[2] Greg. Tur., *HF* v. 38; Gregory I, *Dial.* iii. 31. The former mentions the Byzantine alliance also in *HF* vi. 18 and 43.

[3] Gregory I, *Praef. Moralium in Iob* (PL 75. 510 f.), 'cum . . . te illuc [=to Constantinople] iniuncta pro causis fidei Wisigothorum legatio perduxisset'; idem, *Ep.* i. 41a (p. 60 *ad fin.*), a letter of Licinianus of Cartagena to Gregory, tells us that Leander returned home from Constantinople via Cartagena hurriedly: after his return Gregory wrote him the *De Trina Tinctione*, i.e. *Ep.* i. 41 of April 591. See Goubert, *REB* ii (1944), pp. 26–9; R. Aigrain *apud* A. Fliche and V. Martin, *Histoire de l'Église* (Paris, 1947), v. 232; W. Goffart, 'Byzantine Policy in the West under Tiberius II and Maurice', *Traditio*, xiii (1957), pp. 73–118, at pp. 89 f.

[4] Goffart, loc. cit.   [5] Gregory I, *Dial.* iii. 31 *init.*

[6] See his inscription, quoted on p. 69 n. 2 below; Greg. Tur., *HF* v. 38. On Hermenegild's rebellion in general see F. Görres, 'Kritische Untersuchungen über den Aufstand und das Martyrium des westgothischen Königsohnes Hermenegild', *Zeitschrift für die historische Theologie*, xliii (1873), pp. 3–109; A. K. Ziegler, *Church and*

Spanish author of unimpeachable authority to have been incited by none other than the Arian queen, Leovigild's wife, Goisuintha, who had lately been so unpleasant to Ingundis.[1] If this is true—and it could hardly be better attested—the Queen's motives are unfathomable.

There is no reason for thinking that the forces opposing one another during the revolt were for the most part composed of Goths on the one side and Romans on the other. We hear nothing of any assistance given to Hermenegild by the Romans of southern Spain, nor do we hear of any sympathetic move by the Roman population in central or northern Spain which might have helped him. Indeed, the great landowners in general can have found little fault with a king who had restored peace and unity to the kingdom; and it is certain that not all the Roman inhabitants of Spain supported the rebellion, for in 582 Leovigild was able to send to France two ambassadors who were Catholic Romans, Florentius and Exsuperius.[2] On the other hand, when Hermenegild rebelled, the Visigoths by no means rallied as one man to the aid of their Arian sovereign. According to Isidore, the Gothic people were split in two by the revolt, part supporting the Catholic rebel and part the Arian monarch, and Hermenegild's faction numbered 'many thousands' of men.[3] The revolt was essentially a conflict of Goth against Goth, not of Goth against Roman. It does not follow

State in Visigothic Spain, Diss. Washington, 1930, pp. 28—31; Goubert, REB ii (1944), pp. 20–37; Stroheker, p. 173 ff.; J. N. Hillgarth, Historia, xv (1966), pp. 483–508. For the Frankish and Byzantine background see Goffart, art. cit.

[1] Jo. Biclar., s.a. 579 (ii. 215), 'Hermenegildus factione Gosuinthae reginae tyrannidem assumens'. Giesecke, op. cit. 107, revives the old remedy proposed by H. Florez, España Sagrada (Madrid, 1773), vi. 388 n. 6, of substituting Ingundis's name for that of Goisuintha in this text. This is unjustifiable, even though we read in Hist. Pseudo-Isidor. 14 (ii. 385), 'quae [=Ingundis] marito persuasit ut in patrem insurgens pro eo regnaret'; see Hillgarth, p. 30 n. 18. I have not been convinced by the interpretation of Görres, art. cit. 15–18. Also, there is no reason to think that Hermenegild proclaimed himself king under pressure from the 'fervently Catholic' population of Baetica, as is implied by F. Lot, C. Pfister, and F. L. Ganshof, Les Destinées de l'empire en Occident de 395 à 888, Histoire du Moyen Âge, ed. G. Glotz (Paris, 1928), p. 234, or that he was obliged to rebel because his father's reign had hitherto been intolerably cruel and oppressive: so H. Leclercq, L'Espagne chrétienne[2] (Paris, 1906), pp. 254 ff.

[2] Greg. Tur., De Virtut. Martini, iii. 8 (p. 634).

[3] Isidore, Chron. 405 (ii. 477), 'Gothi per Ermenigildum Leuuigildi filium bifarie divisi mutua caede vastantur'; Greg. Tur., HF vi. 43. The fact that the Romans suffered severely during the war does not necessarily mean that they were fighting on a large scale: John may mean simply that they suffered heavily in Merida, Seville, and other scenes of fighting.

that all the Goths who supported Hermenegild had necessarily been converted to Catholicism along with their leader or that they were inclined to favour Catholicism, though we shall see reason for thinking that this may have been the case (p. 107 below).

At all events, Hermenegild proclaimed himself king at Seville— though he still referred to his father, too, as 'King'—and began to mint coins bearing his own name.[1] The revolt led to Leovigild's losing control of Seville and Merida (two of his five provincial capitals), Cordoba, and other important towns and forts. The rebel was in alliance not only with the Byzantines but also with the Sueves of Galicia. King Miro had evidently been frightened by Leovigild's activities on his frontier in 576 (p. 62 above), and he now seems to have done what he could to ensure that a friend sat on the throne of his powerful neighbours. He sent envoys to Guntramn of Burgundy in 580, and, although the reason why he did so has not been recorded, it is tempting to think that he wished to incite Guntramn to intervene in the civil war (though, if so, his plan came to nothing).[2] Somewhat earlier he had had ambassadors in Byzantium;[3] their purpose, too, is unknown, but perhaps they wanted the Byzantines to make some diversionary move that would prevent Leovigild from advancing in the north-west of the Iberian peninsula.

Byzantine influence on Hermenegild in the early days of his reign has been detected in two small ways. The legend on one of his coin-types reads: REGI A DEO VITA.[4] These words, 'Life to the King from God', appear to echo the acclamation of Hermenegild by the clergy at the moment of his coronation in Seville. The idea of using such a phrase on a coin seems to have been suggested by Byzantine North Africa, where the word VITA occurs on the bronze coinage of Carthage in the reign of Justin II (565–78) and not earlier.[5] Now, this may have been the first time that a Visigothic

---

[1] There seems to be insufficient evidence at present to solve the difficult, but important, questions of the chronology and interrelationship of Leovigild's and Hermenegild's coins: see esp. Tomasini, pp. 67 ff., 130–4. Gregory, loc. cit., refers to Hermenegild as 'king', as do Hermenegild's inscription (p. 69 n. 2 below) and his coins. Incidentally, the inscription and the coins show that Hermenegild's name should not be aspirated; but I have accepted the traditional spelling.

[2] Greg. Tur., *HF* v. 41; cf. *De Virtut. Martini*, iv. 7 (p. 651).

[3] Martin of Braga, *De Trina Mersione*, 257. 31 ff., ed. Barlow.

[4] Miles, pp. 199 f.

[5] See M. C. Diaz y Diaz, 'La leyenda *Regi a Deo Vita* de una moneda de Ermenegildo', *Analecta Sacra Tarraconensia*, xxxi (1958), pp. 261–9; Hillgarth, pp. 39 ff.,

monarch put a legend with a religious content on his coinage, and Leovigild was not slow to follow his example, if indeed he did not precede him (p. 70 below). Even the coinage of the two rivals proclaimed something of the religious character of this struggle of Goth and Goth. Secondly, an inscription has survived from Hermenegild's kingdom. It was carved on the doorway of a building erected at Alcala de Guadaira in the second year of his reign; and it refers to the war with Leovigild—indeed, it speaks of Leovigild's 'persecution' of the prince.[2] The system of dating used on the inscription—by the year of the indiction—is Byzantine, but was not an innovation in Spain, for the same system is found on inscriptions of the reigns of Theudis and Athanagild.[3] But there is neither evidence nor likelihood that the Byzantines had any political influence on the usurper or his policies.

Of his internal administration we know almost nothing. It may be that he expelled the Arian clergy from the cities that were in his power—not to have done so would have been all but unique in a Catholic king at this date—and that he handed over the Arian churches to the Catholics (p. 79 f. below). What is most remarkable is that, although Leovigild was busy elsewhere throughout two successive campaigning seasons, those of 580 and 581, the prince failed to take the military initiative. Even when the King was heavily engaged against the Basques in the north of the country in 581, Hermenegild made no move against Toledo; and this disastrous inactivity has never been explained. The Byzantines, too, made no attempt to extend their province and entrench themselves in the cities occupied by the rebel. It is probable that their commitments in other parts of their empire left them with few military forces to engage in adventures in the far West;[4] and Hermenegild is unlikely to have given them much encouragement to do so—he will have had no wish to live out the rest of his days as their vassal or their prisoner.

The rebellion began in the winter of 579–80, and at first

citing P. Grierson. For a different interpretation see J. Vives, 'Sobre la leyenda *a Deo Vita* de Hermenegildo', ibid. xxxii (1959), pp. 31–4.

[1] This point is stressed in the second part of Hillgarth's paper, pp. 35 ff.

[2] Vives, 364, 'in nomine domini anno feliciter secundo regni domini nostri Erminigildi regis quem persequitur genetor sus dom̄. Liuuigildus rex in cibitate Ispā. indictione . . . ' The last two words must have been *tertia* (or *quarta* or *quinta*) *decima*: J. Mallon, *Memorias de los museos arqueológicos provinciales*, ix–x (1948–9) 320–8. [3] Fiebiger–Schmidt, 254–6.

[4] Goffart, art. cit. 90; Goubert, *REB* ii (1944), pp. 32 f.

Leovigild was unable to give it his full attention. His strenuous efforts to come to terms with his son, together with another enterprise which we shall discuss later (pp. 83 f. below), occupied him throughout 580. In 581 he invaded the country of the Basques, though there is no likelihood that the Basques were in any way co-operating with Hermenegild. The priority given to the Basque campaign is most remarkable. The King knew from first-hand experience gained in 570–1 what powerful enemies the Byzantines were. It was at least possible, so far as he can have known, that they would now occupy the most important cities in southern Spain; and, if they did so, he would have little chance of dislodging them, for in siege-warfare they were at their strongest. Yet instead of forestalling them with all possible speed, he left them alone throughout 581 so as to deal with the Basques.[1] The explanation of his action would seem to be that the Basques had come down from their mountains on an unparalleled scale; and there is numismatic evidence that they won a striking success before the King was able to defeat them. There exists a unique coin of Leovigild minted at Rosas (Rodas) on the Mediterranean coast a short distance south of the French border. This coin bears the legend: CVM D I RODA, which is thought to mean *cum Deo intravit Rodam*.[2] Now, Leovigild never refers to the Deity on his coins except during these years when Hermenegild was in revolt; and the coin of Rosas was unquestionably issued sometime in the period 580–4. But Hermenegild did not win over so distant a city as Rosas to his side; nor did the Franks ever occupy, or even threaten, the city in this period.[3] The only possibility would seem to be, then, that the Basques, whose invasion in 581 is known to have been a large-scale one, had managed to penetrate down the valley of the Ebro, to reach the Mediterranean coast, and in the end to occupy Rosas. But Leovigild recovered the town from them, and he also occupied part of Vasconia. In the hope, no doubt, of overawing his enemies he founded the second of his cities, Victoriacum (unidentified), presumably sited so as to watch the Basque country.[4] And while he achieved all this, Hermenegild made no move.

[1] Jo. Biclar., *s.a.* 581 (ii. 216).

[2] Miles, pp. 85. 18⁻. who rightly, in my opinion, suggests the date 581, the year of Leovigild's expedition against the Basques.

[3] *Contra*, Hillgarth, 38 f.; idem, *Historia* xv (1966), pp. 503 ff.; but see p. 75 n. 1 below.   [4] Jo. Biclar., loc. cit.

However dangerous the Basque attack may have seemed, Leovigild must have known well that there was no risk of the primitive mountaineers being able to hold north-eastern Spain indefinitely, although they could gravely damage the cities and countryside there. On the other hand, there was a serious risk that Hermenegild would march northwards or that the Byzantines would break out of their province, appear north of the Sierra Nevada, and occupy considerable areas of Baetica. The King's action, therefore, in dealing with the Basques first, while reserving the rebel and the Byzantines for later treatment, is no small indication of his strength of will.

For Hermenegild the year 582 was the beginning of the end. In that year his father at last appeared in the south and showed his qualities by at once capturing Merida, the capital of Lusitania.[1] It may be that his coins minted at Merida, and bearing the legend VICTOR and VICTORIA, commemorate this event.[2] In the following year he crossed into Baetica and began the siege of Seville, where Hermenegild and Ingundis were still inertly living; and when Miro and a Suevic army appeared on the scene, Leovigild surrounded them and obliged them to swear allegiance to him. Miro died at Seville, according to John of Biclarum; though according to Gregory of Tours, he was allowed to withdraw to Galicia, where he died soon afterwards. At all events, the Sueves did nothing more to help the rebel.[3] His only allies now were the Byzantines.

Leovigild had already dislodged the rebel garrison from the fortress of Osset (San Juan de Alfarache, across the river from Seville); and, as the siege of Seville lasted through the winter, it may have been the winter months which he spent in capturing Italica and in restoring its walls. Italica lies beside the village of Santiponce, some five miles north-west of Seville (though within sight of it), on the right bank of the Guadalquivir, and was celebrated as the birthplace of the Emperors Trajan and Hadrian. Its capture caused severe hardship to the beleaguered citizens of Seville.[4] Leovigild celebrated its fall with a coin issue of which only a single specimen survives. It bears the legend: CVM DE(O)

[1] Greg. Tur., HF vi. 18.   [2] Miles, pp. 119, 194 ff.
[3] Greg. Tur., HF vi. 43; Jo. Biclar., s.a. 583 (ii. 216). The latter is misunderstood by Isidore, Hist. Suev. 91 (ii. 303), who makes Miro come to help Leovigild.
[4] Jo. Biclar., s.a. 584 (ii. 216).

O(BTINVIT) ETALICA.[1] With the probable exception of the coin of
Rosas, this is the earliest issue to show that the King had begun to
compete with his son in ascribing his successes to divine aid.

The siege of Seville was pressed on with energy. The city was
suffering from famine as well as from the royalist assaults; and
Leovigild even blocked the river Guadalquivir on which it
stands.[2] It was only at this point that Hermenegild called upon
the Byzantines for help, a fact which shows that the imperial
forces had not occupied the rebel cities, but were merely obliged
by their treaty with the prince to give him assistance in the field
when requested to do so. But Leovigild outwitted his son. He
paid the Byzantines no less than 30,000 solidi to withdraw their
support; and when Hermenegild risked a battle against his father
outside Seville, his allies deserted him in the field.[3] Eventually the
King stormed the city about June or July 583, and he commemo-
rated its fall with another issue of coins that again proclaimed that
God was on his side: CVM D(E)O OPTINVIT SPALI.[4] But Hermenegild had escaped from his fallen capital and tried to make his way
to the Byzantine province in spite of his allies' recent treachery.
Leovigild went on to reduce the other cities and forts which his
son had held, and soon afterwards entered Cordoba, where the
prince himself fell into his hands.[5] The fall of Cordoba was also
celebrated on the coinage, but now that the war was over it was
no longer necessary to refer to God's help: CORDOBA BIS OPTINVIT,
where the reference in *bis* is to the reduction of the city in 572 at
the end of the revolt which had broken out in Agila's time.[6]

The end of the war and the capture of Hermenegild can be
dated with some precision to February 584.[7] Hermenegild had left

---

[1] Miles, pp. 111, 192, and his Plate III. 1. Leovigild was the only king to mint at
Italica, which frequently sent its bishop to the seventh-century Councils.

[2] Jo. Biclar., *s.a.* 583 (ii. 216).

[3] Greg. Tur., *HF* v. 38, 'relictus a solacio'. E. Stein, *Studien zur Geschichte d.
byzantinischen Reiches* (Stuttgart, 1919), p. 114 n. 5, thinks it possible that Leovigild
may have paid this money for the return of Cordoba: but the Byzantines never occupied
Cordoba (p. 321 f. below). Goffart, art. cit. 107, dates Leovigild's payment to a time
later than the fall of Seville: but this cannot be reconciled with Greg. Tur., loc. cit.

[4] Miles, pp. 110, 191, and his Plate II. 15–16. The coin bearing the legend CVM
DEO SPALI ADQVISITA (ibid.) seems to be a forgery: Hillgarth, p. 37 n. 37.

[5] Jo. Biclar., *s.a.* 584 (ii. 217).

[6] Miles, pp. 108 (where it is an error to say that Cordoba fell to the Byzantines
c. 567–72), 190 f.

[7] When Oppila reached Tours on 2 April 584 he brought news that the war in
Spain was now over: Greg. Tur., *HF* vi. 40. But a Frankish embassy which returned

Ingundis and her infant son Athanagild in the hands of the Byzantines, and, although Leovigild tried to recover them,[1] the
Byzantines sent them off to Constantinople. Ingundis died on the
journey in Africa, according to one account, or in Sicily, according to another;[2] but Athanagild reached the Eastern capital,
where his ultimate fate is unknown. Hermenegild had taken
refuge in a church in Cordoba, but his brother Reccared was sent
in to him by the King, and persuaded him to throw himself upon
his father's mercy. He fell at Leovigild's feet, and the King raised
him up and kissed him. But he also stripped him of his royal robes,
took him back to Toledo, and sent him into exile at Valencia with
one slave to wait upon him.[3] Evidently the prince was later
moved to Tarragona; for it was in that city a year later, in 585,
that he was killed by a Goth called Sisbert.[4]

Gregory of Tours had no doubt that Leovigild ordered the
murder.[5] That was also the view of Pope Gregory the Great, who
reports that towards the end Hermenegild was kept in chains:
when Easter 585 arrived, an Arian bishop was sent into the prison
in the dark so that the prince might be tricked into accepting
communion from his hands. But Hermenegild was not deceived.
He abused the bishop; and Leovigild, when he heard of this, had
him put to death.[6] Although the Pope's narrative does not
inspire confidence in every respect, we cannot wholly jettison his
evidence. It is difficult to believe that Leovigild, old and sick
though he may have been, would have left Sisbert unpunished if
he had killed the prince on his own initiative; and in fact Sisbert
survived into Reccared's reign. It looks as though Hermenegild
would have been spared if he could have agreed to revert to the
Arian faith; but he preferred to die a Catholic martyr.[7]

from Spain earlier in that same year declared that the war in Spain was still raging
violently: ibid. vi. 33. Between the time when this embassy arrived in France and the
time when Oppila reached Tours, a third embassy had time to travel from Spain to
France: ibid. vi. 34. These data can best be accounted for on the supposition that
the war ended about February.

[1] Greg. Tur., *HF* vi. 43 *fin.*, 'uxorem tamen eius a Grecis erepere non potuit'.
But Paul. Diac., *HL* iii. 21, says that Ingundis fell into the hands of the Byzantines
while trying to return to France, perhaps a more convincing version.

[2] Greg. Tur., *HF* viii. 28; Paul. Diac., loc. cit.

[3] Greg. Tur., *HF* v. 38 *fin.* (cf. vi. 43 *fin.*; viii. 28); Jo. Biclar., *s.a.* 584 (ii. 217).

[4] Ibid., *s.a.* 585 (ii. 217).   [5] Greg. Tur., *HF* viii. 28, 'morti tradedit'.

[6] Gregory I, *Dial.* iii. 31. Cf. J. N. Hillgarth, *Historia*, xv (1966), p. 490.

[7] Greg. Tur., *HF* v. 38 *fin.*; vi. 43 *fin.*; viii. 28; Gregory I, loc. cit. 31; Fredegarius,
ii. 83, 87. On the vexed question of Hermenegild's martyrdom see Garvin, pp. 486 ff.

3. *Leovigild and the Franks*

The attitude of the three Frankish kings to these events in Spain is a nice illustration of the fact that religion was a matter of little consequence in foreign policy in this period. Throughout the entire civil war Leovigild was negotiating with Chilperic I of Soissons with the aim of marrying his second son Reccared to Chilperic's daughter Rigunthis;[1] and there is no reason to think that his negotiations were in reality designed to prevent Chilperic from assisting Hermenegild.[2] On 1 September 584, some months after the civil war had been won, a large Spanish embassy arrived at Chilperic's court to escort Rigunthis to Spain.[3] There is no hint in our authority that the Frankish king at any time believed religious differences to be a hindrance to the projected marriage.

As for Childebert of Metz, Leovigild does not seem to have had any relations with him while the civil war was in progress. But as soon as the war was over he feared that Childebert might attack him because Hermenegild's wife Ingundis, who was Childebert's sister, had been driven off into the Byzantine province. These fears were justified, for in fact Childebert did intend to act against Leovigild, though for an unknown reason he made no move.[4] Now, our authority makes no mention of Childebert's having any religious motives for fighting: his war, if it broke out, would be due to the treatment of Ingundis and would not be designed to crush heresy. Childebert's attitude towards his sister's fate is noteworthy. In 585 he carried out certain undertakings to the Byzantine government (which he had hitherto refused to do in spite of having been paid 50,000 solidi) and led his army into Italy against the Lombards 'because there was a report that his sister Ingundis had now been transferred to Constantinople'.[5] We are reminded of the occasion in 531 when Childebert I invaded Septimania because of the maltreatment of his sister by Amalaric.

---

[1] Greg. Tur., *HF* v. 43, vi. 18 (cf. *De Virtut. Martini*, iii. 8, p. 634), 29, 33 f., 40. On the relations of Leovigild and Reccared with the Franks in this period see G. Reverdey, 'Les relations de Childebert II et de Byzance', *Revue historique*, cxiv (1913), pp. 61–86; P. Goubert, *Byzance avant l'Islam* (Paris, 1956), ii. 95 ff.; Goffart, art. cit.

[2] *Contra*, Stroheker, p. 154.   [3] Greg. Tur., *HF* vi. 45.

[4] Ibid. vi. 40, 42. The Spanish embassy of 582 visited Childebert as well as Chilperic, but with what purpose we do not know: ibid. vi. 18.

[5] Ibid. viii. 18; cf. Jo. Biclar., *s.a.* 584 (ii. 217).

Finally, Leovigild's relations with King Guntramn of Burgundy during the civil war are obscure. The Suevic king, Miro, may have wished to incite this monarch to intervene against Leovigild (p. 68 above), but that is not quite certain. At any rate, as soon as Guntramn heard in 585 of the deaths of Hermenegild and Ingundis, he ordered his forces to subjugate Septimania and then invade Spain. Two disorderly Frankish columns, spreading devastation in their own country wherever they went, moved in the direction of Nîmes and Carcassonne. They entered Carcassonne, but when their commander was killed they panicked and fled back to France. The Visigoths successfully ambushed them several times on their way home. The other column ravaged the countryside around Nîmes, burning the crops and cutting down the vines and olive trees, but could take neither Nîmes nor any other city except one, which is unnamed. The cities were all strongly fortified and well supplied with food, whereas the Franks so wasted the country that they themselves began to die off from hunger. Their losses were said to have amounted to about 5,000 men. The Visigothic defence was organized by the prince Reccared, since Leovigild himself in this year was engaged in his campaign against the Sueves of Galicia (p. 87 below). After repelling the invaders the prince went over to the offensive, took the fort called Ram's Head (modern Cabaret) near Carcassonne, together with Beaucaire (Ugernum), which was strongly situated on the Rhone not far from Arles, and even ravaged the region round Toulouse.[1] None the less, Guntramn rejected Leovigild's two requests for peace in 586, and the Goths under Reccared therefore made another plundering raid on France.[2] These were the only invasions of France the Visigoths ever undertook; and their aim was not conquest.

This was the position at Leovigild's death. There is no evidence that he had feared Frankish intervention until *after* he had crushed Hermenegild. And no one expected at any time, so far as we know, that the Franks would invade Spain or Septimania from religious

---

[1] Greg. Tur., *HF* viii. 28, 30; Jo. Biclar., *s.a.* 585 (ii. 217). It is clear that there was no invasion of Spain itself, though this is stated by Fredegarius, iv. 5, an inferior authority. Hence I cannot follow F. Mateu y Llopis, 'De la Hispania tarraconense visigoda a la Marca hispanica carolina', *Analecta Sacra Tarraconensia*, xix (1946), pp. 1–122, at p. 13, and Hillgarth, pp. 38 f., in supposing that Leovigild's Rosas coin refers to this campaign.

[2] Greg. Tur., *HF* viii. 35, 38.

motives: they would do so, if at all, in order to avenge the exile and death of Ingundis.

4. *Contemporary Views of the Civil War*

What, then, was the character of the civil war? There is a sharp division of opinion among our sources of information. The Catholic Spanish chroniclers look upon Hermenegild with disfavour. They do not speak of him as championing the Catholic Church against an Arian tyrant: rather, he was a subject who rebelled against his king and a son who fought against his father. They do not so much as hint at his conversion to Catholicism. If we had to rely on the Spanish authorities alone, we should never have guessed that Hermenegild was a Catholic when he fought and when he died. They would have us believe that the war was due to a purely personal dispute between the King and the prince, and the prince was in the wrong. The King's attack on him was wholly justified. They suppress the fact that Leovigild sent Sisbert to murder the prisoner: indeed, St. Isidore does not mention Hermenegild's death at all. The documents that emerged from the Third Council of Toledo contain not a single reference to the martyred prince. Reccared, who was his brother, and Leander, who had received him into the Church, spoke at Toledo as though he had never existed. The early-seventh-century author of the *Lives of the Holy Fathers of Merida*, who has much to say about the reign of King Leovigild, is not only silent about Hermenegild but has deliberately suppressed reference to him in a curious passage where he quotes from Pope Gregory the words: 'Reccared, following not his faithless father but his martyr brother, was converted from the perverseness of the Arian heresy.'[1] But for the words 'martyr brother' he substitutes 'Christ the Lord'! In Spain there was a conspiracy of silence on all that related to Hermenegild.

Now, the coins on which both Leovigild and Hermenegild proclaimed their association with the Deity are unique in the whole range of Visigothic coinage; and they indicate that religious issues were at stake in the war. Moreover, Gregory of Tours has no doubt that the revolt was a Catholic one: when Leovigild heard of Hermenegild's conversion, according to Gregory, he

---

[1] *VPE* v. 9. 4, quoting Gregory I, *Dial.* iii. 31.

immediately began to look round for reasons for destroying him.[1] In 594 Pope Gregory went so far as to call the prince a martyr.[2] Why then do the Spanish writers suppress what they know of the character of the rebellion? Even Gregory the Great, who was well-informed about the career of Hermenegild, does not mention him at all in any of the letters which he addressed to Spaniards, letters which were widely read in Spain.[3] The answer would seem to be that after the conversion of Reccared and the establishment of a Catholic State, it was thought unwise to associate Catholicism with rebellion, especially with a rebellion which had caused much devastation in Spain[4] and which had been supported by the Byzantines. Now that Spain had become a Catholic State, revolt against the State authority must not be condoned, much less glorified. Does not Isidore even hint his disapproval of those who had murdered Agila long ago?[5] In his brief chronicle does he not include as many as three phrases which show that in his opinion Athanagild was a usurping tyrant?[6] And when he writes about his brother Leander he says not a word to suggest that Leander had helped to convert the usurper Hermenegild to Catholicism. As for John of Biclarum, he was writing in the reign of the rebel's brother Reccared. If he had described the revolt candidly he would have had to tell how Reccared had supported his Arian father against the Catholic prince, how he had tried to win his pious brother back to Arianism, and, indeed, how he had been the first to benefit from his brother's death.[7] But the puzzle is why the author of the *Lives*, writing in Merida some time in the first half of the seventh century, should have thought fit to follow the official version, particularly as he is fiercely critical of Leovigild (unlike Isidore and John of Biclarum, who find much to admire in him). At all events, no Spanish author speaks well of Hermenegild until

---

[1] Greg. Tur., *HF* v. 38; but in vi. 43 he disapproves of Hermenegild's attempt to to kill his father *quamlibet hereticum*.

[2] Loc. cit. Cf. Hillgarth, pp. 28 f.   [3] Hillgarth, ibid.

[4] Jo. Biclar., *s.a.* 579 (ii. 215).

[5] *HG* 46 (ii. 286): 'fide sacramenti oblita'.

[6] Ibid., 'tyrannidem regnandi cupiditate arripiens', 47 'regnum quod invaderat', 'sumpta tyrannide'.

[7] See Hillgarth, pp. 24 ff., and idem, *Historia* xv (1966), pp. 491 ff., on these points. Cf. Messmer, op. cit. (p. 16 n. 3 above), pp. 132 f. For the date at which Jo. Biclar. wrote see F. Görres, 'Johannes von Biclaro', *Theologische Studien und Kritiken* (1895), pp. 103–35, at pp. 128 f.

Valerius of Bierzo (Bergidum) late in the seventh century includes him in a bizarre list of martyrs—Crispus Caesar, Hermenegild, King of the Goths, Aucuia, King of the barbarians, the Duke Hippolytus, Count George, and Queen Alexandria.[1]

5. Leovigild's Religious Policy

It is against a background of civil war and later of threats from abroad that we must view Leovigild's religious policy. He is the only Arian king of Spain who is said to have been a persecutor of the Catholics in his kingdom; but he is never accused of bloodshed in this connection, and only four specific cases are recorded of persons who are said to have suffered hardship for their religious beliefs in his reign.[2] It is important to establish, if we can, not only the circumstances but also the chronology of these four incidents.

The relations of Leovigild with Masona, a Visigoth who had become Catholic Bishop of Merida, fall into a number of stages. At first the King, impressed by the Bishop's prominence, tried repeatedly to persuade and even bribe him to join the Arians. But Masona responded by rebuking the King for his heresy and by preaching vigorously against Arianism.[3] The King next appointed one Sunna as Arian Bishop of Merida and gave him some churches in the city which had hitherto belonged to the Catholics. Sunna appealed to the King to be given possession of the Church of St. Eulalia also, and Leovigild sent a number of commissioners to Merida to examine the rival claims. The commission, though consisting mainly of Arians, awarded the church to the Catholics.[4] So far there is nothing that could be called 'persecution'.

[1] De Vana Saeculi Sapientia, 8 (PL 83. 426). On this list see Sister C. M. Aherne, Valerio of Bierzo, an Ascetic of the Late Visigothic Period, Diss. Washington, 1949, pp. 41 ff.

[2] There is no conclusive evidence that Leovigild banished Leander: see Stroheker, p. 177 n. 2. In general see F. Görres, 'Des Westgothenkönigs Leovigild Stellung zum Katholicismus und zur arianischen Staatskirche', Zeitschrift für die historische Theologie, xliii (1873), pp. 547–601. On the alleged persecution see the literature cited in Garvin, pp. 445–8.

[3] VPE v. 4. 1 ff., where very strong language is used of Leovigild, though the writer is not ill-disposed towards him in iii. 8 ff. There is a paper on Masona by F. Görres, 'Mausona, Bischof von Merida', Zeitschrift für wissenschaftliche Theologie, xxviii (1885), pp. 326–32.

[4] VPE v. 5. 1 ff.

But now Leovigild summoned Masona to Toledo and once again tried unsuccessfully to persuade him to join the Arians. He then commanded him to hand over the tunic of St. Eulalia so that it might be placed in an Arian church in the capital.[1] This Masona refused to do, and because of his refusal Leovigild exiled him to an unknown place, where he remained for three years or more.[2] Our authority for these events goes on to describe the return of Masona to Merida and then immediately records the death of Leovigild, which we know to have taken place between 13 April and 8 May 586,[3] so that we may date Masona's return to his see to the last year of Leovigild's life. Now, our authority assumes throughout his narrative that the King had control of Merida, which in fact had fallen to him only in 582 (p. 71 above). The episode of Masona, Sunna, and the King, together with the three years of Masona's exile, therefore, falls in the period 582–6. But Masona had become Bishop of Merida at least as early as 573,[4] and there is no reason to think that he had been molested in any way by the King in the earlier part of his career as bishop. He fell into disfavour only when Leovigild recaptured Merida from Hermenegild.

There is no indication in our authority that Leovigild appointed Sunna to succeed an earlier Arian Bishop of Merida; and it seems to be implied that none of the churches of the city was then in the hands of the Arians, for as soon as Sunna was consecrated he proceeded to take over some Catholic churches for the use of his own flock.[5] The inference appears to be that there was no organized Arian community in the city before Sunna was consecrated as bishop. But it is hardly credible that there was no Arian community in so important a centre as the provincial capital of Lusitania at so late a date as 582. Indeed, Leovigild would not have appointed a bishop to a city where there was no congregation, and in fact Sunna certainly found an Arian community there on his arrival. How then are we to explain the absence of an Arian organization in Merida in 582, which our authority's words distinctly imply? The most likely explanation is that when the city fell into Hermenegild's hands in 580 the rebel prince

[1] Ibid. v. 6. 4 ff. [2] Ibid. v. 6. 23 ff.
[3] Ibid. v. 9. 1 ff.
[4] Jo. Biclar., s.a. 573 (ii. 213), with Garvin's edn. of the VPE, pp. 426 f.
[5] VPE v. 5. 4 ff.

suppressed Arianism there, drove out the Arian priests, and made their churches over to the Catholics. Much has been written about Leovigild's alleged persecution of the Catholics: may there not have been a very real persecution of the Arians by Hermenegild in the territories that fell under his control? When we consider what happened to the Arians throughout the entire kingdom when Reccared turned Catholic, it will seem improbable that the Arian Church continued to flourish, or even to exist openly, in Seville, Cordoba, and Merida in the years when a Catholic prince governed them.

If we suppose, then, that Arianism was suppressed by Hermenegild, the position in Merida becomes clear, and we may conclude that in 582–3 Leovigild was simply restoring the situation which had existed before the war: he handed back to the Arians the churches which had been theirs in 579. But he refused to give them the Church of St. Eulalia, which his commission decided had always been a Catholic church. It is unfortunate that we do not know the motives that caused him to go on to exile the Bishop. What was the significance of the request for the tunic of St. Eulalia?[1] Was this the only matter in dispute between Leovigild and Masona? Is it likely that the Catholic Bishop had failed to support the Catholic rebel? Masona was recalled from exile by Leovigild himself soon after the suppression of the great rebellion; but our authorities do not say that the Bishop was ever accused of having supported Hermenegild. Can we be certain that nothing has been held back in this connection? We have already seen something of the Catholic writers' reluctance to mention the Catholic rebel.

When the King exiled Masona he did not suppress the Catholic bishopric of Merida. There was no attack on the Catholic community in general. On the contrary, he appointed to the see of Merida another Catholic, called Nepopis, who was already bishop of another diocese.[2] The attack on Masona was an attack on the Bishop personally, not on Catholicism as such.

Less information has survived about the King's relations with John of Biclarum, the chronicler, our best contemporary source of information for the history of the reign. John had migrated to

---

[1] The tunic probably belonged by right to the Arians: *VPE* v. 6. 19, 'fraudulenter surripuisti'.

[2] Ibid. v. 6. 29; cf. v. 8. 8 ff., with Garvin, p. 473.

Constantinople as a young man and had remained there for seventeen years until about 576,[1] when he returned to Spain. In his chronicle he says nothing of his fortunes under Leovigild; but Isidore of Seville is not so reticent.[2] He says that John, who like Masona was a Goth, returned to Spain at a time when 'the Arian madness' was raging, incited by King Leovigild. The King tried to compel John to believe in the wicked heresy, but John resisted him and was sent into exile at Barcelona, where for ten years he endured much persecution at the hands of the Arians. Now, allowing a year for the King to get to know him and to make his attempt to convert him to Arianism, it would seem to follow that the years of his exile were 577–86, though whether it was Leovigild or Reccared who recalled him from his banishment is unfortunately not recorded. If this chronology is correct, John was exiled *before* Hermenegild's revolt broke out, at a time when there is no other reason for thinking that Leovigild was putting pressure on the Catholics. This is a matter to which we shall return.

The third person whom Leovigild is said to have persecuted is Phronimius (p. 65 above). Phronimius was a native of Bourges in the Frankish kingdom, who had emigrated to Septimania in the time of King Liuva (568–72). Liuva had welcomed him with the generosity that was characteristic of the Arian kings; and Phronimius became Catholic bishop of Agde (Dép. Hérault). Some years later he urged Ingundis, who was on her way from France to Spain to marry Hermenegild, not to allow herself to be persuaded to accept the 'poison' of Arianism. This came to the ears of Leovigild, who set about finding ways and means of expelling him from his bishopric. Certain informants finally warned Phronimius that the King was sending an assassin to kill him, and Phronimius accordingly fled from Septimania to the Frankish kingdom, where in 588 he became Bishop of Vence. This is the story of Gregory of Tours,[3] but whether the King really planned to murder the Bishop is open to some doubt. He would not have shared such a scheme with many advisers, and those who warned Phronimius may have been misinformed. No doubt Leovigild was annoyed with his foreign, mischief-making Bishop; but, like the other Arian kings of Spain, he is never recorded to have put

---

[1] On this date see Mommsen, *Chron. Min.* ii. 207 f.
[2] *De Vir. Illustr.* 62 f. (PL 83. 1105).
[3] *HF* ix. 24. Cf. Görres, art. cit. (p. 78 n. 2 above), p. 574.

a man to death because of his religious faith. Be that as it may, Phronimius's flight took place in 580, that is, when Hermenegild had already rebelled.

Finally, Gregory of Tours tells a story of how a certain un-named priest, who refused to admit that the Son and the Holy Spirit were inferior to the Father, was tortured and then exiled from Spain by Leovigild. The priest 'departed rejoicing and returned to Gaul'. Thus he, too, like Phronimius, was a Gaul, not a Spaniard. Unfortunately, in this case Gregory gives no hint at the date of the events that he is narrating.[1]

What are we to say, then, about Leovigild's attitude towards the Catholics, first, before Hermenegild's revolt broke out, and, secondly, during the course of the revolt? The evidence of Isidore suggests that coercive measures were used against John of Biclarum before Hermenegild went to Seville; and indeed Isidore asserts that Arianism was on the offensive at the time when John returned from Constantinople to Spain *c.* 576. But this is not otherwise attested and is hard to reconcile with two passages of Gregory of Tours. Gregory says that the Frankish envoys who returned to France from an interview with Leovigild in 582 stated that the King was trying to drive out the Catholic faith 'with new guile' (*novo nunc ingenio*). In their opinion the anti-Catholic policy had only recently been put into action, that is, after the rebellion had begun.[2] More important, Gregory reports at length a conversation which he held at Tours in 580 with an Arian Visigothic ambassador named Agila; and he represents Agila as insisting upon the tolerant attitude of the Arians towards Catholicism.[3] But if Leovigild was engaged at that moment, or if he had been engaged in recent years, in persecuting the Catholics in his kingdom, it is hardly credible that Gregory would have omitted to point to the falsity of Agila's position. Besides these two passages of Gregory there are further facts to be taken into account. Early in Leovigild's reign there was some immigration of African Catholic monks into Spain. The fame of one of these immigrants, the abbot Nanctus, came to Leovigild's ears, and

---

[1] *In Glor. Martyr.* 81 (p. 543), where the king is undoubtedly Leovigild. Gregory ends his story with the words: 'sed ut fides dictis adhibeatur, ego hominem vidi qui haec ab ipsius clerici ore audita narravit'. I suppose that many well-established 'facts' of ancient history are no more securely based.

[2] *HF* vi. 18. On the word *ingenium* see Krusch's index, p. 608.

[3] *HF* v. 43.

'although he was an Arian' he wished that Nanctus would commend him to God in his prayers, and hence gave him land so that the abbot and his brethren might have food and clothing from it.[1] In those early years Masona of Merida was able to found monasteries and endow them.[2] But it is John of Biclarum who gives us the most important piece of evidence. Speaking of the outbreak of Hermenegild's rebellion, he says that 'when Leovigild was reigning in peace and quiet a domestic quarrel confounded the security of his adversaries'.[3] He would scarcely have spoken of peace and quiet if a persecution of the Catholics had been raging at the time in question. And who were the King's 'adversaries' if not the Catholics themselves? What the revolt brought about, according to John, was the destruction of the 'security' of the Catholics.

There is, in fact, a conflict in our evidence here, but the inference is unavoidable. Gregory of Tours spoke to witnesses of the highest authority at the very time of the events. John of Biclarum was himself involved in the events. Isidore, on the other hand, was writing more than forty years after the revolt had been crushed; and it is hard to resist the impression that he was mistaken in a point of chronology. He confused the date of John's return from Constantinople to Spain (576) with the date of his exile by Leovigild. Accordingly, John's exile lasted for less than ten years, and Leovigild's attitude towards Catholicism throughout the first ten years of his reign was 'one of consistent toleration'.[4] His anti-Catholic measures coincided with the war against Hermenegild, or, at any rate, cannot be shown to have antedated it. On the other hand, no general council or provincial synod of the Catholic bishops met while he was on the throne. Evidently he continued the ban on such assemblies which seems to have been imposed by Agila and which was maintained by Athanagild and Liuva. But there is no reason to think that the position of the Catholics worsened in the first ten years of the reign.

As for his attitude while the rebellion was in progress, we have seen that when the revolt began in 580 he was not able to give it his full attention immediately: he spent the campaigning season of

---

[1] *VPE* iii. 2 ff.   [2] Ibid. v. 3. 3; Jo. Biclar., *s.a.* 573 (ii. 213).
[3] *S.a.* 579 (ii. 215).
[4] So Scott, 196. Cf. Görres, art. cit. (p. 77 n. 7 above), p. 120 n. 1; Garvin, p. 481; Stroheker, p. 172 n. 5.

581 in action against the Basques and only turned southwards in 582 (p. 70 f. above). But one event is recorded from the time that elapsed between the outbreak of the revolt and the campaign against the Basques. The first recorded action of Leovigild when he heard that his son had risen in revolt (apart from his efforts to come to terms with him) was to call a synod of Arian bishops at Toledo in 580. At this synod the decision was reached that converts 'from the Roman religion' to 'our Catholic faith', that is, to Arianism (p. 40 above), need not be rebaptized: the laying on of hands would be enough if the convert would partake of communion and would offer glory to the Father through the Son in the Holy Spirit, the normal Arian form of the *Gloria*. On these lines the synod published a document which was afterwards denounced by the Third Council of Toledo.[1]

The purpose of this move of Leovigild is superficially clear: it was intended to ease the transition of Catholics to Arianism. The need for rebaptism had hitherto been a stumbling-block for Catholics who might have wished to change their faith. True, some had not been deterred by it, and others had had their children baptized as Arians (p. 39 above), though neither category is likely to have been very numerous. But now the ruling of Leovigild's synod, coupled with the offer of monetary advantages, resulted in many conversions both of priests and of laymen, as our Catholic authorities admit. No less a figure than Vincentius, Bishop of Saragossa, went over to Arianism. What became of him later on, we do not know: the name of the bishop of Saragossa in 589 was Simplicius.[2] But his action caused Severus, Bishop of Malaga in the Byzantine province, to write a pamphlet against him, which unfortunately has not survived.[3] Severus's publication, together with the anxiety which is clearly shown in the pages of Gregory of Tours, illustrates the close attention with which men in the neighbouring Catholic states were following the outcome of Leovigild's synod.

---

[1] For the *libellus detestabilis* see III Tolet. 16. On this doxology see Stroheker, p. 174.

[2] Isidore, *HG* 50 (ii. 288), 'plerosque sine persecutione inlectos auro rebusque decepit' (sc. Leovigild); but he slips in saying (ibid.) 'ausus quoque . . . etiam rebaptizare Catholicos'. Jo. Biclar., *s.a.* 580 (ii. 216), 'plurimi nostrorum cupiditate potius quam impulsione in Arrianum dogma declinant'. But Greg. Tur., *HF* vi. 18, goes too far when he says that the 'Christians', as he calls them (he means the Catholics) in Spain were few in number (*pauci*).

[3] Isidore, *De Vir. Illustr.* 43 (PL 83. 1105).

In 582 the King's attitude seems to have been even more advanced than it was when the synod met in 580. He was now prepared to worship at the shrines of Catholic martyrs and even in Catholic churches, and to assert—a dramatic concession (p. 39 above)—that Christ the Son of God was equal with the Father; but he still denied the full Godhead of the Holy Ghost.[1] That is to say, in the matter of the equality of the Son with the Father he departed from the teachings of the Council of Rimini, which Ulfila had long ago propagated among the barbarians. But in denying the full divinity of the Holy Spirit[2] he took up the position of the heretics known as Macedonians (named after Macedonius who became Bishop of Constantinople when Eusebius of Nicomedia died in 341) or Pneumatomachi, or simply Semi-Arians, a heresy which had been known to Ulfila and had been rejected by him. In fact, the King was orthodox with regard to the Second Person of the Trinity but Arian with regard to the Third. And at the great Council of Toledo in 589 Reccared explicitly named and rejected Macedonianism.[3] Moreover, the Arianism of some of Leovigild's ambassadors was remarkably elastic. Indeed, one of them was prepared to admit that the Father, Son, and Holy Spirit were of one 'power'; and, although he would not communicate in a Catholic church or accept the Catholic form of the Benediction, he was prepared to attend a Catholic church service. It is also significant that one of the few stories told about the war with Hermenegild shows Leovigild restoring to a Catholic monastery of St. Martin, situated between Saguntum and Cartagena, everything which his troops had plundered from it.[4] Again, in dealing with Masona, John of Biclarum, and the unnamed priest whose story is told by Gregory of Tours (p. 82 above), Leovigild tried at first to win them over by peaceful means, and he resorted to force only when persuasion had failed. On the face of it, the King was trying to close the ranks and to win all the support which he could possibly obtain in

[1] Greg. Tur., loc. cit.; cf. Stroheker, pp. 174 f.

[2] This denial was based on a typically Germanic–Arian argument: 'quod in nullis legatur codicibus', Greg. Tur., loc. cit., who undertakes to refute the argument.

[3] Mansi, ix. 980, cf. 985.

[4] Greg. Tur., *In Glor. Confess.* 12 (p. 755). Why was the king operating in that region? Is it possible that he was on the way from capturing Rosas from the Basques (p. 70 above) to begin his attack on Hermenegild?

face of an essentially Catholic revolt. And since many Catholics accepted his compromise, it may be right to believe that his policy 'caused disunion and uncertainty in the Catholic camp, and probably lightened effectively the task of suppressing the rebellion'.[1] If his Goths were Catholics, perhaps we have here the explanation of Hermenegild's curious failure to take the military initiative against his father in 580 and 581.

Leovigild took other measures too. It is likely (p. 79 f. above) that Hermenegild confiscated the Arian churches in the cities that fell under his control; and when the King recovered these cities he restored the churches and their revenues to the Arians, as we appear to catch a glimpse of him doing at Merida. This, and his similar action in Galicia in 586, may be the explanation of St. Isidore's statement that 'he took away the revenues and privileges of the churches'.[2] He is also said to have confiscated the goods of private citizens as well as of the Church. But whether he did this in the earlier years of his reign as part of an attack on the nobility which was designed to finance his wars and put aside usurpers, or whether the reference is to the goods of the rebels whom he crushed in 573 and the following years, is not stated. In either case there is nothing to suggest explicitly that these measures were connected with Hermenegild's revolt; but that they were is indicated by the fact that Reccared restored the money later on.[3]

Our chief contemporary Spanish source of information, John of Biclarum, gives no hint that in his opinion Leovigild was a persecutor of the Catholic Church; and no valid evidence has reached us from any writer that would justify us in describing the King as a persecutor. Now, if his aim had been to take the offensive against the Catholics of Spain in general, he would scarcely

[1] Scott, p. 206. For some good remarks on Leovigild's religious policy see Stroheker, pp. 166 ff.; but for another interpretation see pp. 105 ff. below.

[2] HG 50 (ii. 288), 'ecclesiarum reditus et privilegia tulit'. His further statement (ibid.), 'plurimos episcoporum exilio relegavit', is in my opinion a generalization from the cases of Masona and Phronimius: *contra*, Hillgarth, p. 31 n. 21. Little can be built on Leander's statement in his closing address to the Third Council (Mansi, ix. 1003 A), 'et quorum asperitatem quondam gemebamus, de eorum nunc gaudemus credulitate', a mere rhetorical antithesis; or on Reccared's remark, 'vos tamen Dei sacerdotes meminisse oportet, quantis hucusque ecclesia Dei catholica per Hispanias adversae partis molestiis laboraverit' (ibid. ix. 979 A).

[3] Jo. Biclar., *s.a.* 587 (ii. 218), 'Reccaredus rex aliena a praecessoribus direpta et fisco sociata placabiliter restituit', where note the delicacy of *praecessoribus*. Isidore, HG 55 (ii. 290) is less discreet: 'adeo liberalis ut opes privatorum et ecclesiarum praedia, quae paterna labes fisco adsociaverat, iuri proprio restauraret'.

have directed his chief attack against two Visigoths and two immigrants from France. And whatever his attitude towards the Catholic clergy, there is no hint in our sources that he ever interfered with Catholic laymen. And if we regard the war against Hermenegild as essentially a war of Goth against Goth (p. 67 above), it is not at all surprising that the King took no steps whatever against Hispano-Roman Catholics. In such a war Leovigild would have directed his ecclesiastical policy against the Goths in his opponent's camp. But since his propaganda was certainly directed towards Catholics, it seems to follow that the many thousands of Goths in Hermenegild's entourage at Seville were Catholics.

6. The Conquest of Galicia

The last major exploit of Leovigild was the conquest of the Sueves in Galicia and the incorporation of their kingdom in Visigothic Spain. The attack on Galicia may have been an old plan of the King's; for his actions on the Suevic frontier in 576 had been provocative, and may have caused the Sueves to look round for alliances with France and Byzantium (p. 68 above).

After the fiasco at Seville (p. 71 above) the Suevic king, Miro, had died in 582. His son Eboric succeeded him and made peace with Leovigild;[1] but two years later the new king's brother-in-law Audeca rebelled and dethroned him, ordaining him as priest. Following the example of Leovigild himself he went on to marry his predecessor's wife, whose name was Sisegutia,[2] having presumably rid himself of Eboric's sister. He also imitated Leovigild and Hermenegild by putting his own name—in the form Odiacca—on his coins, of which a single specimen survives. The existence of this coin 'is proof that the kingdom was preparing to follow the example of its Visigothic neighbour in establishing a fully regal coinage at the very moment when its existence was about to be brought to an end'.[3]

But he reigned for only a year, for in 585 Leovigild set out on his last campaign. He devastated Galicia, dethroned Audeca, but did not kill him: he treated him as Audeca himself had treated Eboric—the dethroned King became a priest and was exiled to

---

[1] Greg. Tur., HF vi. 43.   [2] Ibid.; Jo. Biclar., s.a. 584 (ii. 216).
[3] P. Grierson, 'A Tremissis of the Suevic King Audeca (584–5)', Estudos de Castelo Branco (1962), pp. 7–12.

Beja in Portugal (Pax Julia). At this same time Guntramn's forces had invaded Septimania and were in process of being checked by Reccared (p. 75 above). In face of this war on two fronts Leovigild destroyed the ships trading between France and Galicia, plundered their cargoes, and killed or imprisoned their crews.[1] He took over the royal treasure of the Sueves and incorporated Galicia as the sixth province of his kingdom.[2] Later in the year there was a revolt in Galicia led by one Malaric, who tried to establish himself as King and to restore the kingdom. But he was crushed by Leovigild's generals, and no further effort at independence is ever reported from Galicia.[3]

Leovigild at once re-established Arianism as the State religion of his new province, which had been converted to Catholicism in the period 550–60 during the reign of Miro's father, Theodemir. The conversion then appeared to be so complete that the bishops who met at the First Council of Braga on 1 May 561, and who found it necessary to attack Priscillianism, were content to ignore Arianism. And when the Second Council of Braga met in June 572 no fewer than five of the twelve Catholic bishops who signed the minutes had Germanic names. The Arian church organization had been suppressed; and in 572 St. Martin of Braga had been able to say that 'with the help of Christ's grace there is no doubt in this province about the unity and correctness of the faith'.[4] But at the Third Council of Toledo in 589 four Arian bishops from Galicia abjured their Arianism and signed the minutes of the Council as Catholics. These were Beccila of the see of Lugo, Gardingus of Tuy, Argiovittus of Oporto, and Sunnila of Viseu, all of them bearing Germanic names. (But no ex-Arian signed for the remaining sees, not even for the metropolitan city of Braga: evidently not all the Arian Sueves held their opinions lightly.) Now, there is no doubt that these bishops had been installed by Leovigild; for if they had been appointed to their sees before 585 as Catholics we should have to suppose that they abjured their Catholicism in 585, when Leovigild overran their country, and then abjured their Arianism in 589, when the province as a whole

---

[1] Greg. Tur., *HF* viii. 35. These ships are often thought to have been warships, but the phrase *res ablatae* in Gregory's text suggests to my mind that they were merchantmen: so, too, Baynes, op. cit. (p. 21 n. 2 above); A. R. Lewis, 'Le commerce et la navigation sur les côtes atlantiques de la Gaule du ve au viiie siècle', *Le Moyen Âge*, lix (1953), pp. 249–98, at p. 271.

[2] Jo. Biclar., *s.a.* 585 (ii. 217).   [3] Ibid.   [4] Barlow, 117. 18 f.

returned to Catholicism. But had they blown with the wind to that extent the Third Council would hardly have regarded them as suitable men to continue in the episcopal office. Further, there were about a dozen sees in Galicia, and since Leovigild may not have had time to make appointments to all of them, it follows that at least one-third of the Arian bishops there made haste to join the Catholics in 589.

What of Leovigild's religious policy in Galicia? What, in fact, had become of the Catholic bishops of those sees in which the King installed Arian bishops? At the Third Council of Toledo three of the four sees of which the bishops abjured Arianism were each represented by *two* bishops—the Suevic ex-Arians together with Nitigisius of Lugo, Neusila of Tuy, and Constantius of Oporto.[1] (It was contrary to canon law for a city to have two bishops simultaneously, as Pope Hilarus had pointed out to the bishops of Tarraconensis more than a century previously;[2] but the times were exceptional.) These three men had been Catholics throughout and had never been Arians. But had they held their posts before 585 or were they installed by Reccared when he was converted in 586? Fortunately, it seems possible to answer this question. It is known that Nitigisius was already Bishop of Lugo in 572, when he attended the Second Council of Braga,[3] so that it is reasonable to suppose that Neusila (a German) and Constantius had also occupied their sees before Leovigild's conquest of their country. (Presumably the Catholic Bishop of Viseu had died and had not yet been replaced in 589.) It seems, then, that in 585–6 Catholic bishops held office simultaneously with their Arian counterparts in those cities in which Leovigild had time to install Arian bishops.

But perhaps the three Catholic bishops had been deposed by Leovigild in 585 and were reinstated by Reccared two or three years later? That is unlikely, for Leovigild is not known ever to have suppressed a Catholic bishopric. Even when he banished Masona of Merida in 582 he appointed Nepopis to take his place (p. 80 above). The inference is, then, that when Leovigild conquered Galicia he did not do away with the organization of the

---

[1] Mansi, ix. 1000 ff.

[2] Hilarus, *Ep.* 16. 4 (A. Thiel, *Epistolae Romanorum Pontificum* (Braunsberg, 1868), p. 168).

[3] Barlow, p. 123.

Catholic Church there: he simply set up an Arian organization side by side with it. But he will have met the same difficulties there as he seems to have encountered in Merida in 582: the new Arian bishops had to be provided with churches and revenues, and these can only have been supplied as a result of confiscations from the Catholics, who had themselves acquired them, of course, by confiscating them from the Arians c. 560.

Although the King installed a number of Arian bishops in Galicia, surely he cannot have had time to convert many of the population at large? And yet the language used by Reccared in 589 when referring to the Sueves suggests that the number converted by his father was exceedingly high. Reccared did not exaggerate in order to stress the size of the victory which he himself had won for Catholicism by re-establishing the Catholic Church in Galicia; for John of Biclarum also says that Reccared recalled the entire nation of the Goths and Sueves to the unity and peace of the Church.[1] That is perhaps an overstatement, but it would clearly be a mistake to write off all our evidence and believe that Reccared used absurdly boastful language to his bishops in 589. When we recall that pagan practices were widespread in Galicia and that so late as 561 a Catholic bishop admitted that men living in the more outlying parts of this remote country had received little or no knowledge of the true teaching,[2] then it may appear that a change from Catholicism to Arianism and back again was a less unaccountable procedure in Galicia than it would have been had it taken place among the more sophisticated population of Toledo —though indeed something very similar may have come about in Merida when control of that city passed from Leovigild to Hermenegild and back again to Leovigild. At all events, there is no hint in any authority that Leovigild used force to bring the Sueves back to Arianism.

It was reported to Pope Gregory the Great and also to Gregory of Tours, both of them strict contemporaries of these events, that Leovigild before he died came to see the truth of the Catholic belief.[3] No anti-Catholic measures of any kind are reported from

---

[1] Mansi, ix. 979, 'Suevorum gentis infinita multitudo'; Jo. Biclar., s.a. 587 (ii. 218), 'gentemque omnium Gothorum et Suevorum', etc.

[2] Lucretius of Braga at the First Council of Braga: Barlow, p. 106. 6 ff., cf. p. 110. 10. He perhaps means Catholic as against Priscillianist teaching.

[3] Gregory I, Dial. iii. 31, relying on the reports of 'many who come from Spain'; Greg. Tur., HF viii. 46, 'ut quidam adserunt'. There can be no certainty about

the final period of the reign, that is, after the suppression of Hermenegild. On the contrary, this was the time when the King recalled Masona, and perhaps also John of Biclarum, from exile, and when Leander returned from Constantinople to Spain to become Bishop of Seville.[1] It was the time when Leovigild pressed ahead with his plan to marry his second son, Reccared, to the Catholic Frankish princess, Rigunthis (p. 74 above). The years 584–6 were a time of reconciliation in Spain except in the former kingdom of Galicia, where the King was busy reinstating Arianism. Gregory the Great goes on to say that Leovigild did not proclaim his conversion publicly through fear of his people. When his son Reccared turned to Catholicism in 587, according to another authority, he had himself baptized in secret.[2] Similarly, the Burgundian king, Gundobad, became convinced before his death in 516 of the falsity of Arianism and was ready to be received into the Catholic Church—provided that this could be done in secret. According to Gregory of Tours, he was afraid of a revolt of his people if it should become known that he had abandoned Arianism.[3] Clearly, if Leovigild had in fact become converted—and the story is hard to believe—it would have been difficult for him to make his Catholicism public in view of the severe sufferings and losses that the Visigoths had endured in the late war, which had been fought to some extent at least in the name of Arianism. If there is any truth in the rumour of Leovigild's conversion, it is tempting to think that he and Reccared, like Gundobad among the Burgundians in similar circumstances, expected trouble from the rank and file of their people and perhaps from some of the nobility, too, if their conversion were to be proclaimed prematurely. And Reccared did not avoid trouble.

Leovigild's alleged change of faith, and it is inconsistent with *VPE* v. 9. 1 ff. For the view that it never happened, which is nowadays accepted almost universally, see Garvin, pp. 481 f. For an explanation of how the rumour, if it is a rumour, may have arisen, see Scott, p. 211.

[1] Jo. Biclar., *s.a.* 585 (ii. 217).

[2] Fredegarius, iv. 8.

[3] *HF* ii. 34, the authority of which is rejected sometimes for no valid reason. Observe in Greg. Tur., loc. cit. 31, Clovis's fears that his people might not follow him in deserting the old gods.

IV · RECCARED

THE sources for the first four years of Reccared's reign are
good. John of Biclarum continued his chronicle to the year
590. The Acts of the Third Council of Toledo are extensive
and informative. The *Lives* of the Bishops of Merida are, as
always, lively and illuminating. Gregory of Tours and Gregory
the Great are contemporary witnesses of the highest order.

When Reccared succeeded his father between 13 April and 8
May 586 he was still an Arian. Since the Visigoths did not
recognize any hereditary right of succession to the throne it was
thought noteworthy that he succeeded peacefully.[1] The absence of
rivals was partly due to the strength and ruthlessness of his father;
but Reccared himself had shown considerable military ability in
France and probably seemed a formidable candidate for the throne
in his own right. But the peace did not last for long either at home
or abroad.

1. *Reccared and the Franks*

He inherited a dangerous situation on the frontier of Septimania; for the Frankish king, Guntramn, was still threatening an
attack in spite of his set-back at Nîmes and Carcassonne (p. 75
above). There had already been a new frontier incident. A man
named Desiderius had on his own initiative launched another
attack on Carcassonne; but after an initial victory he was killed
outside the city walls, and his men were routed. Whether this had
happened before or after Reccared's accession is not clear;[2] but in
either case it increased the tension on the French frontier.

Reccared immediately sought a reconciliation with his step-
mother Goisuintha, who had troubled Ingundis years before; and
on her advice he sent envoys at once to both Childebert and
Guntramn, asking for peace. Childebert, whose ardour to avenge
his sister had now cooled off, agreed to peace; and the Visigoths
thus succeeded in neutralizing two of the three Frankish kings (for

[1] Jo. Biclar., *s.a.* 586 (ii. 217), 'cum tranquillitate'.
[2] Ibid., *s.a.* 587; Greg. Tur., *HF* viii. 45, who dates the event to the end of
Leovigild's reign. See Garvin, p. 511.

they had had no trouble with Chilperic).[1] But Guntramn, so far
from signing a peace, refused to meet the envoys, and the frontier
between his possessions and Septimania was closed. In reply the
Goths successfully raided the lower Rhone valley.[2] It was at this
stage that Reccared became a Catholic; and he now sent another
embassy to Childebert and Guntramn. Childebert agreed that
Reccared was not guilty of the charge that had been brought against
him of having been an accomplice in the death of Ingundis—for
this, rather than any difference of religion, was still the issue that
interested him—and, in fact, soon after his accession Reccared had
executed Sisbert, the assassin of Hermenegild.[3] When the Goths
offered Childebert 10,000 solidi for a treaty of alliance, he and his
mother Brunhild, who also felt deeply about the fate of Ingundis,[4]
accepted readily. The envoys went on to say that Reccared was
prepared to marry the King's sister Chlodosind—the projected
marriage with Rigunthis had long since fallen through—but
Childebert and his mother said that they could not agree to this
without Guntramn's consent.[5]

Guntramn's reception of the envoys was much less accom-
modating. He declared that he could not trust a people who had
handed over his niece Ingundis into captivity, killed her husband,
and caused her to die abroad.[6] When asked in 588 about the marriage
of Reccared and Chlodosind, he said that he could not agree to
his niece going to a country where her sister had been killed.[7] In
that same year, however, Childebert agreed to the marriage
'since he had learned that that nation [i.e. the Visigoths] had been
converted to the Catholic faith'.[8] This was the only reference
which any of the Frankish kings made to religion throughout
these prolonged and somewhat tedious negotiations; and it is
remarkable that religion was mentioned only when the marriage
of the King's sister was under discussion. True, Reccared had
referred to his Catholicism when asking for peace in 587;[9] but
there is no evidence that this plea carried weight with the Franks

---

[1] Greg. Tur., *HF* ix. 1.
[2] Ibid. ix. 1 and 7.
[3] Jo. Biclar., *s.a.* 585, 587 (ii. 217 f.).
[4] Greg. Tur., *HF* viii. 21. For her later attitude see ix. 28. Note esp. her letter to
the Byzantine Empress: *Epist. Austras.* 44, and her letter to the boy Athanagild,
ibid. 27. There is no evidence, however, that she wished to help Hermenegild before
585: *contra*, Goffart, art. cit. p. 108.
[5] Greg. Tur., *HF* ix. 16.   [6] Ibid.   [7] Ibid. ix. 20, p. 439.
[8] Ibid. ix. 25.   [9] Ibid. ix. 16.

when they were considering the question of peace—they had already signed a treaty with Reccared when he was still an Arian.

At last, in 589, Guntramn moved against Septimania. It was the last attack ever launched by the Franks against the united Visigoths, and it was a total failure. If the century opened with a crushing Visigothic defeat, it closed with a victory so decisive that the Franks only invaded Spain again in 631, when a considerable Gothic party invited them to do so. In 589, led by Claudius, *dux* of Lusitania, the Goths surprised and defeated the Frankish general, Boso, on the river Aude near Carcassonne, killed about 5,000 men, captured the Frankish camp, and took more than 2,000 prisoners. St. Isidore, who was a young man at the time and who liked Franks as little as Gregory of Tours liked Goths, was jubilant: 'No victory of the Goths in Spain was ever greater or even equal to it.'[1] We shall consider the context of this war from the Spanish point of view later on. What is already clear enough is that there is no evidence for thinking that Guntramn had religious or sectarian motives of any kind for attacking Septimania, or that religion played any significant part in any of the Frankish kings' negotiations with Spain. What the Franks wanted was plunder, renown, and Septimania.

2. *The Third Council of Toledo*

Reccared was converted to Catholicism about February 587 and had himself baptized in secret (p. 91 above.) Pope Gregory I, after speaking of Leovigild's alleged conversion, says that the dying King commended Reccared to Leander of Seville so that the Bishop might do with him as he had done with his brother Hermenegild. His brother's merits helped Reccared to bring many to the bosom of God Almighty; and Gregory considered that all this could not have been achieved 'if King Hermenegild had not died for the truth'.[2] No Spaniard thought so, or rather no Spaniard said so in public.

Whatever his personal motives for his change of faith, Reccared held three preliminary meetings before the Third Council of Toledo assembled. He called a meeting of 'the bishops of his

---

[1] Greg. Tur., *HF* ix. 31; *VPE* v. 12. 3; Jo. Biclar., *s.a.* 589 (ii. 218), who says that scarcely 300 Visigoths defeated about 60,000 Franks! Cf. also Fredegarius, iv. 10; Isidore, *HG* 54 (ii. 289), with Fontaine, ii. 835.

[2] *Dial.* iii. 31.

religion', at which he proposed that they should meet the Catholic bishops in order to find out what was the true faith. He next held a joint meeting of Arian and Catholic bishops, at which a debate ensued, and Reccared pointed out that no miracle of healing had been performed by the Arians—he reminded them of how in his father's time an Arian bishop had undertaken to cure a blind man but had failed. Subsequent events showed that the King did not carry anything like a majority of the Arian bishops with him at this meeting (p. 101 below). But he pressed on. He held finally a meeting of Catholic bishops without the Arians, at which he declared himself convinced of the truth of Catholicism, was anointed with chrism, and joined the Catholic Church.[1]

Even before the Third Council opened, the Arian churches and their property had been made over to the Catholics.[2] An inscription survives from the church of St. Mary in Toledo which states that 'In the name of God the church of St. Mary was consecrated *in catolico* on 12 April in the first year of the reign of our master, the most glorious king, Flavius Reccared, in the 625th year of the [Spanish] era', that is, in 587. The words *in catolico* have caused discussion. They are normally taken to mean 'on Catholic ground';[3] but it is difficult to believe that the King or the Metropolitan, Euphemius, thought it necessary to commemorate that they had consecrated a Catholic church on a Catholic site. Now, it is hardly credible that the Arians had allowed the chief church in the capital city of their realm to remain in Catholic hands throughout the sixth century; and what the inscription probably records is the reconsecration as a Catholic church of what had for many years been an Arian one.[4]

When the bishops assembled at Toledo the King delivered a preliminary address in which he proclaimed the end of the ban on Catholic conciliar meetings (p. 35 above). The bishops then adjourned for three days of fasting. Finally, on 8 May 589 they met for their first session, with the King sitting among them like

---

[1] Greg. Tur., *HF* ix. 15. For the incident of the Arian bishop's failure to heal a blind man see idem, *In Glor. Confess.* 13 (pp. 755 f.). Jo. Biclar., *s.a.* 587 (ii. 218), mentions first a meeting of Reccared with the Arian bishops, at which the King persuaded the bishops to go over to Catholicism, and secondly, *s.a.* 590, the Third Council itself.

[2] III Tolet. 9; cf. *VPE* v. 11. 16.

[3] *Thesaurus Linguae Latinae*, s.v. 'Catholicus', 616. 73–5; Vives, 302.

[4] So E. Diehl, *Inscriptiones Latinae Christianae Veteres* (reprinted Berlin, 1961) 1814, '*in fide catholica* potius quam *in catholico loco*'.

Constantine among his bishops at Nicaea.[1] After a prayer he announced that his personal conversion had been made known 'not many days after the death of our father'. (In fact, he had been converted ten months after Leovigild's death.)[2] He ordered a notary to read out a statement written in his own hand,[3] in which he anathematized Arius and all his teachings and recognized the doctrine of the Councils of Nicaea, Constantinople, Ephesus, and Chalcedon. He reminded the bishops that he had won for the Catholic Church the famous nation of the Goths, who had hitherto been kept divided from the Church by the wickedness of their teachers. Moreover, the Sueves, who had been led into heresy by the fault of another (he meant his father), had also been recalled to the truth. What both nations needed now was instruction in the true faith, for it was ignorance that had led them astray.[4] He and his queen Baddo—for he had married at last—then signed the document. The assembly burst into applause and called out slogans in honour of God and the King.

Next, one of the Catholic prelates addressed those bishops and other clergy as well as the leading Gothic grandees who had been converted from Arianism, asking them to state their creed and to condemn Arianism with all its dogmas, rules, and offices, its communion and its books. Whereupon eight bishops who had defected from Arianism—four Visigoths and four Sueves (p. 88 above)—together with other clergy and the foremost Visigothic nobles, anathematized the heresy of Arius in twenty-three articles.[5] One of these articles (no. 18) condemned 'the detestable book published by us in the twelfth year of King Leovigild', that is, the statement issued after Leovigild's Arian synod in 580. They also anathematized any who denied that Christ was begotten of God and was equal and consubstantial with Him; any who denied that the Holy Spirit progressed from the Father and the Son and was coeternal and coequal with Them; any who asserted that the Son and the Holy Spirit were inferior to the Father and were not of the one substance, omnipotence, and eternity with Him; any

---

[1] Mansi, ix. 977; cf. Jo. Biclar., *s.a.* 590 (ii. 219). Curiously, we do not know in which Toledan church the bishops held their sessions.

[2] Mansi, ix. 977 *fin.*; Jo. Biclar., *s.a.* 587 (ii. 218).

[3] Ibid. 590 (ii. 219), 'scriptam manu sua'.

[4] Mansi, ix. 979. There is another reference to Leovigild in the sentence (ibid.) 'meminisse oportet quantis hucusque ecclesia Dei catholica per Hispanias adversae partis molestiis laboraverit'.   [5] Ibid. 984 ff.

who assigned to the Son a beginning in time; any who did not wholeheartedly condemn the Council of Rimini, which had long ago been the basis of the beliefs of Ulfila (whose name was not mentioned). These and other anathemas together with the creeds of Nicaea, Constantinople, and Chalcedon were then signed by the eight bishops (all of whom bear Germanic names), an unspecified number of priests and deacons, and a number of *viri illustres*, of whom only five are named—Gussinus, Fonsa, Afrila, Aila, and Ella—though there were others besides.[1]

The King then addressed the assembly a second time. In his opening speech he had emphasized the need for accurate teaching of the new faith by the clergy. He now proposed to introduce into the kingdom the Oriental custom whereby the congregation recited the creed of Constantinople aloud in unison before the Lord's Prayer on each occasion when communion was celebrated. The people would readily incline to believe what they often repeated, and no one could now plead ignorance of the true faith.[2] This proposal was accepted by the bishops in the second of the twenty-three disciplinary canons which they next went on to agree, for during the long years of Arian rule ecclesiastical discipline had deteriorated (not least in the matter of appointments to bishoprics).[3]

Seventy-two bishops signed the record of the Council's proceedings in person or by proxy; and the assembly ended with an address of thanksgiving delivered by Leander of Seville, who, with Eutropius, abbot of the monastery of Servitanum (p. 23 above) and afterwards Bishop of Valencia, had been the leading figure at the Council.[4] Leander's closing speech dealt solely with spiritual matters: so far from being a eulogy of the King or an expression of gratitude to him, it did not even mention him. And throughout the entire course of the Council not a word was said of Hermenegild, and no reference, however oblique and veiled, was made to his tragic career or to the fact that he had died bravely for the faith.

---

[1] Ibid. 988 f., 'omnes seniores Gothorum'.   [2] Ibid. 990.

[3] Ibid. 993. Decline of discipline: canon i.

[4] Jo. Biclar., *s.a.* 590 (ii. 219. 9 f.). On Eutropius see Isidore, *De Vir. Illustr.* 45 (*PL* 83. 1106). Some of his writings survive. Neither Eutropius nor any other abbot signed the acts of the Council: see C. J. Bishko, 'Spanish Abbots and the Visigothic Councils of Toledo', *Humanistic Studies in Honor of John Calvin Metcalf*, University of Virginia Studies, i (Charlottesville, Virginia, 1941), pp. 139–50, esp. p. 145.

The Council made no ruling about the status of the converted Arian clergy; and it was only in the year 633 that the Spanish bishops enacted that those who had been baptized 'in heresy' were ineligible for a bishopric.[1] The eight ex-Arian bishops who had signed the recantation also subscribed the twenty-three disciplinary canons as Catholic bishops. They came from seven cities, for two of them were from Valencia; and to five of these seven cities Catholic bishops had already been appointed, so that at the end of the Council there was double representation from Tuy, Lugo, Oporto, and Tortosa, and triple representation from Valencia (Murila, Ubiligisclus, and the Catholic Roman, Celsinus). The Arian converts, it seems, were not trusted to act alone; but for some reason no colleague had been installed at Barcelona, which was represented by the ex-Arian Ugnus alone. (It is odd that two bishops, Stephen and Peter, signed for Illiberris, though there is no evidence that either of them was a convert from Arianism.) At the Council of Barcelona which met in 599 Ugnus still signed for Barcelona, while Tortosa was still represented by the two bishops who had signed at Toledo, the Catholic Roman, Julian, and the ex-Arian Visigoth, Fruisclus.[2]

The twenty-three disciplinary canons entailed a major constitutional innovation. The Catholic bishops who assembled at Toledo in 589 became closely associated, as their Arian predecessors are not known to have been, with legislation on secular matters. Either at the King's instigation or after consultation with him—or even without consultation—they published rulings on matters that could not be described as wholly ecclesiastical. Their rulings had not in themselves the force of law, but they became law when the King published his 'Edict in Confirmation of the Council', in which he laid down penalties for those who disobeyed the enactments of the Council. The penalty in the case of 'more honourable persons' (p. 136 below) was the confiscation of half their goods by the Treasury, and in the case of 'inferior persons', exile and the loss of all their property.[3]

The bishops enacted that, although the practice of the Church in general was to hold provincial synods twice a year, it would be

---

[1] IV Tolet. 19.

[2] Mansi, x. 483 f.; cf. ix. 1001. Stephanus of Illiberris is mentioned in Vives, 177, cf. 589.

[3] Mansi, ix. 1000.

sufficient in Spain, owing to the poverty of the Spanish churches and the vast distances involved, if synods met only once a year—a concession already made to Spain in 517 by Pope Hormisdas[1]— the place of the meeting to be decided by the metropolitan bishop. This was a purely ecclesiastical ruling and lay within their competence; but they went on to state that, in accordance with a decree of Reccared, the local judges (*iudices locorum*) and the agents of the Treasury estates (*actores fiscalium patrimoniorum*) should appear at the provincial synod of their province on 1 November each year. The bishops would instruct them on how to deal justly with the people and would not allow them to burden taxpayers with transport services (*angariae*) or excessive *corvées*. According to the king's advice, the bishops were to act as overseers of the judges and were to report their outrages to the king.[2] Reccared followed this up with a law in which he declared that bishops who knew of the excesses of judges and agents, and failed to report them, would have to refund from their own pockets the loss suffered by the oppressed.[3]

These were no mere vague and pious exhortations. The bishops did in fact go on to meet the officials, and a document has survived from such a meeting held on 4 November 592. This document is a letter addressed by the bishops of the financial district of Barcelona (Artemius of Tarragona, Sophonius of Egara, John of Gerona, the chronicler, and Galanus of Ampurias) to the accountants (*numerarii:* p. 127 below) appointed for the year by the Count of the Patrimony. The bishops express their agreement with the rates at which payments of wheat and barley are to be commuted for gold—8 siliquae per bushel, together with 1 siliqua each to the 2 *numerarii* to cover their costs, and 4 siliquae to cover inevitable losses and price changes, in all, 14 siliquae for each bushel. The bishops remark that the officials have asked them for their consent 'according to the custom'—evidently such meetings had been held before 592—and they point out that if any of the agents of the *numerarii* exact more than the agreed sum, they must be punished and the excess returned to those who had been wronged.[4] Clearly, the bishops had won very decided and specific

---

[1] Hormisdas, *Ep.* 25 (p. 89 n. 2 above). The point was repeated at IV Tolet. 3; Conc. Emerit. 7.
[2] III Tolet. 18.   [3] *LV* xii. 1. 2 *fin.*
[4] *De Fisco Barcinonensi*, printed in Mansi, x. 473 f.

control over the finance officers of the central government. How long these meetings continued to be held we do not know.

Another remarkable intrusion into civil affairs by the fathers assembled at Toledo was minuted without any reference to the king. If a cleric lived with a woman who gave rise to 'infamous suspicions', he was to be separated from her and punished according to the canons. To impose such an ecclesiastical penalty lay within the bishops' normal competence; but they went on to enact that the woman in question should be sold into slavery by the bishops and her price given to the poor.[1] This noteworthy ruling also became law, of course, when Reccared published his Edict in Confirmation. In 590, the year after the Third Council had met, the bishops of Baetica were in some cases negligent in enforcing the rule. The First Council of Seville, therefore, enacted that if priests, deacons, and others ignored their bishops' rebuke, the royal judges must arrest the woman in question. The Council went so far as to declare that the judges must swear an oath to the bishops that they would not give back to a cleric any woman whom they had taken from him because he had had an illicit association with her; and if the judges did in fact restore such a woman they would be excommunicated. They repeated that the woman must be sold.[2]

With Reccared's consent the bishops at the Third Council excommunicated anyone who should force widows and virgins to marry when they wished to preserve their chastity.[3] The King confirmed the bishops' ruling in a special law. He declared that no one might marry virgins, widows, or penitents who had vowed their chastity to God, even when they themselves consented. The penalty for both parties was loss of property and exile for life.[4] The law was to be enforced not only by the judges but also by the bishops, and if either judges or bishops neglected to enforce it they became liable to a fine of no less than 360 solidi.[5] This wholly new attitude—the view that the bishop is on a par with the judge in enforcing the secular law—reappears in the bishops' further ruling that the two were to act together in seeking out and suppressing paganism and in putting a stop to the popular dances

---

[1] III Tolet. 5. This harsh ruling was softened somewhat in 653: VIII Tolet. 5.
[2] I Hispal. 3.   [3] III Tolet. 10.   [4] LV iii. 5. 2 (p. 106. 15).
[5] On this subject see also Conc. Ilerd. 6; II Conc. Barcinon. 4; and, in the seventh century, VI Tolet. 6.

and foul songs that often disgraced Christian feast-days (p. 55 above). But it was Reccared himself who ordered the judges to join with the bishops in inquiring into and punishing cases of infanticide.[1]

Again, the prolonged lack of ecclesiastical discipline which had prevailed under the Arian kings had enabled clerics to ignore their bishops and sue one another in the public courts. It was now ruled that those who did so in the future would lose their case and would be excommunicated.[2] The bishops at Toledo did not need to consult Reccared before reaching this conclusion. Further, at the suggestion of the Council, Reccared instructed the bishops to pass a ruling on the Jews, with the result that for the first time in Spanish history forcible conversion of Jews in certain circumstances became legal (p. 111 below).

What is most remarkable is that this dramatic increase in the power of the bishops in civil legislation involved a substantial growth of the influence of the Hispano-Romans on the government of the country; for the overwhelming majority of the bishops were Romans at this date and throughout the rest of Visigothic history. And this procedure—conciliar canon confirmed by royal enactment—continued to be a Visigothic practice until the end of their history.

3. *The Arian Reaction*

Not all the Arians of the kingdom accepted the conversion of the King and the grandees without a struggle. Only four Visigothic bishops at most abjured their Arianism at the Third Council; and, although we do not know the number of Arian bishoprics in Spain, it cannot be doubted that these four were only a small fraction of the total. The fate of the bishops and other clergy, both of Galicia and of the rest of the kingdom, who refused to abjure their Arianism is unknown except for three cases (Sunna, Athaloc, and Uldila) which will concern us in a moment. In fact, between the time of Reccared's personal conversion about February 587 and the opening of the great Council in May 589, the King had to deal with one rebellion and two conspiracies against his life.

---

[1] III Tolet. 17.   [2] Ibid. 13.

One conspiracy was headed by the Arian Bishop of Merida, that same Sunna who had been sent there by Leovigild in 582. He was joined by a number of very rich Visigoths, some of them *comites civitatis* (p. 139 below), and actually by a large number of Catholics. Our authority says that 'Sunna convinced some of the Goths who were of noble birth and exceedingly wealthy . . ., and separated them along with an innumerable multitude of the faithful from the ranks of the Catholics and the bosom of the Catholic Church', and caused them to take part in the conspiracy.[1] The *comites* were Goths who had become Catholic but who now reverted to Arianism. The large number of the people who followed them, however, were Catholics throughout and had never been Arians. According to one authority, the aim of the conspirators was to murder Masona of Merida; and we need not doubt that this was their first objective. According to another source, however—and his reliability, too, cannot be questioned—the ultimate aim of Sunna and two men named Segga and Vagrila, both of them Goths, was to overthrow the King himself.[2] When the conspiracy was crushed, Reccared punished Segga by cutting off his hands before banishing him to Galicia.[3] The amputation of hands was a rare penalty in Visigothic law, but there is some reason for thinking that it was the punishment of usurpers,[4] so that it looks as though the conspirators intended to place Segga on the throne. At all events, the conspiracy was betrayed by Witteric, who was to become King of Spain in 603 after murdering Reccared's son. Claudius, the *dux* (p. 143 below) of Lusitania, crushed it without difficulty. The rank and file of the conspirators were deprived of their estates and their offices and were sent into exile. Vagrila managed to escape from his captors and take refuge in the church of St. Eulalia. When Claudius asked the King what he was to do with him, Reccared replied that he, his family, and his possessions should become the property of the church of St. Eulalia; but Masona generously freed him and his family and gave him back his estates. As for the Bishop, Sunna, Reccared offered to appoint him as bishop of some other city if he would accept the Catholic faith. But Sunna proudly refused and declared himself

[1] *VPE* v. 10. 1 ff.   [2] Ibid.; Jo. Biclar., *s.a.* 588 (ii. 218).
[3] Ibid.

[4] R. S. Lopez, 'Byzantine Law in the Seventh Century and its Reception by the Germans and the Arabs', *Byzantion*, xvi (1942–3), pp. 445–61, at pp. 454 f. See also p. 157 below.

ready to die for the cause of Arianism. He was therefore banished from Spain, went to Mauretania, and made many converts to Arianism there before he died. The churches, together with their revenues, which Leovigild had handed over to Sunna in Merida were now returned to the Catholics.[1]

Early in 589, before the Third Council opened in May, a second conspiracy was discovered. The Queen, Goisuintha, the widow of both Athanagild and Leovigild, had incited Hermenegild to rebel in 579 (p. 67 above). She had later been reconciled to Reccared and had advised him to reach an accommodation with the Frankish kings (p. 92 above). At the time of the King's conversion she and an Arian bishop called Uldila (or Uldida) had momentarily professed their acceptance of Catholicism, but they were soon discovered not only to have relapsed into Arianism but to be plotting to dethrone Reccared. Uldila was sent into exile, and Goisuintha died.[2] The scene of their activities is unknown, but presumably the Queen was living in the capital, and, if so, Uldila is the only known Arian Bishop of Toledo.

When Reccared sent the news of his conversion to Septimania a serious incident took place at Narbonne. Two rich and noble counts called Granista and Wildigern, along with the Arian bishop, Athaloc, and many other Arians, rose in rebellion 'against the Catholic faith' and aimed to dethrone Reccared. They turned for help to the Frankish king, Guntramn, and brought 'an infinite multitude' of Franks into Septimania. This was the army of Boso (p. 94 above). So far from choosing his allies on sectarian grounds, Guntramn had intervened in Septimania so as to help the Arians! When the invaders were routed by Claudius, who had already crushed Sunna, the revolt collapsed, though not before many Catholics had been killed. Athaloc died a natural death; the fate of the other rebels has not been recorded.[3]

A fourth revolt, that led by Argimund, *dux* of a province and a member of the King's *cubiculum*, broke out after the Third Council had closed. Its aim was to dethrone and kill Reccared and to crown Argimund king in his place. But there is no evidence in this case that the conspirators intended to restore Arianism. The

---

[1] *VPE* v. 11. 12 ff.
[2] Jo. Biclar., *s.a.* 589 (ii. 218).
[3] *VPE* v. 12. 1–5, with Garvin, pp. 511 f.; Jo. Biclar., *s.a.* 589 (ii. 218); cf. F. Görres, *Zeitschrift f. wissenschaftliche Theologie*, xli (1891), pp. 95–7.

plot was discovered, and Argimund suffered decalvation and his right hand was cut off.[1] Now, there is no parallel in the reign of any other sixth-century king of Spain for so many revolts and conspiracies against the throne. And yet the Arian protest against the conversion, though led by members of the nobility and supported by some of the rank and file of the population, appears surprisingly feeble and half-hearted. In Spain itself, as distinct from Narbonensis, the protest was made by a handful of bishops and rich men; but the bulk of the Gothic population seems to have stood aside and accepted the new order of things with so little protest that we may once again wonder whether many of them had not already become Catholic before 589 (p. 37 f. above) and whether many of those who had remained Arian may not have been confused and daunted by Leovigild's radical concessions to Catholicism (p. 40 above). But what is even more remarkable is that both Spanish and Septimanian Catholics assisted the protest of the Gothic Arians.

Reccared lost little time in pressing home his victory. He began at once to burn Arian books, a policy in which he was only too successful, for not a single Gothic or Arian text has survived in Spain. (He was not the first German ruler to order the burning of books: he had been forestalled in this occupation by the Vandal king, Huneric, who in 484 learned the practice from the Roman emperors.)[2] Reccared banned Arians from employment in the public service,[3] and the forcible conversion of Arians was not unknown: that Agila who spoke to Gregory of Tours so warmly, and yet so tolerantly, on behalf of Arianism (p. 37 above) was forced to enter the Catholic Church.[4] The Arian church organization was suppressed; and this repression by the King and the bishops was successful, for after Reccared's reign no more is heard of Arians in Spain.

---

[1] Jo. Biclar., s.a. 590 (ii. 219). I use the cowardly term 'decalvation' because I cannot decide whether the victim was scalped or whether he merely had his head shaved: see Averil Cameron, *Revue belge de philologie et d'histoire*, xliii (1965), pp. 1203–16, with bibliography, referring to the Merovingian practice.

[2] Fredegarius, iv. 8; cf. Scott, p. 207. Huneric: Victor Vitensis, *Hist. Persec.* iii. 10.

[3] Gregory I, *Dial.* iii. 31, 'ut nullum suo regno militare permitteret, qui regno Dei hostis existere per hereticam perfidiam non timeret'.

[4] Greg. Tur., HF v. 43 *fin.*, 'necessitate cogente'; and it is wrong of Jo. Biclar., s.a. 587 (ii. 218), to say that the conversion of the Arian bishops was carried through 'ratione potius quam imperio'.

4. *The Conversion to Catholicism*

There is no reason to think that the forces opposing one
another during the revolt of Hermenegild were for the most part
composed of Goths on the one side and Romans on the other.
There is explicit evidence that the Goths were split by the rebellion (p. 67 above); and there is no evidence at all that the Roman
population was involved in the military actions of the revolt.
On the other hand, the rebellions of the Arian bishops, Sunna and
Athaloc, were supported by Catholics, and for these Catholics the
central issue was not a religious one at all. They were prepared to
fight and die—but not, it seems, on religious grounds. They were
ready to join with Arian bishops in fighting for Arianism against
a Catholic king who was trying to establish Catholicism. How then
are we to characterize the movement of opposition to Reccared?
It is clear that the internal struggles of the reigns of Leovigild
and Reccared were more complex than a straightforward struggle
between Catholics and Arians.

Leovigild was following the general practice of the Visigothic
Arians when he termed Catholicism the 'Roman' religion, while
Arianism was 'ours' (p. 40 n. 1 above). That is to say, in some
men's eyes a struggle between Arianism and Catholicism was also
a struggle between Visigoths and Romans. Moreover, the only
two Spaniards certainly known to have been harmed by Leovigild
because of their religious opinions were two Visigoths who had
risen to important positions in the Catholic Church. It is true that
the King is not recorded to have taken steps against Visigothic
Catholics in general: he did not interfere, for instance, with
Theodoric and Ermanric, who were Visigothic Catholic bishops
in 589 (p. 38 above), though that may be due simply to their lack
of distinction and influence or to our lack of knowledge. Again,
the unparalleled series of revolts against Reccared (although
Catholics took part in them) bore an essentially, though not an
exclusively, Visigothic character in that their leaders were Visigoths, whereas it was a Roman called Claudius who suppressed
the conspiracy at Merida and defeated the Frankish invaders of
Septimania when they came to the help of the Arian rebels there.

It is hardly open to doubt, then, that some Visigoths saw the
events of 589 not only as a struggle between Arianism and
Catholicism, but also, and perhaps chiefly, as a conflict between

Visigoths and Romans. The victory of Catholicism was in some sense a defeat for the Visigothic element in the population of Spain; or at any rate it may have been regarded as such by a considerable number, though not by all, of the Visigoths. Accordingly, it is not unreasonable to suppose that Leovigild attacked John of Biclarum and Masona of Merida not because they were Catholics but because they were Visigoths who had gone over to Catholicism. There is no proof that they were in any way connected with Hermenegild's rebellion (though Masona can hardly have failed to support it), but they were in Leovigild's eyes traitors to the Gothic cause at a critical time. If this is not the correct interpretation of Leovigild's actions, why did he not take any measures against the Catholic Romans and especially the prominent Catholic Roman bishops? Why did he not move against Leander of Seville (if he was in Spain at the time) or against Euphemius, Metropolitan of Toledo, or against Eutropius, abbot of the monastery of Servitanum, who was to be so active at the Third Council? If his aim was to take the offensive against Catholicism in general, why did he confine his attentions to two Visigoths and two unimportant clerics from the Frankish kingdom?

The facts can hardly be explained except on the view that the religious faith of the Roman population, who were scarcely involved in Hermenegild's revolt, was of minor interest to Leovigild. He had no wish to change it. The Visigothic Arian Church did not proselytize; and there cannot have been many cases of forcible conversion of Catholics or of Catholics having their children baptized as Arians. On the contrary, the Arians made the transition from Catholicism to Arianism difficult by insisting until 580 on rebaptism as a pre-condition. They cannot have been unaware of how warmly the Catholics felt on this matter. The Council of Lerida had taken stringent measures against the rebaptized (p. 39 above), and only recently Ingundis had objected strongly to being baptized a second time. The Third Council at a somewhat later date did not overlook the question: the bishops who abjured Arianism were obliged to anathematize all who believed in rebaptism.[1] The Visigoths, in fact, did not wish to diffuse Arianism among the Hispano-Romans, just as Theodoric the Great discouraged the conversion of Romans to

[1] III Tolet. 15.

Arianism in Italy. The reason for this was presumably that if masses of Romans were to enter the Arian Church the distinction between Visigoth and Roman would have been blurred in one capital respect—and the kings thought it necessary to keep the distinction sharp and clear-cut. This is not inconsistent with the fact that Leovigild tried to convert the Sueves of Galicia. The Sueves were Germans, and it was over against the Romans that the Visigoths wished to preserve their social identity. Catholicism was the Roman religion and Arianism was the religion of the Goths; and so they should remain.

But in that case, what of Leovigild's synod of 580? The synod offered to accept Catholics into the Arian Church without re-baptism: the imposition of hands would be enough if the convert would partake of communion from an Arian bishop and would offer glory to the Father through the Son in the Holy Spirit (p. 84 above), a form of the *Gloria* that was outlawed by the Third Council.[1] This is sometimes thought to have been an attempt to weaken the Catholics, both Roman and Gothic, in Hermenegild's camp. But if Romans were not substantially involved with Hermenegild, that cannot be precisely the case. Nothing that we know suggests that Leovigild or any of the other Arian kings of Spain, or of any barbarian kingdom, was even remotely concerned with any design to convert this Roman subjects to Arianism. And if it was Leovigild's bizarre plan to build a united Semi-Arian Church of Spain which would include both Romans and Goths, what was to be the language of the liturgy? Were the Goths to surrender their native language? Or did the King think that the Romans would worship in Gothic?

The synod of 580, then, was concerned with Goths alone—and naturally so: Leovigild directed his propaganda at Hermene-gild's soldiers, who were nearly all of them Goths. He thought it the duty of all Visigoths to accept the compromise with Arianism which his synod now offered. In 580 the King was trying to reach a compromise, not between Arian Visigoths and Catholic Romans, but between Arian Visigoths and Catholic Visigoths, while the conversion of such men as Vincentius, Bishop of Saragossa, was incidental.

If this is the correct conclusion, it would seem to follow that the number of Visigoths who had already become Catholic

[1] Ibid. 14.

before 580 was substantial. There would have been little point in changing Arian dogma in basic respects merely in order to recover the allegiance of John and Masona and a handful of others. Many Visigoths had supported Hermenegild in Seville in 579; and Leovigild's actions in the following year could well be accounted for on the supposition that these men had followed the prince not only into a rebellion but also into the Catholic Church. On this hypothesis Leovigild's policies throughout his reign were consistent: he had no quixotic wish to unite Goths and Romans into one people or to bring them together in one Macedonian Church, but he did wish to keep the Goths a united entity over against the Romans.

Why did Reccared and his adherents carry the conversion through? If it is the case that the substantial number of Goths who supported Hermenegild had in fact become Catholic, then Reccared was furthering a tendency in 589 that had gained considerable ground among his people within the past decade or two. But if that is not the case then we cannot understand his motives. Neither he nor any of his close associates has left any document which would throw light on them. What we do know is that he, unlike his father, tried to bring the two nationalities that inhabited his kingdom a step closer to a single administrative system. Besides the religious unification, he also introduced a new principle into the law; for all three of his extant laws were intended to bind Goths and Romans alike. Hitherto the Goths had lived under Gothic law and the Romans under Roman law as set out in Alaric's *Breviarium;* and each nationality had its own courts. Reccared's three laws are the first indication of a common *Reichsrecht* of universal application within the kingdom.[1] And the trend which he initiated in legislation continued until Reccesuinth abolished the Roman law altogether about 654: Leovigild was the last king to legislate for the Goths only. A further change was dictated by no king. Archaeology has shown that the period of the conversion to Catholicism coincides with the final abandonment of the old Gothic form of dress, the disappearance of the traditional 'Gothic' brooches and buckles (p. 151 below), the end of the custom of burying goods along with the dead, and the beginning of a time when the influence of East Roman crafts makes itself strongly felt among the Goths of Spain: in the finds

[1] K. Zeumer, *NA* xxiii (1898), pp. 481 f.; cf. ibid. xxiv (1899), p. 616.

of the seventh century the Germanic element has almost disappeared.[1] The Romanization of the royal court and the introduction of Byzantine ceremonial by Leovigild were quickly followed
by the establishment of the 'Roman' religion as the official
religion of the State. In this period the Goths took a striking step
towards absorption by the Romans. The loss of their traditional
customs, together with the new powers that the Catholic bishops
gained under Reccared, suggests that the period 586–601, the
reign of Reccared, tended on the whole to elevate the Romans to
the level of the Goths and to deprive the Goths in some ways of
their privileged position in the country. If the Visigoths were to
retain any privilege in the future, they had to do so in the political
sphere and by political methods. And this they did.

A full explanation of the conversion of the Visigoths to
Catholicism, then, would show it as part of a widespread move
towards the Romanization of the kingdom that took place in the
reign of the Arian Leovigild as well as of the Catholic Reccared.

5. The End of the Reign

After the Third Council had ended Leander wrote to Pope
Gregory the Great telling him among other matters of the
character of Reccared and of his conversion to Catholicism. The
letter has not survived, but Gregory's answer to it, dated April
591 (no less than two years after the great Council and four years
after the King's personal conversion), stresses that what was now
needed was an even more anxious vigilance over the King so as to
ensure that he continued on the right path.[2] But Reccared never
wavered. He took an intense interest even in the detail of the life
of the Church. Thus, a letter was addressed to him by a monk
named Tarra who had been expelled from the monastery of
Cauliana near Merida after being accused of associating with a
prostitute. In this letter, which is written in a style of excessive
obscurity, Tarra energetically protested his innocence to the
King: since the death of his wife he had kissed no woman in the
whole of Lusitania. Whether Reccared acquitted him is unknown,
but the letter is evidence not only of his eagerness to maintain the

---

[1] Zeiss, 80, 126, 138, *et passim.*
[2] Gregory I, *Ep.* i. 41.

morality of the clergy and the monks but also of his willingness to busy himself with individual cases.[1] His piety is also illustrated by his gift of a golden crown to the shrine of the blessed Felix at Gerona, which long after he died was used to crown a usurper (p. 220 below.)

There is evidence that he sometimes made appointments to vacant bishoprics (p. 43 above); but his nominees do not appear in all cases to have been wisely chosen. Bishop Agapius represented Cordoba at the Third Council of Toledo and at the First Council of Seville and had recently died in 619. Since he had been transferred directly from the public service to his see, his appointment is more likely to have been due to Reccared than to Leovigild. Having had no experience in lesser ecclesiastical offices, his ignorance of ecclesiastical discipline was so profound that he allowed his priests to consecrate churches, and he unfrocked and exiled his priest Fragitanus without consulting his provincial synod. The bishops at the Second Council of Seville referred to him in very harsh terms.[2]

Reccared himself did not write to the Pope until some time in the years 596–9. It is possible that his long delay was due to his suspicion of the close relations between the Papacy and the East Roman Empire.[3] He told the Pope that he had intended to write at the time of his conversion, but pressure of business had prevented him. Three years after becoming a Catholic he had sent to Rome the abbots of some Spanish monasteries bearing gifts and the news of his salvation; but they had been shipwrecked near Marseilles and had returned to Spain without ever reaching their destination. He now sent the Pope a golden, gem-adorned chalice in the hands of a papal emissary who happened to be in the Byzantine province at Malaga.[4] The Pope replied in August 599 in a long letter in which he enthusiastically praised the King for winning so many souls for the faith.

In the course of the letter he mentions a law which Reccared directed against the Jews. The Jews had tried to bribe the King with a sum of money to withdraw the law, and the Pope is pleased

---

[1] *Epist. Wisig.* 10 (676 f.), with F. Görres, 'Miscellen zur späteren spanisch-westgothischen Kirchen- und Culturgeschichte', *Zeitschrift f. wissenschaftliche Theologie*, xlii (1899), pp. 437–50, at pp. 437–9.

[2] II Hispal. 6 f., cf. 3.

[3] So J. N. Hillgarth, *Historia*, xv (1966), p. 486.

[4] Gregory I, *Ep.* ix. 227ᵃ.

name of the Catholic faith before he himself had been reordained, the church would have to be consecrated afresh by a Catholic bishop.[1] But at the other synods of the reign the bishops did not find it necessary to refer to the Arian converts at all. What chiefly interested them was the old problem of the celibacy of the clergy.

At Barcelona in 599 the ex-Arian Ugnus still signed for the see of Barcelona itself, and both Julian and Fruisclus for Tortosa.[2] At Toledo in 597 Masona, who still signed for Merida, and apparently Mutto of Jativa and Baddo of Illiberris were Visigoths.[3] Otherwise, Germanic names are absent from the lists of signatories at these synods. The conversion did not result immediately in any striking increase of Goths in the higher offices of the Church.

---

[1] Conc. Caesaraug. 1–3.   [2] Mansi, x. 484.   [3] Ibid. 478.

V · THE ROMAN POPULATION

KING Alaric II published his *Breviarium* of Roman law in 506 so as to provide his Roman judges with rulings on the questions that arose most often in the courts. The code, which is a selection of laws from the Theodosian Code and other sources, was drawn up at the King's personal command; and it was he who directed that 'interpretations', written in simple language, should be added to each law which might seem to call for explanation. The work was carried out in haste and shows several signs of a lack of final revision. Indeed, the very principle of selection from the Theodosian Code gives rise to difficulties. Thus, the Roman public post (*cursus publicus*) continued to function in some sense in the Visigothic kingdom. The Code of Theodosius contains no fewer than sixty-six laws relating to it, but of all this mass of legislation Alaric's editors selected only a single ruling.[1] This forbids emergency requisitions of horses (*paraveredi*) and ox-wagons (*parangariae*) by anyone who could not produce an official warrant (*evectio*). Those who broke this law were to be reported by certain officials of the locality to the provincial governor, who would fine the wrongdoer 72 solidi for each illegal requisition. The question of emergency requisitions of horses in Spain was one which worried Theodoric the Ostrogoth some twenty years later;[2] but why Alaric included this law while omitting the great bulk of the relevant legislation, and in what conditions the post now worked, we cannot tell. Yet in spite of its shortcomings the *Breviarium* enjoyed a vast reputation north of the Pyrenees in the early Middle Ages.

A Goth named Goiaric, who may have been killed by King

---

[1] *CTh* viii. 5. 59. The *cursus publicus* is still referred to by Chindasuinth: *LV* v. 4. 19 *init.*; and his bishops in 646 were forbidden to take out more than 50 *evectiones* on their annual visitation of their dioceses: VII Tolet. 4. I cite the *Breviarium* from Mommsen's edition of the Theodosian Code. Each reference, unless otherwise stated, is to the *interpretatio* and not to the original law. For the history in Roman times of the various institutions, etc. mentioned in this chapter see the magisterial work of A. H. M. Jones, *The Later Roman Empire* (Blackwell, Oxford, 1964), to which I am heavily indebted.

[2] Cassiodorus, *Var.* v. 39. 14.

Gesalic in the palace at Barcelona in 510,[1] arranged for the work to be done. The compilation and editing were carried out by Roman lawyers and were approved by bishops and members of the nobility—apparently Catholic bishops and Roman nobles—before the master-copy was signed by Alaric himself on 2 or 3 February 506 and deposited in his Treasury. Copies were then despatched to Roman officials, presumably the provincial governors who would have to administer the law, under the signature of a Roman called Anianus. The extant text is a copy of the exemplar addressed to a certain Timotheus, which had been signed by Anianus at Aire-sur-Adour (Aturis). The letter of instructions in this copy states that the purpose of the collection was to remove inadequacies and obscurities from Roman law, and directs that the laws in the *Breviarium* were to be the only laws administered in the courts: to employ any other would be a capital offence, or, at any rate, the guilty judge's property would be confiscated.[2]

This code continued to be the law under which the Roman inhabitants of the kingdom lived until King Reccesuinth annulled it in, or very soon after, 654. A single manuscript preserves the law of King Theudis (p. 13 f. above), which was added to the *Breviarium* in 546; and this is the only evidence for an expansion of the code during the whole period in which the kings used it. The code is practically our sole source for the public life of the Hispano-Romans.

1. *The Great Landowners*

The class of large Roman landowners had in some measure survived the storms of the fifth century and continued to exploit their estates and to enjoy their riches under the Visigothic kings. They were men of enormous wealth, and when Theudis married one of their womenfolk he found himself able to maintain at his own expense a private army of no fewer than 2,000 men (p. 10 above). Such landowners are known to have lived in Lusitania, Baetica, and Tarraconensis; but they could doubtless be found elsewhere, too. They referred to themselves as 'senators', and they

[1] Chron. Caesaraug., *s.a.* 510 (ii. 223), 'his coss. Gesalecus Goericum Barcinone in palatio interfecit'.
[2] The relevant documents are printed in Zeumer, pp. 465–7, and in Mommsen, *CTh* xxxi–xxxvii.

continued to use the old Roman titles of rank.[1] In non-legal literature there are several references to 'senators'; but the word probably meant no more than a very rich landowner of the type who had in earlier days been a member of the imperial senatorial class—and it is never used of a person bearing a Gothic name.[2]

But officially the kings can scarcely be said to have recognized the senatorial order as such. It is true that 'senators' are mentioned three times in Alaric's code. In two laws he forbids 'senators' to lend money at more than half the rate which other men could charge.[3] And in a third law he gives permission to 'senators' to marry women of humble birth provided that they were respectable and born of respectable parents.[4] In the last point, so far from recognizing senators as being distinct from the rest of the population, the King in fact tended to bring them into line with other men. Elsewhere, when he interprets Roman laws, he uses a vaguer term than 'senators' (p. 123 n. 5 below) or he discards the reference altogether.[5] That is to say, the former Roman senators were now distinguished in law from the other Romans of Spain solely by the amount of interest which they were permitted to charge on loans. Presumably they became liable to service on the city councils. The code nowhere exempts them, and the term *honorati*, which the Emperors had applied to members of the aristocracy, is now used more than once of city councillors.[6] On the other hand, there were posts in the royal service which were open to Romans, which exempted their holders from service on the city councils, and which city councillors were debarred from holding.[7] No doubt, these offices usually went to the ex-senatorial class, and it is unfortunate that no list of them survives.

[1] Stroheker, pp. 78 ff., collects the evidence.
[2] Braulio, *Vita S. Aemiliani*, 11 (PL 80. 707) 'Sicorii senatoris ancilla'; 15 (708) 'senatoribus Nepotiano et Proseria'; 17 (ibid.) 'domus Honorii senatoris'; cf. 22; *VPE* iv. 2. 1, 15, etc.
[3] *CTh* ii. 33. 3–4.　　　　[4] Marcian, *Nov.* 4.　　　　[5] *CTh* ix. 1. 1.
[6] Ibid. i. 20. 1 'honorati provinciarum, id est ex curiae corpore'; ix. 19. 1 'curiae dignitate privabitur, id est ut honoratus esse non possit'; Conc. Narbon. 6, 'honorati de civitate'; *VPE* iv. 2. 1 'cuiusdam primarii civitatis ex genere senatorum nobilissimi viri'; 2 'supradictus illustris vir'.
[7] Theodosius, *Nov.* 15. 1. Note *CTh* ii. 14. 1 'qui dignitate praeclari sunt'; iii. 6. 1 'quicumque in administratione constitutus'; ii. 1. 3 'in omnibus personis, quas etiam praesentiae nostrae dignitas comitatur'; ix. 40. 10; xi. 11. 1 'ex his qui provinciarum rectoribus coniunguntur aut militant vel qui agunt in diversis officiis principatus', etc.

The great Roman landowners and high officials still interfered,
as they had done in Roman times, with the administration of justice,[1] avoided paying their due share of the taxes,[2] and oppressed
those poorer and weaker than themselves by forcing them to
sell them their property or even to give it to them as a gift.[3] Like
the king, they managed their estates through procurators and
'agents' (actores)[4]—the provincial governors were especially
warned to prevent the oppression of 'inferior persons' by the
agents of the powerful[5]—or they leased land to lessees, who were
still known as conductores.[6] Agents and procurators, who might be
either slaves or freemen,[7] were also employed by the great Gothic
landowners and are mentioned even in the last days of the
kingdom.[8]

The condition of the coloni who worked on the royal or private
estates was not substantially changed by the arrival of the Visigoths in Spain. Even in the seventh century they were still tied to
the soil, and they paid one-tenth of their produce in rent together
with other unspecified perquisites.[9] But the taxes of the coloni were
now collected not by the landlord but by the State officials.[10]
Alaric also discarded the Roman regulation that permitted the
chaining of coloni who were thought to be meditating flight.[11] But
the colonus who owned any land or other property was still
forbidden to sell it without his lord's knowledge.[12] Anyone who
wittingly harboured another man's colonus was obliged not only
to return him to his owner but also to pay the tax due on him for

---

[1] CTh i. 29. 8; ii. 13. 1, 14. 1. Cf. i. 16. 13, 20. 1.   [2] Ibid. xiii. 10. 1.
[3] Ibid. iii. 1. 9; ii. 1. 3; cf. ix. 11. 1 (private prisons).
[4] Ibid. i. 16. 14, 22. 1; ii. 30. 2, 31. 1, 32. 1; iv. 8. 6, 12. 5, 22. 1, 4; ix. 29. 2;
III Tolet. 18, 21; but rationales in LV x. 2. 6, for which see p. 124 n. 4 below.
[5] CTh i. 16. 14.   [6] Ibid. ii. 30. 2, 31. 1.
[7] Majorian, Nov. 7, 'si ingenuus fuerit is ipse actor'; cf. CTh ii. 32. 1.
[8] LV vi. 1. 1 (antiqua), 5, p. 254 init. (Chindasuinth); 2. 4 (idem); viii. 1. 5
(idem); ix. 1. 9 (Erwig); xii. 3. 19 (idem); ix. 1. 21 (Egica).
[9] Formulae Visigothicae, 36 'decimas vero praestatione vel exenia, ut colonis est
consuetudo, annua inlatione me promitto persolvere'; 37 'et ideo spondeo me annis
singulis secundum consuetudinem de fruges aridas et liquidas atque universa
animalia vel pomaria seu in omni re, quod in eodem loco augmentaverimus, decimas
vobis annis singulis persolvere'. Cf. LV x. 1. 19 (Reccesuinth). The bishops assembled at Seville in 619 write, 'scribitur enim in lege mundiali de colonis agrorum
ut ubi esse iam quisque coepit, ibi perduret'. See, too, LV x. 1. 19 (Reccesuinth).
Chindasuinth, ibid. v. 4. 19, explicitly forbids plebeii to alienate their land, vineyards,
houses, or slaves: the purchaser will lose what he bought, without compensation.
[10] Alaric omitted CTh xi. 1. 14.   [11] Ibid. v. 17. 1.
[12] Ibid. v. 19. 1.

the period during which he had kept him; and the fugitive was reduced to slavery.[1] But if he managed to retain him for thirty years—twenty years in the case of a female—the *colonus* became legally his property. If the *colonus* was discovered before thirty years had elapsed, however, the landowner from whom he had fled could claim him and any children whom he had begotten, together with any property which he had acquired.[2] When a freeman wished to marry a *colona* tied to the soil, he had first to make a declaration in the municipal records to the effect that he would not desert her. He might then marry her and would remain a freeman, but he could not leave the estate to which she was tied.[3]

2. *The Cities*

The kings tried to keep the administration of the cities functioning very much as it had done in Roman times. Like the emperors before them, they went to the utmost lengths until Chindasuinth's reign (642–53) to tie the city councillors (*curiales*) to their councils (*curiae*) and to block every means of escape. They did so because of the vital part that the curials played not only in local administration but also in collecting the State taxes. The local landowners, who in the main were the members of the city councils, were still forbidden strictly to leave their posts.[4] There was no senatorial order now into which the richer of them could hope to escape; but, as we have seen, there were royal offices of one kind or another, and Alaric enacted that 'no one born a curial should aspire to any offices or try by supplicating [the king] to assume any office' without knowing that he would still be liable for his duties on the curia.[5] If a curial did in fact gain one of these offices he was obliged to supply a substitute for himself on his city council; and if the substitute turned out to be unsatisfactory the original councillor was recalled to his post.[6]

The city councillor was forbidden to sell his property secretly and so to avoid his obligations: if he did so, the sale was void, he was summoned back to his council, and the purchaser lost the price which he had paid.[7] Provincial governors were strictly

---

[1] *CTh* v. 17. 1.
[2] Ibid. v. 18. 1; cf., for other refinements, Valentinian, *Nov.* 31.
[3] Valentinian, loc. cit.   [4] *CTh* xii. 1. 170.
[5] Theodosius, *Nov.* 15. 1.   [6] Valentinian, *Nov.* 32 (p. 138. 94).
[7] *CTh* iii. 1. 8.

ordered to exempt no curial from his duties; and if a curial's means were so reduced as to make it impossible for him to carry on, his case was referred to the king for consideration.[1] He could only sell his property if his debts to the Treasury or other creditors were so crushing as to make it imperative to do so; and then his fellow curials, who could vouch for the necessity of the sale, had to subscribe the deed of sale.[2] He could not sell land without first obtaining a decree of his council allowing him to do so; and if he sold slaves he had to have the transaction witnessed by five leading men of his curia.[3] It was expressly ordered that no curial could become a lessee of royal or private estates, nor could he act as surety for a lessee of either fiscal or private land: any estate leased to a curial was confiscated by the Treasury.[4] Curials could not avoid their obligations by moving from the city in which they had been born; for if they did move, they became liable for curial service both in the city of their birth and also in that in which they had taken up residence.[5]

The kings also continued the Roman government's ban on curials' taking Holy Orders.[6] Those who had already become deacons had to supply a substitute to take their place on the city council; otherwise, they were themselves recalled for service. Lower clergy than deacons were recalled unconditionally. Bishops and priests were allowed to continue in their clerical office, but they were not permitted to dispose of their property freely. If the ex-curial bishop or priest had sons or male relatives, one half of his property was at once made over to them so that they could serve on the council of which he himself had formerly been a member. If he had only a daughter, he was obliged to make over to her one half of his property, provided that she was married to a city councillor; otherwise, the property went to the council itself.[7] Clergy were specifically exempted from serving as 'exactors' (p. 129 below).[8] As late as 633 the Fourth Council of Toledo found it necessary to repeat that no one liable to curial

---

[1] Ibid. xii. 1. 1.
[2] Valentinian, *Nov.* 32. [3] Majorian, *Nov.* 7 (p. 174. 153 ff.)
[4] Theodosius, *Nov.* 9; *CTh* x. 3. 2.
[5] Ibid. xii. 1. 12.
[6] Valentinian, *Nov.* 35 (p. 148. 131 f.)
[7] Ibid. 149. 138 ff.; Majorian, *Nov.* 7 (p. 173. 138 ff.) Note *CTh* v. 3. 1, 'nec curiae quicquam debuerint'.
[8] *CTh* xvi. 2. 2: the *allecti* mentioned there are unknown elsewhere.

duties should be consecrated as bishop.[1] Nor could a city council-lor enter a monastery so as to escape his duties.[2]

He could not take flight to the estates of the rich. If the agent of a great estate concealed a city councillor for more than a year without his lord's knowledge he was punishable: indeed, a slave agent was beaten with clubs. If the agent did so with his lord's connivance, the estate where the fugitive councillor was found was confiscated by the Treasury. The daughter of a councillor was forbidden outright to marry a slave or the agent or procura-tor of an estate: in this case the slave was tortured to death. If she refused to marry a councillor of her city or if she went to live in another city, she had to pay one quarter of her inheritance to the council which she abandoned.[3] If she bequeathed all her property to her husband she thereby made him liable for service on the council when she died.[4] But in fact she was urged under threat of severe pecuniary loss to marry a curial in her own town.[5] Again, a councillor who had only illegitimate sons could bequeath his property to them, provided that he first had them enrolled in his city council. If he had no legitimate sons and bequeathed his property to someone who was not a member of his council, one quarter of the property went to the council though the legatee could repurchase it at an agreed price.[6] All these regulations and many other refinements remained in force until the reigns of Kings Chindasuinth and Reccesuinth (642–72).[7]

Apart from its duties connected with the collection of the taxes, the council also administered the city and its surrounding terri-tory. It was concerned in the registration of gifts of land and other property,[8] the registration of adoptions[9] and of wills,[10] the appointment of guardians,[11] various matters relating to minors and their property, and so on.[12]

No curial could accept the municipal office of *defensor* (p. 125

---

[1] IV Tolet. 19, 'qui curiae nexibus obligati sunt'.

[2] Valentinian, *Nov.* 35 (p. 148. 130).   [3] Majorian, *Nov.* 7.

[4] *CTh* xii. 1. 124.   [5] Majorian, loc. cit.

[6] Theodosius, *Nov.* 22. 1 and 2.

[7] *LV* v. 4. 19. If he died intestate and left no close relatives the curia took his property: *CTh* v. 2. 1.

[8] *CTh* viii. 12. 1; cf. iii. 5. 1.   [9] Ibid. v. 1. 2.

[10] Ibid. iv. 4. 4; cf. *Formulae Visigothicae*, 21, 25; Paul, *Sentent.* iv. 4. 2.

[11] *CTh* iii. 17. 2–4.

[12] Ibid. ii. 17. 1; iii. 1. 3; 5. 13; 17. 1; 30. 6; cf. ii. 4. 1; v. 7. 2; ix. 42. 10; Paul, *Sentent.* ii. 25. 4.

below) or that of the highest local official, the *curator*, until he had
served in order in the regular municipal magistracies, the quaes-
torship, the aedileship, and the duumvirate. For breach of this
law he was dismissed from his office and was sent to the king for
punishment.[1] The richest group of curials, the *principales*,[2]
retained their organization in Visigothic times, though the nature
of that organization is unknown.[3]

By no means all city councillors were poverty-stricken, and
they often owned property in more than one province.[4] They
were not exempt from corporal punishment, but Alaric retained
severe penalties for provincial governors who went too far in
punishing them.[5] They could only be subjected to torture after
their case had been referred to the king;[6] and in one case where
they were liable to torture—when guilty of falsifying wills or
public documents—the law stated that they must first be deprived
of their office.[7]

Workmen in the cities continued as in Roman times to be
organized in guilds; and any guildsman (*collegiatus*) who fled from
his city was forced to return to it. A child born to a guildsman and
a slave woman or a *colona* had the status of its mother, while the
son of a guildsman and a free woman had to become a member of
his father's guild.[8] No guildsman was permitted to enter the ranks
of the clergy or to become a law officer of a church. If he managed
to do so, he was subject to the same regulations as the city
councillors.

3. *The Administration of Justice*

In order to administer the Roman law to the Roman inhabitants
of the kingdom and to collect the taxes from them, Alaric and his
successors retained much of the Roman administrative machine.
The kings had not inherited, of course, the great offices of
the Imperial central government; but they did take over the

---

[1] *CTh* xii. 1. 20. By discarding ibid. xii. 1. 21, 5. 2, Alaric deprived the *duumviri*
of their exemption from *inferiora munera*. The *curator* is mentioned in *Formulae
Visigothicae*, 25.
[2] *CTh* viii. 5. 59. The *principales* are mentioned in *Formulae*, loc. cit.
[3] For the *principales* see Jones, index, s.v.
[4] Theodosius, *Nov.* 22. 1, 'quod si, ut adsolet, in duabus provinciis ei possessio
vel habitatio fuerit', etc.
[5] *CTh*. xii. 1. 47.   [6] Majorian, *Nov.* 7 (p. 174. 156 ff.).
[7] *CTh* ix. 19. 1.   [8] Ibid. xiv. 7. 1.

provincial organization of the five provinces; and in 585 they also acquired the province of Galicia from the Sueves.

The Roman governor (*iudex* or *rector provinciae*) was paid by the king.[1] With his pay he was obliged to establish his headquarters (*praetorium*), and it was illegal for him to raise special levies from the provincials for this purpose.[2] Little is known about the officials who made up his staff (*officium*) in Visigothic times. Like his predecessor in the Roman period he was forbidden to appoint his personal assistant (*domesticus*) or the official who controlled access to him (*cancellarius*) from any place other than the province which he governed. But whereas in Roman times the *cancellarius*, at any rate, was chosen by the *officium*, the kings introduced a new principle: these officials were now publicly elected.[3] A little light is thrown on the matter by the fact that the governor's accountants (*numerarii*) were also elected; for in their case the electorate is known to have been formed by the Catholic bishops and the people (presumably the inhabitants of the provincial capital),[4] so these were no doubt the electors in the other cases, too. Other officials of the governor's staff are occasionally mentioned, but their duties are not known to have changed since Roman times.[5] It was enacted that if they were found guilty of accepting bribes to admit litigants and others to the governor or to exclude them, they were either to be put to death or, at any rate, referred to the king.[6] If they obliged a rustic to work for them as if he were their own slave, or if they made personal use of his ox or his slave, or if they accepted 'perquisites' (*exenia* = *xenia*) or gifts of any kind, or if they failed to refuse them when offered, they were put to death

---

[1] In *annonae* and *cellaria*: *CTh* i. 22. 4, with Jones, i. 396 f.; but *LV* xii. 1. 2 (Reccared), 'quod, dum iudices ordinamus, nostra largitate eis conpendia ministramus', refers to the payment not of Roman but of Gothic officials. For a seventh-century reference to the *iudices provinciarum* see IV Tolet. 65.

[2] *CTh* loc. cit.

[3] Ibid. i. 34. 3. The governor's *officium* is also mentioned ibid. viii. 5. 59; xii. 6. 22; Valentinian, *Nov.* 35.

[4] *LV* xii. 1. 2; cf. *CTh* viii. 15. 2.

[5] The *executores*, who summoned the defendants to the governor's court and enforced the court's decisions, appear in Valentinian, *Nov.* 35, the law of Theudis (p. 13 above), and are added to the Roman original of *CTh* x. 17. 3. For the *consiliarius* see ibid. i. 34. 2, ii. 1. 6, but he appears to be identified with the *cancellarius* in i. 34. 3. Note in general xi. 11. 1, 'qui provinciarum rectoribus coniunguntur'. Alaric discarded the laws which obliged sons to follow their fathers in the provincial offices.

[6] *CTh* i. 16. 7.

and their property was confiscated.[1] While in office they were
allowed to buy and sell goods including land, but they lost the
article purchased without compensation if they used the influence
of their office to enforce the sale.[2] The governors' accountants
found ways and means of compelling the provincials to sell their
property to them: when such cases came to light the property was
restored to its rightful owner and the accountant lost the price
which he had paid.[3] If the governor himself were found guilty of
theft or of crime in general, he was dismissed and disgraced; and
his peculations, if any, had to be made good by his heirs.[4]

One of the main functions of the provincial governor was to
act as judge; but now, as in Roman times, those who had formerly belonged to the senatorial class were not tried by the
governor in serious criminal cases but were sent to the king for
judgement,[5] even in cases where they confessed to a serious
crime;[6] and five noblemen were chosen by lot to try them.[7]

When criminal cases arose between soldiers (that is, for the
most part, Goths) and private citizens, the governor heard those
where the Roman was the defendant, and the military (Gothic)
judge, those where he was the plaintiff.[8] Thus, any prejudice
which the judge might feel would benefit the defendant. But civil
cases were heard by the provincial governor.[9] Attempts to by-
pass the governor and to have cases heard by the military judge
which ought to have been heard by the governor were punished
by the exile of the guilty party and the payment by his lawyer of a
fine of no less than 720 solidi.[10] In Roman civilian suits soldiers
were warned not to try to bring influence to bear.[11] It is clear that,
at any rate in criminal jurisdiction, the kings were determined to
keep the two legal systems, the Roman and the Gothic, as distinct
and separate as possible.

[1] Ibid. xi. 11. 1.   [2] Valentinian, *Nov.* 32.   [3] *CTh* viii. 15. 2.
[4] Ibid. ix. 27. 1, 4.
[5] Ibid. ix. 40. 10, where 'in senatorii ordinis viros' of the original law becomes in
Alaric's interpretation 'aliquae maiores personae aut alicuius dignitatis viri'. Cf. ii.
14. 1.
[6] *CTh* xi. 36. 1 'maioribus personis'.   [7] Ibid. ii. 1. 12.
[8] Ibid. ii. 1. 2; cf. Marcian, *Nov.* 1 'ipsi [= militantes] apud conpetentes iudices,
quas conpetere sibi credunt'.
[9] *CTh* ii. 1. 2.
[10] Ibid. ii. 1. 9 'ad illos qui armatis praeesse noscuntur'. It was in general an
offence to sue for interested motives in the wrong court: ibid. ii. 1. 6; Marcian,
Nov. 1. See also *CTh* ii. 7. 1.
[11] *CTh* ii. 12. 6; cf. i. 21. 1.

In Euric's day the social power of the Goths was such that a Roman might find it worth his while to hand over to a Goth an article of which the ownership was in dispute: the claimant who had taken legal action to recover possession of the article would find it out of his reach if it could be shown to be in Gothic hands. This practice was forbidden in Euric's code: the claimant was given possession of the article, whether his claim to it had been weak or strong, and the Roman who made it over to the Goth so as to avoid a trial had to compensate the Goth adequately.[1] This law refers specifically to Romans, but the corresponding law in Leovigild's code applies to Goths: it forbids Goths to make over disputed articles to third parties, irrespective of their nationality. The inference has been drawn from Leovigild's alleged modification of Euric's ruling that the social power of the Goths generally had declined relatively to that of the Roman population of the kingdom. But this does not follow. Euric's law specifically applied to Romans, while Leovigild's law, like all the laws in his code, applied to Goths: he simply wished to prevent the abuse whether it was practised by Romans or by Goths.[2] The law provides no evidence whatever for the view that Leovigild aimed at depressing the legal status of the Goths to that of the Romans (p. 59 above).

There is no trace now of the Treasury courts that had existed in Roman times. If a provincial were wronged by an agent or procurator of a royal estate he was entitled to take his case direct to the king; and the official, if found guilty, was liable to be burned to death.[3] Evidently the king was very much closer to his wronged subjects than the Emperors had been; for no Spaniard wronged in Roman times by an agent of the *res privata* would have dreamed of taking his case in the first instance to the far-distant Emperor. The *coloni* and slaves of the royal estates, however, were subject to the governor's jurisdiction like private persons; and no official of the 'Patrimony' had authority to interfere.[4] Nor was the governor obliged to await the presence of an agent before proceeding to the trial.[4] Agents were explicitly

---

[1] Cod. Euric. 312.   [2] *LV* v. 4. 20.   [3] *CTh* x. 4. 1.

[4] Ibid. ii. 1. 1, where note that the *actores* of the original is replaced by *servos vel colonos*. The term which I have rendered 'official' in this law is *ordinator*, which recurs in ii. 1. 5, x. 1. 2; cf. iv. 8. 6. Whether it is in fact a vague term or whether it indicates a specific office like the Roman *rationalis* (*LV* x. 2. 6) is not clear.

[5] *CTh* ii. 1. 11.

warned not to try to defend their underlings from the governor's jurisdiction; and, on the other hand, governors were instructed not to be vexatious to the agents at the instigation of the leading city councillors of the locality, the *principales* (p. 121 above), as it seems they had frequently been.[1]

Appeals from the governor's judgement were allowed in both civil and criminal cases[2] except, as in Roman times, where the defendant confessed to a serious crime (homicide, adultery, magical practices, or poisoning) or where he was manifestly guilty, or in cases of manifest debt to the Treasury;[3] but we are not told who heard the appeals in the sixth century. Some cases were certainly remitted to the king; but their nature is not defined.[4] When a litigant in a civil appeal lost his case twice he was forbidden to press it further;[5] but where there was no appeal he was allowed to 'supplicate' the king to reopen his case, provided that he did so within two years of the judge's returning to private life.[6]

The governor could not possibly have heard all the cases, civil and criminal, which arose in his province; and hence minor cases were taken before the *defensor*, a municipal magistrate (p. 120 above).[7] In Roman times the *defensor* had been appointed by a resolution of the city council, but under the kings he (like the *cancellarius* and the *numerarius*, two officials on the governor's staff) was elected by the citizens of his city. The result of the election was confirmed by a decree of the city council, apparently without reference to any higher authority. If a man usurped the office without awaiting confirmation by the council he became liable to a fine of 360 solidi.[8] The original function of the office, when it was instituted in the fourth century, had been to defend the council and the people of the city in question against higher authorities; but it quickly became itself oppressive, and in 392 the Emperor Theodosius I had found it necessary to remind the

---

[1] Ibid. ii. 1. 1; x. 4. 2.

[2] Ibid. xi. 30. 2, 15, 20; 31. 6; 35. 1; 37. 1; Marcian, *Nov.* 1. In *CTh* ii. 1. 6 a man may appeal 'apud maioris dignitatis iudices', but these are not specified. In xi. 30. 2 the appeal runs 'ad alium iudicem'. Cf. Valentinian, *Nov.* 35 (p. 151. 194).

[3] *CTh* xi. 36. 1, 8, 21. A man convicted of rape or of a crime of violence could not appeal: ibid. ix. 10. 1; 24. 1. See also Valentinian, *Nov.* 35 (p. 151. 192 ff.). Poisoners were excommunicated by Conc. Ilerd. 2 in 524.

[4] *CTh* ii. 18. 1; cf. i. 22. 2.   [5] Ibid. xi. 38. 1.

[6] Theodosius, *Nov.* 13; cf. Valentinian, *Nov.* 19.

[7] *CTh* ii. 1. 8; cf. 4. 2.   [8] Ibid. i. 29. 6.

defensores that 'in accordance with their name they should defend
the council and people entrusted to them with all justice and
equity', and Alaric thought it wise to repeat this advice.[1] They
are still mentioned in a law of King Reccesuinth published about
654,[2] and they may have continued to function until the end of
the kingdom.

Reccared learned that the *defensor*, like the *numerarius*, when
elected by the bishop and people, laid down his office at the end
of a year, and this he regarded as a hardship for the people. He
enacted, therefore, that the *defensores* must continue in office for
their full term, though unfortunately he does not say how long
this was. He also declared that they must pay nothing to the
governor; and the governor who accepted or exacted a bribe
from them was to be deprived of his office and fined 720 solidi.[3]

4. *Taxation*

The second great function of the Roman provincial governor
under the Visigothic kings was the raising of the taxes. Of the
three Treasuries that had existed in Roman times, that of the
Sacred Largesse, which had been largely concerned with payments
to the army, seems to have disappeared in sixth-century Spain.
But two of the taxes which had formerly been levied by this
Treasury continued to be raised in Visigothic times. One of these
was the customs dues, which were levied in the ports, and, no
doubt, on the frontiers of France, Galicia, and the Byzantine
province, as well as on the provincial boundaries. They were
farmed out for a period of three years; and it continued to be a
capital offence for the tax-farmers to raise more than the statutory
percentage.[4] When disputes broke out between overseas traders in
the ports, they were adjudged not by royal officials but by the
traders' own *telonarii*, whose name may perhaps suggest that they
had the duty of collecting the tax and of forwarding it to the
tax-farmers.[5] Secondly, the tax levied every four years on traders

---

[1] *CTh* i. 29. 7; cf. Isidore, *Etym.* ix. 4. 18 'unde et defensores dicti, eo quod
plebem sibi commissam contra insolentiam inproborum defendant. at contra nunc
quidam eversores, non defensores existunt.' The *defensor* had an *officium* to assist him,
but no details are known about it in the sixth century: *CTh* iii. 30. 6, where the
defensor witnesses inventories of goods administered by the guardians of minors.
[2] *LV* ii. 1. 27.   [3] *LV* xii. 1. 2.
[4] *CTh* iv. 13. 1; Cassiodorus, *Var.* v. 39. 7 'transmarinorum canon'.
[5] *LV* xi. 3. 2.

was also levied in the sixth century; and neither the clergy (to whom trade was ineffectually forbidden) nor soldiers were now exempt if they engaged in trade.[1] On the other hand, there is no reason to think that the kings levied the old *aurum coronarium*, which the Emperors had exacted from the cities on their accession and on various festal occasions thereafter, or the *aurum tironicum*, a money payment in place of supplying recruits to the army.

Of the other two Roman Treasuries and their administration—that of the Praetorian Prefect and that of the *res privata*—much survived under the Visigoths. Unfortunately, since the Visigothic law codes were intended for day-to-day use in the courts, they have little occasion to mention the higher officials of the civil service, and they rarely discuss the king's immediate entourage. Hence, the only high financial officer of the central government of whom we have knowledge is the Count of the Patrimony (*comes patrimonii*), the direct successor of the Imperial *comes rei privatae*. Since it was now his duty to appoint the *numerarii* (p. 99 above), officials who had formerly been on the staff of the Praetorian Prefect, it looks as though he had taken over the running of what remained of the Prefect's staff as well as that of the *res privata*. It may be, in fact, that the financial organization of the kingdom had been unified at the top. At all events, it is no surprise to find that the only sixth-century *comes patrimonii* whom we know by name was a Roman: he held office in 592 and was called Scipio.[2]

The old Crown lands of the *res privata* now passed to the kings and are referred to as the *res* (or *domus*) *dominica*.[3] They still continued to increase as a result of legacies[4] and confiscations, though the governor was not permitted to confiscate a man's goods in the name of the Treasury without reference to the king.[5] The revenues of the *res dominica* were devoted to the maintenance of the king's household. The king would grant some of these lands to individuals, Goths or Romans, who in his opinion had deserved them,[6] or to men who petitioned him for them;[7]

---

[1] *CTh* xiii. 1. 13 'solutio auraria'.

[2] *De Fisco Barcinonensi* in Mansi, x. 473.

[3] *CTh* x. 4. 2, *et al.* But in iv. 12. 3 Alaric appears to draw a distinction between the 'Patrimony' and the king's personal property. This distinction became important in the seventh century (p. 202 below).

[4] *CTh* iv. 4. 2.   [5] Ibid. ix. 41. 1.

[6] Ibid. x. 1. 2; 8. 3; cf. 10. 15; 14. 1; *LV* iv. 5. 5; Marcian, *Nov.* 3.

[7] *CTh* iv. 15. 1; cf. v. 7. 1.

and sometimes individuals usurped them without permission.[1] King Leovigild somewhat arbitrarily, it seems, took a Treasury estate from one of his nobles and gave it to the Catholic abbot, Nanctus.[2] Officials of the *res dominica* were liable to punishment if they questioned the title of the grantees.[3]

There is no reason to think that any substantial change was made in the internal administration of the individual estates which made up the *res dominica*. But there is no indication now that the provincial governor and his staff had to help in collecting the rents of the Crown estates, as they had had to do in Late Roman times.[4] In general, the estates were leased out to *conductores* (p. 117 above), who might be either Romans or Goths; but one novelty was that during the regency of Theodoric the Ostrogoth (511–26), and perhaps later, the *conductores* of the royal estates became salaried officials.[5] Any fiscal lands or buildings granted to individuals by the king were held in perpetuity, provided that the rent and fiscal dues were paid.[6] Extensive groups of leased Crown estates, perhaps all those lying within the one province, were administered by procurators; and below the procurators, agents managed smaller groups either by supervising the *conductores* or by working the estates themselves.[7] We have seen how savagely the misdeeds of these men were punished by the kings (p. 124 above); while the punishment for harbouring a runaway slave of the *res dominica* was a fine of no less than 72 solidi.[8]

The basic tax was levied on arable land and vineyards (which were probably assessed separately, since the documents distinguish between them)[9] together with houses, and the only personal tax which is recorded was levied on slaves, female as well as

---

[1] *CTh* iv. 22. 3.

[2] *VPE* iii. 9 'locum fisci'. An unnamed king in the *Vita S. Fructuosi*, 3, arbitrarily takes land from a monastery and gives it to a nobleman, who had petitioned him for it: the king granted it to him 'pro exercenda publica expeditione'.

[3] *CTh* x. 1. 2; cf. 8. 3, 10. 15, 14. 1.

[4] Note, e.g., how Majorian, *Nov.* 7. 16, is in the part of the law which Alaric omitted expressly 'quia haec, quae continet, usu carent'.

[5] Cassiodorus, *Var.* v. 39. 6.

[6] Marcian, *Nov.* 3. Note that practically all the laws relating to emphyteutic land, including its tax concessions, were withdrawn by Alaric, though see *CTh* iii. 30. 5; cf. iv. 12. 3.

[7] *LV* xii. 1. 2 (Reccared), 'actores fisci'.

[8] *CTh* v. 17. 2.

[9] *LV* v. 4. 19 (Chindasuinth); Erwig's Edict (Zeumer, 479. 41). The assessments seem to have been revised occasionally: *CTh* xiii. 10. 5.

male.[1] The principles on which the tax had been raised by the Praetorian Prefects in Roman times continued in existence with little change. Land could still not escape tax by being sold, or given away as a gift, or inherited: in any event the new owner was liable for all its dues. No private arrangement might be made relating to the payment of tax; and secret conveyancing designed to cheat the Treasury was severely punished.[2] Those who persistently refused to pay the land tax found that their land was sold up by the *exactor* (see below); and ,according to an explicit law, even the king's permission not to pay tax was invalid,[3] for it was a principle of Alaric's law, taken over from Roman law, that any concession granted by the Crown which ran counter to the law was not valid—the point is made time after time in his code.[4]

The work of actually collecting the tax still depended mainly on the city councillors in each locality. The process was supervised locally by a municipal official called the *exactor*, who was elected annually by the city council from among their own number, though in some cities it was the custom (or the small number of available councillors made it necessary) for the *exactor* to hold office for two years. But the governor had to ensure that no one held the office, which offered many opportunities for extortion, for longer than two years.[5] The office had to be taken up publicly in the presence not only of the other city councillors but also of the people. The result of the election had to be entered in the municipal minutes and notified to the governor; and those who were minuted as having elected the *exactor* were bound to make up his peculations.[6] The greatest source of extortion by the *exactores* was their demand for receipts for what had already been paid; if these were not forthcoming they would extort the taxes again, even when they were registered as having been paid, and would pocket the second payment.[7] Again, when ordered to sell

---

[1] *LV* x. 2. 4 f.; Erwig's Edict; III Tolet. 8.

[2] *CTh* iii. 1. 2; xi. 1. 17; 3. 3.   [3] Ibid. i. 2. 9.

[4] Ibid. i. 2. 2; cf. i. 1. 4; 2. 5 and 8; ii. 4. 4–5; 6. 1; 7. 1; iii. 10. 1; iv. 22. 5; ix. 1. 15; xii. 1. 12; Valentinian, *Nov.* 19.

[5] *CTh* xii. 6. 22.

[6] Ibid. xii. 6. 20, where in the original law it is those who had *nominated* him who were responsible for his conduct.

[7] Ibid. xi. 26. 2, where in Honorius' law it is the *discussores* and their henchmen who are guilty of this crime. Observe that the *discussores* are not mentioned explicitly in xi. 36. 21 either.

up the property of a debtor to the Treasury they would sometimes sell it precipitately for a knockdown price, perhaps in
collusion with the purchaser, so that the debtor lost all and the
Treasury gained little.[1] The kings, in their own interests, forbade
tax-collectors and others to remove the agricultural slaves and
plough-oxen of the farmers 'from the labour of which the
tribute is paid', though this does not seem to have been a capital
offence now as it had been in Roman times.[2] Each and every
complaint made by the provincials against the *exactores* was to be
inquired into carefully; and, if the *exactor* were found guilty of
excessive exaction, the penalty was death and fourfold restitution
from his property of what he had extorted. Governors who did
not hold an inquiry into complaints against *exactores* or city
councillors were liable to a fine of 2,160 solidi, one of the highest
pecuniary fines in Alaric's code.[3] In fact, it was one of the duties of
the governor to travel to every part of his province, inquiring
personally into the complaints that landowners made in connection with the payment of taxes.[4]

Below the *exactor* was another municipal official, the *tabularius*,
who had to be a freeman. (The fact that it was found necessary to
ban *coloni* and slaves from holding the office illustrates its low
status.) He sent out the tax demands to the individual tax payers,[5]
and he did so on the basis of the tax registers (*polyptychi*), on which
a man had to have his name entered as soon as he bought, or
otherwise acquired, land or other property subject to tax.[6] When
King Sisebut in 612 freed certain slaves he conferred on them the
privileges of Roman citizenship; and accordingly they were
directed to have their names entered in the tax registers so that
they might be assessed for tax according to their property
(*peculium*).[7] As in Roman times, the *tabularii* sometimes managed

---

[1] *CTh* x. 17. 3. Note the pejorative use of *exactores* in III Tolet. 20.

[2] *CTh* ii. 30. 1; cf. xi. 11. 1. I do not know which official is indicated in the term
cura pacis in the former law.

[3] Ibid. xi. 7. 20; cf. xi. 6. 1; 16. 11 on superindictions, which the king alone
could declare.

[4] Ibid. i. 16. 11; but the Roman original of this law is directed expressly at the
activities of the *compulsores*, who were members of the governor's staff.

[5] *CTh* viii. 2. 5, on which see Jones, iii. 178 n. 89.

[6] *CTh* xi. 3. 5, 'publicis libris'; cf. 26. 2; Cassiodorus, *Var.* v. 39. 2, 'polyptychis
publicis'.

[7] *LV* xii. 2. 13, 'in polipticis publicis'. Freed slaves always became Roman
citizens: *Formulae Visigothicae*, 2–6.

to pass some of the tax burden of the rich landowners on to the poor.[1] Finally, the *susceptores*, who like the *exactores* were elected publicly by the city council, actually went round and collected the tax.[2]

The central authority continued to send officials of their staffs to collect arrears (*compulsores*)[3] and *discussores* to keep the entire machinery of collection up to scratch.[4] These last two types of official tended to be very extortionate.

The kings, like the emperors before them, sometimes remitted outstanding taxes. The practice was that what had already been paid to the exactors when the remission was announced was not returned to the tax payer: it was paid into the *thesauri* by the *retentatores*. But no demand was made for that which was still outstanding from the period covered by the remission.[5] The system was well known to favour the richer taxpayers (p. 233 below).

We can, then, outline the system for administering justice and for collecting the taxes up to the level of the provincial governor. In broad outline it continued to be what it had been in Roman times, though a handful of officials were now elected by the people of the cities, instead of being directly appointed. But the administrative officers higher than the governor are almost unknown to us, owing to the nature of the law codes from which our information comes. The result is that we do not know who it was that instructed the local authorities as to the rate of tax for the year. Still less do we know the rate itself in any one year. But it is unlikely that the peasant in the field or the craftsman in his shop noticed much difference in their relationship with the State when the government of the emperors was taken over by the barbarian kings. Nor did their circumstances change very much after the middle of the seventh century, when, as a result of the reforms of Chindasuinth and Reccesuinth, the Roman administration was swept away and the Goths governed the country alone.

[1] *CTh* xiii. 10. 1: who are 'hi quibus exactionis libri traduntur'?
[2] *CTh* xii. 6. 20.
[3] Cassiodorus, *Var.* v. 39. 2; Marcian, *Nov.* 2. 2. Note the omission of the *compulsor* from *CTh* i. 16. 11 interpr.
[4] Valentinian, *Nov.* 1. 3 § 2.
[5] Marcian, *Nov.* 2.

VI·THE GOTHIC POPULATION

OUR knowledge of Visigothic life in the sixth century is derived almost entirely from archaeology and from what remains of Leovigild's law code (p. 58 above). It is true that the surviving laws are undated, and we do not know which of them were enacted by Leovigild himself and which by his predecessors. Nor can we know the significance of those that Reccesuinth omitted. But the code can be used to describe conditions in the Spanish kingdom during the sixth century. It is a source of the highest value.

1. *The Land*

When the Visigoths settled in the Spanish peninsula in the late fifth and early sixth century, they did not disperse evenly over the entire country. A map of their sixth-century cemeteries shows that most of them lived between the upper reaches of the rivers Ebro and Tagus, in the triangle between the cities of Palencia, Toledo, and Calatayud. They often settled, of course, outside these limits, and the Gothic cemetery of Herrera de Pisuerga, which has been excavated, lies some seventy kilometres north of Palencia. But in general they were concentrated in the modern province of Segovia and in the surrounding provinces of Madrid, Toledo, Palencia, Burgos, Soria, and Guadalajara.[1] They settled both in the countryside and in the cities, but in what proportions we do not know.

When the Patrician Constantius planted them in 418 in the province of Aquitanica Secunda (p. 2 above) he settled them on the land on the system known as *hospitalitas*. That is to say, the Visigoths received two-thirds of each Gallic estate on which they were settled, and the Roman owner had to be content with one-third. What percentage of the labour and of the houses on each estate the Visigoths were given is not recorded. Only the

---

[1] W. Reinhart, 'Sobre el asentamiento de los Visigodos en la Peninsula', *Archivo español de Arqueología*, xviii (1945), pp. 124–39; J. Werner, *Germania*, xxviii (1944–50), pp. 279–81; cf. Zeiss, pp. 17 f., 93 ff. But see p. 290 below.

larger estates, those of the great senatorial landowners, were affected by the settlement: small farms were not partitioned. Nor is
there any reason to think that *every* Visigoth received two-thirds
of an estate: there would not have been enough large estates to go
round. Only the leading men of the Visigoths became landowners,
and it was no part of their plan to set up each of their followers as
an independent gentleman. But Visigothic nobles sometimes gave
land to their 'retainers' (*buccellarii, saiones*).[1]

This system of settlement was welcomed, for whatever reason,
by the large Roman landowners of south-western Gaul as well as
by the Goths themselves. At any rate, there is no evidence that
either side resisted it, or that any attempt was ever made to upset
the arrangements imposed by Constantius in 418. And when the
Visigoths transferred themselves to Spain they took this system of
land settlement with them: in Spain, too, they appropriated
two-thirds of each of those estates on which they planted themselves. Leovigild's code still contains regulations about 'the
two-thirds belonging to the Goth' and the 'third' of the Roman;
and his laws on the matter were taken over by Kings Reccesuinth
and Erwig. Indeed, in 682 Erwig introduced a new regulation
concerning the system. It is clear that *hospitalitas* continued to
exist throughout the entire Visigothic period of Spanish history.[2]
And as well as the land itself the barbarians took over the Roman
system of management. The larger landowners did not work
their new estates with their own hands: they adopted the Roman
practice of managing them through 'agents' (*actores*) and procurators. But that does not mean that they took no personal
interest in the detailed running of their estates. We catch a
glimpse of a military *dux*, the father of St. Fructuosus of Braga, as
he went with his young son into the mountain valleys near
Bierzo (Bergidum) in north-western Carthaginiensis in order to
receive an account of his flocks. He personally listed his sheep and
examined the reports of his shepherds.[3]

Was land owned by Goths subject to taxation under the Gothic
kings? Only one law in the code throws light on the question.[4]
This law instructs the judges of each city to restore immediately to

---

1 *Journal of Roman Studies*, xlvi (1956), p. 68. For the *buccellarii* and *saiones* see
p. 264 below.   2 *LV* x. 1. 8; cf. 6 *fin.*
3 See p. 117 n. 8 above. Cf. *Vita S. Fructuosi*, 2.
4 *LV* x. 1. 16 (antiqua). The *tertiae* of the Romans are also mentioned in Cod.
Euric. 277; *LV* x. 1. 8; 2. 1.

its rightful owner any 'third' belonging to a Roman which a Goth had seized: the purpose of the enactment, according to the legislator, was to prevent the Treasury from suffering loss. The clear inference is that the Roman paid tax on his 'third', but that the 'third' became exempt from tax if it fell into the hands of a Goth. Hence, it can hardly be doubted that the Gothic two-thirds were also exempt from taxation. But it does not follow from this that *all* land, whether part of a partitioned estate or not, became exempt from tax when a Goth secured the ownership of it. The legislator specifically refers only to the 'thirds': he is not speaking of land in general. In other words, the Treasury charged the Goths tax on all land which they might happen to own other than that of the partitioned estates. True, this involved subjecting the Gothic landowners to the attentions of the Roman municipal tax-officials. But, before Reccesuinth abolished Roman law soon after the middle of the seventh century, there was certainly no separate Gothic machinery for collecting taxes independently of the Roman *exactor* and his colleagues.

It was strictly forbidden, then, to upset the division of a Roman estate when once the division had been carried through: the Roman could never lawfully recover the two-thirds of his land that had been made over to his Gothic 'partner' (*consors*), and the Goth could never lawfully encroach upon the one-third that remained in the hands of the Roman, unless the king were to make him a special grant of it.[1] (That each side tried often enough to oust the other is shown by the legislation which forbids them to do so.) Whether a Goth could sell his two-thirds to another Goth and whether he could divide or alienate his holding in his will, we do not know, though Goths certainly bought and sold land.[2]

No information has reached us about any arrangements which may have been made at the time of the original settlements in Spain for the support of the rank-and-file Gothic warriors.

2. *The Law*

A law which probably existed in Euric's code, and which is certainly found in that of Leovigild, asserts that no judge may

---

[1] *LV* x. 1. 8.
[2] Ibid. v. 4. 7. For the position in Erwig's time see ibid. x. 1. 6 *fin.*

hear a case for which the code has made no provision. The judge must refer the parties in such a case to the king for decision, and the king will then be able to legislate for similar cases which may arise in the future.[1] The intention of the kings was to remove the old customs of the people that had existed when they still lived in a tribal society and when a man still looked to his kindred for protection against his enemies. However familiar a dispute may have been to the traditional usages of old, it could no longer be decided in the old way. The State insisted on stepping in and replacing custom by its own legislation.[2] But its task was not an easy one, and the law in question was not regarded as obsolete, even towards the end of the seventh century. Indeed, King Reccesuinth was obliged to introduce a new law dealing specifically with cases where a litigant who had brought an action for theft disregarded the judge's decision and instead accepted composition money from the thief.[3]

Alaric had taken over from Roman criminal law the distinction between penalties inflicted on the rich and those inflicted on the poor, the decision as to whether a man was rich or poor being left, no doubt, to the discretion of the judge. Thus, for one offence a privileged man (*digna idoneaque persona*) was liable to be exiled for two years, and have half his goods confiscated by the Treasury while a poor man (*indigna et pauperior persona*), who owned little or nothing that the Treasury could take, was sent to hard labour in the mines or quarries for two years.[4] A poor freeman (*ingenua et vilior persona*) who harboured a brigand in his home was liable to be beaten, while a rich man (*melior*) was punished at the judge's discretion, and the agent or procurator of an estate was burned alive.[5] And governors were directed to give more weight to the evidence of a rich man than to that of a poor man.[6]

[1] Ibid. ii. 1. 13, with K. Zeumer. *NA* xxiv (1899), pp. 70–2.

[2] Ibid. xxiii (1898), p. 485.

[3] *LV* vii. 4. 1.

[4] *CTh* i. 5. 3. The punishment of hard labour in the mines is mentioned ibid. ii. 14. 1; ix. 10. 4; but is discarded in v. 7. 2; Paul, *Sentent*. v. 17. 2. We do not know what mines or quarries were exploited in Visigothic Spain, but see *LV* x. 19. 4; Isidore, *Etym*. v. 27. 31, 'metallum est ubi exules deportantur ad eruendam venam marmoraque secanda in crustis'; xiv. 4. 28; '[Hispania] gemmarum metallorumque copiis ditissima'.

[5] *CTh* ix. 29. 2; cf. 10. 4; 36. 2; Valentinian, *Nov*. 23; Paul, *Sentent*. v. 18. 1; 20. 6; 21. 2, *et saepe*.

[6] *CTh* xi. 39. 3; cf. 13, 'dummodo idoneos'. Cf. *Formulae Visigothicae*, 40 (p. 594 *init.*), 'per idoneum testem'.

This distinction between the treatment of rich and poor appears only occasionally in Alaric's code; but at an early date it found its way into Visigothic criminal law, where it became almost a general rule. The legislators divide the free Gothic population into two classes and define different penalties for the one crime according to the social class of the offending party. They also distinguish sharply between the penalty to be inflicted on a freeman, whatever his class, and that to be inflicted on a slave. Beginning as early as Euric's time the code frequently mentions two classes of freemen, the *maioris* (or *honestioris*) *loci personae* and the *inferiores personae*. Thus, if a *maioris loci persona* damaged a fence, he was obliged by the law to repair it, to pay for any loss that the owner had incurred, and, in addition, to give him 10 solidi. A *persona inferior* similarly repaired it and paid for the loss, but instead of paying the additional 10 solidi (which might well be beyond his means) he received 50 lashes of the whip. If a slave was guilty, he had to repair the damage and receive 100 lashes.[1] The penalty for refusal to testify in the courts was, in the case of a nobleman, the loss of his right ever to testify, while a poor freeman not only lost his right to testify but also received 100 lashes of the whip.[2] To forge or tamper with a royal document brought upon an *honestior* the confiscation of half his property by the Treasury; but a *minor persona* was liable to have his hand cut off.[3] If a man dragged his slave or his debtor from the altar of a church where he had sought asylum—and the legislator has Arian churches in mind—without the bishop's permission, the matter had to be reported to the judge, who could impose a fine of 100 solidi upon an *honestioris loci persona* and a fine of 30 solidi upon an *inferior*, who, if he was unable to pay, was arrested and lashed 100 times in public. The fine in either case was payable to the church in question.[4] The code by no means spared the *honestiores* the indignity of corporal punishment, but their normal punishment when found guilty of a crime was a pecuniary one.

This distinction between the two classes is found so often that it can be said to be a general principle of Visigothic law.[5] It was

---

[1] *LV* viii. 3. 6.

[2] Ibid. ii. 4. 2. For perjury see ibid. ii. 4. 14, where again there are two penalties.

[3] Ibid. vii. 5. 1.

[4] Ibid. ix. 3. 3. In iii. 4. 15 a distinction is drawn between an *idonea* and an *inferior ancilla*.

[5] The distinction is also drawn in no. 2 of the *Leges ex lege Baiuwar. restitutae*

maintained throughout the seventh century, and indeed King Chindasuinth made it illegal for an *inferior* to sue a nobleman in the courts.[1] Nowhere in the sixth-century laws is there a definition of what exactly is meant by the two free classes, though it is certain that in general they were composed respectively of rich men and poor men. But late in the seventh century the *honestiores* consisted only of the *duces*, the *comites*, and the *gardingi*, whom we shall meet later (pp. 252 ff. below), while even such officials as the *thiufadi* (p. 145 below) ranked as inferiors.[2] At all events, whereas the Visigoths in the fourth century had lived in a tribal society— though sharp differences of wealth had by no means been unknown in it—they were now divided very clearly into those with legal privileges and those with few or none. At this date the social classes were crystallized and rigidly marked off from one another by the law.

The fines imposed by the criminal law were very high, and the kings frequently envisage a situation where wrongdoers cannot pay them. The general principle is therefore laid down in the code that the wrongdoer who cannot pay is to be sold into slavery.[3] This is reasserted in many particular cases,[4] and, although occasionally a whipping is substituted for enslavement,[5] convicted criminals must have ended their days in slavery in so many cases that the question has been raised whether the military power of the kingdom may not have been seriously impaired by the judicial enslavement of so many of the free population.[6] In particular, the law of theft must have been an especially fruitful source of slavery.

The law laid down that the thief, if a freeman, was obliged to restore nine times the value of the stolen property to the man whose goods he had taken. If he was a slave, his master was obliged to repay six times the value. But, whether slave or free, the thief also received 100 lashes of the whip. If the slave's

---

(p. 28 in Zeumer's edn. of the code) and *LV* ii. 4. 2, 14; iii. 6. 1; vii. 2. 20, 22; 5. 1 (cf. 3); viii. 3. 6, 10, 12, 14; 4. 24, 25, 29, all *antiquae*. Fredegar, iv. 82, distinguishes between the *primates* and the *mediogres* (as he calls them) of the Visigoths. In *LV* viii. 1. 10 there is a distinction between *honestiores* and *servi* without any reference to *inferiores*.

[1] Ibid. vi 1. 2 (p. 248 a, *ad fin.*)   [2] See p. 254 below.
[3] *LV* vii. 1. 5.
[4] Ibid ii. 4. 6; iii. 3. 5; v. 4. 11; vi. 4. 2; vii. 1. 1; 2. 14, 3. 2, 3; viii. 2. 1.
[5] Ibid. v. 4. 11; vi. 4. 2, 4. 8; viii. 1. 6, 9; ix. 1. 2; 3. 3.
[6] C. Verlinden, *L'Esclavage dans l'Europe médiévale* (Brugge, 1955), p. 79.

master was unwilling to pay, the slave became the property of the person from whom he had stolen. And if a freeman had not the means with which to pay, he, too, became the slave of the injured party.[1] Now, even in Euric's time some Visigoths had been so poor as to be compelled to sell their own children; and Leovigild was obliged to reissue the law in which Euric had forbidden the practice.[2] But persons who were forced by poverty to sell even their own children into slavery must often have found it impossible to replace nine times the value of anything that they might have stolen. But if they could not do so, they were inevitably enslaved.

In earlier times homicide was punished among the Visigoths by the payment of a *wergild* to the victim's kin, and doubtless this *wergild* had been payable in numbers of cattle. The principle was retained when the people entered the Roman provinces, but by the sixth century the *wergild* was no longer payable in cattle : it was now reckoned in cash and was fixed at the staggeringly high figure of 300 solidi.[3] An optimate might well be able to find such a sum, but it would be far beyond the reach of an 'inferior' person, who, if he were found guilty of murder, would certainly be enslaved. On the other hand, the law distinguished between intentional and unintentional homicide and imposed no penalty for the latter;[4] and in Chindasuinth's time, and probably earlier, killing in self-defence was not a crime.[5]

The sixth-century laws on wounding were discarded in the seventh century in favour of the principle of *talio* (p. 259 below) and so are unknown, though it seems that a man guilty of wounding had at least to pay in composition a sum fixed by the judge.[6] But the cases of murder and theft are sufficient to illustrate the fact that by the sixth century the kindred, which had been the basis of Visigothic society in the fourth century, was of little or no account in the eyes of the law. Men may still have regarded it as of

---

[1] *LV* vii. 2. 14.

[2] Cod. Euric. 299; *LV* v. 4. 12. The Hispano-Romans, too, sometimes did so: *CTh* iii. 3. 1.

[3] *LV* vii. 3. 3. I take it that the extraordinary tariff set out ibid. viii. 4. 16, where the sum varies according to the age and sex of the slain, was worked out for the specific case with which that law deals—the killing of a person by an animal whose owner knew it to be dangerous—and for that alone. On the rarity of such tariffs in primitive law see A. S. Diamond, *Primitive Law*[2] (London, 1950), pp. 317 f.

[4] *LV* vi. 5. 2; cf. viii. 3. 3, etc. For various qualifications and reservations see ibid. 3 ff.   [5] Ibid. vi. 4. 6.   [6] Ibid. vi. 4. 8 f.

importance (though it is unlikely that they did so in Chindasuinth's time, when the kin sometimes did not trouble to prosecute the murderer of one of their kinsmen);[1] but the law gave it little or no recognition. A man no longer depended on his kin for the security of his property or his life. The duty of protecting him was now taken over by the State. The murder of very close kin was not unknown under the sixth-century kings, and it was still regarded with something of the old horror. Only for this type of homicide (as well as for giving drugs so as to cause abortion and for murder by an armed man who had entered another's house with a view to killing the householder) was the death penalty imposed on murderers by Visigothic law (p. 261 below.)[2]

It was illegal for kinsmen to act independently of the State. Punishment for crimes was fixed, not by discussion among the interested parties and their kinsmen, but by the royal legislator, over whom the parties had little or no control. Moreover, the old clan custom of pursuing a wrongdoer's kinsman if it could not punish the wrongdoer himself was explicitly forbidden by the kings: neither kinsmen, heirs, neighbours, nor anyone else must pay for a crime, but only the criminal in person. Nor could feuds be inherited from generation to generation as in olden days: *crimen cum illo, qui fecit, moriatur*.[3] The State emphatically denied that the kindred had any rights or duties in cases of crime. It might or might not award damages to the kinsmen, but that was not for the kinsmen to decide. The criminal now faces the State in isolation from his kin, and individuality is forced upon him.

3. *Administration*

In the sixth century there was a *comes civitatis* supported by a deputy (*vicarius*) in each *civitas* where Goths lived. In some, at least of the secondary towns of the *civitas* was an official who is called the *iudex territorii*, or *iudex loci*, or simply *iudex*—the terms are synonymous. Thus King Sisebut addressed a letter to the bishops and judges (presumably the *comites*) of the three cities of Martos (Tucci), Cordoba, and Montiel (Mentesa) and to the priests and judges (in this case the *iudices locorum*) of nine minor

[1] Ibid. vi. 5. 15.
[2] Ibid. vi. 5. 18 (where the kindred includes both the maternal and the paternal relatives); for abortion see ibid. vi. 3. 1; armed burglary, ibid. vi. 4. 2.
[3] Ibid. vi. 1. 8.

towns in the locality.[1] The count was the chief Gothic administrative officer in his city; but normally neither he nor the judge
had power over the Roman inhabitants.

The *comes* was appointed by the king and was a man of great
wealth and of noble birth.[2] His duties were sharply distinguished
from those of the Roman provincial governor and his staff,
though evidently he sometimes tried to encroach upon them;
for Reccared explicitly warned the counts and their deputies that
they were in no way to levy taxes from the people: that was the
business of the provincial governor. The counts and their vicars
were not to exact a single *annona* from the city or its surrounding
countryside, nor were they to harry the people with any exactions,
transport duties, or forced labour for their own profit: the king
paid them adequately.[3] And, if the count or vicar usurped the
property of others in the king's name without a court order, he
had to restore double that which he had filched.[4] The count's
authority was superior to that of the judge. In the text of the laws
he is always mentioned before him, and in the seventh century,
and doubtless also in the sixth, appeals from the decisions of the
judge were heard either by the count in person or by deputies
appointed by him.[5] In one set of circumstances the count could
even discipline the judge with great severity for neglect of duty.
These circumstances are curious. The count was responsible for
arresting and punishing free-born prostitutes who might be
found in his city, while the judge arrested and punished prostitutes who were slaves (a strange division of labour). But if the
judge omitted to do his duty in this respect, either through
negligence or because he had been bribed, the count imposed on
him a sentence of no fewer than 100 lashes of the whip and fined
him 30 solidi.[6]

---

[1] For the term *iudex territorii* see ibid. iv. 4. 1; vi. 4. 4; xii. 1. 2 (Reccared); III
Tolet. 16; cf. *LV* vii. 5. 1; but *iudex loci* in v. 4. 8 (from Cod. Euric. 289); viii. 4. 29;
III Tolet. 18; *Consensus de Fisco Barcinon.* (p. 99 n. 4 above). But usually he is
simply the *iudex*. The terms *comes* and *iudex* respectively seem to be indicated in
CTh iii. 11. 1, 'his quibus civitates vel loca commissa sint'. I cannot explain the
'tribunes' of *LV* xi. 1. 2. Sisebut's letter is *LV* xii. 2. 13 (why does he ignore the
Bishop of Egabra?).

[2] *VPE* v. 10. 1; *Formulae Visigothicae*, 39 *fin.*, 'vicem agens illustrissimi viri
comitis'. The *iudex* was also appointed by the king in Chindasuinth's time: *LV* ii.
1. 18.   [3] Ibid. xii. 1. 2.

[4] Ibid. viii. 1. 5 (Chindasuinth).   [5] Ibid. ii. 1. 31 (Chindasuinth).

[6] Ibid. iii. 4. 17. For the superiority of the *comes* see also ibid. vi. 5. 12 (Chindasuinth).

The rule was that crimes committed by Goths were reported both to the count and to the judge. The latter proceeded to arrest the accused; but if he found himself unable to do so he appealed to the count for assistance, that is, for military assistance.[1] (The count would also give help when Roman judges could not arrest Roman criminals.) The case was heard by the two officials sitting together, so as to avoid the suspicion of collusion. If the accused were found guilty on a non-capital charge, and had to pay composition-money to the accuser, it was the judge's business to see that this money was paid. When it was fully paid he was allowed to pocket one-tenth of it for his trouble (though if he took more than one-tenth he had to refund double the amount he had taken).[2] But if the accused were found innocent the accuser had to undergo the penalty to which the accused would have been liable if found guilty. The accused was kept in prison by the judge while awaiting trial. If he broke out, or bribed the prison officer (*carcerarius*) to set him free, the prison officer had to suffer the penalty to which the prisoner, if found guilty, would have been liable.[3] The judge received no fee for imprisoning an accused man who was afterwards acquitted; but for each of those found guilty he received one-third of a solidus.[4] If he were found to have been bribed to put an innocent man to death, he was himself executed. If he was bribed to free a man guilty of a capital charge, he had to pay to the plaintiff seven times the amount of the bribe and was dismissed from his post and had to produce the acquitted criminal in court.[5]

Civil cases might be heard by the city count or the judge, but, even when the count is mentioned, it seems usually to be implied by the language of the laws that the *iudex territorii* was judge of first instance. It is rarely assumed that he will be unable to enforce his judgements. Thus, a divorced woman who remarried without having produced written or other attested evidence of the divorce was liable to punishment by the count, or his vicar, or by the judge: the law goes on to speak as though the last of these

---

[1] Ibid. vii. 1. 5; 4. 2. In the criminal laws, then, we might have expected the legislator to have referred to the *iudices* rather than to one *iudex*; but in fact he does so in the *antiquae* only in vi. 4. 8, 10; 5. 18, all of which deal with cases of wounding or homicide. Contrast the singular in vi. 5. 2, 19, etc.

[2] Ibid. vii. 4. 4.   [3] Ibid. vii. 4. 3.   [4] Ibid. 4.

[5] Ibid. 5. In certain cases of debt the creditor was to approach the *iudex* and the *praepositus civitatis*, ibid. v. 6. 3. This latter term is not used elsewhere.

would normally deal with the matter. In the case of 'noble persons' it is assumed that they may be too powerful for the judge to separate and punish them. If so, he is to report the matter to the king.[1] (The king, incidentally, found time to interest himself even in cases of prostitution: it was to a poor man of the king's choice that a woman repeatedly found guilty of prostitution was enslaved, though if the woman were already a slave the king might delegate his powers to the *dux* or the count.)[2] Again, the code recognizes that an important witness might be kept out of court by the patronage of a nobleman or 'by fear of the king': if so, the matter was to be referred to the king himself, if he was in the vicinity, or else to the local bishop or *dux*, whose 'greater authority' would cause the man to be produced in court.[3] On the other hand, the normal assumption is that the count or the judge would be able to deal with the nobility. The judge heard cases involving *honestiores personae* as well as *inferiores*, and in general he seems to have had little trouble in enforcing his decisions on *honestiores* or on clerics.[4] But litigants were sternly forbidden to obtain the patronage and influence of a nobleman (*maior persona, potens*) so as to defeat their opponents in a law suit; and if a noble refused to leave the court when the judge ordered him to go, the judge had authority not only to throw him out forcibly but also to exact from him the heavy fine of 144 solidi.[5]

The decisions of the Roman provincial governor's court were enforced by an official whom King Theudis calls the *executor*, his old Roman name, or the *compulsor*.[6] The corresponding official who enforced the decisions of the Gothic courts was known in the seventh century as the *saio*,[7] though in a sixth-century law he is called by his Roman name *executor* and in another is referred to in a periphrasis.[8] The term *saio* used in this sense first appears in Isidore's *Etymologiae*[9] and recurs in the laws of King Chinda-

---

[1] *LV* iii. 6. 1. For the power of the *potentes* see also vii. 1. 1.

[2] Ibid. iii. 4. 17. Note also the king's interest in iii. 1. 2.

[3] Ibid. vii. 1. 1. But see p. 144 n. 4.

[4] For the latter see v. 4. 17, the only case in the *antiquae* where the *iudex* deals with the clergy.

[5] *LV* ii. 2. 8. On Chindasuinth's drastic reduction of this fine to 10 solidi (ii. 2. 2) see Zeumer, *NA* xxiv (1899), pp. 91 f.

[6] Zeumer, 468. 37.

[7] *LV* ii. 1. 26 (p. 73 a). The metropolitan bishop also had *saiones*: Conc. Emerit. 8.

[8] *LV* ii. 1. 13, 21, 'ille qui a iudice ordinatus ad tollendum fuerat destinatus'.

[9] *Etym.* x. 262, 'saio ab exigendo dictus'.

suinth.[1] It seems that in the sixth century the word *saiones* denoted, not court officials, but what Tacitus had called the 'companions' (*comites*) of the leading men.[2] At all events, both the *comes* and the judge had each his own *saio* or *executor*.[3]

So much of Leovigild's legislation was replaced by Reccesuinth that it is impossible to give anything like a complete description of the judicial functions of the *comes*; and apart from his duties in connection with the army (p. 145 below) his other appearances in Leovigild's laws are not very significant.[4] Although he was the most important official in the locality, the great mass of the law, both criminal and civil, was administered not by him but by the judge; and most of the laws regulating judicial procedure refer to the judge alone.[5] Both the judges and the agents of the royal estates brought down upon themselves the wrath of the bishops in 589. Many complaints had been received that they were forcing the slaves of the bishops, other clergy, and the churches to work for them in their public duties and even in their private business. The bishops excommunicated all such judges and called upon Reccared to stop their malpractices.[6] We never again hear of the judges oppressing the clergy.

Above the *comes*, whose sphere of activity was the city and its surrounding countryside (*territorium*), stood the *dux*, whose power extended over a whole province. We have mentioned the conspiracy of Argimund, who was *dux* of an unspecified province (p. 103 above). The Claudius who suppressed the conspiracy of Sunna, and defeated the Franks in 589, was *dux* of the province of Lusitania.[7] In the seventh century we hear of Ranosind, *dux* of the province of Tarraconensis.[8] King Egica, in the Speech

---

[1] *LV* ii. 1. 18, 26; 2. 4; vi. 1. 5 (p. 253 *ad fin.*); x. 2. 6. Egica uses the term *saio* in ii. 2. 10.

[2] Cod. Euric. 311; *LV* v. 3. 2; cf. 3. But v. 3. 2 was taken over along with the word *saio* by Reccesuinth and Erwig, so that in the seventh century it was understood in two senses. In the title of v. 3. 2, however, there is some explanation of the word in its fifth-century sense, 'saionibus in patrocinio constitutis'.

[3] *LV* ii. 1. 13.

[4] He appears also in viii. 4. 26, 29; ix. 1. 20; cf. xi. 1. 2.

[5] e.g. ii. 1. 23; 3. 2–6; 4. 2, 14, etc.   [6] III Tolet. 21.

[7] Jo. Biclar., *s.a.* 589 (ii. 218). The description of Claudius as *ducem Emeretensis civitatis* in *VPE* v. 10. 7 is an inaccuracy. There was no official called *dux civitatis*, and the author of the *VPE* has loosely written the name of the chief city of the province in place of the name of the province itself. Note also the case of Zerezindo on p. 37 n. 2 above.

[8] See p. 220 below.

from the Throne (*tomus*) which he addressed to the Seventeenth
Council of Toledo in 694, referred to the province of Gallia
Narbonensis as a *ducatus*;[1] and in the seventh-century laws there
are several references to *duces provinciarum*.

No Roman, so far as is known, was ever allowed to become
a city count throughout the history of Gothic Spain. Clearly, a
Roman *comes civitatis* would have been as much of an anomaly as
a Goth would have been in the Roman office of provincial governor.[2] But the case of Claudius, *dux* of Lusitania, shows that
Romans were not excluded from becoming *duces*. The case of
Claudius also shows that *duces* had military duties, though why
the *dux* of the distant province of Lusitania was selected to lead
the campaign against the Franks in 589 is not recorded. In a
seventh-century document we hear of 'the army of the *dux* of that
province' (probably Baetica).[3] Unfortunately, the administrative
duties of the *dux*, his method of appointment, and his relations
with the palatine officials and the king in the sixth century are
not even hinted at in our sources. Practically all our information
dates from the seventh century, and even then it is pitifully
meagre, since the codes by their very nature have little to say
about the highest officers of the kingdom. All that is certain is
that the *dux* ranked higher than the *comes*.[4]

Finally, the composition of the royal court cannot be described.
What is known about the Count of the Patrimony has been
mentioned above (p. 127 above). Whether the offices of *comes
cubicularium*, *comes scanciarum*, *comes spatariorum*, and others
(p. 253 below), which are known from the second half of the
seventh century, existed at all in the sixth century, and, if so, in
what form and with what functions, we cannot tell. The Visigoths
discarded the Roman titles of rank apart from that of *vir illustris*.
This title was borne by the Goiaric who was concerned with
drawing up the *Breviarium* of Alaric II, and is frequently found in
later times. The Third Council of Toledo was attended by a

---

[1] Zeumer, p. 485. 12.

[2] I must confess that I do not know what to make of *Eugenii comitis* in Braulio,
Vita S. Aemiliani, 14 (PL 80. 708).

[3] *Vita S. Fructuosi*, xiv. 30, a document which also refers (ii. 1) to 'ducis exercitus Spaniae proles'.

[4] *Duci* would seem to be the right reading in *LV* vii. 1. 1 (antiqua) at p. 286. 20:
see Zeumer's crit. n. If so, the passage explicitly mentions the *maior auctoritas* of the
dux and of the bishop over that of the *iudex*.

number of Gothic *viri illustres*, who publicly renounced Arianism. Who they were and what their functions amounted to, how they were appointed, what powers they held, whether they received a salary from the Crown, and if so, how much, are questions that we cannot even begin to answer.

4. *The Army*

Practically all that we know about the Visigothic army in the sixth century is derived from a handful of laws in the code (ix. 2. 1–7). It is true that Alaric's code also refers to soldiers, and shows that it was not unknown for Romans to serve in the armed forces; but it is unthinkable that the kings allowed more than a small proportion of their army to be composed of others than Goths.[1]

The largest unit into which the Gothic levy was divided was called the *thiufa* and was commanded by the *thiufadus*. This officer was inferior in authority to the city count, and, if he connived at the desertion of any of his men, it was to the count that he had to pay nine times the amount of the bribe that he had accepted, or 20 solidi if he had not accepted a bribe. Under him stood, in order of rank, the *quingentenarius*, the *centenarius*, and the *decanus*, who had to pay respectively 15, 10, or 5 solidi for conniving at desertion without being bribed.[2] The unit commanded by the *quingentenarius*, presumably consisting of five *centenae*, is never mentioned and may never have had a separate existence; but the *centena* and the *decania* of the other two officers are named in the code; and the money exacted from officers who had connived at desertion was distributed among the men of the *centena* which had suffered from the desertion.

---

[1] *CTh* ii. 10. 6; 12. 6; 23. 1; iii. 5. 5; iv. 8. 9; 22. 4; xi. 11. 1, etc. The reference to *protectores* in iv. 10. 3 is difficult to explain.

[2] *LV* ix. 2. 1. The *thiufadus* is often identified with the *millenarius*, but the two are distinguished in *LV* ii. 1. 27. The *millenarius* is a mystery. In the two passages in which he is mentioned, Cod. Euric. 322 (though he is omitted in Leovigild's version of this law, *LV* iv. 2. 14) and *LV* ii. 1. 27 (Reccesuinth), he is spoken of only as having judicial functions (and not merely in cases where soldiers were concerned), and there is no hint that he was ever a military commander. There were *millenarii* in both the Ostrogothic and Vandal kingdoms, but I cannot find that they were military officers in either case. For the Ostrogoths see Mommsen, *Ges. Schr.* vi. 438 n. 1. The 'chiliarchs' of Procopius, *BV* iii. 5. 18, for example, may have been the Vandal equivalent of the Visigothic *thiufadi*, though Mommsen, loc. cit., p. 438 n. 2, claims that the word simply = *tribuni*. The account of the organization of the Visigothic army given by E. Oldenburg, *Die Kriegsverfassung der Westgoten*, Diss. Berlin, 1909, pp. 38 f., should be read with caution.

The desertion of officers, too, was not unknown. If the *centenarius* deserted in the field he was guilty of a capital crime, though if he managed to take asylum in a church—an Arian church, presumably—he was spared, but had to pay a fine of no less than 300 solidi (which were also divided up among his *centena*). He was not dismissed from the service, but he was reduced to the rank of a *decanus*.[1] The penalty for a *decanus* who deserted in the field is also recorded: he was simply fined 10 solidi. A common soldier who deserted was fined 10 solidi and received 100 lashes of the whip in the market place of his town.[2]

All these penalties were also inflicted on the officer or man who failed to join the colours when called up. The procedure was that, when troops were required, royal slaves named *compulsores exercitus* summoned each Goth whose services were required—it is not stated whether they also summoned Romans—by calling on him in person; and while doing so they were not above pilfering his goods[3] or accepting a bribe to allow him to stay at home.[4] The city count punished these, too. The commanding officer, who is curiously called *praepositus hostis*,[5] appears to have been notified of defections, but it was the local count who punished them.

The commissariat is mentioned in only one law. In each city or fort there was an official called *erogator annonae*, whose function was to distribute supplies to the troops. He was himself supplied by the city count and an official called the *annonae dispensator*, or simply *annonarius*. If these failed to send him the supplies, he notified the commanding officer (*praepositus hostis* or—an otherwise unknown term—*comes exercitus*), who in turn notified the king of the number of days for which the unit had received no supplies. The city count and the *dispensator* were then obliged to provide four times the due amount at their own expense. The same rules relating to the supplies of garrison troops applied also in the case of troops in the field, that is, as the legislator puts it, in the *thiufa*.[6]

The decimal system of organization seems to be an artificial creation, but its creator is unknown. At all events, the relation-

---

[1] *LV* ix. 2. 3.   [2] Ibid. ix. 2. 4.
[3] Ibid. ix. 2. 2. The *compulsor* is also mentioned ibid. ix. 2. 9, p. 375. 9 (Erwig).
[4] Ibid. ix. 2. 5.
[5] Ibid. ix. 2. 3; cf. 5, 'preposito comitis', which must be corrupt: see Zeumer, ad loc. Is he the *dux provinciae*?
[6] Ibid. ix. 2. 6.

ship of the count with the *thiufa* can best be accounted for if we suppose that each *civitas* in which Visigoths were settled was responsible for putting one *thiufa* in the field, that is, a unit perhaps consisting on paper of 1,000 men. But the figure cannot be pressed. On the only occasion for which details are known, a *dux*, who presumably commanded the forces of an entire province, led no more than 300 men (p. 94 n. 1 above). And the forces of the various provinces cannot have been equal in number, for the Visigoths were not equally distributed over the whole face of Spain. But if we are right in believing that each *civitas* put one *thiufa* in the field, it follows that the organization of the army, even apart from the retainers of the nobles, was based on a territorial principle. And since there is no evidence that the Visigoths settled in clans in the various cities, the principle of kinship played little or no part in the organization of the army. The very foundation of the army was different from that of the primitive Germans described by Tacitus and from that which can be inferred to have existed among the Visigoths before they entered the Roman Empire in 376.[1] Moreover, the army now had one function of capital importance that the German levies of which Tacitus speaks did not have. The function of the Visigothic armed forces was not simply to defend the kingdom against foreign attack. They were also used to enforce the law at home, for a judge who could not effect the arrest of a criminal could appeal for assistance to the count (p. 141 above).

5. *Art*

Several Gothic cemeteries of the sixth century have been excavated. The graves contain the bodies of the poorer Visigoths, not those of the great landowners or of the court officials from the king's entourage; and so the objects buried in them throw light on the possessions of the rank and file of the Gothic population and on the craft of the average bronzesmith, but give no information about the art and manners of the court. The Roman urban population had abandoned the practice of burying gravegoods in the fourth century, though country-folk retained it

---

[1] Apart from the fact that it consisted of tribal levies we know practically nothing about the organization of the Visigothic host before the time of the codes: see Oldenburg, op. cit., pp. 16–19.

somewhat longer.[1] Among the Goths grave-goods are found in Arian cemeteries only, never in Catholic graveyards; and when the one cemetery was in continuous use in the sixth and seventh centuries, only the earlier burials include grave-goods. When the Visigoths lived north of the lower Danube in the fourth century they had buried their dead. Cremation was almost unknown among them, and the law codes and church councils of the sixth and seventh centuries never refer to it. Cremation was not a problem. Apparently it was not even known in the Spanish kingdom.

They scooped out shallow graves, usually revetted them with flagstones, and floored and covered them with two further flags, so that the grave somewhat resembled a stone coffin. Husband and wife were often laid in the same grave even if this meant opening it long after the death of one of the partners. The bodies were laid on their backs in an extended position with their arms usually by their sides, facing the east, fully clothed, the women wearing a few ornaments, the menfolk rarely accompanied by any metal object except the bronze buckles on their belts.[2] Even in their pagan days the Visigoths had not buried weapons or armour with their dead, and exceedingly few pieces have been found in the Spanish cemeteries. Unlike their ancestors in the fourth century, the sixth- and seventh-century Visigoths did not provide their dead with pottery, and little is known about Visigothic ceramics. As for glass, the Goths sometimes wore glass beads and had glass inset in their belt-buckles; but a glass vessel is an extreme rarity. Inlay and enamelling were practically beyond the powers of the craftsmen or the means of their customers. Bronze vessels, too, from this period have rarely been discovered. It is the bronze articles of personal wear which give importance to the sixth-century cemeteries.

The most characteristic finds are bronze belt-buckles and brooches with bronze back-plate. Women wore their dress gathered up by a brooch at each shoulder—the head of the brooch pointing downwards[3]—with a leather belt around the waist. In the early years of the century they used a non-radiate type of bronze bow-

[1] H. Schlunk, *Ars Hispaniae*, ii (Madrid, 1947), p. 308.

[2] Photographs of graves in Menendez Pidal, pp. 346 ff.; Lantier, art. cit (p. 56 n. 1 above), p. 179.

[3] J. M. Santa-Olalla, 'Zur Tragweise der Bügelfibel bei den Westgoten', *Germania*, xvii (1933), pp. 47–50; Lantier, art. cit., p. 182.

brooch which is distinguished by the ornamental plates riveted to
the sides and top of the head and by the palmette riveted immediately above and below the bow. They are not otherwise
decorated, the main effect being gained from the bright surface of
the bronze. The foot tapers downwards and often slopes slightly
to either side. This was a type of brooch that the Visigoths had
been wearing with little change since the fourth century when
they lived north of the lower Danube; but it seems to have been
going out of fashion in the reigns of Amalaric and Theudis.[1] It
was replaced by cast-bronze, round-headed, radiate bow-brooches
with or without 'chip-carved' ornament (*Kerbschnitt*) on head and
foot, a type which was developed in Spain in remarkably individual ways. Those with chip-carved ornament were heavily under
the influence of Ostrogothic taste;[2] the others, which are a
development of the non-radiate type, cannot be paralleled in any
other country settled by the Germanic peoples. In particular, the
craftsmen added one, two, or even three pairs of knobs symmetrically on either side of the foot; and these knobs, like the
radiates of the head, sometimes had coloured glass inset in them.
Such side-knobs, apart from a few examples from southern
France, are unique in the Germanic world, but it is hardly
necessary to explain them by supposing that the manufacture of
the brooches had been taken over from the Visigothic by Hispano-
Roman craftsmen.[3]

The 'Gothic buckles', consisting of plain oval loop, tongue
with ornamental plate or rolls at its base, and rectangular buckle-
plate adorned with chip-carving and inset with coloured glass
cabochons or with garnets in the centre and at the angles,[4] were
in use simultaneously among the Ostrogoths of Italy and the
Visigoths of Spain in the first half of the sixth century. They seem
to have made their appearance first among the former and then to
have been taken over by the latter. But the Visigoths went on to
develop them in their own individual way. Instead of ornamenting
the surface of the plate with stones or glass inset in the centre and
obliquely at the four corners, they soon began to cover the entire
surface with cabochons, overcrowding and concealing the bronze

---

[1] Zeiss, pp. 12 f., 97 ff.; Ferrandis *apud* Menendez Pidal, p. 644.

[2] Zeiss, pp. 102 f.

[3] *Contra*, Zeiss, pp. 101, 105, 120, 123, 138, *et saepe*. He supposes that the buckles,
too, were made by Roman workers.

[4] Ibid., pp. 25 ff., 106 ff., and his Plates 9–10.

background. While in the earlier type the garnets were set in cells separately soldered, in the later examples coloured pastes were set in a dense network of cells cast at the one time.[1] The decline in the use of the garnet may have been due to the cutting off of the supply by the war of the Byzantines and the Ostrogoths in Italy. Alternatively, the Visigoths would place an openwork upper plate upon an underplate so as to reveal and frame the stones set in the latter, and so on. But after a period of deterioration in technique and in taste, these buckles, like the brooches, disappeared from the cemeteries towards the end of the century.[2]

Among other forms of buckle-plate the so-called 'lyre motif' plate and its later developments, which are unparalleled outside Spain, are important. The plate on these buckles was originally divided by a raised rim into a circular compartment ending gracefully in two symmetrically arranged leaf- or almond-shaped compartments, all three being filled with a flowing, stylized floral design in low relief. This type of buckle makes its appearance in Spain late in the sixth century; and what is of great significance is that it appears to be based on Byzantine models and that in its more developed and decadent forms it was worn throughout much of the seventh century.[3]

A final type is the large bronze eagle-brooches which are ultimately derived from a type discovered in the fourth-century treasure found at Pietroassa in Rumania. The form of the bird is strongly stylized, and the surface, like that of the buckle-plates, is wholly covered with inset glass or garnets. In some cases these brooches had three rings at the end of the foot on which to hang pendants. A later form is not in the polychrome style but is of cast bronze, the ornament being in chip-carving.[4] The development of the eagle-brooches and the rectangular buckle plaques proceeded

---

[1] Zeiss, pp. 28–30.

[2] The cemetery at Estagel, which began to be used in the first quarter of the sixth century and went out of use before the seventh century, provides brooches and buckle-plaques indistinguishable from those found in the Spanish cemeteries: Lantier, pp. 184 f. The identity of the articles found on both sides of the Pyrenees implies the existence of industrial centres which supplied them to both groups: ibid. 187.

[3] Zeiss, pp. 42 ff., 118 ff. But I do not find it necessary to accept his view (pp. 120, 123) that the deterioration of the ornament is due to Hispano-Roman craftsmen. For an important comment see P. Verdier *apud* M. C. Ross, *Arts of the Migration Period in the Walters Art Gallery* (Baltimore, 1961), p. 17 n. 45.

[4] Zeiss, pp. 18 f., 104 f.

on parallel lines in Spain and Italy in the first half of the sixth century, and is further evidence of the close relations between the two countries during the Ostrogothic period of Spanish history. The development of the eagle-brooches, as of the belt-plates, breaks off in Italy with the fall of the Ostrogothic kingdom in 552 but continued in a less impressive way in Spain, where it may not have survived into the seventh century.[1]

These examples of buckles and brooches illustrate the fact that some of the articles of daily use in Visigothic Spain in the first half of the sixth century were fashioned on Ostrogothic models. They illustrate the depth of Ostrogothic influence on Spain during the period of Theodoric's regency. (No pure-blooded Visigoth sat upon the throne, if we ignore Gesalic, until the accession of Agila in 549.) But they also illustrate something of the independent-mindedness of the Visigoths; for, soon after the arrival of the Ostrogothic prototypes, the Visigoths began to develop their brooches and buckles in ways which were unknown in Italy or anywhere else in the Germanic world. But in the second half of the century, when the Byzantines were entrenched in parts of southern Spain, East Roman styles began to come into fashion. These, too, were developed by craftsmen who were not subjected to continuous Byzantine influence, or who rejected such influence, until they at last produced work of such an individual character as to show that they had forgotten their original models. On the other hand, fashions that became widespread among the other Germanic peoples, and in particular the famous 'animal-style' ornament (apart from the bird-brooches), were all but unknown in the Spanish peninsula. If the animal style was characteristic of the northern Germans, polychrome ornament continued to be characteristic of the Goths as a whole in the sixth century, and of the Visigoths in the seventh.

With the conversion to Catholicism the Visigoths abandoned their custom of burying grave-goods with the dead. The conversion also coincided with a dramatic change in the character of the small finds from Visigothic sites. Germanic styles and tastes

---

[1] Schlunk, op. cit., p. 309; J. M. Santa-Olalla, 'Westgotische Adlerfibeln aus Spanien', *Germania*, xx (1936), pp. 47–52; idem, 'Nuevas fibulas aquiliformes hispanovisigodas', *Archivo español de Arqueología*, xiv (1940–1), pp. 33–54; but the two eagle-brooches from Estremadura (now in the Walters Art Gallery, Baltimore) which he describes are not of solid gold but of gilt bronze: on them see Ross, op. cit., pp. 22 n. 78, 100 f.

disappeared at the end of the sixth century, and their place was taken by peculiarly Spanish varieties of what had once been the tastes and styles of Byzantium. In one case a Latin inscription actually appears on the openwork belt-buckle of a seventh-century Visigoth: *Ch(ristus) sit tecum Ch(ristus)*.[1] It has been said that if we had to rely on archaeology alone we should never guess that Spain was ruled by Germans in the seventh century.[2]

[1] Zeiss, p. 35. According to idem, p. 53, only one buckle (found near Gerona) is inscribed with its owner's name (Trasamundus).

[2] Zeiss, p. 142.

PART TWO

THE CATHOLIC KINGDOM

VII · THE UNIFICATION OF SPAIN

A DEEP gorge of the Tagus surrounds three sides of the granite rock on which Toledo stands. Sheer cliffs fall several hundred feet from the edges of the city to the fast-flowing river. They are so formidable that no man-made defences are needed on the city's east, south, or west sides. 'A small town', Livy had called Toledo, 'but fortified by its site.'[1] Only from the north can an enemy assail it with much hope of success; but throughout the entire history of the Visigothic kingdom no armed attack was ever launched upon it until the Arabs arrived there in 711. To them it fell at last, 900 years after Marcus Fulvius, proconsul of Spain, had won it for Rome.

When the city had become the capital of the kingdom is obscure;[2] but there is no reason to doubt that it was in his capital on 24 November 546 that King Theudis signed his law on legal costs. The kingdom of which it was the centre reached the height of its power in the first quarter of the seventh century. After the general conversion of the Goths to Catholicism in 589 heresy was rarely mentioned again; and although Priscillianism still survived it was no serious threat to the unity of the Church. The Visigoths had been fervently attached to Arianism for over two centuries, but after the Third Council of Toledo it was forgotten almost overnight. Further, during the first twenty-five years of the new century, although Liuva II and Witteric were assassinated like so many of their predecessors in the sixth century, no king was ever again murdered while he still sat upon the throne. Above all, in the second decade of the century the Goths won conclusive victories over the Byzantines; and about the year 624 King Suinthila at last drove them into the sea. Justinian and his

---

[1] Livy, xxxv. 22. 7.

[2] For some speculations see R. de Abadal, *Del Reino de Tolosa al Reino de Toledo* (Madrid, 1960), pp. 63 ff.; E. Ewig, 'Résidence et capitale pendant le haut Moyen Age', *Revue historique*, ccxxx (1963), pp. 25–72, at p. 31. The fact that Amalaric, after his flight from Narbonne in 531, brought his royal treasure with him to Barcelona, does not prove that Narbonne had previously been his capital or that he now intended to make Barcelona his chief city: Greg. Tur., *HF* iii. 10. The royal treasure appears to have accompanied the kings on their campaigns, for Agila took his treasure with him on his campaign against Cordoba in 549: Isidore, *HG* 45 (ii. 285).

successors had clung to Malaga and Cartagena for over seventy years. The grandiose plan was to break out from the bridge-head at those two cities and to absorb Spain into a restored Roman Empire. But the break-out never took place; and now a barbarian monarch claimed to rule the Iberian peninsula.

But there was one area where his writ did not run. The kings never tamed the impenetrable mountains of the Basques. The light-armed mountaineers not only retained Navarra (their earliest known home), Alava, Viscaya, and Guipuzcoa, but also began before the end of the sixth century to filter down the northern slopes of the Pyrenees into Aquitaine, to which they were already giving their name—Guasconia, Gascony. They frequently raided the lands of the Franks as well as of the Goths, and would vanish often enough among their mountains before the kings of Toledo could bring them to battle. Throughout the entire period of the kingdom they preserved not only their independence but also their paganism.[1]

In the rest of Spain the disputes of the Hispano-Romans continued to be heard in Roman courts under the code of Alaric. This code was more than once referred to at the Church councils in the first half of the seventh century.[2] The Roman provincial governors still held office; and in the Visigothic *Formulae*, which appear to date from the second decade of the century, a number of the old municipal offices are mentioned.[3] The city councils still continued to function.

Unhappily, the chronicle of Isidore of Seville is our only continuous source of information for the history of this seemingly prosperous quarter-century. It is as uninformative as ever; and we can supplement it with little more than a couple of anti-Jewish laws of King Sisebut, the minutes of three provincial synods of the Catholic Church, and some curious and difficult

---

[1] *Vita Amandi*, i. 20 (MGH, *SS. rer. Merov.* v. 443), professedly referring to the mid-seventh century; Einhard, *Vita Karoli Magni*, 9. Guasconia: Ravenn. Cosmogr. iv. 10; cf. v. 28 (pp. 296, 418, ed. Pinder and Parthey); cf. Greg. Tur., *HF* vi. 12; ix. 7. References to the Basques down to the year 810 are collected by A. Schulten, *Revue internationale des études basques*, xviii (1927), pp. 225–40.

[2] II Hispal. 1, 2, 3, 6; IV Tolet. 46, with Séjourné, pp. 103 ff. In the *Iudicium inter Martianum et Aventium episcopos* (p. 288 below) there is a reference to Paul, *Sentent.* i. 1. 2: see Zeumer, *NA* xxiv (1899), pp. 120 f.

[3] IV Tolet. 65; *Formulae*, 21 (*ordo curiae*), 25 (*principales, curator, magistri*). Both of these *Formulae* mention the *gesta publica*. Freed slaves still became Roman citizens, ibid. 2 ff., and p. 165 below.

letters by a *comes* of Septimania called Bulgar or Bulgaran. Now, in spite of the apparent peacefulness of the period these sources evidently conceal deep and disturbing undercurrents in the history of these years, for no sooner had this quarter-century come to a close than a storm broke over Spain. There followed a generation of conspiracy, revolt, warfare, repression, and intense insecurity. The factors which ultimately caused the troubles of the thirties and forties were presumably gathering strength in the reigns of Sisebut and Suinthila; but Isidore and our other feeble sources give no hint at their nature.

1. *Liuva II and Witteric*

In the whole history of the kingdom Leovigild was the only ruler to be followed on the throne by his son and his grandson. When Reccared died at Toledo in December 601, he was succeeded by his son Liuva II. Liuva was illegitimate. He had been born in 584 when the negotiations for his father's marriage with a Frankish princess were still in progress and Queen Baddo had not yet appeared on the scene. But he did not survive for long. In the twentieth year of his age, when he had reigned for only about eighteen months, that same Witteric who had long ago betrayed the Arian conspirators of Merida to Reccared proclaimed himself king. He dethroned the virtuous young man and cut off his right hand so that he could never reascend the throne; and, not content with that, he put him to death in the summer of 603.[1] Isidore regards the youth as an innocent victim of rebellion; but Witteric could have argued that he was a usurper, for he had reached the throne as Reccared's son rather than by due process of election.

There is no valid evidence that the new king tried to restore Arianism as the official religion of the State.[2] On the other hand, no record of any synod or council has survived from his reign; and the clergy disliked him. Difficulties of an unknown character seem to have been created for the Church in Toledo, where the Metropolitan Aurasius stood up boldly to his adversaries.[3] Some letters written by Bulgar in 610, soon after Witteric's death, show

---

[1] Isidore, *HG* 57 (ii. 290).

[2] F. Görres, 'Weitere Beiträge z. Kirchen- und Culturgeschichte des Vormittelalters', *Zeitschrift f. wissenschaftliche Theologie*, xii (1891), pp. 77–111, at pp. 102–5; Garvin, p. 497. But the view that he did so has unfortunately been revived by many recent writers.   [3] Ildefonsus, *De Vir. Illustr.* 5 (PL 96. 200 f.)

that the King (unjustly, according to the writer) had exiled him and had imprisoned him in many prisons, vexed him by hunger and thirst, and inflicted punishment after punishment upon him. Unhappily, he does not explain how he had fallen foul of the tyrant; but other innocent persons, too, had met with similar injustice.[1] Bulgar writes harshly of Witteric, though before his death the King, as a result of a vision, had restored him to his office, that of count of some city in Narbonensis. But since Witteric seems to have had the support of Elergius, Bishop of Tarrasa (Egara), the wrong may not have been wholly on the King's side. At all events, among Bulgar's letters are two in which he writes to thank two men who subsequently became metropolitan bishops (Agapius of an unknown see and Sergius of Narbonne) and who had helped him in his time of trouble.

Witteric fought frequently and with energy against the Byzantines in the south of his country but had little personal success. His generals managed to retake the unimportant town of Gisgonza (Sagontia) and to capture some Byzantine troops there (p. 320 below). In 607 he became entangled in one of those marriage proposals with the Franks that had bedevilled other Gothic kings before him. Theuderic II of Burgundy asked for the hand of Witteric's daughter Ermenberga and gave an oath that he would never dethrone her. He was glad when the girl reached Châlons-sur-Saône; but his grandmother Brunhild, herself a Visigoth, and his sister Theudila poisoned his mind against his bride, and the marriage was never consummated. Ermenberga was sent back to Spain without her dowry. The enraged Witteric entered into an alliance with Chlotar II and Theudebert II of Austrasia together with Agilulf, the Lombard King of Italy, to attack Theuderic and dethrone him; but the alliance came to nothing.[2] The Visigoths had now learned their lesson. There is no evidence that they ever again tried to arrange a dynastic marriage with the Franks.

---

[1] *Epist. Wisig.* 15–16 (pp. 682–4). It does not follow that Bulgar had been exiled to Narbonensis, for Sergius became metropolitan there only after Bulgar's tortures had ended. On Bulgar see M. Alamo, *Dict. d'histoire et de géographie ecclésiastique*, x. 1114–16.

[2] Fredegar, iv. 30 f. There is an unconvincing discussion in G. Kurth, *Études franques* (Paris, 1919), pp. 320 ff. Observe that there is no indication that Ermenberga was an Arian or that she had to be converted from Arianism when she married the Frankish king.

Eventually, a conspiracy was formed against Witteric. Its character is unknown; and whether the King was murdered for purely personal reasons or because of his anti-clerical policies—if they *were* anti-clerical—has not been recorded. At any rate, he was assassinated at a banquet in April 610,[1] though in the view of Count Bulgar it was a heavenly rather than a human sword which struck him down.[2]

2. *Gundemar*

The new ruler was Gundemar, whose wife Hildoara died during his brief reign; and a letter of consolation was written to him by that same Count Bulgar who had suffered under Witteric. From this letter it appears that Gundemar had previously been governor of the province of Narbonensis, where he had dealt in a kindly manner with those who were 'exiled and afflicted', presumably some of Witteric's victims.[3] Bulgar refers to that 'most wicked robber', Witteric, who had been devastating the people hitherto. From the Count's correspondence it emerges that Gallia was the scene of wars against the Franks, and of various disasters;[4] and it is characteristic of the nature of our evidence that this information reaches us incidentally and without a single detail to illuminate it. Isidore is silent. The causes of the struggle, the course of the campaigns, and the outcome of the war are alike unknown.

Gundemar differed from Witteric in taking a sympathetic interest in the affairs of the Church. A council of the bishops of Carthaginiensis, which met at Toledo in 610, is the first council known to have assembled since the reign of Reccared.[5] It was attended by fifteen bishops of the province, though in view of the agenda the Bishop of Toledo politely stayed away so as not to prejudice the discussion. Its purpose was to consider the primacy of Toledo within the province; and the question was one that had stirred deep feelings. Cartagena had been the provincial capital and the metropolitan see, though Montanus of Toledo (p. 34 above) had described himself as metropolitan in 527.[6] But

---

[1] Isidore, loc. cit.   [2] *Epist. Wisig.* 14 (p. 683. 10).
[3] Ibid. 16 (pp. 684 f.).
[4] Ibid., 'nequissimus praedo'; ibid. 14 *fin.*; 15 *fin.*
[5] On the council of 610 see esp. Séjourné, pp. 86 ff.
[6] II Tolet. 5 *fin.*, or rather he lived *in metropoli*. He signs as *episcopus*.

Cartagena had been lost to the kingdom at the time of the Byzantine invasion; and at the first Catholic council to be held thereafter, the Third Council of Toledo, Euphemius of Toledo had signed the acts as 'Metropolitan of the province of Carpetania'. Now, Euphemius had a reason for doing this. Cartagena was in Byzantine hands, the Third Council had not discussed the question of primacy within the province, and Euphemius presumably had not wished to prejudge the issue in favour of Toledo: hence, he had used the name of a part of the province. In the twenty years that followed the Third Council some rivalry with Toledo had revealed itself. Another see had claimed the primacy of that part of Carthaginiensis which lay outside Carpetania.[1] Accordingly, the fifteen bishops of the province published a firm statement that Toledo was in fact the metropolis of the entire province. On 23 October this statement was supported by a document signed by the King himself together with twenty-six other bishops, the Bishop of Toledo still remaining absent. (The second meeting was attended by the metropolitans of Lusitania and Baetica. The latter was Isidore of Seville, who had succeeded his brother Leander when Reccared was still alive: and he thus makes his first appearance in history.) The document that the second meeting produced confirmed the primacy of Toledo in the province as a whole and asserted that Euphemius had signed as he did in ignorance, 'for we know beyond doubt that the region of Carpetania is not a province but a part of the province of Carthaginiensis'.[2]

Before this organizational storm had blown up, Gundemar had ravaged the country of the Basques in the campaigning season of 610; and in that of 611 he 'beleaguered' the Byzantines, though with little effect.[3] There was at least a threat of trouble with the Franks, too. Although Gundemar referred to Witteric's reign as a 'usurpation',[4] he inherited Witteric's foreign relations and his hostility towards Brunhild and King Theuderic. Count Bulgar in Septimania was alarmed to hear a report that Brunhild and the King were inciting the ferocious ruler of the Avars to attack Theudebert, with whom Witteric had been in alliance. We never

---

[1] Cf. Gundemar in Mansi, x. 510, 'neque eamdem Carthaginiensem provinciam in ancipiti duorum metropolitanorum regimine contra patrum decreta permittimus dividendam', etc. The same point is referred to by the bishops, ibid. 507 c.

[2] Mansi, x. 510 f.   [3] Isidore, HG 59 (ii. 291).

[4] Mansi, x. 510.

hear whether this rumour was true; but Gundemar and Theudebert began to draw up a treaty of alliance, and the Visigothic king
agreed to pay money to the Franks.[1] It was unique behaviour in a
Visigothic monarch to become so closely involved in the internal
disputes of the Frankish rulers. There is nothing like a parallel to
it throughout the entire history of the Spanish kingdom. At one
stage of the negotiations Theuderic arrested and imprisoned some
noble Visigothic ambassadors. Thereafter two Goths called
Tatila and Guldrimir, *viri illustres*, sent to France as envoys by
Gundemar, were stopped at an unidentified place in France
called Irupinae and were not allowed to complete their journey.
The Visigothic reaction is interesting. Count Bulgar occupied
Juvignac (Iubiniacum) and Corneilhan (Cornelianum), two places
which Reccared had made over to Brunhild in unknown circumstances. And when the Queen demanded their return he refused
to hand them back until the imprisoned Goths had been freed.[2]
How the matter ended we do not know. It seems that the Visigoths did not after all become seriously involved in the inter-
necine struggle of the Franks; and the strong reaction of Bulgar
in seizing the two places shows how Visigothic power and
confidence had grown relatively to that of the Franks during
the century that had elapsed since the day of Vouillé.

In February or March 612 Gundemar died at Toledo.

3. *Sisebut*

Sisebut succeeded him and reigned until February 621 when he,
too, died a natural death. His campaigns were fought both in the
north and in the south of Spain. In the north the Asturians
rebelled, and Sisebut's general Richila crushed them. The royal
generals, one of whom was called Suinthila, also put down the
Roccones in their mountain fastnesses. This people is presumably
identical with the Runcones, whom Miro, King of the Sueves in
Galicia, had fought in 572 (p. 62 n. 4 above).[3] They probably
lived in Cantabria. In his surviving poem King Sisebut implies
that he himself had travelled by sea in 613 when fighting the
Basques and Cantabrians. This is the first hint at the existence
of a Visigothic fleet. It was Sisebut's creation; but its basic

---

[1] *Epist. Wisig.* 11 f. (pp. 677 ff.)   [2] Ibid. 13.
[3] Isidore, *HG* 61 (ii. 291).

function, its size, its organization, its achievements, and its fate, are unknown.[1]

The King fought in person two successful campaigns, perhaps in 614–15, against the Byzantines in the south. When he had brought them so close to total defeat, we might have expected him to fight a third campaign so as to expel them from Spain altogether. Whether his refusal to do this was due to his horror at the bloodshed involved, or whether other factors entered into his calculations, has not been recorded. He was certainly distressed by the loss of life. On one occasion, when the Byzantines were massacred by his men, he was heard to cry out, 'Alas, that there should be such bloodshed in my time!'[2] Isidore records—evidently it was unusual behaviour in a Visigothic king—that he ransomed many of the troops who had been taken prisoner by his forces.[3] The Patrician Caesarius, Governor-General of the Byzantine province, appealed to this quality in his character. He had already made several requests for peace. He now (perhaps in 615) wrote to the King stressing the slaughter caused by the war—and it was Catholic blood that flowed on both sides—and the hordes of men taken into captivity by both armies. As a token of goodwill the Patrician had already freed Caecilius, Bishop of Montiel (Mentesa), who had fallen into his hands.[4] The King in his reply touched on the slaughter, the plague, and the calamities caused by the war. He agreed to negotiate a peace treaty and commended his plenipotentiary, Ansemund, to the Patrician.[5] The four surviving letters of Caesarius and Sisebut give a curious glimpse of the diplomatic procedures of the time. They are written in an excessively obscure style, with extraordinary elaboration of language, and in tones of the utmost chivalry and courtesy.

The King's personal piety is stressed by several authors. He

[1] Isidore, in the *Recapitulatio* at the end of his *HG* (ii. 294. 25 ff.), remarks: 'hac sola tantum armorum experientia hucusque carebant, quod classica bella in mari gerere non studebant. sed postquam Sisebutus princeps regni sumpsit sceptra, ad tantam felicitatis virtutem provecti sunt, ut non solum terras, sed et ipsa maria suis armis adeant.'

[2] Fredegar, iv. 33, a chapter which seems to preserve some echo of the campaign in Cantabria, but I am sceptical of the thesis of M. Broëns, 'Los Francos en el poblamiento de la Península Ibérica durante los siglos VI y VII', *Ampurias*, xvii–xviii (1955–6), pp. 59–77, that there had been substantial immigration of Franks into northern Spain and especially Galicia in the sixth and seventh centuries.

[3] Isidore, *HG* 61 (ii. 291).

[4] *Epist. Wisig.* 3. On this Caecilius see Görres, art. cit., pp. 105–11.

[5] *Epist. Wisig.* 4.

built at Toledo the Church of St. Leocadia, where four plenary councils of the Spanish Church were to be held. At one time Isidore of Seville thought of dedicating to him the *Etymologiae*, one of the great books of the Middle Ages; and in 613 he did in fact dedicate to him his *De Natura Rerum*.[1] Sisebut interested himself deeply in the affairs of the Church, which he sternly ruled. Al etter has survived in which he reprimands Eusebius, Bishop of Tarragona—he took the chair at the provincial synod of 614—for the interest that he showed in the theatre. The King's language is strong, even offensive; but he incongruously adds to his rebuke a direct order to the Bishop to appoint the bearer of the letter to the see of Barcelona, a procedure that was more glaringly contrary to canon law than was theatre-going.[2] The Bishop of Montiel (Mentesa), Caecilius, who had been a prisoner of the Byzantines, wished to retire to a monastery. When Sisebut heard of this, he sharply rebuked him and ordered him to appear before himself and some other bishops in order that he might be recalled to his duties.[3] His deep piety is apparent in his letter to his son Theudila, who had entered a monastery, and in his epistle to Adualduald, the Lombard King of Italy (616–26), in which he tried without tact to convert that monarch from Arianism to Catholicism.[4]

He was the first and only Visigothic king to win and to deserve a reputation as a Latin author. In 613, at the time of the northern campaign, he addressed to St. Isidore his remarkably successful poem on eclipses of the moon, a poem which may have been designed to counteract pagan outbursts following on the eclipses of the moon and the sun that were seen in Spain in 611 and 612.[5] His *Life* of St. Desiderius of Vienne is a competent work of hagiography and also of political propaganda; for his hero had been put to death in 606–7 by Theuderic and Brunhild, the enemies of successive Visigothic kings, and Sisebut's purpose in choosing this saint for his eulogies, we may be sure, was in part that Theuderic and Brunhild might be the villains of his work.[6]

On the other hand, no plenary council of the Church was summoned in his reign. The bishops of Tarraconensis met at

---

[1] J. Fontaine, *Isidore de Séville: Traité de la Nature* (Bordeaux, 1960), pp. 1 ff.

[2] *Epist. Wisig.* 7. Isidore also frowned upon the theatre: see, e.g., *Etym.* xviii. 41. 3; 42. 2; 46. 1; 51. 1 f.

[3] *Epist. Wisig.* 2.   [4] Ibid. 8 f.

[5] It has been beautifully edited by Fontaine, op. cit., pp. 151 ff., 328 ff.

[6] The *Vita* is edited in MGH, *SS. rer. Merov.* iii. 620 ff.

Tarrasa (Egara) on 13 January 614 under the presidency of that Eusebius whose visits to the theatre had earned the King's displeasure. The synod merely confirmed the decisions of the synod of Huesca (p. 112 above) on the celibacy of abbots, priests, and other clergy.

In 619 the second provincial synod of Baetica was held in the Church of Holy Jerusalem in Seville under the presidency of Isidore. It dealt chiefly with disciplinary and organizational matters. The bishops noted, for example, the ignorance of canon law displayed by Agapius, formerly Bishop of Cordoba and now dead (p. 110 above).[1] At this synod a Syrian named Gregory was brought before the assembly. He declared himself to be a bishop of the heretical sect of the Acephali (the first hint at the existence of heresy in Spain since the reign of Reccared). The Acephali, or 'Headless', were an extreme party of Monophysites who had refused to accept the *Henotikon* published by the Eastern Emperor Zeno in 481. They had originated in Egypt and had received their name not because they had no bishops—the case of Gregory himself shows that they had—but because they were originally in communion with none of the five patriarchs of the Roman Empire.[2] Gregory denied the existence of two Natures in Christ and asserted that Deity was sensible to suffering. But after a long struggle St. Isidore was able to convince him of his errors in these important questions; and he was received into the Catholic Church, admitting that there were two Natures and one Person in one and the same Jesus Christ, and agreeing that the nature of Deity cannot suffer.[3] Syrian influences, then, could still penetrate into Spain early in the seventh century; and it is unfortunate that we do not know the size, composition, or fate of the flock which Gregory abandoned. It is hardly credible that so obscure a sect formed a threat to the unity of the Spanish Church. What is indeed remarkable is that this little synod of the bishops of Baetica, meeting at the end of the world, could produce a definition of the Two Natures that (even if it confused Gregory of Nyssa with

---

[1] Canon 7.

[2] Canon 12; cf. Braulio, *Praenotatio* (PL 81. 17); Contin. Isid. Hisp. 16 (ii. 339 f.) But Isidore, *Chron.* 385 (ii. 473), remarks: 'ideo Acephali, id est, sine capite, nominantur, quia quis primus eam haeresim introduxerit non invenitur', cf. *Etym.* viii. 5. 66. He regards the Eastern Emperors from Zeno to Justinian as Acephali.

[3] Canon 12; Braulio and Contin., locc. citt. On this synod see Séjourné, pp. 95 ff., but note also Fontaine, ii. p. 852.

Gregory of Nazianzus) was as learned and as well argued as any disputation of the great theologians of the East.

Sisebut's Christian piety led him to consider the position of the Jews in his kingdom. He has left us two documents bearing on the subject. One of these is a formal law; the other is a letter addressed to Agapius, Bishop of Martos (Tucci), Caecilius, Bishop of Mentesa (p. 162 above), Agapius, the unsatisfactory Bishop of Cordoba, to the judges of those cities, and to the priests and judges of nine other places in southern Carthaginiensis and eastern Baetica. (Why Reccesuinth included the letter in his law code without redrafting it we do not know.) The letter was written very soon after the law had been enacted, and it supplements the law in a few particulars.

Reccared's regulations about the Jews had not been strictly enforced by Witteric and Gundemar;[1] and this Sisebut deplored. The matter was close to his heart, for the law was published a month or two after he had reached the throne in March or April 612, certainly well before 1 July. His first aim was to remove all Christian slaves from Jewish ownership as quickly as possible and to free Christian freedmen from Jewish patronage. (Indeed, Sisebut even says, though he does not develop the point, that no hired workman may be employed by a Jew.) A Jew, therefore, must sell his Christian slave and the slave's property (*peculium*) to a Christian purchaser at a fair price. But he must sell him in the locality, near his normal dwelling-place, for the slave's convenience and also perhaps so as to prevent Jews from handing on their slaves to their brethren in Africa and France. If the slave had no property, he must supply him with some. Alternatively, he might manumit the slave, who would then become a Roman citizen liable to tax; but the Jew could not become the freedman's patron. Fictitious sales were severely punishable. These provisions were to be carried out before 1 July 612; and, if a Jew were found to be in possession of a Christian slave after that date, the Treasury would confiscate one half of his property, and the slave would be freed. The King next turned to proselytism and mixed marriages. In the matter of proselytism Sisebut reverted to the harsh position of Alaric II, which Reccared had mitigated. A Jew who converted a Christian to Judaism was now to be put to death and his property taken by the Treasury. If anyone who was

[1] *LV* xii. 2. 13 (p. 418. 8).

converted to Judaism refused to return to the Church, he was to be publicly whipped, suffer decalvation, and become the slave of a nominee of the Crown. In the case of mixed marriages, which were illegal, if the Jewish partner refused to join the Catholic Church he or she must go into exile for life; but if such persons turned Catholic and were baptized, they were allowed to keep all their property, including their slaves. Slaves born of the marriage of Christian and Jew were Christians, whether they liked it or not. This part of the law, too, was to be put into effect before 1 July of the current year. The King ended his law by calling down a fearful curse on any ruler who should fail to enforce it in the future; and his curse was remembered with lively fear by King Erwig some seventy years later. Sisebut observes that the law was enacted 'with all the palatine *officium*', but makes no mention of the bishops.[1]

If this were all, we might say that Sisebut, like Alaric II and Reccared, was less a persecutor of the Jews than a defender of the Christians. His single aim, we might think, was to stop proselytism. But he took other steps without the enactment of a law and without the authority of any Church council. It was he who began the policy of forcible conversion of others besides the children of mixed marriages. Isidore dates the anti-Jewish measures of the King to the beginning of his reign; and an insertion in his *Etymologiae* suggests that the forcible conversions took place in his fourth year as king. The Saint observes that Sisebut did not act according to wisdom, for he compelled by force those whom he ought to have challenged by the logic of the Faith.[2] No details are known about these forcible conversions, but they clearly did not have the support of the Catholic hierarchy. The Fourth Council of Toledo, at which Isidore was the senior metropolitan, explicitly and firmly condemned the policy of force, and referred specifically to those who had been violently converted by 'the

---

[1] *LV* xii. 2. 13 f. The view that Sisebut's anti-Jewish legislation was inspired by the Emperor Heraclius (so P. Goubert, *REB* iv (1946), p. 120) is not supported by evidence.

[2] Isidore, *HG* 60 (ii. 291); cf. Contin. Isid. Hisp. 15 (ii. 339), 'Iudeos ad Christi fidem vi convocat'. The forcible conversions seem to be referred to in *Etym.* v. 39. 42, 'Heraclius septimum decimum agit annum. [Huius quinto et quarto religiosissimi principis Sisebuti] Iudaei in Hispania Christiani efficiuntur [v. l. baptizantur].' On this passage see W. Porzig, 'Die Rezensionen der Etymologiae des Isidorus von Sevilla', *Hermes*, lxxii (1937), pp. 129–70, at pp. 165 f.

most religious prince Sisebut'. It was the only occasion on which the Spanish bishops ever criticized the anti-Jewish actions of the kings; and their condemnation brought little comfort to the 'converted' Jews. Since they had now been associated with the divine sacraments, had received the grace of baptism, had been anointed with chrism, and had partaken of the body and blood of the Lord, they must be compelled to remain Christian lest the divine name be blasphemed and the faith that they had accepted be held cheap and contemptible.[1] In fact, the Council criticized Sisebut and confirmed what he had done. A number of Jews saved themselves by migrating from Spain to France.[2] But it is unlikely that more than a small percentage of Spanish Jews left the country; and the devout King's laws were not strictly enforced by his immediate successor on the throne. Perhaps he himself did not press home his persecution throughout the whole of his reign: the date of his laws and the words of Isidore show that, although the laws remained permanently in force, his harsher measures were probably confined to the early years of the reign.

But, if the bishops did not go all the way with Sisebut, they were not indifferent to the Jews. Dating from about the time of the King's anti-Jewish measures is a letter written by the Metropolitan of Toledo, Aurasius, to a certain Froga, Count of Toledo. Aurasius had converted some prominent Jews to Christianity— Joseph, the Rabbi Isaac, Nephthali, and others. Levi Samuel, the head of the synagogue (*archisynagogus*) in Toledo, protested to Froga that Aurasius had deceived them or had enticed them in some way to accept baptism. The Count was a man of action. He gave orders that a watch be kept until the new converts should come out of the church for the first time, clad in the white dress of catechumens; and when they did so he sent a man with a cudgel to beat the converts. Aurasius was furious. He publicly excommunicated and anathematized the Count in front of the church; and the letter still survives in which the Metropolitan informed Froga of his excommunication.[3] The reluctance of Witteric and Gundemar

---

[1] IV Tolet. 57.　　　　[2] Addit. ad Chron. maiora, 2 (ii. 490).

[3] *Epist. Wisig.* 20, with the scholion printed by W. Gundlach, *NA* xvi (1891), pp. 46 f., where Froga is described as *comitem et praefectum Toleti*, an otherwise unknown title. I take it that Froga was *comes civitatis Toletanae*, an office explicitly mentioned in Zeumer, p. 486. 15. On *archisynagogus* and *rabbi* at this date see Katz, pp. 80 f. On Aurasius see Ildefonsus, *De Vir. Illustr.* 5 (PL 96. 200 f.)

to enforce Reccared's legislation on the Jews, and the action of Froga, are the first but not the last indication that the anti-Jewish measures of the kings were not unanimously supported by the Catholic population.

Sisebut died in February 621 and was succeeded by his son Reccared II—his Catholic piety is reflected even in the name that he gave to his son. But Reccared died after a reign of only a few days[1] and was succeeded by Suinthila, who had held the office of *dux* under Sisebut and, in addition to his successful campaign against the Roccones (p. 161 above), had played a prominent part in the war against the Byzantines.

4. *The First Years of Suinthila*

At the beginning of his reign the new king had to deal with the Basque mountaineers, who had overrun the province of Tarraconensis.[2] He evidently surprised a large party of them: they laid down their arms and gave hostages. At their own expense and with the labour of their own hands they founded the fortress of Ologicus (unidentified) to serve as a Visigothic strongpoint in their country.[3] But the victory may not have had very lasting results. Braulio, writing to St. Isidore in 625, speaks of disorders in the neighbourhood of Saragossa. The region suffered from famine, plague, and warfare; and the Basques are more likely than anyone else to have caused the devastation, which brought much hardship to the local people.[4]

Suinthila's most striking success was his final expulsion of the Byzantines from Spain (p. 334 below). His victory followed a pitched battle. Two patricians fell into his hands. One of them he took by a stratagem; the other he defeated in battle.[5] He was thus

---

[1] Isidore, HG 61 (ii. 292); but Contin. Isid. Hisp. 17 (ii. 340) gives Reccared II a reign of three months: see Zeumer, NA xxvii (1902), pp. 425 f.

[2] There is a study of Suinthila by F. Görres, 'Die Religionspolitik des spanischen Westgotenkönigs Swinthila', *Zeitschrift f. wissenschaftliche Theologie*, xlix (1908), pp. 253–70. The discovery of two of his coins at Pamplona does not prove that Suinthila was ever in that city: *contra*, F. Mateu y Llopis, 'Sobre los límites de la conquista visigoda en Vasconia y Cantabria', *Ampurias*, vi (1944), pp. 222–5, at p. 223; Miles, p. 100.

[3] Isidore, HG 63 (ii. 292 f.), where Ologicus is described as *civitatem Gothorum*: I do not know the exact import of the words.

[4] Braulio, *Ep.* 3 (PL 80. 650)=*Ep.* 2 at the beginning of Lindsay's edn. of Isidore's *Etym.* On the date see Lynch, pp. 44 ff.

[5] Isidore, HG 62 (ii. 292).

the first Visigothic king to rule over the whole of Spain, apart from Vasconia.[1]

Isidore of Seville, who is our sole authority for the first years of the reign, ends his chronicle with the fifth year of Suinthila, that is, with the year which ran from the spring of 625 to that of 626. Since the campaign against the Basques took place 'at the beginning of his reign'—say, in the campaigning season of 621 or 622—the expulsion of the Byzantines, which Isidore mentions in his chronicle, must be dated to the campaigning season of one of the years 623–5. At that date Suinthila and the kingdom that he ruled reached the height of their power.

Now, Isidore published his *History of the Goths* while Suinthila still sat upon the throne. Accordingly, he is fulsome in his praise of the King's character and administration and also of the King's infant son Riccimir, whom Suinthila, ignoring the tragic fate of Liuva II, had associated with himself on the throne. Among the King's virtues Isidore mentions his good faith, prudence, energy, his vigour in acting as a judge, his painstaking care in administration, and says that his open-handedness to the poor and needy was such that he deserved to be called 'not only the prince of his peoples but also the father of the poor'.[2] A few years later the King was deposed, and the diplomatic Saint found it possible to subscribe to a different picture of the father of the poor. And someone thought it wise to rush out a second edition of the *History of the Goths* from which these unfortunate eulogies had been deleted.[3]

[1] Ibid., 'totius Spaniae intra Oceani fretum monarchiam regni primus idem potitus', where the words *intra Oceani fretum* mean 'inside [i.e. east of] the Straits of Gibraltar' and do not imply that the Byzantines controlled any land outside the Straits. The view that they had occupied part of Algarve has been demolished by Stroheker, pp. 241 ff.

[2] Isidore, *HG* 64 (ii. 293). I ignore the *Dedicatio* to Sisenand, printed in Mommsen, *Chron. Min.* ii. 304. It is undoubtedly inauthentic, as Mommsen, ibid., p. 254, points out.

[3] Cf. Mommsen, ibid., pp. 254–6.

VIII · A DECADE OF REBELLION

FROM the time of Suinthila's victories over the Byzantines until the end of the kingdom we have no continuous source of information about the Goths in Spain. True, an anonymous writer continued Isidore's chronicle to the year 754, but until the accession of Egica in 687 he has little to tell us. The Frankish chronicler known as Fredegar gives valuable information about the accession of Sisenand and about the reign of Chindasuinth; but thereafter no contemporary Frankish historian ever again refers to the history of the Goths.

We are confined, therefore, to a single source for the history of the kings from Sisenand to Tulga (631–42). This is the minutes of the successive councils of Toledo which met frequently in this period. At these councils the bishops often commented on political and constitutional matters; but they concerned themselves only with those public events that the kings placed on their agenda. Thus, if a rebellion broke out and was crushed, the bishops might be invited to deal with the general problems of revolt and usurpation, but they would have no cause to outline the course of the revolt itself. That is to say, the conciliar canons leave us in the peculiar and difficult position of knowing the bishops' reaction to certain events while remaining in ignorance of the events themselves. We have to infer what happened from the bishops' comments on what happened. In these circumstances the details of the historical events cannot now be known.

Finally, in one remarkable case, that of the usurper Iudila, our literary sources tell us nothing whatever, and all that we know is that two coins have survived bearing his name. These coins can be fitted into a context supplied by the other sources; but that the result is no more than a hypothesis needs hardly to be mentioned.

1. *Sisenand*

St. Isidore praised the virtues of Suinthila while he was on the throne. But in 633 he was the first bishop to sign the minutes of the Fourth Council of Toledo; and those minutes spoke of

Suinthila's 'crimes', his 'iniquity', and his accumulation of property at the expense of the poor! In the new circumstances it might have been fatal for Isidore to repeat his published view that Suinthila was the 'father of the poor'. The chronicler of 754 seems to regard Suinthila with favour, whereas the Frank Frede-gar says that he was excessively harsh to his subjects and incurred the hatred of the magnates of his kingdom. (He does not mention the attitude of the poor of his kingdom.)[1] Moreover, his reign, like those of Witteric and Sisebut before him, saw no general council of the Church. But provincial synods were not banned, and at least one was held in his reign, though its minutes have not been preserved. It met at Seville about 624; for Braulio, while still an archdeacon, wrote to the King asking him for a copy of its acts. He received no reply and hence wrote to Isidore asking him to intercede for him. (Since Isidore had presumably presided over any synod held at Seville, it is puzzling that Braulio had not written to him in the first place.) As for what happened at the synod, Braulio remarks only that a certain Sintharius, who is otherwise unknown, 'was not purified but was at least melted by the fire of [Isidore's] examination'.[2] We also know that at this synod as a result of almost unbelievable intrigues the Bishop of Ecija (Astigi) was deposed (p. 287 below). There is no hint in the canons of the Fourth Council at oppressive measures against the Church. Indeed, the King dedicated, probably in a church at Guarrazar in Carthaginiensis, a famous gold crown, which still survives,[3] so that he was presumably a man of some personal piety. The contradiction in our sources appears to mean that Suinthila was popular with the rank and file of the population—and perhaps even with St. Isidore[4]—and equally unpopular with the nobility.

At all events, the nobles eventually plotted to overthrow him; but they could not do so with their own resources. They found it necessary to bring a foreign force to Spain to dethrone him; and they therefore sent one of their number, Sisenand, to the Frankish King Dagobert of Neustria to ask for an army to destroy Suinthila. In return for a bribe consisting of a golden dish weighing 500 lb.,

---

[1] Contin. Isid. Hisp. 18 (ii. 340); Fredegar, iv. 73.

[2] Braulio, *Ep.* 3 (*PL* 80. 650)=*Ep.* 2 (Lindsay). On this synod see Séjourné, pp. 30-2; Martínez Díez, pp. 318 ff.

[3] Vives, 375.   [4] So Görres, art. cit., p. 265.

which the Patrician Aetius had long ago given to King Thorismud (451–3), a Frankish army from Burgundy assembled at Toulouse and in 631 marched south to Saragossa. It was the last Frankish invasion of Visigothic Spain; and Suinthila's army capitulated to the united enemy. When the Franks arrived in Spain Suinthila recognized his position as hopeless and abdicated. Even his brother Geila had deserted him and had gone over to the enemy.[1] The nobles thereupon proclaimed Sisenand as king on 26 March 631; but Suinthila was still alive in December 633, when the Fourth Council banished him, his wife, and his children, undertook never to promote them to the offices which they had formerly held, and confiscated their goods. The same sentence was passed on Geila, who was already plotting against Sisenand.[1] The final fate of Suinthila is unknown: a late and unreliable authority says that he died a natural death at Toledo before 641.[2]

Apart from the circumstances of his accession and the information given in the minutes of the Fourth Council of Toledo practically nothing is known about Sisenand. Happily, the minutes of the Fourth Council—the 'great, universal council', as it was called—are long and informative.

On 5 December 633 the new king opened the Fourth Council in the Church of St. Leocadia in the capital, the church that Sisebut had built.[3] Entering with the most illustrious men of the kingdom, the King in the presence of sixty-two bishops prostrated himself on the ground. With tears and groans he asked the bishops to intercede for him with God and exhorted them to correct the abuses that had arisen in the Church. The bishops left political matters to the end of their deliberations and, under the leadership of St. Isidore, began their discussions by trying to enforce a remarkable uniformity in ecclesiastical matters upon the whole of Spain and Septimania. Thus, Easter had been celebrated on different dates in different places. In future, therefore, the metropolitans were to consult together by letter three months before Epiphany so that they might proclaim an agreed date to their comprovincials.[4] The triple as well as the simple immersion at baptism was still practised in spite of the efforts of Pope Gregory

[1] Fredegar, loc. cit.; IV Tolet. 75 (Mansi, x. 640 c).
[2] *Epit. Ovet.* 16 (ii. 373).   [3] Isidore, *Chron.* 416ᵃ (ii. 480).
[4] The bishops of Tarraconensis revert to this point in III Caesaraug. 2, where it is presumed that it is the bishop's duty to inquire of the metropolitan as to the date of Easter.

the Great and Leander of Seville to make the simple immersion the standard (p. 41 above). Certain churches were closed on Good Fridays, the Divine Office was not celebrated, and the Passion of the Lord was not preached to the people. Some Catholics ended their Good Friday fast at the ninth hour of the day, when they sat down to a hearty banquet. Spanish priests often repeated the Lord's Prayer on Sundays only. In some churches Lauds were read after the Epistle before the Gospel was preached, although the Spanish canons directed that the Gospel should follow immediately after the Epistle. Some priests omitted to sing the Song of the Three Children at Sunday Mass. Many refused to accept the Book of Revelation as canonical.[1] All these and other abuses were condemned by the bishops, who also detected certain differences between the practices of Spain and those of Gaul and Galicia. At the Easter vigil the Paschal lamp and candle must be blessed in Gaul as they were in Spain; and the Galician form of the tonsure must be brought into line with that of Spain.[2]

The case for uniformity did not convince everybody; and not long afterwards even so eminent a bishop as St. Braulio of Saragossa, who himself was present at the Council and signed its decisions, advised his brother Fronimian to choose what he found acceptable and to eliminate what he thought offensive.[3]

The assembled fathers then agreed twenty-nine canons on the discipline and administration of the Church, eight canons on monks and penitents, ten canons on the Jews, and eight canons on the freedmen of the Church. But in the seventy-fifth canon they turned dramatically to public affairs. This long canon was inspired by the King himself.[4] It is written in tones of the utmost solemnity and was remembered until the last years of the kingdom. It was the most famous canon ever agreed by the Spanish Church. Its purpose was to add strength to the kings of Spain and stability to the Gothic race. Ignoring the new king's revolt against Suinthila, the bishops thundered against the iniquity of breaking

---

[1] Canons 5–19 deal with these and similar matters. But in 675 the Eleventh Council had to insist that all rites and offices in each church should be identical with those of the metropolitan church. Abbots in particular were warned, especially in connection with vespers, matins, and the mass. In 666 Lusitania had enforced uniformity in a matter concerning vespers. On the liturgical canons of IV Toledo see Séjourné, pp. 137 ff.

[2] Canon 9 (Gaul); 41 (Galicia).   [3] Braulio, *Ep.* 14 (*PL* 80. 661).

[4] 'Sisenando regi, cuius devotio nos ad hoc decretum salutiferum convocavit.'

the oath of allegiance to the sovereign. They begged that there should be no usurpations in Spain, no attempts to stir up rebellion, no plots against the lives of the monarchs. In future, when a king died, his successor must be appointed by the magnates of the whole kingdom sitting along with the bishops in a common council. Three times the bishops repeated their awful anathema against any who should conspire to break his oath of allegiance, or make an attempt on the king's life, or try to usurp the throne. Three times the anathema was read out to the concourse with profound solemnity, and three times the notaries copied it into the minutes. All the clergy and laymen present shouted out their agreement. Then the bishops called upon Sisenand and his successors for ever to rule moderately and mildly, with justice and piety, over the peoples entrusted to them by God. Any successor of Sisenand's who ruled harshly or oppressively would be anathema. After this impressive scene the bishops condemned and sentenced Suinthila and his family (p. 172 above).

By recognizing Sisenand as king the Council contradicted the spirit of its own extraordinarily earnest enactment. As for the succession to the throne, the bishops made no concession to the principle of hereditary succession: they merely removed any rights to which the people may still have clung. Future kings would be appointed by the grandees and the bishops and by nobody else. But the seventy-fifth canon gives rise to a difficult question. What it shows above all else is the King's insecurity. It is hardly possible to believe that so emphatic a statement would have been published by the bishops if the King had had nothing more to fear than the plotting of Geila. In fact, since the death of Witteric in 610, each Visigothic king had died in his bed. There is no hint in our sources at the outbreak of rebellions against Gundemar, Sisebut, or Suinthila until Sisenand himself rose. Sisenand's is the only revolt known from the period. What then did he fear? What reason had the bishops to condemn usurpation with such tremendous emphasis and at the request of a king who was himself a usurper?

Moreover, the seventy-fifth canon, though inspired by Sisenand, reads peculiarly like a condemnation of Sisenand's own revolt. Though it was intended to support and safeguard him, it is in fact a tirade against nothing other than what he himself had done when he rebelled against Suinthila. No one present at the

Fourth Council could have failed to see that what the bishops anathematized was what the King had done and what they themselves by their very presence at the Council had condoned.

These difficulties would disappear if, between the time of Suinthila's deposition and the opening of the Fourth Council, a further revolt had broken out, and if someone else had tried unsuccessfully to do to Sisenand what Sisenand had succeeded in doing to Suinthila. In fact, a crisis arose in 632 that led Sisenand at the very last moment to postpone the opening of the Fourth Council: he had arranged the Council for 632, but he was obliged to delay it until the end of 633. This crisis may well have been due to the rebellion of Iudila.

No literary source and no inscription mentions the name of Iudila. We know it only from two coins, one of which was minted at Merida and the other at Granada (Illiberris).[1] They are inscribed with the name of IVDILA REX, and they are known to have been struck either in the reign of Suinthila or in that of Sisenand. Now, we know of no context in Suinthila's time into which Iudila's usurpation would fit. On the other hand, the seventy-fifth canon and the postponement of the meeting of the Fourth Council would be explained if Iudila had tried to usurp the throne sometime in the years 631–3. If Iudila's revolt had immediately preceded the opening of the Council, then to a contemporary the seventy-fifth canon would read like a condemnation not of Sisenand but of Iudila. And its tone of alarm would be due to the seriousness of a rebellion that spread to parts of at least two provinces, Lusitania, where the provincial capital fell to the rebel, and Baetica.

With this hypothesis, then, it would follow that Sisenand's accession to the throne was not undisputed, that while he and his Franks were victorious in the north of Spain a considerable area of the south refused to accept him, and that his opponent Iudila was successful for a long enough time to organize some of the local mints to issue coins for him. Whether the usurper was in any way a supporter of Suinthila, and whether his revolt was in any sense a protest against Suinthila's overthrow, is unknown. But it might not be wide of the mark to suppose that he disputed

[1] On Iudila see Miles, pp. 30, 321, with bibliography. But there is no reason for identifying him with Geila; and the suggestion that he is the Bishop Uldila who had rebelled in Reccared's reign is far-fetched.

Sisenand's accession, that he failed to win the support of the magnates and the bishops in general, and that he was suppressed in the campaigning season of 633. This reconstruction of the events would account for the curious fact that Sisenand waited so long before dealing with the deposed Suinthila, who must have remained a threat to him until the assembled bishops had condemned him. The hypothesis gains support from the fact that Sisenand did indeed intend originally to hold his great Council not in 633 but in 632. The royal summons to attend the Council had already gone out to the bishops in 632. St. Isidore had started on his journey to the capital and was already nearer to Toledo than to Seville when the King at the last moment countermanded his summons and advised the bishops to return home.[1]

The truth may be, then, that Sisenand planned to condemn Suinthila in 632, that he had suddenly to cancel the projected Council because of Iudila's rebellion which broke out in southern Spain in the campaigning season of 632, that he crushed the revolt in the season of 633, and that he was able to reissue invitations to his Council only late in that year, for the bishops did not meet until December. The revolt may have had repercussions as far north as Saragossa, where there was trouble in 632. Perhaps it was caused by Sisenand's own invasion of 631, for his army of Franks reached Saragossa.[2] But the turmoil caused by the Franks ought to have died down by 632, and it may be that the disorders were due to Basque raiders who took advantage of the confusion caused by Iudila's revolt to pick up some plunder in the neighbourhood of Saragossa.

That a revolt broke out in 632 is probable. That its leader was Iudila is a guess (though if the guess is rejected we must find room for his revolt elsewhere in this troubled reign). What else can we learn about the uprising? The Fourth Council gave special attention to clerics who should take up arms in a sedition voluntarily, or who had already done so: such men were to be banished to a monastery to undergo penance.[3] Had some of the clergy of southern Spain supported the rebellion? Again, for the first but not the last time the authorities show some hint of alarm in case Catholic priests may communicate with foreign powers (as

---

[1] Braulio, *Ep.* 6 (*PL* 80. 654) = *Ep.* 5 (Lindsay).
[2] Idem, *Ep.* 5 = *Ep.* 4 (Lindsay); cf. *Ep.* 10, with Lynch, p. 183.
[3] IV Tolet. 45.

Leander had communicated with Byzantium during Hermenegild's rebellion in 579–84, though the bishops did not mention the
precedent). The Council enacted that priests living near the
frontier must not receive secret messages from a foreign people
unless they had the king's permission, nor must they send secret
messages out of Spain.[1] It is not likely that the bishops had in
mind the frontier between Septimania and France, for Iudila's
revolt (if that is what they were talking about) broke out in the far
south of Spain, and, indeed, the Franks were Sisenand's allies.
Nor would a southern rebel have been likely to invite the plundering Basques into what he hoped would some day be his
kingdom. Is it possible, then, that the rebels were in communication with the Byzantines in Africa or the Balearics? Finally, it
may be that Sisenand had directed some bishops to take part in the
trial of the defeated rebels; but if so he was condemned by the
Council, which ruled that no bishop should undertake such a
task, for no bishop must be guilty of shedding blood, even the
blood of traitors.[2]

The Fourth Council of Toledo also discussed other matters
that were of more than ecclesiastical interest. They laid down
that anyone who had a legal complaint against bishops, judges,
the nobility (*potentes*), or, indeed, against anyone else, should
present it to the provincial synod of bishops. If the synod found
that there was a case, a royal *executor* should see that the proper
authorities put the matter right (p. 283 below).[3] Moreover, if the
bishops should see judges or noblemen oppressing the poor, they
were to rebuke them; and if the rebuke was ineffective they were
to inform the king.[4] This canon supplemented canon 18 of the
Third Council (p. 99 above), which had given the bishops this
power over the judges but not over the nobility. But it was St.
Isidore's opinion that many bishops failed to speak up against the
oppressors of the poor: they had no wish to lose the friendship of
the powerful oppressor, or perhaps they were themselves engaged
in criminal activities.[5] On the instructions of Sisenand himself the
Council enacted that all clerics of free birth (though not the lands

---

[1] Ibid. 30, where note 'praeter eos qui a regia potestate licentiam acceperunt':
for what purposes was permission given?

[2] Ibid. 31.   [3] Ibid. 3.

[4] Ibid. 32. Cf. Eugenius of Toledo, Appendix, *carm.* 25, 'censoribus populi
obediant [sc. iudices] ut postulet ordo'. On the corruption of judges see Ziegler,
p. 141 n. 32.   [5] Isidore, *Sentent.* iii. 45. 2 f. (*PL* 83. 714).

of the Church) should be exempted from all taxes and forced labour.[1] The clergy had little reason to be disappointed with the change of government from Suinthila to Sisenand.

Another great matter with which the bishops concerned themselves was the position of the Jews in the kingdom. Although the Council disowned Sisebut's policy of forcible conversion (p. 166 above), it drew up no fewer than ten canons dealing with the Jews. Two of them were enacted on the explicit instructions of the King himself. The Third Council of Toledo had banned Jews from holding any public office which gave them power to punish a Christian. The Fourth Council now banned on pain of a public whipping Jews and persons born of Jewish parents from holding *any* public office, because, it was alleged, they used such offices to inflict injury on Christians. Roman provincial governors (*iudices provinciarum*)—for the Jews were Roman citizens—and bishops were to see that this law was enforced, governors who connived being liable to excommunication.[2] The second canon adopted on the King's instructions reaffirmed laws of Reccared and Sisebut: Jews could not legally own or buy or receive as a gift any Christian slave. But Sisebut's penalty for breach of this law was modified: the slave was to be restored to freedom, but nothing was said now about the confiscation of the Jewish slave-owner's property.[3] It is clear that Suinthila had not strictly enforced the anti-Jewish legislation of his predecessor, just as Witteric and Gundemar had not enforced that of Reccared. The bishops went on to rule that the circumcising of a slave by a Jew who had relapsed into Judaism—and there were many who had done so—would entail the freeing of the slave and the recall of the Jew to the worship of Christ by the local bishop. If such Jews had circumcised their own children, the children were to be taken from them. The bishops made this ruling after consultation with Sisenand.[4] A more sinister canon laid down—if our text can be trusted—that the sons and daughters of Jews must be separated from their parents and brought up in monasteries or Christian households. But it is difficult to believe that so drastic a measure was passed at this date, and the reference is doubtless to the baptized children of Jews.[5] Again, the Third Council had banned

---

[1] IV Tolet. 47.   [2] Ibid. 65.   [3] Ibid. 66.   [4] Ibid. 59.
[5] Ibid. 60. The reading *filios vel filias baptizatos* is proposed by Hefele and Leclercq, *Hist. des Conciles*, iii. 1. 274 n. 1; cf. Juster, p. 311 n. 2; Katz, p. 50 n. 3.

once more intermarriage between Jews and Christians; but intermarriage had continued and was far from unknown in Sisenand's time. The bishops, therefore, declared again that Jews married to Christian women, if they refused to accept Christianity, had to separate from their wives and children. Christians married to Jewesses had also to leave their wives; and in either case the children were to be brought up as Christians.[1] All these enactments related to matters that had been considered by earlier councils and legislators; but there is no earlier parallel to the canon that enacted that Jews who had been converted to Christianity should have no further association with Jews who had not been converted. The penalty for breach of this ruling was harsh. The unconverted Jew was to be given as a slave to a Christian, while the convert was liable to a public whipping.[2] Lapsed Jews could not testify in the courts.[3]

But the bishops did not believe that these laws would be enforced without opposition. Even in 633 *many* bishops and laymen protected the Jews, and the Council believed that they did so in return for bribes. Anyone who should help the Jews in future, therefore, whether bishop, priest, or layman, would be anathematized and excommunicated.[4] It is clear that in Sisenand's time, as before it and after, many Christians, both clerics and laymen, disregarded the anti-Jewish laws of their kings (whatever their motives may have been), and that so fanatical a king as Sisebut went considerably beyond even the bishops in his fervour.

The seventy-fifth canon of the Fourth Council is the first document to mention the oath of allegiance to the king which was sworn by all the population of Spain. We do not know when this oath had been instituted; but in Egica's time the palatine officials were obliged to present themselves in person to the King so as to swear it, while royal officials (*discussores iuramenti*) travelled through the provinces administering it to the whole free population.[5]

Sisenand died on 12 March 636 and was remembered in later times as an orthodox Catholic king, though the chronicler of 754 regarded him simply as a usurper and has no word of praise for him.[6] Sisenand evidently kept in his own hands the appointments

---

[1] IV Tolet. 63.   [2] Ibid. 62, correctly interpreted by Juster, p. 312 n. 1.
[3] IV Tolet. 64.   [4] Ibid. 58.   [5] *LV* ii. 1. 7.
[6] *Epit. Ovet.* 16 (ii. 374); Contin. Isid. Hisp. 19 (ii. 340).

to the highest offices of the Church. In 632 Isidore received a letter from Braulio of Saragossa informing him that the Metropolitan of Tarraconensis, Eusebius of Tarragona, was dead. Braulio urged Isidore to suggest to the King that he should appoint to the vacant see a man whose holiness and learning would be a model to others.[1] Isidore replied that the King had not yet made up his mind.[2] (It is noteworthy that even so eminent a prelate as Braulio did not approach the King directly.) Although the great Metropolitan of Seville, then at the height of his enormous reputation, had evidently spoken to Sisenand about the matter, it is clear that the King was not at all bound to take his advice. Sisenand alone appointed metropolitans and was recognized to have this right. In this case he appointed the Audax who signed at the Fourth Council, and whether the appointment won the approval of Braulio and Isidore is not recorded. We also hear of the King's friendship with a Toledan priest called Gerontius, who, relying on the King's favour, was able to oppose and even to display some contempt for his metropolitan, Justus (633–6); but Heaven, we are told, was able to punish him suitably.[3]

There is no reason to think that the news ever reached Sisenand—nor would he have been interested by it—that on Monday, 7 June 632, Mahomet had died at Medina.

2. *Chintila and Tulga*

The new procedure for choosing a king was put to the test when Sisenand died, but we do not know how Chintila reached the throne. In fact, of all the remaining kings of the seventh century Wamba alone was properly elected by the nobility and the bishops in accordance with the ruling of the Fourth Council. Chintila gets a passing notice in one or two late chronicles, but practically all that we know of him is derived from the acts of the Fifth and Sixth Councils of Toledo, which met in his reign.

He was no sooner seated on the throne than he summoned another Council of the Church, for the bishops assembled in the Church of St. Leocadia at Toledo and had finished their deliberations by 30 June 636. After the extraordinarily fruitful work of the Fourth Council it is not remarkable that they had practically

---

[1] Braulio, *Ep.* 5 *ad fin.* (PL 80. 654) = *Ep.* 4 (Lindsay).
[2] *Ep.* 6 = *Ep.* 5 (Lindsay).
[3] Ildefonsus, *De Vir. Illustr.* praef. 5 (PL 96. 197).

no ecclesiastical business to discuss, and all the canons except one (which instituted three days of litanies beginning on 13 December each year) deal with the King's safety and with the question of the succession to the throne. In them we can detect that same note, though it is now more shrill, of alarm and insecurity to which the Fourth Council had testified two and a half years earlier. It is evident that, although he may have been the choice of the courtiers and the bishops, Chintila felt himself to be acutely menaced from the moment of his accession.

Attended by his optimates and the *seniores* (p. 253 below) of his palace he opened the Council in person and commended himself to the bishops' prayers and obliged his *fideles* (p. 252 below) to do likewise. As though mere repetition of the anathemas would solve the problem of usurpation it was enacted that canon 75 of the Fourth Council should be read out in public at the end of every council of the Spanish Church. (It was, in fact, read out three times with great solemnity at the Sixteenth Council in 693, after Sisebert's revolt had been crushed.)[1] The King's first aim now was to protect his descendants. They were to enjoy all the goods that they had justly acquired or that their parents had provided for them: anyone who molested them or injured them in the future would be anathema.[2] Moreover, any loyal *fidelis* of the king would remain in the enjoyment of his property when the king died. He would also be allowed to retain the presents given him by the late king.[3] The problem of usurpation was also considered directly. Excommunication was the penalty of those who inquired of soothsayers concerning the fate of the king or who cursed the king or who should form a party to support another with a view to making him king.[4] Anyone aiming at the throne without being duly elected 'by all' and without noble Gothic birth was excommunicated and anathematized. This is a 'new cure' for a 'new sickness'; for the bishops explicitly asserted that men 'whose origin is no ornament' and 'whose virtue is no adornment' thought that they could indiscriminately ascend the throne.[5] Finally, the King published a statement confirming the Council's decisions, which now had the backing of the State power.

The bishops clearly imply that one or more than one Hispano-Roman of humble birth had aimed at the throne in the last year or

[1] V Tolet. 7; XVI Tolet. 10. [2] V Tolet. 2. [3] Ibid. 6.
[4] Ibid. 4, 5. [5] Ibid. 3.

two of Sisenand's reign or perhaps in the spring of 636; and their words suggest that this was a new phenomenon. The Fifth Council looks like a panic move by a king who at the earliest possible moment tried to protect himself, his family, and his *fideles* to the best of his feeble ability. Had there been no recent disturbance he could well have been content with the decisions of the Fourth Council, to which those of the Fifth added little except in the matter of property. Moreover, if the country had been afflicted with revolt and unrest, we could account for the fact that only twenty-four bishops signed the minutes in person or by proxy. In one striking way the Fifth Council is almost unique among the Church assemblies of seventh-century Spain: the bishops of Gallia Narbonensis were not present. The acts specifically refer to this Council as a meeting of 'bishops from the various provinces of Spain'. There is no comment and no explanation. Can it be that Septimania was in revolt (as it was later to be in Wamba's time) and that the danger which threatened Chintila came from the north? Perhaps it is no coincidence that Chintila and Wamba, alone of the seventh-century kings, minted no coins in Narbonensis.[1]

But even the Fifth Council did not satisfy the King. Only eighteen months after the bishops had dispersed, Chintila recalled them to the Sixth Council, which he does not appear to have attended in person. This time fifty-three bishops hastened to the capital, and on this occasion they referred to themselves as the 'bishops of Spain and Gaul', and three Gallic bishops (Narbonne, Elne, Lodève) were present. It was still the King's desperate hope that by repeating the relevant canons he would strengthen his position on the tottering throne and protect his doomed descendants. On 9 January 638 the bishops once again crowded into the Church of St. Leocadia, and once again they discussed the familiar themes. They re-enacted their previous decisions that the children of Chintila should continue after his death in the enjoyment of their wealth and that no one should injure them;[2] that no one should unjustly take their property or their office from the king's *fideles* unless they had been disloyal;[3] that no one, whether cleric or layman, should form a party to set up a new king: anyone who had already joined such a plot would be pardoned if

---

[1] Miles, p. 76. I ignore the brief reigns of Liuva II, Gundemar, and Reccared II.
[2] VI Tolet. 16.   [3] Ibid. 14.

he were to betray it to the king. Again, when the king died, no one was to usurp the throne, and no one might become king who was tonsured or decalvated or of servile origin or who belonged to a foreign race. Only a Goth might succeed to the throne.[1] The Council dealt with men—and they were many—who, having been guilty of wrongdoing, took refuge among the enemy, gave them military aid, and so brought loss and damage to Spain. Such men, if they fell into the king's hands, were to be excommunicated. (It is lamentable that the bishops give no hint at the identity of the foreign enemy whom they have in mind.)[2] A solemn imprecation was called down upon those who might attack the king, dethrone him, usurp his position, or gather a band of conspirators against him. And the successor of a murdered king together with the entire Gothic people would be dishonoured above all other peoples of the earth if they did not punish the regicide as they would avenge the murderer of their own father.[3]

That the cause of these frenzied repetitions was the outbreak of one or more rebellions against the throne is not a matter of conjecture: the revolts of Chintila's reign are mentioned in later times. In a law published in 642, less than two years after Chintila's death, King Chindasuinth, himself an old plotter and a hardened conspirator, refers to the problem of those who came to be called *refugae*, that is, men who went to foreign powers with a view to launching attacks on Spain from abroad. He goes on to lay down penalties upon all such men who had gone abroad *from the time of Chintila*.[4] There also survives a letter written about 652 by Fructuosus, later Metropolitan of Braga. Fructuosus addresses King Reccesuinth and his bishops and asks them once again—for he had evidently asked in vain before—to pardon those imprisoned since Chintila's time.[5] Finally, as much as forty years after Chintila's day, in the reign of Erwig, persons were still alive who had been disgraced in the time of Chintila; and in 683 they were at last pardoned.[6] Chintila's bishops, then, were not

---

[1] Ibid. 17.   [2] Ibid. 12.   [3] Ibid. 18.

[4] *LV* ii. 1. 8 (p. 54), 'ex tempore reverende memorie Chintilani principis'.

[5] *Epist. Wisig.* 19 (pp. 688 f.), with W. Gundlach, *NA* xvi (1891), pp. 45 f. In his edition of the *Epist. Wisig.*, p. 688, crit. n., Gundlach takes the phrase *de tempore domni Scindani* to refer to Sisenand; but K. Zeumer, *NA* xxiv (1899), p. 66 n. 1, shows that Chintila (read *Scindilani*) is meant.

[6] XIII Tolet. 1, 'qui ex tempore divae memoriae Chintilani regis simili hucusque infamationis nota respersi sunt'.

legislating for hypothetical situations that might or might not arise in the future. They were concerned with an alarming situation which already existed in the present.

One rebellion in the reign of Chintila may have broken out in the province of Galicia, where in due course Fructuosus became interested in the fate of the survivors. On other occasions the rebels had received help from abroad, though whether this help came from the Byzantines in Africa and the Balearics, or from the Franks or the Basques, we have no means of saying. Further, Chindasuinth and his bishops later on were clearly troubled not by a single revolt but by a series of outbreaks. Their language constantly suggests that rebellion supported from abroad was a phenomenon that occurred repeatedly. The revolts had led to heavy fighting, and Spain had been gravely damaged. And, finally, one or more Hispano-Romans, who did not belong to the Roman aristocracy, had tried to win the throne.

It is remarkable that Chintila should have seen fit to summon two national councils in the space of eighteen months. It looks as though the problems that he tried to solve in June 636 were shown before January 638 to be calling still for solution. And, in view of the very strong language with which the bishops over and over again condemned usurpation, it may seem not unreasonable to suppose that one or more rebellions assisted by a foreign power had broken out both in the spring of 636 and during the course of 637. More we cannot say.

At the Sixth Council the bishops found time to deal with other matters than the King's safety. While they were still in session, a deacon named Turninus arrived from Rome carrying a letter (now lost) from Pope Honorius I. In this letter—the first papal letter known to have reached Spain since Gregory the Great had died in 604—Honorius urged the Spanish bishops to be more robust in the faith and to show more alacrity in crushing the 'unbelievers', by which term he meant the Jews. Perhaps he had heard belatedly of conditions under Suinthila, who had not enforced the anti-Jewish legislation of Sisebut.[1] The Pope even went so far as to say of the Spanish bishops that 'They are all dumb dogs: they cannot bark', a quotation which he ascribed to Ezekiel.

The Spanish bishops entrusted their reply to the pen of Braulio, Bishop of Saragossa (631–51); and his answer to the Pope still

[1] So Lynch, p. 134.

survives. He fully recognizes the primacy of the bishop of Rome
(*Romanus princeps*). He agrees that it is entirely right for the Pope
to show a holy solicitude for all the Churches and to cleanse the
house of God of those who do not believe. What the Pope
proposed had long been in the mind of King Chintila: the
coincidence that both Pope and King, though separated by so
many lands and seas, had conceived the same plan simultaneously
shows that it was divinely inspired. But the Spanish bishops had
not been forgetful of their duty. They were proceeding slowly on
purpose, not because of negligence or fear: they were subduing
the native hardness of the Jews by constant preaching. The
criticisms that Honorius had made of them were unfair. The
words of Isaiah 56: 10 about 'dumb dogs'—the Pope had gone
wrong in attributing them to Ezekiel—could not in fact apply to
the bishops of Spain. In support of their argument they were now
sending to Honorius the acts of their Council together with
canons 57–66 of the Fourth Council. Braulio then passed over to
the offensive. The Pope must not be misled by false rumours: the
bishops of Spain had not been deceived by the report, which had
reached them, that the venerable prince of Rome had himself
allowed baptized Jews to revert to their old superstition. They
would therefore urge the Pope to press on—to press on and to
bring into the bosom of Mother Church the enemies of the Cross
of Christ. After asking for Honorius's prayers, Braulio ends
solemnly by saying that men guilty of any crime whatsoever
should not be struck with so severe a punishment as the Pope had
suggested: such a penalty was supported neither by the canons of
our ancestors nor by the pages of the New Testament. Evidently
Honorius had suggested a treatment for the Jews at which even
the Spanish bishops blenched.[1]

Braulio has often been admired for the sturdy independence of
this composition. But, of course, it is the letter of one persecutor
to another. On the fundamental issue of penalizing the Jews there
is no difference of opinion between the Pope and the bishops of
Spain. The question is simply one of the degree of rigour with

[1] Braulio, *Ep* 21 (*PL* 80. 667–70); better text in F. Dahn, *Die Könige der Germanen*,
vi² (Leipzig, 1885), pp. 641–4, with commentary, ibid. 644–50. For further discussion with bibliography see Lynch, pp. 55 f., 100 f., 131 ff., 145–7. On Braulio's
eminence at the councils see Contin. Isid. Hisp. 20, 22 (ii. 340). Braulio himself is
not above false ascriptions: in *Ep.* 11 (*PL* 80. 658) he misquotes Horace, *Ars Poet.*
21 f. and ascribes the lines to Terence!

which the persecution is to be enforced and its victims coerced. The acts of the Council, of which they sent a copy to Honorius, included one canon relating to the Jews. In it the bishops applauded Chintila's desire to eradicate the Jewish superstition completely and to permit no non-Catholic to live in the kingdom. This is an innovation in the history of Western Europe. Nothing like it had been known in the Western Roman Empire or in the Arian kingdom of Spain. Even Sisebut had not gone so far. The new policy clearly originated with Chintila, not with the bishops. But now the bishops joined with all the optimates and 'illustrious men' in declaring that all future kings before ascending the throne must swear an oath that they would not allow the Jews to violate the Catholic faith and would not be led by indifference or bribes to show favour to the unbelievers. Any who acted otherwise would be *anathema maranatha* in the sight of the Everlasting God and would become fuel for the Eternal Fire. The Spanish bishops ended by confirming the anti-Jewish enactments of the Fourth Council.[1]

The King did not confine himself to words. An enforced profession of faith, known as a *placitum*,[2] still survives from his reign and is the oldest formula of abjuration for Jews. It was signed by the baptized—that is, the forcibly baptized—Jews of the capital on 1 December 638 in the Church of St. Leocadia, the church that had echoed to the devout sentiments of the Fourth, Fifth, and Sixth Councils. In this document the Jews renounced their former beliefs and undertook to abandon the Jewish rite and festivals, the Sabbath and circumcision and their dietary rules. They proposed to surrender to the authorities all Scriptures used in the synagogues together with the Mishnah;[3] and they promised to stone to death anyone of their number who should deviate in the slightest degree from the Catholic faith.[4] This *placitum* flagrantly contradicted the ruling of the Fourth Council that Sisebut's policy of forcible conversion should be abandoned. But

---

[1] VI Tolet. 3.

[2] Cf. Isidore, *Etym.* v. 24. 19, 'alii dicunt pactum esse quod volens quisque facit; placitum vero etiam nolens compellitur', etc. The other Visigothic formulae of abjuration are those of 654 and 681: *LV* xii. 2. 17; 3. 14–15.

[3] *Deuterosis*: Katz, p. 71.

[4] I have read the text as printed in Dahn, op. cit., pp. 650–3. Zeumer does not seem to have known it. For literature on this *placitum* see Katz, p. 14 n. 7; Lynch, p. 130 n. 25.

Chintila had gone far beyond the position of Sisebut and far beyond all the laws and canons.

From time to time he would recommend men to be ordained as priests; and, although the bishops sometimes found his nominees embarrassing, they dared not disregard the royal commendation. Shortly after the poet Eugenius II reached Toledo in 646 to take up the office of metropolitan he was confronted with the case of a priest who had been ordained by his predecessor Eugenius I (636–46) on Chintila's orders. Eugenius I had believed the man to be unsuitable for ordination but had not had the courage to disobey openly the King's instructions. Accordingly, he had stooped to a curious device. He 'led him to the altar, he did not lay his hand upon him, and while the clergy were singing aloud he poured forth a malediction in place of a benediction, as he himself afterwards admitted to friends of his whose testimony can be believed, conjuring them to be silent about this as long as he was alive'.[1] Eugenius II raised with Braulio the question whether this man had been truly ordained and whether sacraments administered by him were valid. St. Braulio, whose theology in this matter has been found defective, answered affirmatively to both questions.

Eugenius I was also unlucky with his deacon Lucidius, who had powerful friends. Relying on these friends he was able to compel the Metropolitan to ordain him as priest and to extort a number of estates from him; and there is no record that Eugenius or his successor was able to bring him to book.[2]

Chintila survived until December 640, when he died a natural death, having already nominated his son Tulga to succeed him. This was a glaring breach of the procedure laid down by the Fourth Council for selecting a king (p. 174 above). Tulga was still of tender years, and Chintila evidently expected that the imprecations and anathemas of the Councils would keep him safe.[2] But anathemas and *maranathas* held no terrors for Chindasuinth.

The dozen years that ended with Chindasuinth's deposition of Tulga in 642 saw at least five major revolts against the throne. Those of Sisenand and Chindasuinth resulted in victory for the

---

[1] Braulio, *Epp.* 35 f., of which the best text is that in Vollmer's edn. of Eugenius of Toledo, pp. 283 ff.; cf. Séjourné, pp. 192 ff., Lynch, pp. 88 f. But Grosse, p. 302 thinks that the king in question is Chindasuinth.

[2] Ildefonsus, *De Vir. Illustr.* praef. 6 (*PL* 96. 197 f.)

[3] For the dedication of a veil by Chintila at Rome see Vives, 389.

rebels. That of Iudila was crushed, but it involved an extensive area of southern Spain, and it lasted long enough to allow Iudila to issue coins in his own name. The two or more rebellions that broke out in Chintila's reign were sufficiently serious to cause that king to summon the almost wholly unnecessary Fifth and Sixth Councils of Toledo. The revolt of Sisenand and those of Chintila's reign were supported from abroad, and apparently Iudila's was, too.

Now, these rebellions differed in one important respect from the insurrections of Athanagild's reign in the previous century (p. 63 above). The sixth-century revolts had been led by men who aimed to free their part of Spain from the control of Toledo. Their purpose was to set up local independent states in various regions of the peninsula. But the rebellions of the fourth decade of the seventh century had no such aim, so far as we know. They were directed solely against the person of the monarch. The purpose of the rebels was not to break the kingdom into a number of independent fragments but to replace the existing monarch by another of their own choice. Spain was now accepted as a unit, it seems, and the disputes centred on the question of who was to rule it. Leovigild had not fought in vain.

There is no means of saying whether the conflicts were caused by differences of policy or whether they were due simply to personal rivalries among the Gothic nobility. The repeated conspiracies against Chintila and Chindasuinth have been taken to mean that the Gothic nobility opposed, not simply these two individual kings, but a strong monarchy as such.[1] There is no hint in the sources, however, of such a purpose; and the successful usurpers, Sisenand and Chindasuinth, introduced no new principle of government. They did indeed try to make usurpation more difficult in the future; but they did not alter the character of the monarchy or of the society over which they ruled, though Chindasuinth planned to do so. Sisenand's attitude towards the Jews was certainly different from that of Suinthila; and Chindasuinth's view of the Jews differed from that of Sisenand and Chintila. But it will hardly be thought that the storms of these years centred on the position and liberties of the Jews in Spain. It is safest to think that the conspiracies were the outcome of the rival ambitions of different Gothic noblemen.

[1] e.g. Zeumer, *NA* xxiv (1899), p. 58.

Another novelty in the seventh century was that some of the Hispano-Romans now aimed at the throne of Spain. The language used by the bishops at the Fifth and Sixth Councils of Toledo suggests that men who were not Goths had tried to become king; and it was thought necessary to prohibit any such attempts.[1] (It is a calamity that the aims of the Roman rebels have not been preserved.) But apart from these hints there is not a single piece of evidence to indicate that Gothic and Roman nobles were divided on any major question of policy, a fact which will present us with a puzzle later on.

No Spanish document of the time records that in 638, the year of the Sixth Council, Jerusalem capitulated to the Arabs.

---

[1] V Tolet. 3, 'nec Gothicae gentis nobilitas', etc.; VI Tolet. 17, 'nisi genere Gothus', etc.

IX · REBELLION AND REFORM

PART from the short chapter about him in the Frankish writer Fredegar (p. 170 above), we know of Chindasuinth and his son Reccesuinth from the minutes of the Toledan Councils that met in this period (642–72), though in the last sixteen years of Reccesuinth no general council met at all. But ninety-nine laws of Chindasuinth and eighty-seven laws of Reccesuinth are included in the law code that the former planned and the latter published. A majority of these laws are concerned with the sort of suit that arose from time to time in the courts; but a few of them have a wider interest.

1. *Chindasuinth*

Fredegar observes that the Gothic race becomes restless when it has not a strong yoke upon its back; and, true to custom, the turbulence that characterized Chintila's reign continued under Tulga. Eventually, one of the nobles, a vigorous man some 79 years old, called Chindasuinth, gathered together at a place called Pampilica (perhaps Pampliega near Burgos) several of the 'senators' of the Goths and a number of the people; and in defiance of so many episcopal imprecations he proclaimed himself king.[1] In April 642—the year in which the Arabs first occupied Alexandria —he dethroned Tulga and tonsured him, thus making him ineligible under canon 17 of the Sixth Council to rule over Spain.

Chindasuinth was well aware of the 'Gothic disease', as our authority calls the propensity of the Goths to dethrone their kings, for he had often been involved in conspiracies himself. He therefore somewhat callously ordered the death of all whom he knew to have conspired against earlier kings. Others he exiled and heartlessly gave their wives, daughters, and property to his faithful followers. The slaughter and the confiscation of property went on through much of his reign. No fewer than 200 Gothic optimates and 500 *mediogres* (as Fredegar calls them) were put to

[1] *Chron. Min.* ii. 260 *fin.* For the identification see E. Ewig, 'Résidence et capitale pendant le Haut Moyen Age', *Revue historique*, ccxxx (1963), pp. 25–72, at p. 32.

death. It was said that 'he demolished the Goths'.[1] A coin of his
that was minted at Merida, the capital of Lusitania, with the
legend VICTOR, has been taken to imply a military success in that
region;[2] and if that is a correct interpretation Chindasuinth
actually undertook a military campaign against some of his rivals
in that province. In the upshot, as a late author says, 'Spain was
quiet in his time'.[3]

The bishops cannot well have complained of Chindasuinth's
ruthless slaughter of former conspirators; for at the Sixth Council
they had themselves called upon each future king to put to death
the murderers of his predecessor as though he were avenging the
death of his own father (p. 183 above). In the second year of his
reign the King published his great law against treason which
gave him the power and the duty to proceed harshly against
conspirators and rebels. In it he stressed the frequency of the
disasters caused by _émigrés_ (_profugi_): the State was obliged to
take up arms against them more often than against foreign
enemies. The aim of the law was to put a stop to all such activities
and to punish those who had been guilty of them in the past.
Chindasuinth declared, therefore, that anyone who from the
time of Chintila had gone, or who would in the future go, to a
foreign power, or who had even wished to do so, in order to
incite that power against the Goths, would be put to death.
Death was also the penalty for anyone who raised opposition to
the throne inside the kingdom. Intention to act was as grave an
offence as the act itself. If the king were to decide to spare the
life of such a person, then the criminal would be blinded 'so
that he may not see the destruction in which he had wickedly
delighted'. In either case all his property would be confiscated by
the Treasury. And, if the Treasury should present some of it to
any individual, that individual would possess it for ever, and no
future sovereign would have the right to take it back from him.
If the king in his mercy should restore some possessions to a
man who had been found guilty under this law, it would be
illegal for him to restore more than one twentieth part of the
total; and what he did bestow upon the culprit would not be

[1] Fredegar, iv. 82; Contin. Isid. Hisp. 26 (ii. 341). In the _Iudicium_ added to the
minutes of the Eighth Council the bishops write: 'ecce etenim ita ex gentis nostrae
mediocribus maioribusque personis multos hactenus conruisse reperimus et de-
flemus', etc.

[2] Miles, p. 31.   [3] _Epit. Ovet._ 16 (ii. 374).

property that he had previously owned: it would come from some other source. But 'many' men, before engaging in treason, made over their property to their church or to their wives, sons, or friends so as to prevent confiscation and in the hope of one day recovering it. All such fraudulent gifts were now void: the Treasury would take all.[1] Now, Goths, like Romans (p. 125 above), were permitted to 'supplicate' the king for pardon for their crimes; but in another law Chindasuinth abolished this right in cases of treason. And, if the king even so felt pity, he would be unable to grant a pardon unless the bishops and the *maiores palatii* (p. 253 below) should give their consent.[2]

The law on treason was made retrospective to Chintila's time in the case of those rebels who had sought help from abroad, the *refugae*. (If he had not put a limit at Chintila's reign, he would have ensnared those surviving nobles who had supported Sisenand.) In the case of those who had conspired inside the kingdom the law was retrospective only to the date of his own accession. Chindasuinth himself had often been guilty of conspiracy, and he had no wish to find himself punishable under his own law!

He next went on to ensure that his law would be enforced. He obliged the whole people, or at any rate the leading circles of the people, to swear an oath that they would carry out its terms and that they would never pardon traitors.[3] When exactly the King required his grandees to swear this oath is not clear; but it was called for because of certain events that are mentioned in general terms by the bishops who met at the Eighth Council of Toledo in 653.[4] An uprising of *refugae*, said the bishops, had often brought about devastation and destruction. Hosts of captives had been led away, and lands had been left desolate. It was this revolt that had called forth the oath; but no details are known about it except that it was aided from abroad.

---

[1] *LV* ii. 1. 8, with Zeumer, *NA* xxiv (1899), pp. 57–67. For a case where the law was applied see p. 225 below. On the Visigothic laws of treason see F. S. Lear, *Treason in Roman and Germanic Law* (University of Texas Press: Austin, 1965), esp. pp. 136 ff.

[2] *LV* vi. 1. 7.

[3] VII Tolet. praef., where the bishops say that the oath had been sworn by 'omnes pene Hispaniae sacerdotes omnesque seniores vel iudices ac ceteros homines officii palatini'; but according to Reccesuinth in his *tomus* to VIII Toledo (Zeumer, p. 473. 29) 'vos omnemque populum iurasse recolimus', etc. See Zeumer, art. cit. 62.

[4] Mansi, x. 1211 C.

Such legislation might have been expected to lead to a swarm of unfounded and vexatious accusations. Chindasuinth therefore passed a further law in which he dealt with those who brought accusations of treason or of other major crimes—forging or tampering with royal documents, counterfeiting, poisoning, magic, adultery—crimes, that is, which carried a penalty of death or confiscation of property. If it turned out that such accusations were baseless and malicious, the accuser was handed over to the accused to suffer the penalty which he had hoped to inflict by his false accusation.[1]

Unlike Sisenand and Chintila, the new king was in no hurry to call a general council of the Church, for he was well able to look after himself without the aid of the bishops' futile fulminations against usurpers. But he eventually had his treason law confirmed, and the penalties for traitorous clerics defined, at the Seventh Council of Toledo, which he summoned to meet in 646. He does not seem to have been present at it himself, and only forty-one bishops attended in person or by proxy. They echoed the words of the law. They recalled that everyone knew the damage that had been done by usurpers and *refugae*, and how these men had imposed endless toil on the Gothic armies. This might perhaps be tolerable if done from time to time by laymen; but—what was far worse—the clergy also frequently engaged in these activities. Henceforth, any cleric from the highest rank to the lowest who went to a foreign country for any purpose whatever, or who acted or planned to act in such a way as to damage the Gothic race and king, or who was an accomplice of such a man, would be instantly deprived of his rank and made a penitent for ever and would be given Holy Communion only at the end of his life. If any priest should administer Holy Communion to such a person, *even when the king ordered him to do so*, he would be anathema for ever and would be subject to the same penalties as the man to whom he administered it. In this matter no priest must obey the king, for a king might arise in the future who would be hostile to the Catholic faith. The bishops then confirmed the King's ruling that a guilty man's property should go to the Treasury: if a king should wish to waive his right of confiscation, he should not be allowed to concede to the traitor more than the value of one twentieth part of his goods.[2]

---

[1] *LV* vi. 1. 6.   [2] VII Tolet. praef.

The bishops returned to the matter in their first canon. When a layman successfully rebelled inside the kingdom and established himself as king, any bishop or priest who aided him would be excommunicated (and the bishops stressed the large number of clerics who had forgotten their oath of allegiance). But, if the wicked usurper, having succeeded in reaching the throne, prevented this punishment from being inflicted, then such a priest would be subject to the punishment as soon as the usurper died. As for laymen who collaborated with foreign powers against the interests of the kingdom, they would be deprived of all their goods and excommunicated. The Council begged the King never to suspend the sentence of excommunication on traitorous clergy and laymen unless the bishops should ask him to do so; and they ended by declaring that if any future king should upset these rulings he would be guilty in the eyes of God of betraying the Catholic faith.[1]

There is some reason for thinking that Chindasuinth's legislation was rigorously enforced. Shortly before the year 656 no less a person than St. Fructuosus, then Bishop of Dumium, the greatest monastic founder of seventh-century Spain, formed a secret plan to visit the Orient. He had not the King's permission to leave the country, so his project was illegal. His plan was known only to a few chosen disciples, but one of them betrayed it, and the Saint was instantly arrested and gaoled. He had made himself liable to the severe penalties laid down by Chindasuinth and his bishops and ran the risk of being excommunicated. But in fact he not only was spared but was shortly afterwards (in 656) translated to the metropolitan see of Braga.[2] What is noteworthy in the incident is the promptness with which he was arrested.

The King did not live to complete what might have been his permanent achievement, the revision of Leovigild's law code. He formed the plan of revising it and evidently began a large-scale programme of legislation with this end in view, for his son was eventually able to include in the new code no fewer than ninety-nine of his laws. The old King, apart from issuing new laws, had also begun the task of revising the laws in Leovigild's code; and there still exists a law in the code of Reccesuinth that is described

---

[1] VII Tolet. canon 1.

[2] Vita S. Fructuosi, 17 (ed. Sister Frances Nock, Diss. Washington, 1946). The passage is discussed in Hermathena, xc (1957), pp. 58–63.

as '*antiqua* but revised by Chindasuinth'.[1] In his own legislation
Chindasuinth sometimes took over old Roman enactments and
sometimes brought old Gothic laws up to date.[2] There is reason
for thinking, too, that the plan to abolish Roman law and to
oblige all the inhabitants of the kingdom to live under Visigothic
law originated, not with Reccesuinth, but with his father. He
began to work on his great scheme in the second year of the
reign, but it was only completed twelve or more years later by
Reccesuinth, who for carrying out his father's plan has been
called the 'Visigothic Justinian'.

In his dealings with the Church Chindasuinth showed the
strength which he also displayed in dealing with the nobility.
Just as Sisebut had appointed a bishop of Barcelona (p. 163 above)
and as Sisenand appointed Audax to Tarragona in 633 (p. 180
above), so Chindasuinth kept in his own hands appointments to
at least the metropolitan sees. In 646 Braulio of Saragossa wrote
to him begging him not to transfer his archdeacon Eugenius to
the metropolitan see of Toledo, where Bishop Eugenius I had
just died. Braulio was nearly blind, and without the help of his
archdeacon he would be unable to administer his diocese.[3] The
King replied courteously but firmly, stating that Eugenius would
be appointed to the royal see; and Braulio submitted sadly
though with good grace. The eminent poet occupied the see
until his death in 657.[4]

Chindasuinth's strong position over against the Church showed
itself in other matters besides the appointment of bishops. With
a couple of exceptions his laws include no appeals to the Divine
Power and none of those pious platitudes and religious sanctions
that had been so dear to Reccared and Sisebut, though not to
Leovigild.[5] His position is also illustrated by his law on certain
cases of contempt of court. If a layman who was defendant in a
suit showed contempt by not appearing before the judge after

---

[1] *LV* ix. 1. 17.

[2] On the origins of his laws see Zeumer, *NA* xxiii (1898), pp. 483 f.; and for the
question of Chindasuinth's projected revision of the entire code, ibid. pp. 511–16.
The evidence is in *LV* ii. 1. 5.

[3] Braulio, *Ep.* 31 (*PL* 80. 677 f.), where note 'sic . . . semen tuum regnum
possideat tuum': I do not know whether Lynch, p. 80, is right in saying that these
words are 'almost a threat'. On Eugenius II of Toledo see Vollmer's edn. of his
works in the MGH, and Lynch, pp. 56 ff.; but there is no reason to think that he was
of Gothic descent.

[4] Braulio, *Ep.* 32 f.   [5] The exceptions are *LV* iii. 5. 3; iv. 2. 19.

being duly summoned, he had to pay 5 solidi to the plaintiff for causing delay and 5 solidi to the judge for contempt; and if he lacked the means to pay he received fifty lashes of the whip. But if a bishop failed to appear or to send a representative he was liable to be forced by the judge or by the *dux* of the province and the *comes* of the city (both of them Gothic, not Roman, officials) to pay a fine of no less than 20 solidi to the judge and 30 solidi to the plaintiff. If a priest, deacon, subdeacon, or other cleric or a monk were guilty, he was to receive the same punishment as a layman, except that, if he could not pay, the bishop was liable on his behalf.[1] This was one of the few cases where the kings imposed a monetary sanction on the bishops.

He also interfered with the churches' right to give sanctuary to criminals. In future there must be no escape for persons found guilty of homicide or magical practices. If such a man should escape to a church, the pursuer must consult with the bishop and swear an oath not to put the fugitive to death. The bishop was then obliged willy nilly to deliver him up, and the fugitive was to be blinded. No other Visigothic king is known to have restricted the churches in such a manner.[2] The documents give no explanation of the curious ruling at the end of the minutes of the Seventh Council which obliged the bishops of the sees near Toledo to spend one month each year, though not the months of harvest or vintage, in the capital 'for reverence of the king', for the 'honour of the royal see', and for the 'consolation' of the metropolitan.[3] Was this canon agreed for political or for ecclesiastical reasons? Were the bishops to act as some sort of advisory council? Or did Chindasuinth simply wish to keep an eye on them? At all events, the ruling is never heard of again.

Chindasuinth showed no enthusiasm for persecuting the Jews. He passed no new laws against them, and we do not know what his attitude would have been towards the anti-Jewish legislation of his predecessors if he had lived to publish his code. But he acted vigorously against Christians who practised Jewish rites, especially that of circumcision, and condemned them to death.[4] His aim was to prevent proselytism, and it is remarkable that

---

[1] *LV* ii. 1. 19, with further refinements.
[2] Ibid. vi. 5. 16. According to VI Tolet. 12, if *refugae* fled to a church, 'regia in eis pietas reservetur comitante iustitia', a diplomatic phrase.
[3] VII Tolet. 6. [4] *LV* xii. 2. 16.

even at this date, after the furious intolerance of Sisebut, Sisenand, and Chintila, Christians were still prepared to attach themselves to Judaism. The Seventh Council is almost unique among the plenary councils of the century in inflicting no new hardships on the Jews. On the other hand, Chindasuinth tried hard to suppress magical practices (p. 308 below).

He gave much attention to the position of slaves (pp. 269 f. below), and he also showed some care for the humbler of his subjects who came before the courts. He acted against judges who fraudulently delayed to hear suits because of their friendship with the defendants. He warned them to be no respecters of persons; and, although a rich witness was more likely, he thought, to be reliable than a poor one, he urged the judges to moderate somewhat the severity of the law when dealing with poor persons.[1] He prescribed the manner in which the judge must deliver his judgement, and he considered the problem of legal costs, which King Theudis had dealt with long ago. Chindasuinth found that in civil actions his judges were taking one-third of the value of the disputed article in return for hearing the case: he reduced this amount to 5 per cent, and the *saiones* (p. 13 above) might now take no more than 10 per cent.[2] But his practice may have been less attractive than his theory; for after he was dead Reccesuinth found it necessary to publish a law that granted immunity to all judges who had delivered corrupt or illegal judgements at the King's order or in fear of the King.[3]

In 648 a letter was addressed to Chindasuinth by Braulio of Saragossa and Eutropius, bishop of an unknown see,[4] along with their priests, deacons, and all the faithful of their dioceses, together with one Celsus, who may have been *dux* of the province of Tarraconensis. In flagrant defiance of canon 75 of the Fourth Council, which Braulio himself had signed, the writers urged the aged King to associate his son Reccesuinth with him on the throne while he himself was still alive and in good health. They recalled the dangers and hostile attacks to which the country had been exposed, and respectfully pointed out that the younger man would be able 'to bear the sweat of wars' and give refreshment to his father until 'the attacks and tumult of enemies' had died

---

[1] Ibid. xii. 1. 1; ii. 1. 24, 'ac praesertim pauper'; ii. 1. 20; cf. 22. Note ii. 4. 3 *fin.* on rich and poor witnesses. For Chindasuinth on perjury in the courts see ii. 4. 6, 9.
[2] Ibid. ii. 1. 25 f.   [3] Ibid. 29.   [4] On him see Lynch, pp. 65 ff.

down. There is no hint in the letter that Reccesuinth would be able to relieve his father of the burdens of administration: the whole emphasis is upon the military duties that the son would be able to shoulder.[1] The letter implies not only that warfare had hitherto been extensive but also that it was still going on. It looks as though Chindasuinth had indeed massacred his rivals ruthlessly but was still even in 648 faced with enemies from without. But who were they? The writers of the letter give no hint of their identity or of their nationality or social class or even whether they were foreigners at all. The Basques had certainly been troubling the kingdom at the beginning of the reign; and there still exists the tombstone of Oppila, a nobleman of Villafranca de Cordoba, who was called up to fight them. He was cut off from his companions and killed in the course of a battle or skirmish on 12 September 642. His *clientes* rescued the body, carried it home, and buried it on 10 October.[2] Braulio and his fellow writers imply that life at Saragossa had not been without its dangers; and it is not out of the question that the Basques, as they had often done before, had come down into the neighbourhood of the city. Braulio also mentions in a letter written in the years 640–6 that men of Saragossa were afraid to travel to the Bishop of Valencia because of the brigands who beset the roads.[3] However that may be, it is not likely that the idea of co-opting Reccesuinth had originated with the bishops. The Eighth Council of Toledo, which met as soon as Chindasuinth was dead, reaffirmed the elective principle without any reference to Braulio's letter.[4] And probably the idea of crowning Reccesuinth was put forward by Braulio and his friends because they already knew that it would be acceptable to the old monarch. But it cannot be argued on that account that Braulio suggested a defiance of the procedure laid down by the Fourth Council for electing a new king simply because Chindasuinth ordered him to do so. There is no evidence that the King ordered him; and in cases where there was no question of royal interference Braulio had himself broken the canons of the Council and had recommended his brother to do the same.[5]

---

[1] Braulio, *Ep.* 37 (*PL* 80. 684 f.)

[2] Vives, 287. Oppila was aged 46, not 27.

[3] Braulio, *Ep.* 24 (*PL* 80. 673), 'quoniam regionis nostrae homines pergere illuc pavent ob latrones'.

[4] VIII Tolet. 10.   [5] Braulio, *Ep.* 14, 17.

Fructuosus. What he had wanted was the pardon of men who had been exiled and presumably left without property; and such cases were not affected by the bishops' new ruling.

What is most curious is that after the crushing of Froia's revolt neither kings nor bishops ever again referred to the problem of the *refugae*. In our documents these *émigrés* first make their appearance in the acts of Chintila's second Council, though Sisenand might have been called a *refuga* in 631. Much is said of them in Chindasuinth's reign and in the early years of Reccesuinth, though no clue is given to their character or to the identity of the foreign power or powers to whom they appealed for help. But now they disappear from the documents as mysteriously and abruptly as they had entered them.

By 653 Reccesuinth had made good progress with the revision of Leovigild's law code, which his father had begun. Braulio had written a letter to him sometime in the period 649–51 in which he spoke of a huge codex that the King had sent him to correct. This codex seems to have contained the text of the new code. The Bishop dwells upon the vastness of the task that the King had laid upon him. The number of necessary corrections and alterations was so enormous that he often despaired of being able to complete his work: there was scarcely a sentence that did not call for correction. He had often put the work aside but had always returned to it, adding lines here and removing words there.[1] In another letter Reccesuinth encourages him to persevere with the interminable labour; and at last Braulio is able to announce the end of his work and says that he 'divided the text of the codex into titles, as you ordered'. In a final letter the King thanks him for his work and asks for his prayers.[2] Unhappily, there is no means of identifying Braulio's personal part in the completed text of the code.

But even now Reccesuinth was not satisfied. In his opening speech to the Eighth Council he invited the bishops to review the laws and to draw attention to whatever in them was wrong, obscure, or superfluous. Presumably, this was the final stage in the preparation of the code, which cannot have been published very much later. When it appeared, Reccesuinth declared that he

[1] Braulio, *Ep.* 10 (PL 80. 685): the letter has survived incomplete. On the episode see Lynch, pp. 135–40.
[2] Braulio, *Ep.* 39–41.

published it 'presiding upon the judicial throne before all the holy bishops and all the palatine officials', who together with God approved the work.[1] His own new laws contain many scriptural quotations, religious sanctions, pious and grandiose commonplaces, and bombast of numerous kinds; but through the clouds of verbiage we can detect much good law.

After placing before the bishops his proposals for modifying the oath and for confirming the law code, the King somewhat rashly went on to urge the Council to propose any other reforms that they might think desirable, and he promised in advance that he would confirm their suggestions.[2] The bishops replied quickly, and, apparently on the second day of the Council, 17 December, they presented Reccesuinth with a vigorously phrased document. That they should have agreed on the point that they wished to make to the King, and that they should have drawn up their statement of it within twenty-four hours, shows the depth of feeling and the unanimity that the matter in question aroused among them. In their statement they pointed out that the rulers of the kingdom in the past had been harsh and extortionate.[3] Certain kings had drained away the resources of the people to their own personal profit. Instead of defending the people, they had plundered them. The profits that they had won from this robbery they used not for the honour and glory of the kingdom but for the enrichment of their own children. What ought to have become Crown property had in fact become the kings' personal possession. When men were condemned in the courts and their property was confiscated, the proceeds benefited neither the Treasury nor the palatine officials.

Throughout most of their document the bishops spoke of oppressive kings in the plural, but towards the end they came boldly out into the open. They meant Chindasuinth, and they named him expressly. What they were demanding was that the property of Chindasuinth's defeated opponents—and they were many—should be distributed among the palace grandees.[4]

---

[1] LV ii. 1. 5 ad fin.

[2] Zeumer, p. 474. 26 ff. For a discussion of the incident see idem, NA xxiv (1899), pp. 45 ff.; cf. Ziegler, pp. 107 ff.

[3] For the document see Mansi, x. 1223 ff., 'Decretum in die secunda universalis concilii editum'; but the words in die secunda do not appear in Vives's text.

[4] At the Sixth Council (canon 14) the bishops had asked that the goods of disloyal fideles (p. 252 below) should be confiscated and given to other fideles.

Accordingly, all the palatine officials and all the bishops, priests, and other clergy unanimously asked that property of every kind, movable and immovable, that had been acquired in any manner by Chindasuinth from the day of his accession, should be taken over by Reccesuinth but should not be regarded as his personal property to be bequeathed to his personal heirs. What had been wrongfully confiscated should be restored to its rightful owners, and the rest should be distributed to those noblemen of the court whom the King might select. Only the property that Chinda-suinth had owned before his accession should be regarded as Reccesuinth's private property : this alone should be inherited by him and his brothers with the right to bequeath it as they pleased.[1]

Within a matter of days Reccesuinth had drawn up and had laid before the Council the text of a law on this matter. In some ways he appeared on the surface to accept the bishop's proposals, but what in fact he did was to change them into their opposite. What the prelates had suggested was wholly to the King's disadvantage. The terms of the law brought him nothing but gain.

Like the bishops he heartily condemned the 'immoderate greed of the kings in previous times', the plundering of the people that increased the kings' private wealth, and so on. But he did not recognize Chindasuinth as the villain of the piece. He declared to be Crown property all those possessions that the kings by virtue of their office had accumulated since the time of Suinthila[2] and all that would in future be amassed by them. That is to say, the property obtained by Suinthila in his later years and the whole of that accumulated by Sisenand, Chintila, and Tulga by virtue of their royal office was Crown property, not the King's personal possession. (He and his brothers had doubtless already pocketed what had been taken by Chindasuinth.) So far, so good. But Reccesuinth added one reservation. He had in mind only that part of the kings' property that they had not disposed of in their wills.[3] He thus assured himself the right to dispose of the remain-der as he wished, and he disturbed the heirs of his predecessors only when they had taken royal property that had not been

---

[1] We do not know the names of Reccesuinth's brothers. His wife, Recciberga, died at the age of 22 years and 8 months, after seven years of marriage: Eugenius, *carm.* 26. There is no mention of a son.

[2] The *praescriptio tricennalis* prevented him from going further back.

[3] *LV* ii. 1. 6 (p. 50. 21), 'quecumque forsitan princeps inordinata sive reliquid sive reliquerit'.

explicitly willed to them—and such property was doubtless extensive. He tacitly rejected the bishops' suggestion about the ways in which he should dispose of Chindasuinth's gains: in this respect he gave himself a free hand.[1] But he very naturally agreed with the bishops that any property that the king had owned before his accession should remain his personal possession; and this also was to apply to what he acquired from his relatives, as indeed Chintila's Councils had already decreed.[2] Finally, all his successors before mounting the throne should swear to observe these regulations about their predecessors' property; and, if any member of the palatine offices should so much as murmur against the provisions of this law, he would be stripped of his office, lose one half of his property, and go into exile.

The bishops showed their utter disappointment with the King's attitude by including among the minutes of the Council the text not only of the new law but also of their original proposal. Later readers of the minutes could then see how far Reccesuinth's enactment fell short of, and even contradicted, the demands of the clergy. But they were obliged to accept in full and to confirm the King's point of view.[3]

Towards the end of the same law Reccesuinth anathematized and excommunicated any who should in the future be helped to the throne by 'the rebellious plebs' or by plotting. The bishops took up this somewhat negative point and went far beyond it. At the Fifth Council they had declared vaguely that no one should ascend the throne unless he had been approved by 'the choice of all', and, more specifically, that only a Gothic nobleman could become king (p. 181 above). But now they stated that future kings must not succeed to the throne through the conspiracy of a few men or 'by a seditious uprising of the rustic plebs'. They must ascend the throne either in Toledo or at the place where the previous king had died, and must be chosen, not 'by all', but by the bishops and the *maiores palatii* (p. 253 below). The king must be a champion of the Catholic faith and must defend it against all heretics as well as against the Jews.[3] But Reccesuinth had given no such right of election to the clerical and lay aristocracy (though the Fourth Council had done so), and the circumstances of his

---

[1] *LV* ii. 1. 6 (p. 51. 2), 'ita habita potestate ut quidquid ex his helegerit facere, liberum habeat velle'.

[2] V Tolet. 2; VI Tolet. 16.   [3] VIII Tolet. 10.

own accession can hardly have made him welcome any such proposal. Were they now reminding him of a privilege that he would have been glad to see forgotten? In all, it is not a coincidence that, although he had promised in his opening speech to confirm the decisions of the Eighth Council,[1] there is no evidence that he ever did so.

He took a further step to protect himself and his dead father. At the Fifth Council the bishops had excommunicated anyone who spoke ill of the king.[2] Insults and verbal affronts were not a crime in Gothic law (though Alaric's code had punished them capitally). But they were forbidden by Exodus 22: 28, 'Thou shalt not . . . curse the ruler of thy people', a passage which the bishops quoted. In Chindasuinth's reign they had returned to the matter: they again doomed to excommunication anyone who spoke slightingly or insultingly of the monarch.[3] But it was Reccesuinth who made insults to the king a criminal offence.[4] Citing the same passage of Exodus, he enacted that if a nobleman, whether cleric or lay, were guilty of verbally insulting the king he would forfeit one half of his possessions. A humbler person would be liable to whatever penalty the king should decide to impose. It also became an offence to speak ill of a dead king; and for this the penalty was fifty lashes of the whip.

In his opening speech to the Eighth Council Reccesuinth had denounced the 'life and habits' of the Jews. The soil of his kingdom was polluted by them. God had extirpated all other heresies root and branch from this region of the world, and this sacrilegious belief alone remained. Some had always been Jews, but others—and these were more detestable and blasphemous—after being baptized, had now relapsed. He bade the bishops deal with them without favour or respect for persons.[5] The bishops accordingly enacted (though they observed that they did so 'at the most pious request of the most sacred king') that the decrees of the Fourth Council relating to the Jews should be enforced now and hereafter, 'for it is unworthy that a prince of orthodox faith should rule over the sacrilegious, and that a people of believers should be polluted by association with unbelievers'.[6] It may be

---

[1] Zeumer, p. 474. 25. Cf. Ziegler, op. cit. 111 f.   [2] V Tolet. 5.
[3] VII Tolet. 1; cf. Paul, *Sentent.* v. 29. 1.
[4] *LV* ii. 1. 9, with Zeumer, *NA* xxiv (1899), pp. 69 f.
[5] Zeumer, p. 474. 36 ff.   [6] VIII Tolet. 12.

doubted whether this was enough to satisfy the King, who had already shown them the text of his law code.

The code contains no fewer than ten laws enacted by Reccesuinth against the Jews, who were henceforth until the end of the kingdom (except perhaps in the reign of Wamba) to face a sustained and savage attack from the State, though some bishops and judges were reluctant to press it home. Reccesuinth began with a law against heresies of all kinds. Any Spaniard, or foreigner visiting Spain, who spoke against the Catholic faith or who had heretical thoughts in his heart would be exiled for ever and would suffer the confiscation of all his property.[1] As for the Jews, no baptized Jew could leave the Christian faith or assail it in word or deed, nor might he take to flight so as to escape from it, or transgress against anything written in the *placita* (p. 186 above), or hide anyone who did so. No Jew might celebrate the Passover or the Sabbath or marry by other than Christian rites. The practice of circumcision was banned. Jews might pay no regard to their dietary rules. No Jew might testify against a Christian, however humble, not even against a Christian slave, though Jews could still take legal action against one another before Christian judges. Although no Jew, whether baptized or not, could give evidence in the courts, the offspring of baptized Jews might do so provided that their honourable character and the fullness of their Christian faith showed them to be suitable; and even then the king or a bishop or judge must approve their character and faith. The penalty for breach of any of these ten laws or of any of the undertakings given in the *placita* was death by burning or by stoning at the hands of men of their own race. If the king should not insist on death, the guilty Jew would be the slave of anyone to whom the king might give him, and his property would be granted to others: he would never recover his freedom.[2] Moreover, when he abolished Roman law, Reccesuinth removed the Jews' immunity from being sued or summoned on the Sabbath; and, when Jews brought their disputes before their own clergy, the ruling no longer was held to be as binding as a verdict of the secular courts. In fact, to be a practising Jew now was a capital crime.

The King felt (not without reason, as it turned out) that some Christians would try to evade these laws. In a final enactment,

---

[1] *LV* xii. 2. 2.   [2] Ibid. 3–11.

therefore, he proceeded against any person, layman, bishop, or other cleric, who assisted unbaptized Jews to continue in their unbelief, or who helped baptized Jews to relapse into their former errors or to assail the true faith openly or secretly. All guilty of breaking this law would be excommunicated, and the Treasury would confiscate one quarter of their goods. The tremendous curse that Sisebut had called down on such people was repeated.[1]

Like Chintila, he did not confine himself to words. There survives a copy of a forced profession of faith which the baptized Jews of Toledo were compelled to sign on 18 February 654. In it they refer to the document that they had been obliged to sign in Chintila's reign (p. 186 above). But 'the obstinacy of our unbelief', they say, had prevented them from truly recognizing the Lord Jesus Christ and from attaching themselves sincerely to the Catholic faith. Accordingly, they now undertook on behalf of themselves, their wives, and their children that they would have no association with unbaptized Jews and that they would not intermarry with them. They would not practice the circumcision of the flesh, nor would they celebrate the Sabbath, the Passover, or the other feasts of the Jewish rite. If they did not like pork, they would not abstain from food cooked with pork. They would be Christian in every respect. And if they found any of their number transgressing against any of these undertakings even in the slightest degree, they would burn or stone him to death (as Reccesuinth's legislation demanded). Should the king spare such a man's life, he and his goods would become the property of anyone whom the king might appoint.[2]

Such was Reccesuinth's attack on the Jews. Sisebut and Chintila had used force to 'convert' Jews from their errors to the true faith; and Chintila had enunciated the principle that no non-Catholic might live in the kingdom. But this was the first systematic attempt to use the whole power of the State to eliminate Judaism in Spain. True, it was not an economic attack on the Jews' capacity and opportunity to earn a living: that was still to come. Nor did Reccesuinth make it obligatory for the Jews to have themselves baptized: unlike Erwig later on, he did not interfere with Jews if they did not practise their rites.[3] But to

---

[1] Ibid. 15. Sisebut: p. 166 above.   [2] Zeumer, pp. 425 f.
[3] Juster, pp. 284, 290.

partake in Jewish ceremonies or to subscribe to Jewish beliefs was now, and for nearly thirty years remained, a capital crime. The policy originated with the King rather than with the bishops, who simply re-enacted their previous decisions—and even in doing so they made it clear that they had been invited by the King to act. But there is no record that on this or any later occasion they protested against the persecution, as they had so mildly done under Isidore's leadership in 633. On the other hand, there is no reason to think that the population at large wished the Jews to be persecuted; and there is explicit evidence that individual bishops and laymen defied the massive anti-Jewish legislation of the kings. Indeed, a flagrant series of breaches of one of the laws was soon to be discussed at the Tenth Council.

In November 655 the bishops of Carthaginiensis held a provincial synod in the Church of St. Mary in the capital, which is known as the Ninth Council of Toledo. The kings are never recorded as having attended provincial synods; and Reccesuinth was not present at this one. There was little on the agenda to interest him, and the whole of the meeting was given up to ecclesiastical business, especially to the perennial problems of the protection of Church property against misappropriation by bishops and others and to the celibacy of the clergy. The bishops also turned to the baptized Jews, and on this occasion they give no hint that Reccesuinth had incited them to do so. They ordered all baptized Jews to spend the Christian feasts in the company of the local bishop so that he could approve their faith and conversation. If they failed to do so, they would be whipped or subjected to a fast, according to their age.[1] Before dispersing, the bishops decided to hold their next provincial synod on 1 November of the following year; but in fact Reccesuinth summoned another plenary council to meet on 1 December 656.

It is not clear why he did so; and the bishops did not react to the Tenth Council with any great enthusiasm, for only seventeen of them attended the meeting, though five others sent deputies. It was the worst attended of all the general councils. Nearly all the bishops who were present came from Carthaginiensis and Galicia. No bishop except the metropolitan came from Baetica, and no one at all represented Gallia or Tarraconensis. In their second canon the bishops referred to the oath of allegiance that was sworn by

[1] IX Tolet. 17.

clergy as well as by laymen. They ruled that if any cleric, from the bishop to the humblest monk, broke his oath, he would be unfrocked and exiled, though the king would have the right to decide whether he should be subjected to one or both of these punishments.[1] It is hardly likely that Reccesuinth called the council merely so as to have this resolution passed. In their seventh canon they dealt with a scandal. They had been astonished to learn that *many* priests and deacons were still selling Christian slaves to the Jews in defiance of so many canon and secular laws. The abuse was widespread among the clergy, who either disapproved of the laws or rated profit above piety. With a wealth of scriptural quotation the bishops excluded from the Church all persons found to have engaged in this unchristian trade in the future.[2]

With the close of the Tenth Council Spain all but disappears from history for the rest of the reign. Reccesuinth survived until 672 (two years after the Arabs had founded Kairwan), but he never summoned another plenary council; and relations between Crown and Church, which had been strained since the accession of Chindasuinth in 642, remained cool for the rest of Reccesuinth's life. When at last another synod met at Toledo under Wamba in 675 the bishops spoke with bitterness of the long years during which they had not been allowed to assemble. When the light of the councils had been withdrawn from the Church, Ignorance, the mother of all errors, had grown. There had ensued 'Babylonian confusion'. Bishops of the Lord had been ensnared by dissolute morality and had yielded to the invitations of the scarlet-clad harlot. In fact, the word of God had been sent into exile.[3] But his estrangement from the bishops did not prevent the King from founding, apparently in 661, his peculiarly attractive church of San Juan de Baños, or rather of St. John the Baptist at Baños de Cerrato in the modern province of Palencia. A Latin inscription over the horseshoe arch of the chancel proclaims to the world, or at any rate to that part of the world which visits Baños de Cerrato, that it was dedicated by 'King Reccesuinth, Lover of Thy Name'.[4]

[1] X Tolet. 2.

[2] Ibid. 7. On possible reasons why some Christians did not enforce the anti-Jewish laws see Juster, pp. 291 ff.

[3] XI Tolet. praef.

[4] Vives, 314. The best descriptions of the church are those of E. Camps Cazorla in Menendez Pidal, pp. 511 ff.; Schlunk, pp. 273 ff.

Only one document has survived to throw light on the King's last sixteen years. This is the minutes of a synod of the bishops of Lusitania which opened in the Church of Holy Jerusalem in Merida on 6 November 666. Reccesuinth appears to have been at war at the time of the meeting, and the bishops dutifully prayed that he should be victorious over his foes.[1] They resolved that whenever he was campaigning against his enemies prayers should be offered up each day in each church for his safety and that of his *fideles* and his army, that all might be preserved and victory granted to him by God.[2] The bishops also passed resolutions on slavery (p. 306 below) and on the incomes of clergy. They made it a crime to speak ill of a dead bishop, and they published a tariff of penalties for those found guilty of such outrageous conduct.[3] But on the life of the kingdom at large they said nothing.

3. *The Reform of the Administration*

Reccesuinth's reign saw the completion and publication of the revised code of laws which his father had begun to draft. It contained 324 laws from the code of Leovigild, which Reccesuinth calls *antiquae*, 99 laws of Chindasuinth, which are headed *Flavius Chindasuinthus rex*, and 87 new laws, which appear in the code under the heading *Flavius Reccesuindus rex*. The three laws of Reccared and the two laws of Sisebut are not included under any heading but are simply ascribed to their authors. A few of the *antiquae* were amended by Reccesuinth and one of them (*LV* ix. 1. 17) by Chindasuinth: the others were taken over from Leovigild with little or no change. Being intended explicitly for use in the courts, the code has as little to say about constitutional law as have the *antiquae*.[4] It has survived intact in two manuscripts, the older of which entitles it *liber iudiciorum*; and it was published in or very soon after 654.[5] The King foresaw such a large demand for copies of it that he made it an offence to charge more than 6 solidi per copy; and anyone who charged or paid more than this sum was to receive 100 lashes of the whip.[6]

---

[1] Conc. Emerit. praef., where the bishops pray that God may grant 'vitae felicitatem cum pacis quiete, sicque eum de suis hostibus reddat victorem ut suorum inimicorum colla ditioni eius subdat', and so on.

[2] Ibid. 3.   [3] Ibid. 17.

[4] The fundamental work on Reccesuinth's code is Zeumer, *NA* xxiii (1898), pp. 484–92.   [5] Ibid. 486.   [6] *LV* v. 4. 22.

What is of the first importance is that the new code was intended to bind all the inhabitants of the kingdom alike, Roman as well as Gothic, without distinction.[1] In a special enactment the King banned the use of foreign and especially of Roman law in his courts.[1] If a judge used any law other than that which was now published, he would be liable to the huge fine of 30 lb. of gold (2,160 solidi).[2] All suits that were in process of being heard in the courts on the day on which the new code was published should be adjudged under the new law; but no case that had already been concluded could now be reopened.[3] Reccesuinth reaffirmed the old law of Leovigild, or perhaps of Euric, that forbade the judge to hear a case for which the code had not provided. The judge or the *comes civitatis* was to have both parties to such a suit presented before the king, who could then decide the issue and provide for similar cases in the future;[4] for in publishing his code Reccesuinth had reserved the right to add to it such new laws as he should think necessary after taking counsel with the bishops and the palatine officials.[5]

Chindasuinth had had radical ideas on the reform of the administration. He did not live to carry them out completely; but one step he did take. He published a law on the Roman city councils, the *curiae*. In it he reminded the curials that they ought never to alienate their property by sale, gift, or exchange. He evidently concluded, however, as Justinian had concluded long ago, that it was impossible to tie the curials rigidly to their office any longer. Accordingly, he declared that, if they did sell, donate, or exchange their property, the man who acquired it or any part of it—whether land, slaves, vineyards, or houses—was liable respectively for the whole or for a proportionate share of the tax. Anyone acquiring such property who did not declare his obligation to pay tax, or who omitted to pay for one year, would lose the property without compensation as soon as the king, the *comes civitatis*, or the *iudex* heard of his omission. (We shall see presently the significance of the fact that in connection with taxation Chindasuinth mentions, not the Roman provincial governor, as we might have expected, but Gothic officials only.) The King went on to reserve the right to restore the property to

---

[1] Ibid. ii. 1. 10. [2] Ibid. 11.
[3] Ibid. 14, with Zeumer, *NA* xxiv (1899), pp. 72–4.
[4] *LV* ii. 1. 13. [5] Ibid. 5.

the vendor or to give it to a third party. At all events, the curials could now safely sell land provided that the purchaser undertook to pay the tax on it. With this measure the old Roman system of local government in Spain, which had existed for so many centuries, came at last to an end.[1] Reccesuinth transferred some, if not all, of the duties of the city councillors in connection with wards, minors, wills, and so on, to the bishops and the judiciary.[2] The councils may have continued to exist in some form; but, if so, their functions are unknown, and it is not a coincidence that no reference to them is ever made in the documents of the second half of the seventh century.

Again, when Reccesuinth carried out his father's plan to annul Alaric's code and to unify the legal system of the kingdom, he deprived the Roman provincial governor and his staff of one of their major functions, the administration of justice: there was now no Roman law for them to administer, and in later times we look for them in vain. Thus, the officials who are mentioned in Wamba's army law of 1 November 673 are the *dux*, *comes*, *thiufadus*, and the vicar of the *thiufadus*; and these recur in Erwig's law on the same subject.[3] In a matter concerning the army this is not surprising. But, when Wamba two years later wished his judges to proceed against bishops who had misused their churches' funds, he mentioned these same officials and said nothing about the Roman *rector provinciae*.[4] In Egica's ferocious law on runaway slaves (p. 273 below), the King refers to the *thiufadi* and their deputies and other lesser, unnamed, judges as well as to the *comes*, but of the Roman governor he says nothing.[5] In fact, after the publication of the new code there is no reference whatever in any document to the Roman governor and his staff.[6] Just as Chindasuinth substantially abolished the Roman city councils, so Reccesuinth almost completely abolished the Roman side of the provincial administration.

There exists in Reccesuinth's code a list of the various judges of

---

[1] *LV* v. 4. 19.   [2] Ibid. iv. 3. 4; ii. 5. 11, 14; iv. 2. 13*, etc.

[3] Ibid. ix. 2. 8, p. 371. 12 f.; ix. 2. 9.

[4] Ibid. iv. 5. 6, p. 203. 28 f.

[5] Ibid. ix. 1. 21, p. 364. 28, 33, where the *comes* is loosely called the *comes territorii* just as in Conc. Emerit. 15 he becomes *iudex civitatis*.

[6] Erwig's *tomus* addressed to XII Toledo in 681 (Zeumer, p. 476, 17) contains the phrase *religiosi provinciarum rectores*; but the context puts it beyond doubt that he is referring to the Gothic provincial governors, i.e. the *duces*.

his courts.[1] With two exceptions they are all holders of Gothic offices. The *dux provinciae* and the *comes civitatis* with his vicar head the list, as we might expect; but, oddly enough, there is no reference to the *iudex territorii*, who had been so prominent in the laws of Leovigild. Chindasuinth certainly refers to the *iudex territorii*[2] and (a synonym of that term) the *iudex loci* as well as to the *comes* and the *dux*.[3] But Reccesuinth says nothing of him, and the term *iudex territorii* (or *loci*) never occurs in his or his successors' laws.[4] It looks as though he not only did away with the Roman side of the administration but also simplified the Gothic judiciary by handing over the functions of the *iudex territorii* to the *thiufadus*, who now becomes prominent. It was certainly he who gave the *thiufadus* the right to try criminal as well as other cases; and it was he who instituted the office of vicar of the *thiufadus*.[5] He seems, in fact, to have combined the office of *thiufadus* with that of the *iudex territorii*: the titles became interchangeable, so that Erwig did not find it necessary to substitute *thiufadus* for *iudex territorii* in his revision of the laws. But *thiufadus* is the only term used in the second half of the century.

Reccesuinth's list of judges next includes the *pacis adsertor*, a commissioner appointed by the king to hear a specific case;[6] and there then follow the military judges, the *millenarius*, the *quingentenarius*, and the *centenarius*. Then, somewhat surprisingly, comes the *defensor*, the old Roman municipal judge; but his appearance in the list is not necessarily evidence for the continued existence of the city councils, for in the Visigothic kingdom he was not appointed by the council but elected by the citizens (p. 125 above). He presumably continued to hear minor cases in the cities. The list ends with another Roman official, the *numerarius*. We might have expected him to hear cases involving the Treasury, were it

---

[1] *LV* ii. 1. 27.   [2] Ibid. ii. 4. 5; cf. vi. 3. 7.

[3] Ibid. vi. 5. 12. But what does he mean when he says, ibid. vi. 3. 7, 'provincie iudex aut territorii'? The first is certainly the *dux*; but, if the second is the *iudex territorii*, why is the *comes* omitted?

[4] But an exceptional case will be found in one of Erwig's anti-Jewish laws (*LV* xii. 3. 25); and in *LV* xii. 3. 26 we read 'iudices universi per diversa loca vel territoria constituti' (Erwig). I assume that the phrase is not used in its old technical sense. For a parallel see n. 6, p. 212 above.

[5] *LV* ii. 1. 16 (I do not follow Zeumer, ad loc., in equating *thiufadus* with *millenarius*). It may have been Chindasuinth who upgraded the *thiufadus*: note the position of this official, ibid. ii. 1. 24.

[6] Ibid. ii. 1. 17; cf. *Vita S. Fructuosi*, 15, 'de praesentia regis . . . iudicem . . . comitem nomine Angelate'.

not that Chindasuinth explicitly enacted that if anyone had to bring an action on behalf of the Treasury he must take his case before the *comes civitatis* and the *iudex*.[1] Only one reference to the *numerarius* is found elsewhere, and this, unhappily, is obscure. At the beginning of his reign Wamba, incited by Festus, Metropolitan of Lusitania, ordered a certain Theudemund to take up the office of *numerarius* in Merida. Theudemund held the post for a year, but his action was illegal because 'it was against the usage of his race and his class' (*contra generis vel ordinis sui usum*). It looks as though the *numerarius* had in law to be a Roman.[2]

All these judges, except the *pacis adsertor*, could hear both civil and criminal cases.[3] They were all appointed by the king, and it was the duty of the *dux provinciae* to see that no one else presumed to set himself up as a judge. In practice, priests and deacons sometimes decided cases between laymen, but in 666 the Lusitanian bishops forbade them to do so any longer, at any rate without their bishop's consent; and the secular law took no cognizance of their activities.[4]

Whether Romans now became eligible for all or any of these judicial posts is doubtful. Romans had held the highest of them, that of *dux provinciae*, even in the sixth century, when the Roman Claudius had been *dux Lusitaniae* (p. 102 above).[5] Among the signatories of the latest Councils of Toledo we occasionally find royal officials bearing Roman names (Vitulus, Severinus, Paulus, David), who describe themselves as *comites*.[6] But we do not know that *comes* in this context means *comes civitatis*; and they are in a small minority as compared with officials who bear Germanic names and, indeed, may well have been Goths. It looks as though the law was now administered almost wholly by Goths, apart from the minor work of the *defensores* and *numerarii*; and it would hardly be an exaggeration to say that the Goths now ousted the

---

[1] *LV* ii. 3. 10; cf. ix. 1. 21 (Egica), p. 364. 29.

[2] Ibid. ix. 1. 21, p. 364. 29. For Theudemund see the end of the *acta* of XVI Toledo.

[3] *LV* ii. 1. 17.   [4] Ibid. ii. 1. 18; Conc. Emerit. 11 *fin.*

[5] Another possible case is the Celsus mentioned in Braulio, *Ep.* 37 (PL 80. 684), where he is 'Celsus . . . cum territoriis a clementia vestra [i.e. Chindasuinth] sibi commissa'. The Paulus *dux* who led the great rebellion against Wamba in 673 may also have been a Roman, though only late and worthless authorities say so.

[6] Zeumer, p. 486: Goths might well have taken the biblical names Paul and David. It would be interesting to know more about that *Laurentium comitem* who lived at Toledo and is mentioned by Braulio, *Ep.* 25 (PL 80. 674).

Hispano-Romans from the chief judicial offices apart from that of *dux*.

But, if Reccesuinth abolished the Roman provincial governor and his staff, what were the arrangements now for collecting the taxes? Only one document throws light on taxation in the second half of the century. This is the Edict of 1 November 683 in which King Erwig remitted all arrears of taxes on slaves that were outstanding from 681 and the preceding years.[1] Taxes that had already been collected but had not yet been paid into the Treasury were not refunded to the taxpayer: the King directed that they must be handed over at once by the officials who had collected them on pain of having to pay four times the amount that they had collected together with any such fine as the King might impose. Moreover, if these officials failed to collect the taxes in full in future years, or if, having collected them, they did not pay them promptly into the Treasury, they would be obliged to pay double the amount out of their own pockets. If they insisted on collecting the taxes for the years covered by the remission, they would be forced to restore fourfold; and, if they had seized arable or vineyard on the ground that these taxes had not been paid, they had to restore them at once to their owners.

Who are these officials who now collect the taxes? Happily, Erwig tells us. The old Roman officials have practically all disappeared. It is true that the Edict includes the word *exactor*, and while this may be a vague term indicating no more than 'collector' it may also be evidence that the Roman official of that name still survived.[2] (If so, the term is evidence for the continued existence of the *curiae*, for the *exactor* was elected not by the people but by the city councillors.) But, even so, it is clear that the duty of collecting the taxes had now been taken over by the Gothic side of the administration, for the chief officials whom Erwig names are the *dux provinciae*, the *comes civitatis* and his vicar, the *thiufadus*, and lesser men. It is they who are to be subject to the penalties laid down in the Edict. Even in the reign of Chindasuinth, who initiated but did not complete the great reform of the administration, Treasury officials who brought an action on behalf of the Treasury were heard not by the Roman governor but by the *comes civitatis* and the *iudex territorii* sitting together; and Chindasuinth says that this was an innovation (p. 211 above).

---

[1] Zeumer, pp. 479 f.   [2] Ibid., p. 480. 1.

Some Goths had held positions of high financial responsibility long before this date. The Second Council of Seville, which met in 619, was attended by a Gothic *vir illustris* who is described as *rector rerum fiscalium*.[1] It is not clear whether he represented the Treasury in the province of Baetica or whether he was the chief financial officer of the whole kingdom, the *Comes Patrimonii* himself. What is important is that even at that date Goths were capable of understanding and directing the intricacies of the Imperial financial system. At the Eighth Council in 653 two of the palace officials who signed the minutes held the office of *Comes Patrimonii*: perhaps one of them had previously held it, while the other was still in office. At any rate, they were both of them Goths, called Requira and Riccila respectively. The latter still held the post in 655, and he certainly held it alone in that year. At the Thirteenth Council in 683 both a *Comes Thesaurorum* (an otherwise unknown official) and a *Comes Patrimonii* were present. Both of these appear to have been Romans; at any rate, they bore Roman names, Isidorus and Vitulus, and the latter still held his post in 693.[2] In the case of the highest financial office of the kingdom, then, Romans may well have been as eligible as Goths even in the last years of the kingdom. But among the high palace officials as a whole Romans were few and far between.

We shall see later on (p. 295 below) that the year 653 also brought a curious innovation in the meetings of the plenary councils of the Church. It seems that in that year for the first time Goths may have been given—as a result of a deliberate act of policy—a majority of the votes; and they certainly had a majority at the subsequent general councils. As they now took over practically the whole of the civil administration, so they simultaneously deprived the Romans of the power of outvoting them (if they should ever wish to do so) in ecclesiastical matters. It is difficult to believe that the date of this innovation is a coincidence.

It is calamitous that we have no information whatever on the motives which led Reccesuinth and his father to deprive the Romans of practically all political, executive, and ecclesiastical power; but that is what they appear to have done. The clear implication of the two Kings' actions (if we have stated the facts

[1] II Hispal. praef.
[2] See the lists of signatories in Zeumer, pp. 485 f., supplemented by more complete lists in Vives's text of the *acta*.

correctly) would appear on the surface to be that acute tension had arisen between the Roman and the Gothic inhabitants of Spain, and that in the opinion of the kings the Romans had now become something of a threat to the whole position of Gothic overlordship. But in the rest of our evidence there is scarcely a hint of any such danger, and certainly no trace of it will be found in the works of St. Isidore.[1] At the Fifth Council in 636 the rule was laid down that Goths alone might sit upon the throne of Spain; and from this it is a reasonable conjecture (p. 181 above) that at least one Hispano-Roman had tried to make himself king before that date. But that was nearly twenty years in the past, and in itself it is hardly enough to justify the guess that Roman unrest had become so dangerous as to oblige the kings to put an end to nearly all Roman influence on the government.

The reasons which led to the great reforms of Chindasuinth and Reccesuinth are one of the darkest mysteries of Visigothic Spain.

---

[1] Isidore's attitude towards the Goths, and its eulogistic character, deserves further study. There is little of interest in P. B. Steidle, 'Der heilige Isidor von Sevilla und die Westgoten', *Benediktinische Monatsschrift*, xviii (1936), pp. 425–34; but see Messmer, op. cit. (p. 16 n. 3 above) 89 ff.; A. Borst, 'Das Bild der Geschichte in der Enzyklopädie Isidors von Sevilla', *Deutsches Archiv für Erforschung des Mittelalters*, xxii (1966), pp. 1–62.

X · THE LAST KINGS

T HE rebellion of Paul against King Wamba in 673 is the one military campaign of the entire period about which we have detailed information. Indeed, it is the first European campaign to be fairly well documented since the battles of 552, with which Procopius had ended his *History*. The course of the rebellion may therefore be recounted at somewhat disproportionate length.

Four documents relating to it have survived, and all of them were written immediately after the revolt had been crushed. The longest is a vivid and accurate *History* of the expedition and victory of Wamba written by Julian, deacon or priest, who was to be Metropolitan of Toledo from 30 January 680 until his death on 6 March 690. He wrote this work in or very soon after 673, certainly before the end of Wamba's reign in 680. Most of his information is derived from oral sources, but he also had access to a letter addressed by Paul to Amator, Bishop of Gerona, and to the *Iudicium*, which we shall mention in a moment.[1] The *History*, which is very eulogistic of Wamba, does not suggest that its author had marched with the King: indeed, Julian goes wrong in his geography by placing Wamba's capture of Clausurae after instead of before his capture of Collioure (Caucoliberi),[2] an improbable slip had he been an eyewitness. He intended his work to be a moral tract rather than a scientific history; yet it is full of valuable historical information.

At the end of his work he adds a curious *Insultatio*, in which he mocks the Gallic province of the kingdom as though it were a woman of many vices, proud, wanton, treacherous, and ungrateful. In doing so he throws light on the relations of the Spaniards with the Gauls of the kingdom.

The third source is the *Iudicium in tyrannorum perfidia promulgatum*, which appears to have been written at Nîmes in 673 by

---

[1] Text of all the documents in B. Krusch and W. Levison, MGH, *Script. rer. Merov.* v. 486–535.

[2] Ibid. 511 n. 4. Clausurae is now L'Écluse or La Cluse near Perthus, Dép. Pyrénées-orientales: ibid., n. 6.

someone who was familiar with Gothic secular and ecclesiastical law. The work was completed before final sentence was passed by the King on the defeated rebels. It includes a brief summary of the events, more accurate even than that of Julian, and it happily gives the names of a large number of Paul's supporters.

Finally, we have a document that was not known either to Julian or to the author of the *Iudicium*. Written by the rebel leader Paul himself, it is the text of a challenge sent by him to Wamba, urging the King to descend from the heights of the Pyrenees to Clausurae and fight there.

1. *Wamba*

Reccesuinth died on Wednesday, 1 September 672, and on that same day Wamba was chosen king by the magnates and the people who were present at the villa of Gertici, about 120 miles from Toledo in the territory of Salamanca. At first Wamba refused the crown, protesting that he was advanced in years and unequal to the disasters that were threatening the kingdom (though our authority does not specify what these disasters consisted of). But, when one of the *duces* threatened to kill him if he did not accept the crown, he submitted.[1] It was not illegal to be crowned at the place where the old king had died (p. 204 above); but Wamba insisted on returning to Toledo for the ceremony of coronation so as to win the consent of the capital and avoid any suspicion that he had usurped the throne. He was finally crowned by Quiricus, Metropolitan of Toledo, on Sunday, 19 September 672, in the Church of the Holy Apostles in the capital.[2] Nothing is known of his previous career, unless he is to be identified with that *vir illustris* called Wamba, whom Reccesuinth had ordered to produce the will of St. Martin of Braga at the Tenth Council in 656.[3]

The first recorded action of the reign was an attack on the Basques; and in the spring of 673 Wamba himself marched to Cantabria. On his way there he was informed of events in the Gallic province.[4] A revolt had broken out under the leadership of the *comes* of Nîmes, a certain Ilderic, supported by Gumild, Bishop of Maguelonne, and the abbot Ranimir, all of them Goths.

---

[1] Julian, *Hist.* 2 f.
[2] Ibid. 3 f., 'in praetoriensi ecclesia, sanctorum scilicet Petri et Pauli'; *Laterculus*, 44 (iii. 468).
[3] Mansi, xi. 42.   [4] Julian, *Hist.* 9.

Aregius, Bishop of Nîmes (who also has a barbarian name), had refused to join them and had been deposed and handed over in chains to the Franks. The rebels promoted Ranimir to take his place. At his installation only two bishops—and they from the Frankish kingdom—were present, though the Fourth Council of Toledo (canon 19) had required that at least three bishops of the same province should be present at the consecration of a new bishop. The rebels controlled the eastern part of Septimania from Nîmes to the river Hérault and a little beyond it as far as the Mons Cameli; but the provincial capital, Narbonne, did not join them.[1] They proceeded to raise money from the citizens who had fallen under their control.[2]

Wamba appointed a *dux* called Paul to crush the revolt. Paul marched northwards, but he quickly formed the plan to take over the kingdom himself. He was joined by Ranosind, the Visigothic governor of the province of Tarraconensis, and by Hildigisus, a *gardingus* (p. 252 below). Pretending still to be on his way to attack Ilderic, he named a place and time at which troops should assemble to attack the rebels. But his treachery came to the ears of Argebad, Bishop of Narbonne, who passed his information on to the King. Before the Bishop could shut the rebel army out of Narbonne, however, Paul made a rapid march, and entered and occupied the city;[3] and the Bishop seems later to have compromised himself with the insurgents.[4] It was in Narbonne that Paul declared himself king, had himself anointed,[5] and was crowned with the golden crown which Reccared had long ago presented to the shrine of the Blessed Felix at Gerona.[6] It may be that he intended, at any rate for the time being, to reign simply as 'the eastern king' in Gallia and Tarraconensis, leaving Wamba to rule as 'the southern king', for he uses these terms in his letter to Wamba.[7] At all events, he obliged the people subject to him to swear an oath of allegiance and to undertake to fight to the end against Wamba and his supporters.[8] Moreover, he was joined by Ilderic and the other rebels at Nîmes, so that Wamba lost control of the entire

[1] On the Mons Cameli, the rebels' frontier, see Krusch and Levison, p. 505 n. 7.
[2] Julian, *Hist.* 5 f.   [3] Ibid. 7.   [4] Ibid. 21.
[5] *Epistola Pauli* (p. 500, Krusch), *unctus*.
[6] Julian, *Hist.* 26, with Krusch and Levison, p. 522 n. 4.
[7] Krusch and Levison, p. 500. 3. But, if we may press Julian's words, Paul called for the deposition of the King at Narbonne: *Hist.* 8 (p. 507. 6 f.).
[8] *Iudicium*, 6 (p. 534. 5 ff.).

province of Narbonensis and a part of Tarraconensis including Barcelona and Gerona; and at any rate in Gaul there was no opposition to Paul, and no support for the King revealed itself.[1] By gifts and promises Paul tried to win the help of a considerable number of Franks and Basques and began to look about for a suitable time to invade Spain and dethrone the legitimate ruler.[2] It was precisely the kind of rebellion supported by foreign powers which earlier kings and bishops had deplored and denounced. But, in spite of the laws and the councils, Paul had begun his revolt with vigour and initiative. But he was no match for Wamba.

The King was in Cantabria on the point of attacking the Basques when he heard of this new and more formidable revolt. He debated with the *primates* (p. 253 below) of his palace, who were with him, whether to advance on Gaul at once or to return home and collect more forces and sufficient supplies for a distant campaign in Gaul. According to Julian, a confident and fiery speech by the King decided the issue.[3] The whole army entered Basque territory, and for seven days they plundered the country-side and burned the houses (though remaining on the open plains and not venturing into the hills) until the Basques of the locality gave hostages and gifts. A peace was arranged; and it is noteworthy that Paul is not recorded as having received the help from the Basques that he had hoped for.

Wamba marched at once through Calahorra and Huesca to Barcelona, where he captured the local rebel commanders, Eured (who apparently had attended the Eighth Council in 653 as a *comes*), Pompedius, Guntefred, the deacon Hunulf, and Neufred.[4] He next marched to Gerona, which also fell to him. Its bishop, Amator, had not sided with the rebels, though Paul had written him a letter which fell into Wamba's hands and from which Julian quotes an extract: it confirms that the insurgents had intended to invade Spain.[5] The King now sent three columns ahead of his main force. One of these columns was to march up the valley of the Segre, pass through Cerdagne (Cirritania), and enter Septimania down the valley of the river Tet. The second was to go northwards through Vich (Ausona), the seat of

---

[1] *Insultatio*, 5 *init.*   [2] Julian, *Hist.* 8.   [3] Ibid. 9.
[4] *Iudicium*, 3.
[5] *Hist.* 11. The *Iudicium* says nothing of Gerona. On the next stage of the campaign see Krusch and Levison, p. 511 n. 4.

222 THE CATHOLIC KINGDOM

a bishopric, descend the valley of the river Tech to Ceret, where it would link up with the King; while the third column was to march along the Roman road near the coast.[1] The King himself followed the coastal road, and, when his men showed some tendency to plunder and outrage the country through which they passed, he punished them severely, circumcising those guilty of fornication.[2]

At the foot of the Pyrenees he rested his army for a couple of days, and then attacked the mountains, where he received the surviving letter of Paul, 'the anointed eastern king' as he calls himself, challenging him to come down to Clausurae (some twenty-five kilometres south of Perpignan, not far from Ceret), where he would be mightily repulsed.[3] In fact, Wamba's advance party broke into Clausurae and captured Ranosind, governor of Tarraconensis, and the *gardingus* Hildigisus, who were in charge of the defence,[4] together with a number of other rebels, most of whom bore Germanic names. A force of Franks, whom Paul had sent to defend the place, took to flight.[5] The news of the fall of Clausurae was brought to Paul by Wittimir, who had shut himself up in Sordonia, a fort near Llivia (Castrum Libiae),[6] but who now fled to the usurper at Narbonne. The news greatly distressed the rebels, for the King was now free to descend to the plains of Narbonensis and all hope of invading Spain had disappeared. The two royalist columns in the interior had also marched successfully, and the entire army was now united in France with no rebels behind them. Castrum Libiae itself had fallen, and in it Wamba's men captured Iacintus, a bishop (perhaps of Elne),[7] and Arangisclus, who were in charge of the defence. They took other prisoners, too, and a quantity of gold and silver.[8]

The objective now was Narbonne, the capital of the Gallic province. Wamba detached a picked force under four commanders to attack the city and sent a naval force to assist (the first reference to naval operations since the reign of Sisebut). When Paul had heard that the royalists were in Septimania, he had retreated to Nîmes but left a strong force at Narbonne under the command of Wittimir. Wittimir refused a call to surrender, and

---

[1] On the three routes see ibid., p. 509 n. 8.   [2] Julian, *Hist.* 10.
[3] Krusch and Levison, p. 500.   [4] Julian, *Hist.* 11.
[5] *Iudicium*, 3.   [6] On the site see Krusch and Levison, p. 512 n. 4.
[7] So Krusch's Index, p. 798.   [8] *Iudicium*, 3.

an attack which began at the fifth hour of the day ended three hours later, in spite of a vigorous defence, when the royalists forced their way inside the walls. Wittimir took refuge in the Church of St. Mary, and sword in hand prepared to defend himself beside the altar. But when one of Wamba's soldiers picked up a plank and was about to bring it down with some force on his head, he fell trembling to the ground and was taken prisoner. He was loaded with chains and was whipped, along with his associates.[1] The King's men also captured at Narbonne a certain Argemund and the *primicerius* Gultricia; but Ranimir, the usurping Bishop of Nîmes, had managed to escape before the city was stormed. He was later caught in the territory of Béziers when it fell to Wamba; for soon after the fall of Narbonne the King occupied Béziers and Agde, where he captured the Bishop Wiliesind, his brother Ranosind, and another Arangisclus.[2]

Wamba's forces now moved by land and sea on Maguelonne, where the Bishop Gumild, one of the original supporters of Ilderic, was particularly impressed by the dangers of an attack from the sea. He consequently deserted his city (as Ranimir had deserted Narbonne) and fled to Nîmes. Maguelonne fell to the King.[3]

The way was now open to Nîmes itself, where Paul was supported by a body of Franks. Once again, a picked force under four commanders advanced some thirty miles ahead of Wamba and after a rapid night march appeared unexpectedly outside the city walls at daybreak on 31 August 673. The defenders, seeing only a small force before them, thought for a moment of going outside the city and engaging them. But in fear of an ambush they remained within the walls and awaited the arrival of a further force of Franks. As soon as the sun rose the royalists began an attack and maintained it throughout the day without decisive result.[4] But they felt some fear that the Frankish reinforcements would arrive and perhaps take them in the rear or else that they might be overwhelmed by a sally from the city (for the defence of Nîmes was perhaps rather more active than Julian would have us believe). With great speed, therefore, Wamba sent reinforcements, said to number 10,000 men, under the *dux* Wandemir: they marched throughout the night and reached Nîmes before dawn on

---

[1] Julian, *Hist.* 12.   [2] *Iudicium*, 4.   [3] Julian, *Hist.* 13; *Iudicium*, 4.
[4] Julian, *Hist.* 13; *Iudicium*, 4.

the second day of the siege. The exhausted force of attackers had been obliged to stay awake all night fearing a sally and were deeply relieved to see Wandemir's army arrive through the darkness.[1] The assault on the walls was now resumed and maintained until about the fifth hour of the day; and then, although Paul vigorously encouraged his Franks, the royalists burned the city gates and entered. The defenders withdrew into the vast amphitheatre of Nîmes.[2]

Within the amphitheatre fierce fighting broke out among the defenders, for the Gallic citizens of Nîmes suspected some of their supporters of treachery, and began to kill them. Paul could not stop the slaughter. Indeed, he was himself suspected by the Gauls of trying to win his own liberty by betraying his followers; while the Spaniards who had come to Gaul with him were thought by the native Gauls to want to kill the citizens and go over to the King.[3] On this day, 1 September, the first anniversary of Wamba's accession to the throne, Paul put off his royal robes amid scenes of bloody slaughter and with his men wholly out of control.[4]

On 2 September, after taking counsel with his lieutenants, he sent Argebad, Bishop of Narbonne (p. 220 above), to beg Wamba to put a stop to the massacre and to spare the rebels' lives. The King had approached to within four miles of the city when the Bishop met him. He agreed to do as Argebad asked and undertook to shed no blood, but he angrily refused the further request that the rebels should not be punished at all.[5] In due course the fighting was stopped, the city was occupied, and forces were posted to prevent any attack from France. Paul was dragged from the arena, and great treasures along with numerous Gallic and Frankish prisoners were taken.[6] The names of nearly thirty prisoners (including Gumild, Bishop of Maguelonne) have been preserved: scarcely half a dozen of them are Latin.[7] Eighteen days after the surrender Wamba sent back to France his Frankish prisoners, whom he had treated well, we are told, because some of them were nobly born and had been given as hostages; but even the rank and file, among whom some Saxons were serving, were sent away with gifts.[8] Before leaving Nîmes Wamba repaired

---

[1] Julian, *Hist.* 15.   [2] Ibid. 18.   [3] Ibid. 19.
[4] Ibid. 20.   [5] Ibid. 21 f.   [6] Ibid. 24.   [7] *Iudicium*, 4.
[8] Julian, *Hist.* 25.

the damaged city, restored the burnt gates, buried the dead, and gave back to the citizens the plunder that had been taken from them. Paul had looted the churches of their treasures in his efforts to raise money; and these treasures were now returned.[1]

On 4 September[2] Paul, mockingly dressed in royal robes, was brought with his accomplices before the King in the presence of all the *seniores* of the palace (p. 253 below), all the *gardingi*, and all the palatine *officium*, as well as the entire army. The King asked them one by one whether he had done them any injury that might have incited them to rebel; and one by one they replied that he had not. The oath of allegiance which Paul and the others had sworn and signed at the election of Wamba was next read out, and the rebels' signatures were shown to them. This was followed by a reading of the oath that Paul had obliged his followers to swear to him, that they would be faithful to him and would fight unanimously against Wamba. Next, canon 75 of the Fourth Council (p. 174 above) was read to the defeated rebels together with Chindasuinth's law on rebellion (p. 191 above). The by-standers did not doubt that if Wamba should spare the lives of the guilty men, he would at least have them blinded, as canon and secular law demanded.[3] But they were not blinded. They suffered decalvation, and in accordance with the seventy-fifth canon the Treasury confiscated their goods.[4]

It was now rumoured that the Franks would try to rescue Paul. Wamba is said to have hoped for an opportunity to 'punish' the Franks for their offences on this and previous occasions; and when they did not come he thought of attacking France himself, but in the interests of peace on the frontier changed his mind. In fact, an eminent Frankish *dux* called Lupus[5] launched a raid in the vicinity of Béziers, but left the province on 6 September on hearing of the King's approach.[6]

Wamba entered Narbonne peacefully and left a garrison there. He expelled the Jews from the city—his only recorded anti-Jewish action—and installed milder governors (presumably *comites*) in the Gallic cities.[7] At a place called Canaba, south of Narbonne, he disbanded his army and returned to Spain.[8] About four miles from Toledo, Paul, with a sham crown on his head,

---

[1] Ibid. 26.   [2] Ibid. 27.   [3] On the whole scene see *Iudicium*, 5–7.
[4] Julian, *Hist.* 27; *Iudicium*, 7.   [5] On him see Levison, pp. 486 ff.
[6] Julian, *Hist.* 27.   [7] Ibid. *Hist.* 28.   [8] Ibid. 29.

together with his companions, their beards shaved off, their feet bare, and their clothing squalid, were placed in carts pulled by camels and were drawn into the capital through throngs of mocking people. Accompanied by this triumphal procession Wamba returned to the city in the sixth month after he had left it.[1] Throughout the campaign he had shown speed, initiative, and much military talent.

According to late and worthless authorities, Paul was a Roman, and that is what his name would suggest (though it does not prove it). But it was illegal for a Roman to become king of Spain; and Julian nowhere in his detailed narrative suggests that Paul's aim was illegal in this respect. But the revolt as a whole was certainly a revolt of Goths against the Gothic king. More than forty persons bearing Gothic names and a mere half-dozen men with Roman names are known to have supported the movement.

So far as we can tell, no question of fundamental policy divided these Goths from those who remained loyal to Wamba. The rebellion seems to have been due, not to any profound social causes, but simply to a mere personal quarrel among the Goths themselves. First Ilderic and then Paul wished to be Reccesuinth's successor and to oust Wamba. All the secular officials who appear in the narrative are Goths—Ranosind, the *dux provinciae Tarraconensis*, Ilderic, *comes* of Nîmes, and Eured, presumably *comes* of Barcelona. Of the bishops, the Metropolitan of Gallia was Argebad, and the Bishops of Nîmes, Agde, Elne (probably), and Maguelonne were respectively Aregius, Wiliesind, Iacintus,[2] and Gumild. No Roman bishop in Gallia is mentioned, though Amator of Gerona appears in the story. Moreover, all the subordinate military commanders on either side are without exception Goths. It is odd that there is no mention of a *dux provinciae Galliae* or of a bishop at Barcelona. Nor is there any reference to the bishops or the *comites* of the other cities of Gaul— Lodève, Carcassonne, and Béziers; and we do not know who was *comes* of Agde. But judging by the names that have been recorded, it would seem that the Goths proportionately to their numbers in the kingdom as a whole held far more than their fair share of the

---

[1] Julian, *Hist.* 30.

[2] Since he sided with the rebels he was presumably a Goth. I am not wholly convinced, therefore, by Krusch and Levison, Index, p. 798, in equating his name with 'Hyacinthus'.

high offices, civil and ecclesiastical, in the province of Gallia. After Reccesuinth's reforms this is no surprise.

The hostility which all Goths felt for the Franks comes out several times in the documents. It appears in Wamba's speech to his officers in Cantabria,[1] and in Julian's account of the panic which broke out in the Frankish cities on 5 September when it was thought that the King might attack them, and in the army of Lupus when it, too, feared an attack by Wamba.[2] Indeed, Julian describes the Franks as 'nations of barbarians'.[3] The attitude was reciprocated; and Frankish contempt for the Goths was as lively now as it had been in the days of Gregory of Tours. It is reflected in Paul's speech to his Frankish allies in Nîmes. The Goths' valour in defending themselves and in striking terror into other peoples was famous in days gone by; but now all their energy has withered away, and their knowledge of war has vanished. They are not in the habit of waging war and have no military experience. If once they begin to fight, they will fly immediately to their hiding-places because their degenerate spirits cannot sustain the weight of a battle.[4]

All this might have been expected; but the mutual contempt of the Gauls of Narbonensis and the Spaniards who ruled them is a surprise. The Gauls used to say that the strength of the Spaniards was inferior to that of Gallic women. They despised associating with Spaniards. They boasted of their own wealth. They would spurn the orders of their Spanish commanders.[5] But Wamba contrasts the Gauls, living in that 'remote corner of the world', with the Spaniards, who ruled a wide kingdom. He remarks that the Spaniards have always been their protectors: the Gauls could never achieve anything without 'our men'.[6] Whenever the news arrives that Gaul is beset by the enemy, Spaniards quickly come in arms to her defence, and, disregarding their own safety, fight with the enemies of Gaul. And if they do not beat off the foe they buy him off. But all they get in return is treachery and destruction.[7] In the late rebellion, with only a part of their

---

[1] Julian, *Hist.* 9 (p. 508. 13, 20).   [2] Ibid. 27 (p. 523. 12 ff., 22 ff.)
[3] Ibid. 29 (p. 524. 26), *barbarorum gentes*. But perhaps the phrase means no more than *externis gentibus* in the previous line. Note also *Iudicium*, 1 (p. 530. 7), *nefandorum societatem*.
[4] Julian, *Hist.* 16 (p. 515. 19 ff.)   [5] *Insultatio*, 1 (p. 526. 9 ff.)
[6] Julian, *Hist.* 9 (p. 508. 14 ff.)
[7] *Insultatio*, 8. Note ibid. 6, *fortiores, validioribus* (p. 528. 7 f.)

strength they defeated the entire power of Gaul.[1] And worst of all, the Gauls give better treatment to the Jews than the Spaniards give: Gaul is 'a brothel of the blaspheming Jews'.[2]

True, all this comes from the writings of a single man, Julian of Toledo. But it is improbable that he would have stressed such attitudes if he had not had reason to think that they would find a sympathetic echo in Spanish hearts. What is not so clear is whether these sentiments were shared by the Romans and the Goths alike in the two areas; and it may be that they were mainly held by the Roman population, for many of the Goths in Narbonensis will have been officials temporarily resident there—and in fact the charges are levelled, not at the *Gothi* in Gaul, but at the *Galliarum terra*. In spite of this hostility, however, and in spite of the willingness of the Gauls to call in Frankish aid when it suited them to do so, we never hear that the Gauls wished to detach themselves from Toledo and to declare themselves independent or to hand themselves over to the Frankish kings. Paul's title of 'the eastern king' does not in itself suggest that the Gauls wished sometimes to be independent of both their powerful neighbours: it merely indicates his own ambitions.

According to Julian, the entire campaign went off without a hitch. But that was not Wamba's opinion; for immediately after his return to Toledo he began work on the great army law which he published on 1 November of that same year (p. 262 below). What he had seen on his expedition had evidently caused him some alarm, and his severe law obliged even the clergy to rally to the defence of their country against foreign enemies and usurpers. Although the clergy had taken an active part in the rebellion, this obligation to fight may well have been the first cause of tension between them and the King.

In the third year of the reign Wamba 'renewed the city of Toledo with wonderful and elegant work'; and two epigrams have survived which he carved on the city's marble gates.[3] In 675, after the long years in which Reccesuinth had allowed no general councils of the Church to meet, Wamba summoned the Eleventh Council of Toledo and the Third Council of Braga. But these were provincial synods (of Carthaginiensis and Galicia

---

[1] *Insultatio*, 7.
[2] Julian, *Hist.* 5 (p. 504. 14 ff.); *Insultatio*, 1, 2 (p. 526. 16 f., 23 ff.)
[3] Contin. Isid. Hisp. 46 (ii. 348).

respectively), and he called no plenary council. The bishops insisted in 675 on the need for annual provincial synods; but there is no evidence that any further meeting was held throughout the rest of the reign. Again, the bishops can scarcely have welcomed his abolition of the rule of thirty years' prescription in cases where bishops had appropriated the possessions of their parish churches (p. 301 below). Worst of all, Stephen, Metropolitan of Merida, complained at the Twelfth Council, which met after the reign had come to an end, that he had been forced by Wamba to install a bishop in the monastery of Aquae in Lusitania, where the body of St. Pimenius lay, though this monastery was not a bishopric at all. The King had also made up his mind to install bishops not only in various villages and small villas but also in the Church of the Holy Apostles Peter and Paul in a suburb of Toledo, the church in which four plenary councils met and in which he himself had been crowned. He thus broke a ruling of the Council of Nicaea itself, that there must not be two bishops in one city, though this rule had already been broken in the exceptional circumstances of the years following on the general conversion of 589 (p. 98 above). The Twelfth Council reasserted the old rule that there should be no bishop where there had never been one. As for Cuniuld, whom Wamba had installed at Aquae, he was not condemned to punishment since he had taken the post only under pressure from the King. In fact, the bishops ruled that he should be translated whenever a vacancy arose in an established see.[1] Wamba took no action against the Jews, except in Narbonensis, though we do not know the attitude of the bishops to this omission. In general, however, the bishops were hostile to Wamba.

The circumstances in which the reign came to an end were carefully described at the Twelfth Council of Toledo, which opened on 9 January 681. The senior metropolitan at that Council was Julian of Seville, but it was also attended by Julian of Toledo, the author of the *Historia Wambae*, whom Wamba had appointed as Metropolitan of the royal see on 30 January 680. The minutes of the Council relate that on Sunday, 14 October 680, at the first hour of the night,[2] Wamba, feeling himself to be mortally ill,[3]

---

[1] XII Tolet. 4. Is Cuniuld to be identified with the Cuniulf of Italica who signed the minutes of XIII Tolet. in 683? This bishop is 'Cuniuld' at XV and XVI Tolet.

[2] The date is given in the *Laterculus* in Zeumer, p. 461.

[3] The strangely vague phrase is 'dum inevitabilis necessitudinis teneretur eventu'.

took on the penitential discipline—for at that date all took on the discipline of penance before death. He was dressed in a monastic habit and was tonsured in the presence of the *seniores* (p. 253 below) of his palace. In fact, however, he survived his sickness, but being under penance he found himself barred by the seventeenth canon of the Sixth Council from ever again sitting upon the throne of Spain. Accordingly, in a document which he was able to sign with his own hand, he nominated the Count Erwig as his successor, an action that was sharply contrary to the canons of the Church. This document, which the bishops at the Twelfth Council one by one examined with close attention, was witnessed by the *seniores* who were present when he signed it. He also composed another document; and this, too, was produced for inspection by the bishops at the Twelfth Council. It was addressed to Julian of Toledo, who had now been Metropolitan for more than eight months, and directed him to anoint Erwig as soon as possible.[1]

That is the story as told in the minutes of the Twelfth Council. There is evidence that Wamba protested strongly that he was not barred from reascending the throne (p. 232 below); but his opposition was overruled. The truth is that canon law, if strictly applied, prohibited him from resuming the throne, and it is no coincidence that in 642 Chindasuinth had tonsured Tulga when he deposed him. But, if the nobility and the bishops had wanted Wamba to continue his reign, the law could easily have been waived.[2]

The events were strange, and Erwig undoubtedly expected that contemporaries would find them suspicious. In order to anticipate accusations, we may suppose, he and the bishops thought it important to set out as solemnly as possible their version of what had happened; and in the tome (p. 278 below) which he handed to the Twelfth Council Erwig urged the bishops to publish the facts.[3] Our sources of information give no

---

[1] XII Tolet. 1. There is a scholarly discussion of the whole episode by F. X. Murphy, 'Julian of Toledo and the Fall of the Visigothic Kingdom in Spain', *Speculum*, xxvii (1952), pp. 1–27, who takes a more lenient view of Erwig than I do. Here and elsewhere I would reject even more strongly than he does the evidence (if it is evidence) of Alphonsus III. See also Ziegler, pp. 114 ff.

[2] Those who deposed Wamba could have appealed to the canons of many Spanish and Frankish councils: for a list of them see Ziegler, p. 114 n. 70.

[3] Zeumer, p. 475. 19.

hint that for the next two hundred years any other version of the events was current; and it was only towards the end of the ninth century that the story was recorded of how Erwig had given the King a potion that caused his sickness and led to his dethronement. In the actual circumstances it was inevitable that such a tale should have been told; and it may have been the truth. Indeed, the mere fact that the Twelfth Council tried at such length to excuse Erwig suggests that there was something that called for excuse.

Wamba was dead before the Thirteenth Council of Toledo opened on 4 November 683.[1]

2. *Erwig*

On the day after the mysterious events of that Sunday night, Erwig, who had hitherto held the rank of *comes*, was appointed king; but he deferred his coronation until the following Sunday, 21 October, to which date he assigned the official opening of his reign. During his years as king, there was a severe famine in Spain. No details are given by any of our sources, but the fact that a chronicler thought it worthy of mention in his brief chronicle indicates its severity.[2] And in the following January the King himself referred to it in the address which he delivered to the bishops at the Twelfth Council.[3] But there is no reason to think that it contributed materially to the fall of the kingdom before the Arab attack.

His first need was to secure himself upon the throne. Therefore, twelve weeks after his accession, on 9 January 681, he opened the Twelfth Council. The bishops set out the circumstances in which he had reached the throne, they released the population of the kingdom from its oath of allegiance to Wamba, and they declared Erwig to be the legitimate ruler of Spain: any man who should act or raise his voice against him was anathema. All this was included in the first canon of the Council. The bishops then significantly turned to discuss the case of those who, appearing to be at the point of death, were given penance while unconscious: what should be done if, unexpectedly recovering their health,

---

[1] Zeumer, p. 478. 8.   [2] Contin. Isid. Hisp. 49 (ii. 349).
[3] XII Tolet. praef., 'quibus malis terra prematur quibusque plagis proventu dierum succedentium feriatur'.

they tried to reject the venerable sign of the tonsure and the religious habit? What if they declared 'most impudently' that they were not bound by the rules of ecclesiastical discipline since they had not asked for penance and did not know that they were receiving it? Such men were now condemned: they must never be allowed to return to the civil or military service. It is hardly open to doubt that the reference was to Wamba: it looks as though the old King on his recovery had struggled in vain to resume the royal office.[1]

But an embarrassing question was raised at the Thirteenth Council by Gaudentius, Bishop of Valera de Arriba (Valeria in Carthaginiensis), who asked it through his deputy. He had fallen gravely ill and had been subjected to the rules of penance: could he now lawfully perform his episcopal duties? The bishops made a lengthy reply to this ill-timed question. They assured Gaudentius that he could indeed continue to perform the duties of his office. Penance does not deprive a man of his heavenly rights, but he must refrain from sin and from 'the tumults of secular business'.[2] There was one rule for Gaudentius and another for an unpopular king.

The earliest actions of Erwig's reign reveal a consistent policy that extended over several fields of government. It was a policy of far-reaching concession, perhaps almost of total surrender, to the nobility and the bishops. It looks as though he had had to pay a high price for being recognized as king; and the price was exacted to the full. His concessions lay in his attitude towards the Church, in taxation, in his revision of Reccesuinth's law code, and in other matters.

He brought to an end the period—it had lasted for no less than a quarter of a century—in which no general council of the Church had been allowed to meet in Spain. He himself opened the Twelfth Council in the Church of the Holy Apostles at Toledo on 9 January 681, less than three months after his coronation. And less than two years later, on 4 November 683 in that same church, he personally opened a second plenary council, the Thirteenth of Toledo. No monarch had summoned two general councils in so short a period since Chintila had called the Fifth and Sixth in 636

---

[1] XII Tolet. 2. (The phrase *militare cingulum* indicates the civil as well as the military service.) The first four canons of XII Tolet. deal in one way or another with Wamba.   [2] XIII Tolet. 10.

and 638. Chintila did so in fear of armed rebellion; but Erwig did so in compliance to the Church. Again, no monarch had appeared in person at a council since Reccesuinth had opened the Eighth Council in 653. Erwig issued an Edict in Confirmation of the resolutions of both Councils, though no other king had done so since Chintila.

That he did not intend to capitulate abjectly to the nobility of Church and State was perhaps shown by his revision of Wamba's army law, and by that alone. This law had been directed chiefly against the slave-owning nobility and the clergy, and Erwig did not repeal it. But he rehabilitated those who had already been condemned under its provisions; and the bishops went on to add a dubious piece of legislation. They allowed those who had lost their right of testifying in the courts under this law to offer their evidence in cases that had been heard while they were still under ban. Apparently, suits that had been closed might now be re-opened.[1] But when Erwig revised this law he made no concessions to the clergy (p. 264 below).

On 1 November 683, however, he made a major concession to the nobility. The Roman emperors had from time to time re-mitted outstanding arrears of taxes.[2] It was well known that such remissions favoured the rich, who had been strong enough to postpone payment of their taxes, and penalized the poor, who had had to pay up on demand. But the Emperors rarely remitted taxes for the years immediately preceding their act of indulgence. The extreme case was the Emperor Majorian, who, when he succeeded to the throne in 461, cancelled all debts to the Treasury up to the previous financial year. But even he was not much more extreme than Erwig (the first Visigothic king known to have remitted taxes at all). In an edict published at Toledo on 1 November 683 he annulled all taxes on slaves that had not yet been paid and that were due before his accession in 681. This was a blatant sop to the slave-owning nobility.[3]

Three days later, on 4 November, ten years after the sup-pression of the revolt of Paul, we hear once more of the rebels, or at any rate of those of them who still survived. Erwig directed the bishops at the Thirteenth Council to review the sentence of 'the profaners of their country'.[4] Accordingly, the bishops decreed

---

[1] XII Tolet. 7. [2] Jones, i. p. 467.
[3] Zeumer, p. 479. [4] Ibid., p. 478. 6 ff.

that 'all whom the wicked conspiracy of Paul once drew into treachery against their race and their country' should be restored to their former status and bear no further disgrace for their perfidy. Less delicately than the King, they pointed out that the amnesty applied only to those conspirators who had been noblemen. They extended the amnesty to the children who had been born to the defeated rebels after the suppression of the revolt, and they went on to forgive and rehabilitate all who had been similarly disgraced since the time of Chintila over forty years earlier. Any of their property which still remained in the possession of the Crown was now restored to them.[1] It may not be a coincidence, then, that three signatories of the acts of the Council of 683 —Trasaric, Trasimir, and Recaulf[2]—bear names that are identical with those of three of the men who had been taken prisoner by Wamba's forces at Nîmes.

The bishops lamented the fact that forced confessions had driven many palatine officials to death or 'perpetual ignominy'. Henceforth, according to the Thirteenth Council, no palatine official or bishop may be the victim of the king's guile. If his guilt were not manifest, a palatine official could not be driven from his office or banned from the court, imprisoned, interrogated, tortured, or whipped, or suffer the confiscation of his property, or be so treated as to make a false, secret, and fraudulent confession of guilt. If charged, he should be tried at a public meeting of bishops, *seniores*, and *gardingi* (p. 252 below), that is to say, he should be tried before his peers. Even those who lived where flight to another country was possible, and those who had to be carefully watched so as to avoid disturbances within the country, could not be kept under close arrest. They could be watched, but not terrorized. The date of their trial could not be postponed until they were obliged to make a false confession because of being separated for so long from their wives, relatives, and property. Any such confession would be invalid. Now, Erwig had said nothing of this in the tome that he addressed to the Thirteenth Council; and the ruling is one that the Council wrested from him.[3]

He was almost as fanatical as Reccesuinth in his attitude to the Jews. He drafted no fewer than twenty-eight laws against them, and in doing so showed a haste which was scarcely less indecent

---

[1] XIII Tolet. 1.   [2] Zeumer, p. 486.   [3] XIII Tolet. 2.

than that of Sisebut when he had come to the throne in 612 (p. 165 above). In the twelve weeks that intervened between his accession and the opening of the Twelfth Council he completed the drafting of the whole of his anti-Jewish legislation; and he was able to beg the Council to 'extirpate the pestilential Jews root and branch'. The bishops confirmed his laws in the ninth canon of their acts.

The King emphasized Reccesuinth's law against heretics in general (p. 206 above): any public defence of heretical opinions would be punished by exile and the confiscation of property. If a man were found to hold heretical views through ignorance, he should be sent to the local bishop or priest for instruction; and if he failed to correct his beliefs he would be liable to the same penalty as the public champion of heresy.[1] Jews were not allowed to read, or to be in possession of, books in which the Christian faith was criticized. The penalty was public decalvation and 100 lashes. Erwig directed that all children above the age of 10 years should be subject to the full ferocity of the punishment.[2]

He repealed that part of Sisebut's law which gave Jews the right (and the duty) to manumit Christian slaves. They held Christians illegally and therefore could not be said to manumit them. They might sell them, however, under the supervision of the local bishop, but they should do so within sixty days beginning on 1 February. After 1 April no Jew might own a Christian slave on pain of losing half his property. But the remainder of Sisebut's law was reaffirmed, apart from the death penalty for proselytism.[3] Erwig reaffirmed the whole of Reccesuinth's anti-Jewish legislation, except that he repealed the law that laid down a single penalty of death by stoning or burning for breach of any one of the laws. This uniform punishment of death for all offences alike, great and small, was too harsh.[4]

Unlike Reccesuinth, Erwig made baptism obligatory. Any Jew who failed to have himself, his family, and his slaves baptized within one year of the publication of the new law would receive 100 lashes, suffer decalvation, be sent into exile, and forfeit his property to the king.[5] This, too, was the penalty for a Jew who

---

[1] *LV* xii. 3. 1. [2] Ibid. 11. [3] Ibid. 12 f.
[4] Ibid. 1; but both Sisebut's and Reccesuinth's offending laws were retained in Erwig's code.
[5] Ibid. 3.

celebrated the Passover or any other Jewish festival. But the penalty for circumcision, whether of Jews or Christians, was far worse: both the circumcised and the operator were condemned to have their genitals wholly amputated as well as to lose all their property. A woman who circumcised, or who gave over others to be circumcised, would have her nose cut off and would lose her property. This, too, was the penalty for proselytism.[1] Again, from the day of the opening of the Twelfth Council on 9 January 681, no Jew might have power to punish or to issue orders to Christians, unless the king should explicitly give him authority to do so.[2] Thus, no Jew might be appointed 'agent' (*actor*) of an estate. Now, it appears that the Church and the monasteries often enough appointed Jews to such offices; and Erwig therefore singled out bishops and monks for special warning against such offences.[3] Exasperating restrictions were imposed on Jews who wished to travel. If a Jew journeyed from one city or province to another, he had immediately on his arrival at his destination to present himself to the local bishop, priest, or judge, who would see to it that he did not celebrate the Jewish Sabbath or any other festival. He had to lodge with devout Christians and eat with them and take the Christian communion. The local priest would inquire where he proposed to go next, and would write ahead to the priest of that place to warn him of the Jew's intended arrival. He might not return home until he had received a letter from the bishop or priest of each locality through which he made his way, stating the date of his arrival, the length of his stay, and the date of his departure.[4] But he was not allowed to travel at all on the Jewish Sabbath or other feasts: on those days each Jewish community had to congregate with the bishop or judge. And it was necessary to declare that on these occasions bishops should not be left alone with Jewish women: any bishop who raped or had intercourse with them was to be unfrocked and exiled.[5]

All punishments prescribed in these Christian laws were to be inflicted by the bishop, and the Jewish defendant was to have no advocate to speak for him.[6] But Erwig, like other kings before him, expected that some bishops and judges would be reluctant to enforce such savage laws or would be bribed to ignore them: the fine for such an omission was 72 solidi.[7] Judges should not act

---

[1] *LV* xii. 3. 4. [2] Ibid. 17. [3] Ibid. 19. [4] Ibid. 20.
[5] Ibid. 21. [6] Ibid. 23. [7] Ibid. 24.

without the bishops' knowledge: otherwise, they might be open to bribery[1]. A penalty was also prescribed for any cleric or layman who accepted a bribe from a Jew in return for concealing Jewish practices.[2]

Finally, in order that no Jew might plead ignorance of the law, Erwig instructed each of his bishops and priests to assemble the local Jewish community in his church and to read out the text of the laws to them. Each Jew's statement of abjuration and of adherence to Christianity was to be preserved in the archives of the local church. And a note at the end of the manuscript text of Erwig's code informs us that the twenty-eight laws were read out to the Jews of Toledo in the Church of St. Mary on 27 January 681, three days after the Twelfth Council had closed.[3]

It can at least be said for Erwig that he abolished the death penalty which Sisebut had imposed for proselytism and which Reccesuinth had prescribed for each and every breach of his ten furious laws against Judaism. A Jew who refused to abandon the faith of his fathers might now expect at least to remain alive, in however terrible a condition. Again, the new laws, like those of Reccesuinth, were directed solely at the practice of the Jewish religion; and a Jew who professed himself to have been converted to Christianity was left unharmed, though he had to submit to severe tests, to sign a formula of abjuration—Erwig appended such a formula to the text of his laws—and to bind himself by a lengthy oath. If he were then discovered to have continued to practise the Jewish rite in secret, he lost all his goods, was whipped 100 times, suffered decalvation, and was sent into exile.[4] Economic sanctions were not yet imposed, though the conditions to which a Jew had to submit if he wished to travel must have interfered gravely with the livelihood of Jewish merchants. But what emerges clearly from the laws is their futility. The similar legislation of Reccesuinth and others had been unenforceable. In spite of the judicial terror, Jews had continued to practise their religion, to own Christian slaves, and to hold offices that gave them power over Christians. Moreover, Christian clergy and laymen alike, at least in some cases, had been willing to turn a blind eye to the 'offences' or had thought a bribe a good reason for saying nothing.

---

[1] Ibid. 25.   [2] Ibid. 10
[3] Ibid. 28.   [4] Ibid. 13–15.

A majority of the bishops who attended the Twelfth Council may well have welcomed this legislation; and one of them certainly did so. This was the powerful Metropolitan of Toledo, Julian, the most eminent scholar of his day. Though born of Christian parents, he was of Jewish extraction.[1] He had written a (lost) treatise, the *Responsiones*, in defence of the laws and canons that denied the right of Jews to hold Christian slaves. He had also composed a reply to the Jewish claim that the Messiah had not yet come. This last work is extant. It begins with an address to Erwig, who, says Julian, had instructed him to write it; and the address ends with a bold warning to the King that his work would be respected on the Day of Judgement only if he pressed on the neck of the enemies of Christ and valiantly upheld the standard of the Christian faith.[2] He dedicated his *Prognosticon* to Idalius, Bishop of Barcelona, who was taken aback to find that Julian sent him his copy of the book in the hands of a Jewish porter called Restitutus.[3]

It was this Julian, no doubt, who now won for Toledo the position of primatial see of all Spain (p. 275 below). And if any bishop were henceforth summoned to Toledo by the king and the metropolitan either to celebrate the major festivals of Easter, Pentecost, or Nativity, to attend a lawsuit, to help in consecrating bishops, or because of some order of the king, he should arrive at the appointed time on pain of excommunication.[4]

Erwig's most noteworthy achievement was his revision of Reccesuinth's law code. In the tome that he handed to the Twelfth Council he asked the bishops to correct inconsistencies in his laws and to eliminate whatever seemed contrary to justice.[5] He was not referring to his legislation against the Jews, which he had mentioned a little earlier. Nor was his reference to his amendment of Wamba's army law; for this, too, he had mentioned already. What then were the laws that he instructed the bishops to correct?

---

[1] Contin, Isid. Hisp. 50 (ii. 349), 'ex traduce Iudeorum . . . qui etiam a parentibus Christianis progenitus'. Cf. Murphy, art. cit. 5. Murphy gives a brief but valuable account of Julian's life. The chief source is Felix (soon afterwards himself Metropolitan of Toledo), *Vita S. Iuliani* (PL 96. 443–52).

[2] PL 96. 538 ff. The fact that Julian wrote against the Jews does not prove, despite Juster, pp. 293 f., that Jews were still publishing attacks on Christianity.

[3] PL 96. 458. We do not know the circumstances of the 'bellica profectio gloriosi principis ab urbe regia', which Julian mentions in his letter to Idalius (PL 96. 456).

[4] XIII Tolet. 8.   [5] Zeumer, p. 476. 13 f.

Did he refer to the few novels that he later incorporated in his code? Or was the revised code itself already complete? Had he and his lawyers carried through the work in the three months that had elapsed since he reached the throne?[1] It is certain only that the code was completed and published before 21 October 681, the first anniversary of his accession; for on that date it came into effect.[2] Its price was 12 solidi, double the price of Reccesuinth's.[3] In its original form it survives in a single manuscript.

His reason for undertaking the revision was the obscurity and ambiguity of many of the laws in the earlier code.[4] But he omitted altogether Reccesuinth's law which punished those who mutilated their slaves;[5] and he replaced a few other enactments by wholly new laws of his own.[6] He also included Wamba's legislation, which cannot have been very popular with the clergy. But what he mainly did was to go through Reccesuinth's code, law by law, line by line, making an extraordinary number of small changes and small additions that were designed to clarify the meaning of the laws or in some cases to change their sense. The diligence of the King and his lawyers is impressive: a huge number of the laws were amended or clarified. Not least important, he made many concessions to the nobility, lightening the penalties to which they were subject under the criminal law,[7] and protecting their privileges.[8]

In return for all this—his summoning of two plenary councils of the Church, his modification of Wamba's army law, his cancellation of outstanding taxes on slaves, his amnesty for nobly-born rebels, his laws against the Jews, and his concessions in the revised law code—Erwig got very little apart from recognition as the lawful ruler of Spain. At the second session of the Thirteenth Council, on 5 November 683, the bishops passed a resolution which they described as a 'return' for the King's kindness. Following in the futile footsteps of Chintila, Erwig tried to protect his family. The bishops called, therefore, 'before God and His holy angels' on all future kings to inflict no injustice on Queen Liuvigoto, her sons and daughters, and their wives and husbands. No one might kill them or strip them of their property,

---

[1] Zeumer, NA xxiii (1898), p. 496, leaves the question open.
[2] LV ii. 1. 1; cf. 14. [3] Ibid. v. 4. 22. [4] Ibid. ii. 1. 1.
[5] Ibid. vi. 5. 13. [6] Zeumer, art. cit. 498.
[7] Examples are LV ii. 1. 8, 21; vi. 1. 2.
[8] e.g. ibid. ii. 2. 9; v. 2. 2; vi. 5. 12.

or tonsure the males (the fate of Wamba, though the bishops wisely omitted to recall the fact), or clothe the women in the religious habit, or without good cause exile, mutilate, or flog them. Anyone who did so would be anathema for ever. Secondly, no one might marry Liuvigoto or have intercourse with her, even if he were a king, should she outlive Erwig. Anyone who did so would be doomed to the sulphurous fires of the Devil.[1] But no king is known to have married his predecessor's widow since Leovigild married Athanagild's unprepossessing relict more than a century earlier; and the bishops give no hint at Erwig's reasons for requesting these useless resolutions.

The Thirteenth Council closed on 13 November 683, and the bishops had scarcely returned home when there arrived in Spain a papal regional notary called Peter. He brought with him a letter addressed by Pope Leo II (April 682–July 683) to all the bishops of Spain, asking them to confirm and subscribe the decisions of the Third Council of Constantinople, the Sixth Ecumenical Council. The Pope sent similar letters to Quiricus, Metropolitan of Toledo (not knowing that he had died more than two years previously), to an otherwise unknown Count Simplicius, and to Erwig.[2] The Sixth Ecumenical Council had condemned Monotheletism and had asserted the Two Wills and Operations in Christ; and the Pope's request was one that called for the meeting of a general council in Spain. But that winter was severe, and the bishops had only recently travelled to and from Toledo. They could not reasonably be summoned to the capital a second time, and Erwig therefore called a provincial synod of the bishops of Carthaginiensis which was also attended by representatives of the metropolitans of all the other provinces. But this was not enough. The King directed provincial synods to meet in the other provinces at which the representatives who had attended at Toledo would report the decisions of the bishops of Carthaginiensis; and the provincial bishops would then confirm the resolutions of the Ecumenical Council.

---

[1] XIII Tolet. 4 f.

[2] PL 96. 414–20. The episode (of which I give a drastically shortened account) is carefully discussed by F. X. Murphy, 'Julian of Toledo and the Condemnation of Monothelitism in Spain', *Mélanges J. de Ghellinck* (Gembloux, 1951), i. 361–73. He points to the curious fact that the Pope knew of Erwig's succession in 680 but was unaware of Quiricus's death in that same year. The chronology of the whole episode needs further research.

The Fourteenth Council of Toledo met on 14 November 684 to consider the replies of the provincial synods; and in due course it sent the Pope its approval of the conclusions of the Ecumenical Council.[1] It also issued a warning to the people of Spain that these divine matters must not be discussed: they must simply be believed.[2] All this had taken time, and the new Pope, Benedict II, wrote to Peter urging him to hurry things up.[3] But when he received the Spanish bishops' letter of approval he was deeply disturbed by it, for in his opinion some of its phrases, and particularly the phrase 'Will engendered Will' (*voluntas genuit voluntatem*), were doctrinally incorrect. The matter led to a clash between Julian of Toledo and the Papacy. Julian was firm and uncompromising, as Braulio had been in his correspondence with Pope Honorius I more than forty years earlier (p. 185 above). His language was offensive. He accused the Pope of reading his document carelessly and of radically misunderstanding his contentions; and he was able to support his positions by numerous quotations from the Fathers, particularly Athanasius, Ambrose, Augustine, and, of course, Isidore of Seville. Eventually, his argument was substantially adopted by the Fifteenth Council of Toledo in 688 with the consent of King Egica; and the somewhat extreme view has been expressed that, had it not been for the Muslim invasion, the Spanish Church might have been led into schism.[4]

Since the death of Gregory the Great in 604 this was only the second occasion on which the Popes had officially communicated with the Spanish bishops; and the experience of Benedict II was no more happy than that of Honorius.[5]

Erwig's later years were afterwards criticized, though not by a reliable critic. After he was dead, Egica spoke of his cruelty to many men, whom he unjustly deprived of office and property, and of his enslavement of noblemen. He hinted at torture and violent judgements. But the documents give no details, and Egica had cause to overstate his case. There is no reason to doubt that Erwig was the first and last Visigothic king to be the puppet of the lay and ecclesiastical nobility throughout his reign.

---

[1] XIV Tolet. 4.   [2] Ibid. 10.   [3] *PL* 96. 423 f.
[4] Murphy, art. cit. 371, who himself rejects the opinion.
[5] On the rarity of communication between Spain and the Papacy in the seventh century see Magnin, pp. 1–31.

On 14 November 687, now mortally sick, he nominated as his successor, not one of his sons, but Egica, the husband of his daughter Cixilo.[1] On the following day, which was a Friday, he took penance and allowed all the *seniores* to leave him—we do not know where he was—and to go to Toledo with Egica.[2]

3. *Egica*

On the following Sunday week, 24 November 687, Egica was anointed in the Church of the Holy Apostles at Toledo;[3] and in that same church, on 11 May 688, he opened in person the Fifteenth Council. Like earlier kings, when opening the plenary councils, he prostrated himself on the ground and commended himself to the bishops' prayers. (We do not know the significance of the fact that at the Sixteenth and Seventeenth Councils he merely bowed his head.) Apart from his desire to reaffirm the position taken up by Julian in the matter of the Two Wills, he had only one reason for summoning the Fifteenth Council.

When giving him his daughter in marriage, Erwig had required him to swear an oath to protect and champion the royal children. At the time of his death he had exacted another oath: Egica had to undertake that before sitting upon the throne he would bind himself not to deny justice to the people. But he now declared that these two oaths, to protect Erwig's children and to give justice to the people, had turned out to be contradictory. The wrongs that Erwig had inflicted upon the people, he declared, could not be righted without harm to Erwig's children. Perhaps he meant that Erwig had given to his children property that he had taken from those persons whom (according to Egica) he had wrongfully condemned: this could not be restored to its rightful owners without loss to Erwig's children.[4] The new king, there-fore, asked the bishops to release him from one or other of these contradictory oaths. He told them to put aside all fear and favour in coming to a decision; but the wording of his tome (p. 278 below) left them in no doubt as to which of the oaths he wished to discard. The bishops obliged him to the extent that they

---

[1] Her name is given in XVII Tolet. 7.   [2] Zeumer, p. 461.

[3] Ibid. Egica may be identical with the *Egica comes scanciarum et dux* who signed the minutes of the XIII Toletanum.

[4] Zeumer, 481. 2, 'ex hoc [=the oath to protect his family] cunctis quasi aditum reclamandi obstruxerit'.

declared the public interest to be more important than the interests of a single family. But the oath in favour of Erwig's family must not be wholly disregarded: the King must love his people and his family equally. Justice must be done to both parties.

Egica also asked the bishops to reconsider canon four of the Thirteenth Council, the canon that called for the protection of Erwig's family. But in this case he was rebuffed: nothing in the canon forbade the imposing of a just punishment on Erwig's family if they deserved one. If Erwig's sons were guilty of a crime, the canon could not save them from the penalties of the law. But the tone of the bishops' answer is tart and impatient and shows something of the strong hand of Julian of Toledo. What the bishops did insist upon was that all judgements should be just.

There was no other business for the Council to discuss; and there is little doubt that, apart from wishing to settle doctrinal questions, Egica summoned it because he wanted to ruin his wife's relatives. But for this project he was far from having won the full support of the bishops. He therefore followed up his partial failure at the Fifteenth Council by a curious move: he summoned a provincial synod of the bishops of Tarraconensis to meet at Saragossa on 1 November 691, where a resolution was passed that directed Queen Liuvigoto to abandon the world and spend the rest of her days in a convent.[1] This was a remarkable decision for a provincial synod to take, especially as it directly repealed part of canon four of the plenary Thirteenth Council. Although nothing is recorded of Egica's motives, it may be that he was convinced that a general council headed by Julian of Toledo would have agreed to no such decision. He therefore waited, we may think, until Julian was out of the way—he died on 6 March 690—and then continued his attacks on Erwig's family by the more tractable means of a provincial synod.

It is scarcely a surprise that the chronicler of 754, in the five words in which he characterizes Egica, says that 'he persecuted the Goths with bitter death'.[2] He followed Erwig's example in remitting taxes, but we have no details, and even this did not save his reputation.[3]

[1] III Caesaraug. 5.   [2] Contin. Isid. Hisp. 53 (ii. 349).

[3] III Caesaraug. 5 fin., 'populum per oracula regni sui voto gratioso ab inpensione tributi reddidit absolutum'; XVI Tolet. 8, 'tributorum impensione populis moderamine discreto remittit'.

In 693 there was a conspiracy against him; and on this occasion the leading rebel was so eminent that his name has survived. He was the Metropolitan of Toledo himself, Julian's successor, a Goth called Sisebert. His immediate aim was to assassinate Egica and some of his leading men, whose names were Frogellus, Theodomir, Liuvila, Tecla, and others, as well as the unhappy Queen Liuvigoto herself.[1] A coin that dates from this period and that was minted at Toledo bears the name of Suniefred; and it is almost certain that the ultimate aim of the conspiracy was to place this man upon the throne; and the rebels would seem to have controlled Toledo for a while.[2]

The rebellion was discussed at the Sixteenth Council of Toledo, which opened in the Church of the Holy Apostles on 2 May 693. In his tome Egica spoke of 'many' who broke their trust, and he declared that any palatine official who conspired to murder the king or to ruin the Gothic people, or who caused any insurrection in Spain, would be driven from every office, and so would his descendants after him. He would become the slave of the Treasury and would lose all his property.[3] The bishops then unfrocked Sisebert and excommunicated him: he would receive communion only on his deathbed, unless the King should pardon him earlier. They also stripped him of all his goods.[4] Sisebert himself was brought before the assembly to hear the episcopal sentence pronounced; and he confessed his guilt.[5] It was decided that in future the punishment of rebels was to be prohibition from ever again holding a palatine office—it seems to have been assumed that usurpers would be drawn exclusively from the palatine officials—and enslavement to the Treasury. Their descendants, too, would not be permitted to hold such office. The king might present their property to the Church, to his children, or to anyone else of his choice; and the rebels' descendants would never be allowed to reclaim it. A curse was called down on any future monarch who failed to enforce this ruling. The bishops then read

[1] Observe that none of the men whom Sisebert proposed to murder signed the minutes of the XVI Toletanum.

[2] Miles, pp. 37 f., 405, with literature. The minutes of the Thirteenth Council were signed by *Suniefredus comes scanciarum et dux*, the same offices as those held by the Egica who also signed the minutes. I do not know the significance of a coin of Egica that was minted at Guadix (Acci) and bears the legend VICTOR: Miles, pp. 92 f., 392.

[3] Zeumer, p. 483. 8 ff.   [4] XVI Tolet. 9.

[5] *Decretum Iudicii*, printed after XVI Tolet. 11.

out three times—and three times the notaries copied into their minutes—an extract from the seventy-fifth canon of the Fourth Council, in which usurpers were declared anathema (p. 174 above). At the end of the third reading all the bishops, the *seniores* of the palace, all the clergy and people in the Church of the Holy Apostles called out that those who broke the canon might be *anathema maranatha* and share the fate of Judas Iscariot.[1]

Felix of Seville, the biographer of Julian, was translated to Toledo to take Sisebert's place; and Faustinus of Braga was moved to Seville. This translation of metropolitans was without parallel in seventh-century Spain, and the bishops were careful to point out that the moves were made 'with the consent of the clergy and people'. Egica confirmed the acts of the Council and reasserted the penalty of excommunication for usurpers which had been laid down in canon 75 of the Fourth Council. But the bishops of Gallia Narbonensis had been unable to attend the Council owing to the plague (*inguinalis plaga*) that was raging in their province. Egica therefore instructed the suffragans of Narbonensis to meet with their metropolitan in Narbonne and, after reading through the minutes of the Sixteenth Council, to sign them. Any who infringed these canons would be excommunicated and would forfeit one-fifth of his goods.

The King followed up the decisions of the Council by adding a law to Erwig's code. He referred to the canon of the Thirteenth Council that protected palatine officials from premature dismissal and arrest. Apparently, Sisebert and his accomplices had used that canon to their advantage. The King was not strong enough to revoke the canon entirely; and he therefore made it illegal for any persons to bind themselves with any oath other than the oath of allegiance to the Crown and the oaths taken in the law courts. A man who swore any other oath whatsoever would now be guilty of conspiracy and subject to Chindasuinth's law on usurpers.[2] Since we do not know how Sisebert had used the concessions granted by Erwig to the nobility, we cannot see this law in its context.

In his address to the Sixteenth Council in 693 Egica asked the bishops to revise the laws apart from those of the kings from Chindasuinth to Wamba.[3] He had the laws of Erwig in mind, and

[1] XVI Tolet. 10.
[2] *LV* ii. 5. 19, with Zeumer, *NA* xxiii (1898), pp. 506 f.
[3] Zeumer, p. 483. 15 f.

in fact he repealed more than one of them. The most notable example was his criticism of Erwig's repeal of Reccesuinth's law on the mutilation of slaves, a law which he restored to the code with a hostile reference to his father-in-law.[1] But he did not subject the code to a systematic revision, as Erwig had done, nor did he produce a new edition. He added over a dozen laws to Erwig's code but left the code itself basically unchanged. The novels deal with a wide variety of topics and are in some cases merciful, as in the re-enactment of Reccesuinth on the mutilation of slaves, and in others merciless, as in the law on fugitive slaves (p. 273 below). Although he was not afraid to attack the nobility, his assault leaves the impression of ineffectiveness.[2]

Like others before him, Erwig had failed to extirpate Judaism from Spain; and Egica continued the persecution. But his attack took a wholly new direction: he aimed to deprive the Jews of the capacity to earn a living. In the tome (p. 278 below) addressed to the Sixteenth Council he set out his aim of destroying Judaism once and for all. He referred to a law which he had already enacted and which he added to Erwig's code. It declared that any Jew who was truly converted to the Catholic faith would be freed from paying the tax on Jews (a tax that we have not heard of hitherto): the amount of this tax would be added to that paid by unconverted Jews. The convert might also trade freely, but a Christian who was not sure of his conversion might not buy anything from him until the Jew had first declared himself to be a Christian and had recited before witnesses the Lord's Prayer and the Apostles' Creed and had eaten Christian food. But a Jew who remained unconverted might not go to the harbour to carry on overseas trade, nor might he trade with a Christian: Jews could only trade among themselves. Moreover, a Christian who traded with an unconverted Jew, if he were a *maior persona*, would be fined 216 solidi, while an *inferior* would be whipped 100 times and fined a sum fixed by the king. What of Jews in agriculture? Slaves and any immovable property—buildings, land, vineyards, olive groves—that they had at any time acquired from Christians would be taken over by the State, though the Treasury would pay compensation for them. The bishops confirmed this law and once

---

[1] *LV* vi. 5. 13 f., where note 'hanc legem iustissime editam, iniuste abrasam'. For further criticism of Erwig see ibid. ii. 4. 8, with Zeumer, *NA* xxiv (1899), p. 104.   [2] *LV* ii. 1. 7; 5. 19.

again remarked that they did so at the King's request.[1] In the course of his tome Egica observed incidentally that synagogues were now banned and in ruins. No extant law had directed them to be closed and destroyed; but no doubt each outburst of royal anger against the Jews throughout the century had caused more and more of the synagogues to be demolished by the more pious elements in the Christian population.[2]

When the Seventeenth Council met on 9 November 694, the first subject that Egica mentioned in his tome was the Jews. He had heard an alarming piece of news. It was reported that in some parts of the world the Jews had rebelled against their Christian rulers and that many of them had been killed by the kings. He had now learned from 'confessions' that the Jews of Spain had conspired with Jews overseas (perhaps he meant in Africa) to rise one and all against the race of Christians and to destroy the Christian religion. The confessions would make this clear to the bishops. He was himself personally offended. Had he not shown mercy to the Jews from the very beginning of his reign? Had he not allowed them to keep their Christian slaves, demanding nothing whatever in return except that they should become Christians? But his kindness had been misplaced: they had persevered in secret in their unbelief. Now, therefore, their wickedness must be ended, except for the Jews in Narbonensis, which was so ravaged by plague and Frankish raids that there were few inhabitants left there. The Jews of that province (*ducatus*) were simply to hand over their property to the *dux*.

In their eighth canon the bishops followed up the news of this 'conspiracy'—it was, of course, a figment or an invention of Egica's—with the last and most ruthless of all the laws relating to the Jews in Spain. Since the Jews had tried to bring ruin upon the fatherland and all the people, their cruel and astonishing presumption must be extirpated by an even crueller punishment. The bishops therefore decreed 'on the order of our most pious and most religious prince Egica' that they should be stripped of all their property, and that they and their wives and children should be taken from their homes and enslaved for ever throughout all the provinces of Spain. They would never be freed or given an opportunity to practise their religion. Some of their Christian slaves would be chosen by the King to take over their property,

---

[1] Ibid. xii. 2. 18; XVI Tolet. 1.   [2] Zeumer, p. 482. 16; Juster, p. 316.

and these men would pay the taxes that the Jews had hitherto paid. (The tax on Jews, as a French scholar has put it, outlived the Jews themselves.)[1] The persons upon whom the King bestowed the enslaved Jews would have to sign an undertaking never to allow them to practise their rites. Finally, their children would be taken from them when they reached the age of 7 years and would be handed over to devout Christians to be brought up and in due course married off to Christians.[2]

No doubt some bishops and judges found ways and means to avoid enforcing these appalling regulations. No doubt, too, the law was rigorously enforced in several areas of Spain; and for nearly twenty years the victims had to wait before their liberators landed at Gibraltar. A Jew named Paragorus has left us a melancholy memorial dating from Egica's second year, 688. His three children had died of the plague that was ravaging Gallia Narbonensis at that time; and he set up their tombstone in Narbonne. The inscription includes a Hebrew phrase written in Hebrew characters, and has carved upon it a five-branched candlestick.[3] Paragorus at least was not afraid to proclaim his Jewish faith.

In return for thus saving the Catholic Church from destruction the bishops compensated the King in their own puzzling way: they passed a resolution anathematizing anyone who should injure Egica's queen and his children after his death. (In the list of injuries that were banned was that of unjust tonsure.)[4] The reason why Egica accepted this form of gratitude is mystifying. He had himself illustrated how frail such a guarantee could be, and Chindasuinth had long ago made short work of the guarantees that the Fifth and Sixth Councils had given to Chintila. The bishops crowned their gratitude by enacting that prayers should be offered up for the safety and well-being of the King and the royal family in every cathedral church in the kingdom on every day of the year except Good Friday, when mass was not celebrated.[5] Their prayers were effective: Egica died in his bed in 702. It was only in 698 that the Arabs had finally occupied Carthage.

4. Wittiza and Roderic

With the close of the Seventeenth Council we lose our best source of information on the last decades of the kingdom's

[1] Juster, p. 334.   [2] XVII Tolet. 8.   [3] Katz, pp. 148–51.
[4] XVII Tolet. 7.   [5] Ibid. 8.

history. No further conciliar documents have survived. We know that on 15 November 700, the thirteenth anniversary of his accession, Egica anointed his son Wittiza as joint king with himself; and late in the year 702 he published his fierce law on fugitive slaves (p. 273 below). Before the end of that year he was dead, and Wittiza reigned alone until the end of 710. The chronicler of 754 describes him as merciful, though he adds a mild word of criticism at the way in which he had reached the throne. He recalled those whom his father had exiled, restored their property and their slaves, publicly burned the statements of debt to the Treasury which Egica had forced them to sign, and gave them back their palatine posts. He is not said, however, to have alleviated the misery of the Jews. In his reign Felix of Toledo ruled the Church with dignity and prudence and during the joint reign of father and son held distinguished councils of the Church.[1] The acts of an Eighteenth Council of Toledo are said to have survived the Middle Ages in a single manuscript; but that manuscript is now lost, and nothing is known of the problems with which the bishops wrestled, the disputes that divided them, and the acts of oppression that they condoned or initiated on the eve of their destruction.[2] Felix was succeeded by a Goth named Gunderic, of whom the chronicler holds a high opinion;[3] but after Gunderic came another Goth, Sindered, a man of zealous piety, who at Wittiza's instigation harshly ruled and oppressed his venerable clergy.[4] A fragment of that same chronicle records the astonishing fact that in the joint reign of Egica and Wittiza a commander called Theudimer repelled a Byzantine naval descent on Spain. We know nothing whatever of the context of this strange event.[5]

When Wittiza died after a reign that brought prosperity and joy to Spain, according to the chronicler, the throne was illegally usurped by Roderic 'at the exhortation of the senate', a phrase that doubtless means that the palatine officials supported him. But if the bishops also supported him Roderic was no usurper. At all events, his accession shows that the measures taken by recent kings to check and overawe the palatine officials had in fact been ineffective. But Roderic lasted for no more than a year,

---

[1] Contin. Isid. Hisp. 58–60 (ii. 350 f.) There is a paper on Wittiza by F. Görres, 'Charakter und Religionspolitik des vorletzten spanischen Westgotenkönigs Witiza', *Zeitschrift f. wissenschaftliche Theologie*, xlviii (1905), pp. 96–111.

[2] Martinez Diez, pp. 166 f.   [3] Contin. Isid. Hisp. 63 (ii. 351).
[4] Ibid. 69.   [5] Ibid. 74 (ii. 354).

and the few coins of his that survive were minted by only two mints, those of Toledo and Idanha (Egitania).[1] Musa, the Arab governor of Africa, sent his general Tarik ibn Ziyad to Spain. Tarik set out from Ceuta (Septem)[2] and landed at the rock that still bears his name, Gebel Tarik, Gibraltar, and began to ravage the cities. In a battle at the unknown 'Transductine promontories' Roderic engaged the invaders with an army that was disaffected because of the circumstances in which he had reached the throne. Presumably he was opposed either by another member of the official aristocracy or by a relative of Wittiza. At any rate, in a single battle, according to the chronicler, he lost his throne and his country—and presumably his life, too, for he is never heard of again, though his widow, Egilo, lived to marry an Arab governor of Spain.[3] Sindered, Metropolitan of Toledo, in fear of the Arab incursion, deserted his flock and fled to Rome, where in 721 he attended a synod and signed its minutes as 'Sindered, a bishop from Spain'. He was 'an hireling, and not the shepherd' (John 10: 12).[4]

Musa himself soon crossed to Spain, where civil war was now raging among the Goths, though the identity of the leaders on each side is unknown.[5] He managed to enter Toledo and put to death among others Oppa, a son of Egica and brother of Wittiza; and he then advanced to beyond Saragossa, though it was at Cordoba that he established his headquarters.[6] The only man recorded explicitly to have resisted the Arabs with vigour is the Theudimer who had some years previously repulsed the Byzantine fleet; but even he made peace with Musa's son, Abd el Aziz.[7] And by 716 the invaders were in Narbonensis.[8]

That is an outline of what we learn from the chronicler of 754, who wrote less than half a century after the events. Later Latin and Arabic writers report many tales, not least about a Count Julian, Byzantine governor of Ceuta, and his daughter Florinda, whom King Roderic violated, so that Julian assisted the Arabs to Spain. Of this famous story the chronicler knows nothing, though he does report that a few years after Tarik's landing a very noble African Catholic called Urban was advising the Arabs in Spain.[9]

---

[1] Miles, pp. 39 f., 442 f.   [2] Paul. Diac., *Hist. Langob.* vi. 46.
[3] Contin. Isid. Hisp. 68 (ii. 352); 79 (ii. 356).   [4] Mansi, xii. 264.
[5] Contin. Isid. Hisp. 70 (ii. 353).   [6] Ibid. 71.
[7] Ibid. 74.   [8] Ibid. 80.   [9] Ibid. 77.

And he knows, too, that some years later a certain Urban, perhaps the same man, had become Metropolitan of Toledo and, with his archdeacon Euantius and the Bishop of Guadix (Acci), Fredoarius, brought much comfort to the Church until his death eighteen years later.[1]

It is certain that Roderic was succeeded by a king named Achila, who is said to have reigned for three years.[2] For some reason the chronicler passes over him in silence, though his reign is put beyond doubt by the survival of some of his coins. They were issued by mints in the north-east of the kingdom, at Narbonne, Gerona, and Tarragona. Indeed, he lasted long enough to issue two types of coin at the Gallic mint;[3] but what he achieved and how he met his end cannot now be told.

[1] Ibid. 87 (ii. 358); cf. 111 (ii. 363).
[2] Zeumer, pp. 461. 25. The Ardo mentioned there as having followed Achila is otherwise unknown.
[3] Miles, pp. 40 ff., 444 f.

XI · ADMINISTRATION

APART from the law codes and the acts of the various councils we have practically no documents that throw light on the life, public or private, of the inhabitants of the kingdom in the seventh century.

1. *Palatini and Gardingi*

The king's immediate entourage was formed by two groups of men, the *gardingi* and the *seniores* (or *primates* or *maiores*) *palatii*, who are also called the *viri illustres aulae regiae* (or *officii palatini*), or the like.

The *gardingi* are mentioned under that name only in documents of the time of Wamba and Erwig;[1] but they are no doubt identical with the king's *fideles*, whom Chintila had tried to protect at the Fifth Council (p. 181 above)—the only plenary council which a king is known to have opened in the company not only of his *seniores* but also of his *fideles*. These men accompanied the king on his campaigns, and in 666 the bishops of Lusitania directed prayers to be said not only for the king but also for his *fideles* and his army whenever they went out on an expedition.[2] They are mentioned a few times in the laws. Thus, an informer who could give information about a major crime (one involving the death penalty or confiscation of property) should bring it to the notice of one of the *fideles*, who would lay it before the king. The wording of the law implies that the *fideles* accompanied the king and would not be available except in his immediate neighbourhood.[3] But the

---

[1] *LV* ii. 1. 1, p. 45. 30 (Erwig), 'cunctis sacerdotibus Dei senioribusque palatii atque gardingis'; ix. 2. 8, p. 371. 13 (Wamba), 'seu sit dux aut comes, thiufadus aut vicarius, gardingus vel quelibet persona'; ix. 2. 9, p. 375. 6 (Erwig), 'si maioris loci persona fuerit, id est dux, comes, seu etiam gardingus'; ibid. 377. 6; xii. 1. 3, p. 408. 24 (Erwig); XIII Tolet. 2 (A.D. 683), 'in publica sacerdotum, seniorum atque gardingorum discussione'; Julian, *Hist.* 7 (p. 506), 'Ranosindum Tarraconensis provinciae ducem et Hildigisum sub gardingatus adhuc officio consistentem'; *Iudicium*, 5; *Vita S. Fructuosi*, 15, 'Benedicta claro genere exorta atque ex gardingo regis sponsa'.

[2] Conc. Emerit. 3.

[3] *LV* vi. 1. 6. Note that *fidelis* is mentioned in one MS. of iv. 5. 5, p. 201. 22. But ibid. v. 1. 1 *fidelium*, I think, means 'Christians', despite the doubt of Zeumer, Index, s.v. *fideles*. Other passages cited by Zeumer there also seem doubtful.

case of Hildigisus (p. 220 above) suggests that they were some-times detached for special service. Wamba's army law mentions the defence of 'the king, nation, fatherland, and the king's *fideles*'.[1] There seems little reason to doubt that the *gardingi* or *fideles* were the king's 'retinue' (*comitatus*, as Tacitus would have said), and one of them is referred to as 'a *gardingus* of the king' (p. 252 n. 1 above). Their function was to guard the person of the king, to whom, of course, they had direct access.[2] But the only one whom we know by name, Hildigisus, betrayed his trust and joined the rebellion against Wamba in 673. The king supported them by gifts of land and other property; and Chintila's aim at the Fifth Council was to ensure that this property and their position were not taken from them when a new king came to the throne, unless after the death of the old king they were discovered to have been unfaithful to him.[3] If they were 'companions', as Tacitus would have understood the term, their tie was with the king personally; and we do not know the outcome of Chintila's attempt to allow them to continue in 'office' under a succession of kings. It seems, somewhat unexpectedly, that Romans could be found among the king's *gardingi*.[4]

The noblemen who signed the renunciation of Arianism at the Third Council were not Reccared's *gardingi* or *fideles*. The minutes of the Council describe them as the *seniores Gothorum*; and it was the *seniores*, too, who signed at the Eighth and subsequent plenary councils of the Church (p. 295 below). At the Third Council they described themselves simply as *viri illustres*, but at later councils they sometimes gave the specific name of their office—Count of the Chamberlains (*cubiculariorum*), Constable (*comes stabuli*), Count of the Notaries,[5] Count of the Patrimony (whom we have already met), Count of the *spatharii*, Count of the City of Toledo, and so on. We can find offices with similar or identical names among the Romans and the Franks; but in the absence of detailed information it is fruitless to try to infer the exact functions of the Gothic officials from those of the corresponding Roman or Frankish officials. Thus, in Roman times the *spatharius* was a member of the Imperial bodyguard. Are the Gothic *spatharii*, then, identical with the *fideles* and the *gardingi*? Is it likely that

---

[1] *LV* ix. 2. 8, p. 373. 2.   [2] *Vita S. Fructuosi*, loc. cit.; VI Tolet. 14.
[3] Ibid.; V Tolet. 6.   [4] *LV* ix. 2. 9, p. 377. 6 f.
[5] For the royal *notarii* see *LV* vii. 5. 9, of which the legislator is unknown.

three terms, drawn from three languages, were used officially to describe the one man? However that may be, we do not know the relative importance of these various offices or their relationship with the executive officers (the *duces* and *comites*) in the provinces.

An amendment by Erwig of one of Chindasuinth's laws contrasts the *inferiores humilioresque*, who appear so often in Visigothic legislation (p. 136 above), not with the *maioris loci personae*, as is the usual practice, but with 'noble and powerful persons, such as are the *primates* of our palace and their sons'.[1] So the *maioris loci personae*, whom the laws so often mention, included (as we might have guessed) the *primates palatii* or *seniores* together with their sons. But the phrase shows that the *primates* did not by themselves make up the whole category of *maioris loci personae*. Who else fell into that category? We know from another law that this category comprised not only the *duces* and *comites* but also the *gardingi*,[2] and these three groups alone. It follows that the *seniores* were those who had held the specific offices of *dux* or *comes*, along with their sons. It also follows that the *gardingi* were not classified as part of the *officium palatinum*, a fact which is confirmed by a passage of the anonymous *Iudicium*, where a distinction is drawn between the *seniores*, the *gardingi*, and the palatine *officium* (p. 225 above). The distinction is a natural one: the *gardingi* were retainers of the king personally, whereas the *seniores* were top-ranking military and civil servants. Now, Reccesuinth distinguishes between the *mediocres* and the *primi* of the palace;[3] and other documents draw a distinction between the *seniores*, on the one hand, and, on the other, the *officium palatinum* or 'the rest of the men of the *officium palatinum*',[4] a more accurate phrase. The *primates palatii* were a more restricted and distinguished group than the *officium* as a whole: they were the highest officers within it. The lesser members of the palace were required by the Sixth Council to show due honour and respect towards their superiors.[5] The number of the *seniores* is never stated. Twenty-six of them

---

[1] *LV* vi. 1. 2, p. 248, 'nobiles . . . potentioresque personae, ut sunt primates palatii nostri eorumque filii'. In iii. 1. 5 Chindasuinth equates the *seniores gentis Gotorum* with the *primates palatii*.

[2] Ibid. ix. 2. 9, p. 375.

[3] Ibid. xii. 2. 15.

[4] *Iudicium* 5 (p. 533); VII Tolet. 1, 'omnesque seniores vel iudices ac ceteros homines officii palatini'.

[5] VI Tolet. 13.

attended the Thirteenth Council in 683, but this was only a selection of the total number.[1]

Occasionally, Romans could be found among them. Helladius, who became Metropolitan of Toledo under Sisebut, had previously been 'an *illustrissimus* of the royal court'. Nicolaus, father of the poet Eugenius of Toledo, 'won magnificent triumphs over the enemy', and so probably held high office.[2] The Count Simplicius, to whom the Pope wrote in 683 (p. 240 above), must have been a prominent official; and the signatures at the later Councils of Toledo include four Roman names. But there is no reason to doubt that the Goths were in a vast majority at the royal court.

In private life Roman and Gothic noblemen corresponded on equal terms in the seventh century. St. Braulio of Saragossa, who was a Roman,[3] sent some of his letters of consolation to Gothic men and women when he heard of the death of their close relatives. He addressed such letters to two Gothic women called Hoio and Eutrocia, to a man named Ataulf, and to Wistrimir, a *vir illustris*, who had written to inform him of the death of his wife, and to others.[4] Rich Goths were very rich. At the time of the Arab conquest the richest man in Spain was a Goth called Athanagild, and the Arabs were able to fine him the sum of 27,000 solidi or 375 lb. of gold.[5] On 12 January 645 Chindasuinth, following an example set by Sisebut in 615–16, tried to limit the quantity of goods that a man of the royal court might give in return for his bride. These goods were known as *morgingeba*, and their value, according to Chindasuinth, was not to exceed 1,000 solidi together with ten boys, ten girls, and twenty horses. The bride and her relatives were now forbidden to demand more than this amount, though after a year of marriage the husband might give his wife additional riches, if he were satisfied with her. The bride's gifts to the groom were similarly limited.[6] Erwig more generously allowed the *primates* to give one-tenth of their property. But there were also rich men who were not *primates*,

---

[1] Zeumer, p. 474. 27, 'ex aula regia rectoribus decenter electis'; 478. 37 f., 'sublimium virorum nobilitatem, qui ex aulae regalis officio in hac sancta synodo vobiscum consessuri praeelecti sunt'. Cf. Contin. Isid. Hisp. 27 (ii. 341), 'palatinum collegium, qui electione collegii interesse meruerant'.

[2] Ildefonsus, *De Vir. Illustr.* 7 (PL 96. 201 f.); Eugenius, *carm.* 27 f.

[3] Lynch, pp. 5 f.   [4] Braulio, *Epp.* 19 f., 28 f., 30.

[5] Contin. Isid. Hisp. 75 (ii. 354).

[6] *LV* iii. 1. 5; *Formulae*, 20; Zeumer, *NA* xxiv (1899), pp. 584–7.

and a tariff was also prescribed for the *morgingebae* of these. Chindasuinth takes as an example a man who was worth the considerable sum of 10,000 solidi: such a man was permitted to give a *morgingeba* of up to 1,000 solidi. If he were worth 1,000 solidi, he might give 100 solidi; and so on. In another law Erwig speaks of persons who, 'intent on working their fields, lash multitudes of slaves'.[1] Did a man worth 10,000 solidi, who was not a *dux*, *comes*, or a *gardingus*, rank as a *persona inferior* in the criminal law? If the definitions above are correct, he did. Wealth alone did not make a man a *maioris loci persona*: he must also be a *dux*, *comes*, or *gardingus*.[2] And we may suspect that the latter would normally be worth more, and in some cases very much more, than 10,000 solidi.

Some members of the palace *officium* (though not the highest members) were slaves. In fact, many slaves and freedmen had made their way into the *officium* by royal command: their presence there was not illegitimate. But Erwig found that they would sometimes use their power to injure their former masters. Accordingly, in 683 he directed the bishops at the Thirteenth Council to forbid all slaves and freedmen and their descendants, and all 'agents' (*actores*) even of the Treasury estates and of the king's private estates, together with all their descendants for ever, to enter the palatine *officium*. An exception was made only of the slaves and freedmen of the Treasury.[3] We shall mention later on some of the posts which the slaves of the *officium* held (p. 268 below).

Egica ruled that, as soon as a new king mounted the throne, the palatine officials should present themselves to him in person unless they were sick or engaged on business of public importance; and, if they failed to do so, the king had authority to do with them and their property what he pleased.[4] Like the *gardingi*, the *seniores* would accompany him on his military expeditions, and he would discuss strategy and high politics with them, as Wamba did in 673 (p. 221 above). He might also consult them about his legislation. Sisebut's law against the Jews was enacted 'with all

---

[1] *LV* ix. 2. 9, 'cum quidam illorum laborandis agris studentes servorum multitudines cedunt'.

[2] Note the contrast in *LV* ii. 1. 9 (Reccesuinth), 'si ex nobilibus idoneisque personis fuerit, . . . si de vilioribus humilioribusque personis fuerit aut certe quem nulla dignitas exornabit'.

[3] XIII Tolet. 6; Zeumer, p. 409. 12 ff. [4] *LV* ii. 1. 7.

the palatine *officium*';[1] and presumably other kings besides Sisebut discussed individual laws with some at least of the *primates* before publishing them. Again, the king could pardon a man found guilty of treason only if the bishops and *maiores palatii* consented (p. 253 above). A number of them were selected by the king to attend the general councils of the Church; and in these they took an active part. In confirming the acts of the Twelfth Council, Erwig is explicit in saying that the decrees of the Council had been enacted at his own command by the bishops and the '*seniores* of our palace'.[2] Along with the bishops they confirmed the law code of Reccesuinth.[3] Some versions of Erwig's law introducing and ratifying his edition of the code make him say that, as the code was ratified in the presence of the bishops, the *seniores* of the palace, and the *gardingi*, so it must be reverenced in all the provinces of the kingdom.[4] But, since the *gardingi* did not attend the councils (except in Chintila's reign), the reference, if it is based on fact, must be to some special ceremony at which the code was confirmed.

According to Chindasuinth, if a slave behaved disrespectfully or disobediently to a noble *illustris*, he was guilty of a criminal offence. An *idoneus* slave (p. 267 below) was punished by forty lashes, and a *vilior* by fifty lashes. But Chindasuinth characteristically added that if the nobleman had provoked the slave to show disrespect he had no redress: he could put the insult down to his own behaviour.[5]

2. The Law

In this vast subject, where a huge mass of evidence lies at our disposal, it will be possible here to mention only a few points that are of general relevance to the public life of the kingdom.

Whether the nobility could be subjected to torture in the law courts before the middle of the seventh century is not clear. A law in which Chindasuinth dealt with the matter seems rather to limit previous practice than to introduce a wholly new principle that noblemen might henceforth be tortured.[6] He begins by considering charges of treason, homicide, and adultery that were

[1] Ibid. xii. 2. 14.   [2] Zeumer, p. 476. 39.   [3] *LV* ii. 1. 5.
[4] Ibid. ii. 1. 1, crit. n.   [5] Ibid. vi. 4. 7.
[6] *LV* vi. 1. 2 *init.*, 'si in criminalibus causis discretionis modus amittitur, criminatorum malitia nequaquam frenatur,' with Ziegler, p. 77 n. 75.

brought against noble members of the palatine *officium* by their peers. (It is in this same law that he forbids 'inferior' persons to lay charges against a noble.) He has in mind charges that could not be proved outright by the evidence of witnesses or by documents or the like. The accuser had now to deliver secretly to the king, or to judges appointed by the king, a written statement of the charges confirmed by the signatures of three witnesses. This written statement of the accusation was known now, as it had been in Roman times, as an *inscriptio*. The inquiry then began and the defendant was tortured. If he did not confess the crime, the accuser was at once handed over to him to be his slave, though he was forbidden to put him to death. (Erwig, always lenient to the nobility, allowed the accuser to pay compensation at a sum to be fixed by the innocent accused.) Now, the contents of the *inscriptio* had not been revealed to the defendant, and if his confession agreed with the charges he was held to be undoubtedly guilty. But, if the confession did not square with the contents of the *inscriptio*, the charge was not proved, and the accuser was punished as before. But, if the accuser or another had informed the defendant beforehand of the nature of the charges contained in the *inscriptio*, the defendant could not be tortured at all: the purpose of torturing him had been lost. How this procedure differs from that of the sixth century we have no means of knowing.

Chindasuinth next turns to other free persons and to lesser charges, such as theft. If the case involved a sum of 300 solidi or more, the *inscriptio* was sent in as before and the accused was tortured. But at this point in the text of the law Erwig rightly detected an ambiguity: is the legislator concerned with 'other free persons' alone or with the nobility as well? Erwig made it explicit, as we might expect, that the *primates* of the palace were on no account to be tortured in cases other than those concerning treason, homicide, and adultery: in cases of theft and lesser crimes, which could not be conclusively proved by the accuser, the nobleman could clear himself by swearing an oath that he was innocent. Erwig also raised the lower limit of what constituted a major theft from 300 to 500 solidi. In lesser cases of theft, according to Chindasuinth, the accused, if convicted, was subject to the ordinary law of theft (p. 137 f. above). If the charge against him could not be fully made out, he could clear himself by swearing an oath.

The practice was to torture free persons of any social class for no more than three days in the presence of the judge and other honest men whom the judge might invite to attend with him. If the judge through malice or bribery allowed the accused to die under the torture, he was himself handed over to the relatives of the dead man to suffer the same fate. And if he swore an oath that he was innocent, and if the honest men testified to his innocence, he was none the less obliged to pay the full *wergild* of 300 solidi to the dead man's heirs. The accuser was put to death.[1]

What is perhaps the latest law in the code is ascribed to Egica, though there is some reason for thinking that it was enacted by Egica's son, Wittiza. It introduces a startling innovation into the law of theft, the ordeal of hot water (*caldaria*). Freemen believed, according to the legislator, that the man accused of theft was tortured in cases that involved 300 solidi—he says nothing of Erwig's substitution of the figure of 500 solidi—and many complaints had been received by him. He now therefore enacted a different law: however small the sum involved in a case of theft, the accused must submit to examination by boiling water, and, if he confessed, he would be subject to the penalties laid down by the ordinary law of theft. Not only the accused, but also suspect witnesses, would be sent to the ordeal.[2] What is curious is that, if the accused were found to have been unhurt by the ordeal, the accuser had to fear no punishment. This ferocious law the legislator regards as an improvement on what had gone before. In fact, it is the nadir of Visigothic legislation.

Chindasuinth introduced the principle of the *talio* into the Visigothic law of wounds, but his introduction is only partial: it applies only in cases of premeditated wounding. Any freeman who dared to decalvate another freeman or to mark him foully on the face or elsewhere on his body by striking him with a whip, club, or otherwise, or to mutilate him, to tie him up, or to detain him against his will, must suffer the *talio*: he must undergo what he had inflicted. But even in these cases the victim, if he so chose, might accept composition at a rate fixed by himself. The only exception that Chindasuinth insisted upon was the case of blows to the head. In these it would be all too easy for the victim to inflict graver

---

[1] *LV* vi. 1. 2.
[2] Ibid. vi. 1. 3. There is no reason to think that the ordeal was an old Germanic custom which the Goths now saw fit to resurrect.

injury than he had received, and he might even endanger the life of his opponent. For these injuries, therefore, the punishment was usually pecuniary. But the bulk of the law concerns injuries that were not premeditated and that resulted from a sudden quarrel; and for these the penalty was pecuniary. Chindasuinth included in the text of his law a prodigious tariff of penalties ranging from 100 solidi downwards for a great variety of wounds to the eye, nose, ear, mouth, hand, fingers, toes, and so on. Even the man who had been made to suffer a hernia (*ponderositas*) was not forgotten. For injuries inflicted on another man's slave the penalty in some instances is a whipping—for the king goes on to give a tariff for these injuries when inflicted on a slave, or by a freedman on a freeman, or by a slave upon another slave (whether with or without his master's knowledge), and so on. The king forbade any distinction to be drawn between injuries to a man and injuries to a woman. A judge who did not enforce the law was to be dismissed from his office by the bishop and the *dux* of his province.[1]

The sixth-century law rarely inflicted the punishment of mutilation upon the convicted criminal: the only case appears to be that of the man who tampered with a royal document (p. 136 above). A law of uncertain date modified the sixth-century procedure. The penalty now was 200 lashes of the whip, decalvation, and the amputation of the right thumb.[2] But Chindasuinth dealt with homosexuality. The penalty that he prescribed for this crime was castration, a penalty that is not otherwise known to the codes except for Jews in certain cases (p. 236 above). The guilty man was also handed over to the local bishop to be exiled. If he were married, his property was taken by his heirs, his wife recovered her dowry, and the marriage was annulled.[3] In 693 Egica directed his bishops to reconsider the matter; and the prelates at the Sixteenth Council, 'burning with the zeal of the Lord', as they said, gave their attention to this crime, which they declared to be widespread. The rigorous penalty of Chindasuinth's law must be enforced. In addition, the guilty criminal must receive 100 lashes of the whip; he must suffer decalvation and go into exile for ever. The bishops were right in saying that the crime was widespread. It extended, for example, into the ranks of the bishops, priests, and deacons, who were also expected to be found guilty from time to time. But in their case the penalty was

[1] *LV* vi. 4. 3.   [2] Ibid. vii. 5. 9.   [3] Ibid. iii. 5. 4.

different: they were simply to be unfrocked and exiled.[1] Unhappily, Egica himself regarded homosexual clergymen with a less
tolerant eye. In a law that was published, it seems, after the
Council had met, he condemned clerics and laymen alike to
castration and the additional penalties imposed by the Sixteenth
Council.[2]

The sixth-century kings had been reluctant to impose the death
penalty. The man or woman who gave drugs so as to cause an
abortion,[3] the murderer of a very close kinsman,[4] the armed man
who entered another's house with a view to killing the householder,[5] the *centenarius* (p. 145 above) who sent his men against
the enemy while himself returning home,[6] were all put to death.
The slave who robbed a tomb, the man who set fire to a house
within a city were burned to death;[7] and so were the free woman
who committed adultery with, or who proposed to marry, her
slave or her freedman, and the slave who raped a free woman.[8]

The seventh-century kings added little to this list except in the
matter of treason. Chindasuinth imposed the death penalty on
the woman who was found guilty of infanticide, though if the
judge should wish to show mercy he might blind her instead. Her
husband was punished similarly if he had ordered the crime or if
he had connived at it.[9] The man who directed his slaves to kill a
freeman, according to Chindasuinth, was also liable to be put to
death.[10]

The procedure for appeals in civil cases is in some respects
obscure owing to bad drafting in one or two laws of Chindasuinth (an unusual shortcoming in the Visigothic codes). It is not
certain whether an appeal from the *iudex*, the *comes*, the vicar of
the *comes*, and the *thiufadus* was heard by the *dux*, or whether
an appeal from the lower courts was heard by the *comes*, and only an
appeal from the *comes* was taken to the *dux*.[11] At all events, when

---

[1] XVI Tolet. 3; Egica in Zeumer, p. 483. 6.
[2] *LV* iii. 5. 7. For the chronological difficulty see Zeumer, p. 165 n. 5.
[3] *LV* vi. 3. 1.   [4] Ibid. vi. 5. 18.
[5] Ibid. vi. 4. 2. What is the reference in the laws of theft, ibid. vii. 1. 4, 'si autem
talis sit fortasse condicio, ut necesse sit illum, qui fur probatur, occidi', and vii. 2. 4,
'quod si capitalia forte conmiserint, simul servus cum ingenuo morte damnentur'?
[6] Ibid. ix. 2. 3.   [7] Ibid. viii. 2. 1; xi. 2. 1.
[8] Ibid. iii. 2. 2; 4. 14.   [9] Ibid. vi. 3. 7.   [10] Ibid. vi. 5. 12 *fin*.
[11] Ibid. ii. 1. 24 (Chindasuinth). The wording certainly suggests that the *dux*
heard appeals from all the lower courts, but contrast ii. 1. 31. Zeumer, *NA* xxiv
(1899), p. 80, leaves the question open.

one party appealed, the judge of first instance sat with the bishop of his city and reconsidered his verdict. If judge and bishop agreed in their verdict, the litigant could appeal to the king, though the penalties were heavy if he then lost his case; and doubtless most litigants would be satisfied with a joint ruling of bishop and judge. But what if the bishop and the judge failed to agree? According to Reccesuinth, the bishop's verdict in that case was to prevail.[1] But Erwig enacted that, in such a case of disagreement, the bishop was to write down his own judgement, drawing attention to the points in which it differed from that of the judge, and was then to forward this statement to the king, who would decide the issue.[2]

The Third and Fourth Councils of Toledo had given the bishops general powers of supervising the judges. We have repeatedly seen how specific duties in this connection were laid upon them. But nowhere were they more specific and important than here.

3. *The Army*

On 1 November 673, soon after his return from the campaign in Septimania, Wamba published his great law on the army. He had found that when enemy raids took place—and the enemy were presumably the Basques and the Franks—some of the inhabitants of the raided area would indeed defend themselves, but their neighbours on the frontier, who ought to have gone to their aid, gave various excuses for not doing so (p. 318 below). The King, therefore, laid down severe penalties for all offenders, even if they were clerics. (This is the first indication that the clergy were liable to military service.) Bishops or other clergy, *duces*, *comites*, *thiufadi* and their deputies, and anyone else living in the raided district or within one hundred miles of it, and anyone who happened to be in the neighbourhood by chance, were liable to punishment if they did not fly at once to the assistance of their country. Such persons must present themselves with all their forces as soon as they were ordered to do so by their *dux*, *comes*, *thiufadus* or his deputy, or by anyone else in authority, or, indeed, as soon as they heard of the raid even if nobody gave

---

[1] *LV* ii. 1. 30.
[2] Ibid. There is a careful discussion in Zeumer, art. cit. 79–88.

them orders to take the field. Any who delayed or failed to appear through ill-will, cowardice, or indifference would have to contribute to make good the damage inflicted by the enemy. If a bishop, priest, or deacon had not the means to contribute, he would be exiled at the king's pleasure. The penalty for lesser clerics and for laymen, whether noble or *viliores*, was loss of the right to testify in the law courts and enslavement; and their property would be used to make good losses caused by the enemy. These rules were also to apply in the case of revolts inside the kingdom: everyone must take the field who lived within one hundred miles of the outbreak, whether bishop, other clergy, *dux*, *comes*, *thiufadus*, the vicar of a *thiufadus*, or private citizen. The law applied also to members of the palatine *officium*. If a man was sick, he must none the less send his forces, and he must produce a suitable witness to prove his sickness.[1]

The outcome of this piece of legislation provides evidence not only of the morale of the population but also of the rigour with which Visigothic laws were enforced. Only seven years later, on 9 January 681, Erwig told the Twelfth Council that about one half of the population of Spain had lost their right to testify in the courts. Whole villages and small villas contained not a single person who could lawfully appear as a witness, and the courts could no longer function satisfactorily. No doubt he exaggerated, or perhaps he had in mind some of the frontier areas only. But his statement must not be written off as absurd. When St. Fructuosus founded his monastery of Nono (apparently in Baetica) so great a throng of candidates for the religious life applied to be admitted to it that the *dux* of the province protested to the king: a restriction must be imposed on the number of prospective monks. He gave the curious reason that if the number were not restricted there would be no one left to 'set out on a public expedition'.[2] It looks as though the number of men who could undertake military service was severely limited; and the picture that emerges is that of a government which could enact and enforce stern legislation but which could not make its subjects fight in its defence.

Erwig therefore asked the bishops to moderate the severity of the law and to restore their freedom and the right to testify to those who had lost them.[3] And the bishops agreed. But he, too,

---

[1] *LV* ix. 2. 8.   [2] *Vita S. Fructuosi*, 14.
[3] Zeumer, p. 476. 3 ff.; XII Tolet. 7.

deplored the reluctance of the rich to defend Spain. Therefore, when the king went out to war in future, or ordered his *duces* and *comites* to do so, none of those who were ordered to join the expedition might refuse to go. Each must be present at the time and place named by the king, *dux*, *comes*, *thiufadus* or his vicar, or by anyone in authority. A new tariff of penalties (which did not include loss of the right to testify) was prescribed: the *maioris loci persona* lost his property and was exiled at the king's pleasure, while the *inferior* received 200 lashes of the whip, suffered decalvation, and was fined 72 solidi—if he could not pay, he was enslaved. Since the majority of *viliores* could not possibly find 72 solidi, the penalty was in practice even harsher than that laid down by Wamba. Sick persons still had to prove their sickness and to send their men to the *dux* and *comes*. The law includes penalties for the *dux*, *comes*, *thiufadus*, and anyone else who released his subordinates from taking part in the expedition, whether or not he did so in return for a bribe. The officer who took a bribe, even if he belonged to the *primates* of the palace, must restore four times the sum that he had taken and must pay a further 72 solidi to the king. Lesser persons were enslaved.[1] Erwig, then, was far indeed from repealing Wamba's law. Indeed, he made it more specific, and he gave no concession whatever to the clergy.

Who were the men whom the high officials and others were obliged to take with them to the wars? In the fifth and sixth centuries rich Goths had two types of free follower, the *buccellarius* and the *saio*, to whom they would present articles of property. Of the former we hear only that if his patron gave him weapons or any other gift he had to return them when he went to serve a new patron. Being a freeman, he was at liberty to change patrons whenever he wished. If he had won booty or the like while serving his original patron, he had to give one half of it back when he left the patron's service. If he died leaving a daughter and no son, the daughter was to remain under the protection of the patron, who would provide her with a suitable husband.[2] Of the *saiones* we are told simply that the weapons given them by their patrons became their own property, and the patrons might not take them back. But any booty that was won by these men belonged to the patrons.[3] Such were Euric's laws, and Leovigild

---

[1] *LV* ix. 2. 9.   [2] Cod. Euric. 310; *LV* v. 3. 1.   [3] Cod. Euric. 311.

confirmed them, adding that if a *buccellarius* went to serve a new patron the latter must provide him with land, for the land that his first patron had given him would now revert to its original owner.[1] From this legislation it is clear that something like the old 'retinue' (*comitatus*), which Tacitus had described long ago, still survived among the fifth- and sixth-century Visigoths. It is true that the Germanic chief of the first century had not given land to his retinue, but he did give them arms and other equipment. Just as we do not know the relationship of the retinue of Tacitus' day to the kindreds in which the rest of the levy fought, so we do not know how the *thiufae* (p. 145 above) of the sixth century combined with the *buccellarii* and *saiones* of the Visigothic nobility when all alike reached the battlefield. Perhaps they fought as separate units, but they were certainly under the command of the king or the *dux*.

Now, in the second half of the seventh century the *thiufadus* and the *compulsor exercitus* (p. 146 above) still existed and presumably commanded those persons who are called *inferiores vilioresque*. The *thiufa*, the *centena*, and the other units also seem to have been in existence still, for Reccesuinth and Erwig took over some older laws that mention them. But the characteristic force that the noblemen now took to the battlefield was their slaves. Erwig complained that they did not bring even one twentieth part of their slaves. He enacted therefore that the *dux, comes, gardingus*, whether Roman or Goth—it is the last time that the distinction is drawn in any Visigothic document—all freemen and freedmen and Treasury slaves, must bring one tenth of their slaves with them on the campaign. (According to some manuscripts of the text, they had to bring one half of their slaves up to a maximum of fifty.) Moreover, each of these slaves must be suitably armed. Some must have breastplates (*zabae*), the majority must have shields, swords (*spathae* and *scramae*), lances, or bows and arrows. There must be some slingers with whatever equipment they had received from their masters. The number of a man's slaves would be carefully calculated; and, if he were found to have presented himself with less than one-tenth of the total, the king would confiscate those whom he had left behind.[2]

Egica returned to the matter. He remarked that, although by God's favour the peoples of his kingdom had an abundance of

[1] *LV* v. 3. 4.   [2] *LV* ix. 2. 9, p. 377.

warriors (a point that the rest of his law contradicted), no harm would be done if their number were increased. Therefore, to repulse foreign enemies those of the Treasury slaves who had been lawfully freed—that is, those who had had their charters of manumission signed by the king's own hand—must join the levy; and so must all their descendants after them. At the time of a public expedition they must present themselves to the king personally without delay. Those who failed to do so would be reduced to slavery again, unless the king, *dux*, or *comes* had given them work of national importance to perform or unless they were too patently ill to attend.[1]

Of tactics we know almost nothing. The Visigoths fought both as infantrymen and as cavalry, but the main strength of their army lay in the cavalry, who were armed with javelin and lance.[2] Like the other Mediterranean Germans, they were mounted spearmen. It is unfortunate that Julian of Toledo had no occasion to linger over the composition, numbers, commissariat, and tactics of the two rival armies that fought in Septimania in 673; and little can be deduced from his narrative. The one figure that he gives, the 10,000 men who were sent to reinforce the attack on Nîmes (p. 223 above), may or may not be an exaggeration. He mentions that when the royal army camped on the plains outside Nîmes it surrounded its camp with a very strong wall.[3] But otherwise he speaks only of the methods of attacking walled cities. Shouting, the calling out of insults, and the blowing of trumpets appear to have been important features of any such attack. The besiegers of Narbonne hurled missiles, arrows, and stones at the defenders on the walls. After three hours of this activity, they made their way to the city gates, set them on fire, scaled the walls, and so entered the city.[4] The procedure at Nîmes was similar. A cloud of stones, spears, and arrows was fired by each side throughout the whole of the first day's attack.[5] And the second day's fighting had a similar character. But if we look a little more closely at the narrative we may wonder whether the royalists were not using *ballistae* or the like in their assaults. At Narbonne there is no hint that they managed to breach the walls; but we do hear that they hurled such storms of stones into the interior of the city

[1] *LV* v. 7. 19.   [2] Isidore, *HG* recapitulatio (ii. 294).
[3] *Hist.* 27 (p. 523. 16).   [4] Ibid. 12 (p. 512. 20 ff.)
[5] Ibid. 13 (p. 514. 1 ff.)

that the place was thought to be submerged beneath 'whistling rocks'.[1] At Nîmes 'they attacked the walls of the city with the blows of rocks', and Wamba had to repair the walls after his victory.[2] The Frankish defenders were terrified by the loud noise (*fragor*) made by the 'powerful hurling' of stones: the attackers discharged 'showers of stones with a mighty crash'.[3] All this scarcely suggests the throwing of stones by hand.

Events were to show that this army, which was largely composed of pressed slaves, was found wanting when it faced the disciplined fervour of the Arabs.

4. *Slavery*

We can say something of the palatine officials at the top and of the slaves at the bottom of Visigothic society. But the vast bulk of the population, those who were neither noblemen nor slaves, have left practically no trace in our records. We know the savage punishments that they suffered when they broke the law; but the documents have no occasion to mention them when they went about their daily tasks lawfully.

The slaves of the Goths were used for agricultural as well as for domestic work. We hear, too, of servile craftsmen and building-workers.[4] Slave women were sometimes put out by their owners as prostitutes at an early date, but this was stringently forbidden by the kings.[5]

A distinction is sometimes drawn between slaves (or freedmen) who were *idonei*—they seem to have been domestic or skilled or city slaves and freedmen—and agricultural labourers (*rustici, rusticani, vilissimi, inferiores*); and different penalties were laid down for offences committed by or against these two categories. Such cases are rare, but they are found in the sixth century as well as in the seventh. Thus, according to a sixth-century law, when a freeman had intercourse with another man's slave girl in her owner's house, he was to receive 100 lashes if she were an *idonea*,

---

[1] Ibid. 12 (p. 512. 25).

[2] Ibid. 13 (p. 514. 4); cf. 18 (p. 516. 23), 'continuis proeliorum ictibus moeniam civitatis inlidunt'. Cf. 26 (p. 521. 25).

[3] Ibid. 17 (p. 516. 16 f.); 18 (p. 516. 23 f.)

[4] *LV* viii. 1. 12; ix. 2. 9 *init.*; xii. 3. 6, etc. Craftsmen: vi. 1. 5. Builders: Vives, 303 *fin.*

[5] *LV* iii. 4. 17.

but only 50 lashes if she were an *inferior*. When a slave did so, he received 150 lashes in either case.[1] In Chindasuinth's great law on wounds, the freeman who decalvated the slave of another man had to pay him 10 solidi if the outraged slave was a *rusticanus*; but if he were an *idoneus*, he had to pay the same sum and in addition receive 100 lashes of the whip.[2] Again, according to Erwig, if a slave raped a freedwoman, both of them being *idonei*, the slave's master was obliged to pay 100 solidi in composition; but, if a slave who was a *rusticus* raped a freedwoman of similar description, his master had to pay the woman a sum of money equal to the value of the slave, but the slave himself received 100 lashes and suffered decalvation.[3]

There were also slaves of the Treasury or royal slaves, some of whom held important palatine offices, such as those in charge of the grooms (*stabularii*), the butlers (*gillonarii*),[4] the silversmiths (*argentarii*), the cooks, and others. Royal slaves sometimes owned land and slaves of their own. Leovigild had forbidden them to sell such property without the royal consent; and even when they had the king's permission they could sell them only to other royal slaves. If they wished to make donations to the Church or to the poor, they had to use other kinds of property for the purpose.[5] The kings set such store on keeping their slaves that Reccesuinth enacted that the rule of thirty years' prescription did not apply to escaped fiscal slaves; but Egica repealed this law.[6] Chindasuinth found it necessary to enact that no slave of the Treasury could be manumitted unless the king himself signed the charter of manumission: evidently the agents of the royal estates had been setting them free too generously.[7] The same king allowed royal slaves to give evidence in the law courts without being tortured, whereas all other slaves, if called upon to testify, could do so only under torture.[8] But he gave some cold comfort by enacting that if a slave were accused of a crime he could not be tortured until the accuser undertook to supply his owner with another slave of equal value when the accused, after being tortured, turned out to

---

[1] *LV* iii. 4. 15.   [2] Ibid. vi. 4. 3.

[3] Ibid. iii. 3. 9. For other references to *idonei* see vi. 1. 5; 4. 7; xi. 1. 1; Conc. Hispal. (A.D. 590) 1. Cf. Conc. Emerit. 17.

[4] Cf. *VPE* ii. 10, 'vasa vinaria quae usitato nomine gillones aut flascones appellantur'; and see the Thesaurus, s.v. *gello*; *LV* ii. 4. 4.

[5] *LV* v. 7. 16.   [6] Ibid. x. 2. 4 f.

[7] Ibid. v. 7. 15, with Zeumer, ad loc.   [8] *LV* ii. 4. 4.

be innocent. And he had to supply two such slaves if the accused died or was maimed as a result of the torture. The judge who tortured him so savagely as to cause his death had also to recompense the owner by giving him a slave of similar value.[1]

Before Chindasuinth's reign slaves had tried in vain to sue freemen in the courts. The defendants failed to appear, alleging that they ought not to plead since they could not collect composition money from the slave if they won their case. But Chindasuinth ruled that, if the slave's master were more than fifty miles away, the slave could sue a freeman (though not his own master) not only in the master's interest but also in his own; and the free defendant must appear and answer the charges and pay composition if defeated. If the slave failed to make out his case, the defendant would receive the 5 solidi which, under another law of Chindasuinth's,[2] had to be paid to successful defendants. If the action had concerned an article worth less than 10 solidi, the slave had to find half the sum due to the defendant, that is, $2\frac{1}{2}$ solidi.[3]

Before Chindasuinth's reign slave-owners appear to have had complete power over their slaves and could kill them with impunity. According to Chindasuinth, they often did so. The only surviving sixth-century law on the relations of slave and master expressly forbids judges to interfere in cases where slaves had stolen from their masters or their fellow slaves: the master alone was to decide what was to be done.[4] Under Chindasuinth, however, it became an offence in some circumstances for a slave-owner to kill his slave. The King wished to put a stop to the widespread practice of putting a slave to death without a public hearing of the case. If a slave were guilty of a capital crime, then, his master had now to go to the judge of the locality or to the *comes* or the *dux*; and only if it were established that the slave was in fact guilty could he be executed. This rule was modified by Erwig, the puppet of the nobility, who allowed more latitude to the master. He declared that if a slave were guilty of a capital offence the master could put him to death first and only then go to the court, where he would be required to prove that the dead

---

[1] Ibid. vi. 1. 5.   [2] Ibid. ii. 2. 5.

[3] Ibid. ii. 2. 9. If the master were within 50 miles the slave could not sue, unless the master was unable to attend the court in person, in which case he had to give the slave written authorization to appear for him.

[4] Ibid. vii. 2. 21.

slave had in fact been guilty. Chindasuinth went on to allow a master to kill a slave in self-defence with impunity, but he had to produce witnesses, or, if there were none, he had to swear an oath that the killing was in fact done in self-defence. But what if a man killed his slave arbitrarily and without any adequate reason? Chindasuinth prescribed the penalty of lifelong exile and penance, while the property of the criminal would be taken by his heirs. But the egregious Erwig modified this also: he changed the penalty to a fine of 72 solidi and permanent loss of the right to testify. If a man killed another man's slave, according to Chindasuinth, he had to give two slaves of equal value with the dead slave to the owner of the latter, and he had also to go into exile (though Erwig abolished the sentence of exile); but he went free if he killed a slave of his own or of another man while punishing him for an offence and could prove by the evidence of witnesses or of his own oath that the killing was unintentional. If slaves under torture accused their master of having incited them to kill a fellow slave, the slaves who had done the deed were liable to 100 lashes and to suffer decalvation, while their master was guilty of homicide. But Erwig again rescued the master: if he swore that he had given no such order, he would go free and have the right to do what he pleased with the slaves who had committed the murder. According to Chindasuinth's law, if a master ordered his slaves to kill a freeman, and this was alleged against him by his slaves under torture, the slaves were lashed 200 times and decalvated; but the master was put to death. According to Erwig, however, the slaves must not be believed unless they could produce a witness, and the master had the right to clear himself by swearing an oath before the judge. If he confessed, however, he was liable to punishment.[1]

Erwig, in fact, restored much of their old immunity to cruel slave-owners, or at any rate he modified the sanctions that Chindasuinth had imposed. But he was less successful when he repealed the legislation of Reccesuinth. Chindasuinth had dealt only with the killing of slaves: he said nothing of maltreating or mutilating them. Reccesuinth declared that a master was innocent if his slave died as a result of a beating that he had given him while enforcing a due and proper discipline.[2] But he banned the

---

[1] *LV* vi. 5. 12. For Chindasuinth's law on the separation of slave families see ibid. x. 1. 17.　　　　　[2] Ibid. vi. 5. 8.

physical mutilation of slaves. He made it illegal for a slave-owner, without a court hearing and without a 'manifest crime' having been committed by the slave, to cut off his hand, nose, lip, tongue, ear, or foot, to gouge out his eye, or to amputate any part whatever of his body. The penalty was exile for three years and penance with the local bishop. The property of the accused was to be managed in his absence by his sons or other relatives and was to be restored to him on his return home.[1] This legislation may date from about the year 666, for in that year the bishops of Lusitania forbade bishops to cut off any member of a Church slave's body; and the opening words of their canon may echo the King's law (p. 306 below). But Erwig had no use for measures such as these, and when he revised the Visigothic code he omitted Reccesuinth's law altogether. But the slaves did not remain for long without protection against mutilation: Egica quickly replaced Reccesuinth's law in the code (p. 246 above).

No subject interested the legislators of the sixth and seventh centuries more than the recovery of escaped slaves; and this interest led to Egica's passing one of the most remarkable laws in the code. Leovigild declared that the man who concealed a runaway slave for more than a week—'until the eighth night', as the law puts it—must give the owner two other slaves of the same value.[2] This eight-day rule is mentioned more than once. If a stranger was given lodging, it was obligatory for the householder to bring him before the judge before the eighth day so that the judge could find out who he was and why he had come. Greater care had to be taken on the provincial boundaries: indeed, the arrival of a stranger in districts near these boundaries had to be reported on the day of his arrival or on the following day.[3] If a man gave hospitality to a runaway slave for twenty-four hours, he was guiltless only if he could swear to the owner that he had not known that the stranger was an escaped slave.[4] But to give hospitality to one who was known to be a fugitive was as bad as inciting another man's slave to take to flight: the guilty person had to supply the slave-owner with two slaves of the same value as the runaway, or with three similar slaves, if the fugitive

---

[1] Ibid. vi. 5. 13.   [2] Ibid. ix. 1. 3.
[3] Ibid. ix. 1. 6. The eight-day rule applied also to fugitive clergy and monks: XIII Tolet. 11.
[4] *LV* ix. 1. 4.

could not be traced.[1] It was also a grave offence to free a runaway slave who had been caught and tied up. The penalty for this was 10 solidi. If the guilty person could not pay such a sum, he was whipped by the judge one hundred times and then had to hunt down the runaway and restore him to his owner. If he could not find him, he had to provide a slave of equal value with the runaway; and if he were unable to do this he himself became the slave of the fugitive's owner.[2]

The sixth-century code directed a reward to be given to any member of the public who caught an escaped slave and restored him to his owner. If the captor had to travel up to thirty miles in order to do this, he must be given one third of a solidus. If he travelled 100 miles, the reward was one solidus, and so on.[3] Even so, escaped slaves might sometimes remain at liberty for a considerable time (though they had to remain at large for fifty years before they became legally free).[4] Anything that they earned during their time of freedom became their masters' property when they were recaptured.[5] Or an escaped slave might pass himself off as a freeman and marry a freewoman. In the sixth century the children of such a marriage were held to be free when the father's real status was discovered; and, if his master agreed, he might remain with his wife. But Erwig, of course, changed this: the children were now considered to be slaves and became the property of their father's owner.[6]

These regulations interfered with a poor man's liberty to travel inside Spain. One day when St. Fructuosus was travelling in the neighbourhood of Idanha (Egitania), barefoot and shabbily dressed, a rustic, who caught sight of him as he lay praying in a wood, despised him because of the cheapness of his dress, 'such is the rustic mind', and at once took him to be a runaway slave and started to beat him. Only a miracle saved the saint.[7]

But all these and other laws failed to achieve their purpose; and at Cordoba in the last weeks of the year 702 King Egica published a new and terrible law. He found that there was not a city, fort, village, villa, or inn where slaves were not hiding. He therefore reaffirmed previous laws and added some new provisions.

---

[1] *LV* ix. 1. 5, where note that it was an offence to cut the hair of a fugitive slave: slaves evidently wore their hair long, while freemen were close-cropped.
[2] Ibid. ix. 1. 2.   [3] Ibid. ix. 1. 14.   [4] Ibid. x. 2. 2.
[5] Ibid. ix. 1. 17.   [6] Ibid. ix. 1. 15 f.   [7] *Vita S. Fructuosi*, 11.

Whoever encountered an escaped slave must immediately produce him before a judge, who would inquire into his status. He must do so even if the slave declared himself to be a freeman. (To obey this ruling he must in practice have been obliged to produce before the judge every poorly dressed stranger whom he met in his locality.) Any slave or freedman who did not do this would be lashed 150 times in public. A freeman would be lashed 100 times and would in addition have to pay the slave's owner no less than 72 solidi. If he did not possess this large sum, he would receive 200 lashes. The other inhabitants of the district, no matter what was their status, including the slaves of the Church, of the Treasury, and of private owners, would be liable to the same punishment if they did not inform on the escaped slave and drive him from his hiding-place. But now the legislator warms to his work. If fugitive slaves arrived in any locality, all the inhabitants of that locality had at once to assemble together and find out, by torture if necessary, whose slaves they were, when they had fled from their masters, and from what district they had come. If the inhabitants held no such inquiry and initiated no inquiry by the judge, then all the residents of that region, male and female, whatever their race, class, or office, would be lashed 200 times by the judge. Further, if the law were not enforced by the *thiufadi* and their deputies, and all other judges, or by the agents and procurators of the local estates, or by the priests, or the servants of the Treasury, of the king, and of private persons, or by anyone else in whose district slaves were hiding, they would be publicly whipped 300 times by the bishops and the *comites*. (In the entire code there is no semblance of a parallel to such treatment of priests.) If in spite of a request from the *comes* the bishop failed to carry out the provisions of the law either from humanity or bribery or indifference, he had to undertake on oath to the *comes* and the *thiufadus* to submit to the rigours of excommunication for the space of thirty days. During that period he must not dare to touch a glass of wine or any food except a biscuit of barley bread and a cup of water in the evenings. Judges and *comites* who did not enforce the law were liable to a fine of 216 solidi.[1]

The entire population of Spain, then, clerics and laymen alike, except the *comites* and their superiors and the bishops and metropolitans, became liable to almost unparalleled floggings if they

---

[1] *LV* ix. 1. 21.

failed to hunt down escaped slaves. By prescribing penalties for such high officials as the *comites* and the bishops Egica appears to have had a foreboding that his law would not often be enforced in practice. The law seems to be a symptom of a society in which the administrative machine is breaking down. Slaves can no longer be bound to their work. They have already escaped in masses. Egica himself admits that there is not a city, fort, village, villa, or inn where they are not hiding. What will their attitude be when the Arabs land at Gibraltar?

XII · THE CHURCH

MOST of our information about the seventh-century Church in Spain is derived from the minutes, which are extensive, of the numerous councils and synods that met throughout the century. In nearly all cases the minutes end with a list of signatures of the bishops who were present together with the names of their sees. A list of the plenary and provincial councils that met at Toledo is given on the following page. The documents never speak of 'national' councils: they refer to them as 'general' or 'universal'.

For purposes of organization the Church retained the old territorial divisions of the Roman Empire. The Roman provinces were the Church's provinces, and the Roman cities, or some of them, were its dioceses. There were eighty-two bishoprics distributed among the six provinces of the kingdom (Gallia, Gallaecia, Tarraconensis, Carthaginiensis, Lusitania, and Baetica). The metropolitan sees were the provincial capitals (respectively, Narbonne, Braga, Tarragona, Toledo, Merida, and Seville). Although Toledo was often known as the 'royal see', it was in no sense a primatial see throughout most of the period. All the metropolitans signed the minutes of the general councils in order of seniority, and the bishops of Toledo signed first at the Fifth and Tenth alone of the plenary councils until the reign of Erwig. But in 681 Erwig, acting no doubt under the influence of Julian of Toledo, granted the see remarkable powers. At that time the king had the unquestioned right to appoint bishops; but the news that a bishop had died often took a long time to reach Toledo, and hence there was sometimes an unfortunate delay in appointing a successor. During the interregnum the Divine Office was neglected, and Church property might be purloined. Henceforth, therefore, the king would choose, and the metropolitan of Toledo would approve, a candidate for each vacancy. The bishops at the Twelfth Council, when they agreed this canon, emphasized that it had been subscribed 'by all the bishops of Spain and Gaul'. They evidently wished to give all possible authority to a debatable measure. To preserve something of ancient rights, they made it obligatory for a new bishop to present himself to his metropolitan within three months of his appointment so as to receive his authority and instruction. If he negligently failed to do so, he

THE SEVENTH-CENTURY COUNCILS OF TOLEDO

Number	Date	Character	Church where sessions were held	Number of bishops & proxies present	
Gundemar's Council	ended 23 Oct. 610	General	?	(a)	15
				(b)	26
IV	5 Dec. 633	,,	St. Leocadia		69
V	ended 30 June 636	Spain only	,,		24
VI	9 Jan. 638	General	,,		53
VII	18 Nov. 646	,,	?		41
VIII	16 Dec. 653	,,	Holy Apostles		60
IX	2–24 Nov. 655	Carthaginiensis	St. Mary		17
X	1 Dec. 656	General	?		22
XI	7 Nov. 675	Carthaginiensis	St. Mary		19
XII	9–25 Jan. 681	General	Holy Apostles		38
XIII	4–13 Nov. 683	,,	,,		77
XIV	14–20 Nov. 684	Carthaginiensis	St. Mary		24
XV	11 May 688	General	Holy Apostles		66
XVI	25 Apr.— 1 May 693	,,	,,		61
XVII	9 Nov. 694	,,	St. Leocadia		?

Note. Unless otherwise stated, the dates are those of the opening of the Councils. Observe that the Church of St. Mary was used for provincial councils only.

would be excommunicated. But even then they added that he need not meet his metropolitan 'if he could prove that he had been prevented by royal command'.[1] In fact, nowhere else in Europe at this date had a metropolitan the right in canon law to appoint bishops in provinces other than his own. The phrase in the canon

---

[1] XII Tolet. 6, with Magnin, pp. 97 ff. The metropolitan of Toledo was never given the title of Patriarch. Note that the king and the metropolitan could also appoint priests.

that 'the privilege of each province' was to be 'preserved' cannot be reconciled with the context: the right of the metropolitan of Toledo extended into every province. But even the metropolitan of Toledo could take part in the appointment only after the king had selected the candidate: he could then approve (or disapprove) the king's choice. It has been said that the canon marks a veritable surrender of the rights of the episcopacy into the hands of the king. But that is hardly the case. The metropolitan now had *some* rights in making the appointments, whereas hitherto the king's power had been unrestricted.

But when the century opened all that lay in the future; and the metropolitan of Toledo had no privileges over his fellow metropolitans in the other provinces.

1. *Councils and Synods*

Throughout the seventh century plenary councils met, not when the Church was confronted with a problem, but when it pleased the king to summon one. But on paper the rule was that a general council was held when there was an article of faith to discuss or when a matter had arisen that affected the Spanish Church as a whole. Otherwise, a provincial synod was to meet in each province once a year.[1] But the practice was not so clear-cut. The provincial Second Council of Seville, which met in 619 in the time of Isidore, published a long and learned statement on the two Natures and the one Person of Christ (p. 164 above), a matter of doctrine that affected the whole Spanish Church. The Eleventh Council of Toledo, which was a synod of the bishops of Carthaginiensis alone, directed 'the bishops and priests of every province' to sing the Psalms in an identical way (as the Fourth Council had long ago directed); and, when it laid down a penalty for bishops who interfered with the womenfolk of the palace nobility, it is hard to believe that its ruling bound only the bishops of Carthaginiensis (p. 301 below).[2] Most remarkable of all, the Council of Tarraconensis, meeting on the orders of Egica in 691, made a ruling on royal widows (p. 243 above) which, if it was an ecclesiastical matter at all, ought to have been considered at a general rather than at a provincial council.

---

[1] IV Tolet. 3.   [2] XI Tolet. 3, 5. Note also III Caesaraug. 1.

Again, two councils, the Fifth and the Sixteenth, were not attended by any bishops from Gallia Narbonensis. At the time of the Fifth Council Gallia may have been in revolt (p. 182 above); and at the time of the Sixteenth Council the province was stricken by a plague. These two councils, therefore, did not rank as fully plenary; and their canons, alone of all those of the century, had to be ratified either at the next following general council or at a Gallic synod called specially for the purpose.[1]

A fact of the utmost importance is that the councils considered matters which were by no means wholly of ecclesiastical interest. The conception was Reccared's. He directed the bishops to discuss some matters that were of purely secular concern (p. 98 ff. above), and he also indicated what conclusions he wanted them to reach. Sisenand had one of the most important of all Visigothic enactments—that ordering the ruin of Suinthila and the condemnation of usurpers—passed at the Fourth Council, although he never issued a secular law on the subject. All the councils from the Fifth to the Eighth fulminated against usurpers and rebels. At the Eighth and subsequent councils the procedure for making known the king's wishes became more formal. Reccesuinth and his successors, after opening the plenary councils in person, would hand over to the bishops a *tomus* or written statement of the matters that they wanted the bishops to consider. They then left the meetings, for no king after Gundemar stayed to sign the minutes. The bishops proceeded to discuss these subjects and to pass the resolutions that the king's tome had indicated. They also debated, of course, purely ecclesiastical questions of which the tome had said nothing. Although they considered the legal relations of the Church with private persons, as, for example, with freedmen, they were silent on all public affairs apart from those that the king had brought to their notice. The records of the councils, therefore, include discussions of those issues that the kings considered to be of capital importance to themselves, to the nobility, and to the bishops; and in each case the king's decision was confirmed by the authority of the Church. Erwig, it is true, was in a weak position; but in general, so far from being a check on the royal power, the councils were regarded by the kings as an important support for their power. In fact, the Toledan councils had no parallel in any other kingdom of the sixth or seventh

[1] VI Tolet. 2; Edict confirming the XVI Toletanum.

century. They were a peculiarly Spanish instrument of government.[1]

The councils were a national institution. Bishops whose dioceses lay within the kingdom never attended councils in the Byzantine province (if any were held there) or in Galicia before 585 or in the Frankish realms. Nor were foreign bishops ever present at the Visigothic councils. These neither influenced nor were influenced by the Byzantines or the Franks. After the conversion of 589 the Church in Spain became a national Church. It was highly centralized and closely associated with the court and the administration, in which the bishops took an increasingly active part. It busied itself with its own affairs and ignored the world outside Spain. It recognized the primacy of the Bishop of Rome, but it rarely communicated with him. It is not known ever to have taken the initiative in corresponding with him; and when the Pope wrote to the bishops of Spain—and he rarely did so—he received on each occasion an arrogant and critical reply (p. 185, 241 above).

The Fourth Council of Toledo ruled that provincial synods should meet on 18 May in each year, when the grass was green and pasture was available.[2] But the Third Council had already ruled that provincial synods should assemble on 1 November, and this was reaffirmed by the Twelfth Council in 681.[3] In fact, of the seven provincial synods of the century which we can date precisely—Tarrasa (Egara) in 614, II Seville, IX, XI, and XIV Toledo, III Saragossa, and the Council of Merida in 666—six opened in the first fortnight of November. (The exceptional case is Egara, which opened on 13 January.) The ruling of the Fourth Council had been ineffective, and that of 589 had prevailed. The great national councils met in the winter months (late October to January), except for XVI Toledo, which opened on 2 May 693 on the morrow of Sisebert's revolt, and V Toledo, which ended on 30 June 636. (Chintila had come to the throne only in March of that year, and external circumstances made it advisable for him to call a council as quickly as he could.) But the winter months were not always suitable; and one reason why the Fourteenth Council

---

[1] There is an excellent discussion of the character of the Toledan councils in Zeumer, NA xxiii (1898), pp. 500–4, and in Magnin, pp. 88 ff.
[2] IV Tolet. 3.
[3] III Tolet. 18; XII Tolet. 12.

was restricted to the bishops of Carthaginiensis was the extreme severity of the weather. The meetings might last for as long as three weeks, though the Second Council of Seville completed twelve items of business in three sessions.

The Church attached the utmost importance to the regular meeting of councils. Nothing caused such damage to ecclesiastical discipline as the neglect of bishops to summon them. When Reccesuinth prevented Church assemblies from meeting for sixteen years on end, the bishops were loud in lamenting the decline of morals that ensued.[1] The Eighth Council pointed to the dangers of disputes becoming chronic if no synods met to resolve them.[2] In his opening address to the Twelfth Council Erwig stated that 'the assistance given by the councils is the best help for a falling world'.[3]

In strict canon law a provincial synod should have met twice a year in each province; but in the peculiar circumstances of Spain it had long ago been conceded that one annual meeting would be enough (p. 36 above). This concession and the pressing need for regular meetings were reaffirmed in 589, 633, 666, and 675;[4] but the very repetition shows how negligent the bishops continued to be. The Council of 675 eventually went so far as to rule that if twelve months elapsed without the holding of a synod all the bishops of Carthaginiensis should be excommunicated for a year—unless the king had directed them not to meet.[5] We still possess the minutes of fourteen provincial synods that met between 589 and 711; and it is certain that others met although their minutes have not survived. But it is ominous that we hear of only one synod that met in Gaul throughout this long period; and it is not open to doubt that provincial synods met far less regularly than the rules called for.

But in fact no council, whether plenary or provincial, could meet at all in the seventh century unless the king directed it to do so; and the bishops nearly always began their proceedings by remarking that they had met at the royal command. True, in 633 they stated that the provincial synod should meet at a place appointed by the metropolitan; but in 666 the Lusitanian bishops

[1] IV Tolet. 3; XI Tolet. 15; Contin. Isid. Hisp. 47 (ii. 349). See p. 209 above.
[2] VIII Tolet. 11.   [3] Zeumer, p. 481. 23.
[4] III Tolet. 18; IV Tolet. 3; Conc. Emerit. 7; XI Tolet. 15; XII Tolet. 12.
[5] XI Tolet. 15.

were careful to add that the meetings should take place 'not without the king's wish', and they remarked explicitly that synods were summoned at the metropolitan's wish and the king's command. And in 675 the bishops declared that the meetings should be held in the metropolitan church at a time fixed by the king and the metropolitan.[1] The king explicitly directed the bishops of Narbonensis to hold a provincial synod in 693 (p. 245 above). Similarly, he might cancel the meeting of a council if he thought fit to do so; and Sisenand cancelled the meeting that he had planned for 632 (p. 176 above).

He did not attend the provincial synods, but he was usually present at the opening session of the plenary councils.[2] Accompanied by the grandees of his court,[3] he would commend himself to the bishops' prayers and would deliver the opening address. In and after 653 he would then hand over to the bishops his tome (p. 278 above), but would withdraw before it was read aloud. After listening to its contents the bishops would make a statement of their Catholic faith (except at V, VII, and X Toledo) and would then begin their formal discussions. The minority had to yield to the majority, and excommunication was the penalty for any bishop who failed to uphold and champion the council's decisions.[4] In not a single case did they dare to disregard the instructions set out in the royal tomes, although they are not known to have been consulted on the contents of them before the meeting began. They might criticize a king after his death, as they criticized Sisebut's anti-Jewish measures, Reccesuinth's failure to summon councils, and so on. But they never criticized him to his face. They never failed to enact what he wished them to enact, and before Erwig's time they never made a ruling of which he might disapprove. Of the two parties to the councils, the Crown and the Church, the Crown was dominant and the Church was subordinate. However distasteful many of the decisions of the

---

[1] Conc. Emerit. 5; XI Tolet. 15.

[2] The king opened IV, V, VIII, XII, XIII, XV, XVI, XVII Toledo, but IX and XI were provincial synods, and XIV dealt solely with doctrinal matters. But the absence of Chindasuinth and Reccesuinth from VII and X denotes some strain between Crown and Church. The puzzle is why Chintila did not attend VI Toledo: perhaps he was militarily engaged with his enemies.

[3] IV Tolet., 'cum magnificentissimis et nobilissimis viris'; V Tolet., 'cum optimatibus et senioribus palatii sui . . . suosque fideles'; XVII Tolet., 'illustre aulae regiae decus ac magnificorum virorum numerosus conventus'.

[4] VIII Tolet. 11.

bishops may now appear, the ultimate responsibility for them lay with the king. Seventh-century Spain was not an example of ecclesiastical rule and clerical terror. It was the kings, not the bishops, who governed Spain and with it the Spanish Church.

The procedure adopted at the provincial synods was laid down at the Fourth Council in 633.[1] Before sunrise on the opening day all worshippers were excluded from the metropolitan church, in which the meetings took place. All doors except one were locked, and the doorkeepers (*ostiarii*)[2] took their stand at the unbarred door, through which the clergy would enter. The bishops processed into the church and sat down in an order that was determined by the date of the consecration of each of them.[3] After the bishops had taken their seats in a circle, those priests were summoned who were entitled to attend; and care was taken to ensure that no deacon insinuated himself among them. The priests sat behind the bishops; and the deacons, who next entered the church, did not sit down but throughout the proceedings remained standing where the bishops could see them. Finally, such laymen as had been selected to attend were admitted along with secretaries (*notarii*), who would read out documents and take the minutes. The door was then locked, and after a period of silence an archdeacon called for prayer. All those present prostrated themselves upon the floor, praying with tears and groans, until one of the elderly bishops arose and prayed aloud to God, while the others still lay flat on their faces. At the end of the prayer the archdeacon called upon them to arise. The bishops and priests took their seats; and as they sat in silence a deacon clad in an alb brought before them a book of conciliar canons and read out the chapters relating to the holding of synods. The metropolitan, who presided over the sessions, then called upon anyone who had an item of business to declare it. When such items had been completed—and each had to be decided before a new one was raised—it was the turn of those clerics and laymen who had remained outside the church. All men were entitled to lay before

---

[1] IV Tolet. 4; cf. Séjourné, pp. 147 ff.

[2] For what is known of the *ostiarii* in Visigothic Spain see Mullins, p. 166. For the tombstone of an *ostiarius* dating from 528 see Vives, 489.

[3] VI Tolet. praef., 'debitis sedibus', and similar phrases at VIII, XII, XIII, XVII Toledo. Note esp. XVI Tolet. praef., 'dum . . . unusquisque nostrorum ex more secundum ordinationis suae tempus in locis debitis residerat'. The point is made explicitly in I Bracar. 6.

the synod complaints against bishops, judges, grandees, or anyone else.[1] Each complainant now made his case known to the archdeacon of the metropolitan church, who reported it to the meeting. The complainant was then admitted and had the right to speak. If the meeting found his complaint to be valid, the wrong of which he complained was righted by the appropriate public officials, and a royal executive officer (*executor*) was appointed by the king at the metropolitan's request to oblige judges and other laymen to appear before the synod. The meeting closed with an expression of thanks to God and the king, and the minutes were signed by each individual bishop in turn, the metropolitan heading the list. The order in which the bishops signed, both at plenary and at provincial councils, seems often to be arbitrary: they certainly did not sign rigidly in order of seniority or date of appointment. The metropolitan presided over the provincial synod, but the general councils are never said to have had a chairman or 'presiding' metropolitan. The senior metropolitan signed the minutes first, irrespectively of whether he occupied the see of Toledo. But after 681 Toledo always signed first.

These dignified arrangements were sometimes marred by clerical uproar; and the Fourth Council declared that God was present among his bishops only when the business of the meeting was completed in tranquillity.[2] But in 675 the bishops took stern measures against trouble-makers. Speeches must not be interrupted. There must be no disorderly uproar, no idle chatter or laughter or noisy shouts. A penalty of expulsion from the meeting and excommunication for three days was prescribed for those who disturbed the solemn deliberations by heckling, by shouting insults, or by bursting into laughter.[3] Moreover, the Eighth Council had to insist that the decisions of the synods were binding on all: any cleric who disregarded them, or who murmured against them, or, indeed, who failed to champion them positively, was to lose his rank and to be barred from Holy Communion. The minority had to yield to the majority or be expelled from the meeting and excommunicated for a year.[4]

But how did the public learn what decisions the councils had reached? It was only in 693 that the bishops considered the question of publishing their decisions. At the Third Council of

[1] IV Tolet. 3 *ad fin.* [2] IV Tolet. 4 *fin.*
[3] XI Tolet. 1. [4] VIII Tolet. 11.

Saragossa, which had met two years earlier, the bishops of Tarraconensis pointed out that freedmen of the Church might perhaps overlook one of their duties because they did not know the canons.[1] The decision was reached in 693 that each bishop, within six months of the end of a synod, should call an assembly of all the abbots, priests, deacons, and other clergy together with all the populace of his city and should inform them fully of the synod's decisions. Thus, no one could fail to know them, and any who opposed them or who even whispered against them would be excommunicated for two months.[2]

A glance at the Table on p. 276 will show that, since there were eighty-two bishoprics in all, the attendance of the bishops at the meetings left much to be desired. A bishop might be prevented from attending, of course, by sickness or old age. Thus, Riccila, Bishop of Guadix (Acci), attended the councils of 675, 681, 684, and 688; but at that of 683 he was represented by his priest Tuencius. Gavinius of Calahorra attended in 633 and 653, but in 638 he was represented by his priest Citronius. These and many similar examples are no doubt to be explained by the bishop's illness at the time of the relevant councils. Indeed, in 693 an epidemic in Narbonensis prevented all the bishops of that province from attending the Sixteenth Council (p. 245 above). Again, Pimenius of Medina Sidonia (Asidona), who had been consecrated in 629, attended the councils of 633 and 638, but sent his priest Ubiliensus to take his place in 646: the see was not represented at any of Reccesuinth's councils, and this is doubtless to be explained by Pimenius's old age, for he still occupied the see in 662.[3] Winibal of Elche (Ilici) attended in person in 646, 653, and 655, but in the following year his deacon Agricius deputized for him. Presumably, towards the end of his life he, like Pimenius and many others, became too old to travel.

It may also have been the case that, at the time when a council met, the bishop was dead and his successor not yet appointed. Some such circumstance may explain the case of Cazlona (Castulo) at Gundemar's council in 610. At the first meeting, when fifteen bishops attended, this see was represented by Theodorus. At the second meeting, Cazlona, alone of these

[1] III Caesaraug. 4.   [2] XVI Tolet. 7.
[3] Vives, 305 f., 309. He survived apparently until 667, when Theoderacis succeeded him: ibid. 310.

fifteen sees, put in a second appearance; but this time it was represented by Venerius. Had Theodorus died in the interval between the two sessions?[1]

Other reasons why bishops could not attend the conciliar meetings were the great distances that separated the Spanish dioceses, and the poverty of the Spanish churches (or some of them). These matters had been mentioned at the Third Council in 589, which ruled that, 'in view of the length of the journey and the poverty of the churches of Spain', only one provincial synod, instead of two, need be held each year.[2] Swollen rivers and bad weather also prevented long journeys.[3] But, if distance and poverty, flooded rivers and vile weather made it difficult for some bishops to attend provincial synods, they will have made it even harder to attend the general councils, which were held far away in Toledo. This fact would account, for example, for the behaviour of the bishops of the see of Ossonoba (in the neighbourhood of the modern Faro in Algarve). Peter, Bishop of Ossonoba, attended the Third Council in 589. But thereafter the see sent no representative to any council until 653, when the deacon Sagarellus signed as deputy for his bishop Saturninus.[4] But the bishops of Ossonoba were more energetic than many of their brethren. Tarrazona and Lerida attended no council between 638 and 683. The exposed city of Pamplona on the threshold of the Basque country sent its bishop

---

[1] What is the explanation of the position at Auca in 683? The bishop Stercorius signed the minutes of XIII Toledo, but later down the list we find among the *vicarii episcoporum* the signature of *Iohannes abba Areginei Aucensis episcopi*.

[2] III Tolet. 18, 'consulta itineris longitudine et paupertate ecclesiarum Hispaniae'; cf. III Caesaraug. 2, 'aut longinquitate itineris praecaventes'; XII Tolet. 6, 'dum longe lateque diffuso tractu terrarum conmeantum inpeditur celeritas nuntiorum'; XIV Tolet. 3, 'sparsis sedibus'; Contin. Isid. Hisp. 27 (ii. 341), 'quos languor vel inopia presentes fore non fecit', referring to VII Toledo.

[3] Conc. Emerit. 6, 'per nimiam intemperantiam aerum'; XIII Tolet. 8, 'aut fluminum aut aerum procellosa inmensitas'.

[4] I have chosen the case of Ossonoba (on its site see Goubert (p. 320 n. 1 below), pp. 99 f.) because scholars have based an astonishing series of hypotheses on the failure of the Ossonoban bishops to attend synods between 589 and 653. It has been inferred that after 590 Algarve must have been occupied by the Byzantines, who prevented the Ossonoban bishops from attending the meetings. We are told that Algarve formed a Byzantine province in itself, distinct from that centred on Malaga and Cartagena, and that it was governed by a separate patrician of its own: so Goubert, pp. 72 f., 100; Görres, *Byzantinische Zeitschrift*, xvi (1907), p. 516, *et al.* But the Byzantines were expelled from Spain about the year 624: why then did the bishops of Ossonoba fail to attend the councils of 633, 636, 638, and 646? The explanation is, we are told, that, although the Byzantines were expelled from Malaga and Cartagena in 624, they retained their possessions in Algarve until 650!

to no council between 610 and 683. But the worst offenders were the bishops of Gallia. True, Elne, which lay nearer to Spain than the others, was represented in 633, 638, 656, and 683. Carcassonne was represented at all these except that of 638. But Agde attended only in 653 and 683, Béziers and Maguelonne in 633 and 683, Lodève and Narbonne in 638 and 683, while Nîmes saw fit to send no representative to any council at all after 633.

Thus, there were numerous valid reasons why a see should not be represented at a council. But allowing for them all, it is difficult to resist the conclusion that in general the attendance was little short of disgraceful (p. 293 below). And often enough nothing more may have been involved than the personal indifference and lack of energy of the bishop—that 'neglect' of which the canons speak. Thus, the diocese of Cabra (Egabra) in Baetica was not represented at the Second Council of Seville in 619.[1] Yet the agenda of the synod included an item of direct importance to the see. When the Byzantines had occupied Malaga, they did not succeed in overrunning the whole diocese of that city; or, if they did, Leovigild or some other king had recovered part, though not all, of the diocese. This part, which was in the hands of the Goths, had been divided between the sees of Ecija (Astigi), Granada (Illiberris), and Cabra. But, before the Second Council of Seville assembled in 619, Malaga and the rest of the diocese had fallen to Sisebut. The question, therefore, was raised by Theodulf, the new Visigothic Bishop of Malaga, whether the whole diocese should now be reunited and reconstituted in the form in which it had existed before the Byzantines landed in Spain, that is to say that Ecija, Granada, and Cabra should restore to Malaga what they had gained as a result of the Byzantine landing there. The Council found for Theodulf, and Cabra lost some of its parishes. We might have expected that this debate would have held some interest for the Bishop of Cabra— the Bishops of Ecija and Granada were present—yet he did not attend the Council. If he himself were ill or aged, he could have sent a deputy. But he did not do so. Why he did not is unknown. Lack of energy and interest is as good an explanation as any.

All this is particularly remarkable in view of the fact that the bishops were summoned not merely by the metropolitans but

[1] There is no reason to follow Goubert, art. cit. p. 91, in thinking that Cabra was then in Byzantine hands.

also by the king. Attempts were made to put pressure on them to attend, but these attempts met with little success. A bishop was excused if he was ill or if he was engaged on royal business; but at any rate in Lusitania he was obliged to make his excuses known to his metropolitan in a letter written in his own hand, and he was obliged to send a deputy to represent him at the synod.[1] The penalty for absence without excuse was excommunication until the date of the following synod, that is, in theory, for one year. The bishop was required to spend the year in question wherever his metropolitan directed him to go; and the metropolitan would see to the care of his palace and his property during his absence. As the bishops truthfully said, there was nothing frightening in this penalty.[2] In Carthaginiensis the penalty was similar; and it became the general rule in 681.[3]

But, of course, there were numerous cases of bishops who attended regularly and conscientiously, like Conantius of Palencia, the spiritual instructor of St. Fructuosus.[4] He occupied his see for more than thirty years. He attended Gundemar's Council in 610; and he was present at the Councils of 633, 636, and 638, when he was probably over seventy years of age, without ever sending a deputy to save him the long journey to Toledo.

A remarkable document that has survived from the Sixth Council suggests that the plenary councils could be impressive when they acted as courts of appeal from the decisions of provincial synods.[5] About the year 625, in the reign of Suinthila, the Bishop of Ecija (Astigi), Marcianus, had been deposed by a majority vote of the bishops who met at a synod in Seville. Presumably St. Isidore voted against him, for he would scarcely have been condemned otherwise; but even the authority of St. Isidore did not secure a unanimous vote of the synod. Marcianus wished to appeal against his deposition to a plenary council, but he had to wait until the Fourth Council[6] met in 633 before his

---

[1] Conc. Emerit. 5.
[2] Ibid. 7.   [3] XI Tolet. 15; XII Tolet. 12.
[4] Ildefonsus, De Vir. Illustr. 11 (PL 96. 203); Vita S. Fructuosi, 2. He published much church music.
[5] Exemplar Iudicii inter Martianum et Habentium Episcopos, printed on the unnumbered pages at the beginning of H. Florez, España Sagrada², vol. xv (Madrid, 1787). But there is a better text in F. Dahn, Die Könige der Germanen, vi² (Leipzig, 1885), pp. 615–20, with commentary on pp. 623–41.
[6] Séjourné, pp. 196, 328, seems right in taking the previous 'universal Council' to be the Fourth, not the Fifth (as Dahn, 624): the Fourth was the 'universal'

case was heard; and even then the bishops found time only to restore him to the rank of bishop but not to his old see. The Fifth Council in 636 was apparently too engrossed in political matters and the protection of Chintila to consider the case at all. But the Sixth Council at its first session went into the case fully, and unravelled an extraordinary tale of perjured witnesses (some of them clerics) and forged evidence. The whole plot against Marcianus had been engineered by a certain Aventius, whose intrigues had been so successful that not only did he have Marcianus deposed but he also had himself appointed as Bishop of Ecija. In that capacity he attended the Fourth Council and, indeed, occupied the diocese for upwards of a dozen years. Several charges had been brought against the unfortunate Marcianus, and some of them were very dangerous. He had been accused of having spoken against the King and of having consulted a female diviner called Simplicia about the life of the King and his own future. He seems to have been charged with illicit relations with a lady called Bonella. He was certainly accused of having a female slave called Ustania to look after his wardrobe, whereas in fact his valet was her brother, Belisarius. In the matter of Simplicia Aventius had used as a witness a person called Reccesuinth, who, it turned out later, had given his evidence when under the age of 14, which was illegal. But if this Reccesuinth's evidence was eliminated, the charge was based only on the testimony of a single witness, a certain Dormitio; and in Alaric's code the testimony of a single witness was inadmissible.[1] Aventius had also persuaded two illiterate women, Franca and Honorata, to sign a statement of evidence that they could not read: the evidence contained in it was contrary to what they knew to be true. In any case, they were such *viles personae* that their evidence ought not to have been used against such a dignitary as a bishop.

What is impressive in this document is not only the abysmal behaviour of Aventius (who was condemned to penance, but retained the rank of bishop) but also the extreme diligence and perseverance of the Sixth Council in finding out the truth. They

council *par excellence*; and note its canon 28, which may have been inspired by Marcian's case. Marcian had succeeded Isidore's brother Fulgentius at Astigi some time after 619.

[1] *CTh* xi. 39. 3.

cross-examined seventeen witnesses (five of them Goths) with the utmost rigour and did all that could be done to uncover the truth. The one shortcoming in the procedure—and the bishops were well aware of it—was the lack of general councils to which Marcianus could have appealed. He had had to wait nearly ten years for his preliminary hearing at the Fourth Council and a further five years before his case was finally settled. By that time most of those who had condemned him, including St. Isidore, were dead.

2. Gothic and Roman Bishops

We know the names of several hundred seventh-century bishops of Spain. Let us compare the number of those who bore Germanic names[1] with the number of those who bore Roman names. It must be stressed that the Germanic names are a minimum and the Roman names a maximum, for, while Goths sometimes took on Roman names, Romans are not known ever to have called themselves by Gothic names. Thus, we might well take the Felix who represented Iria at XII, XIII, and XV Toledo to be a Roman, were it not that in 675 at the Third Council of Braga he had signed himself *Ildulfus qui cognominor Felix*. At that same Council of Braga the see of Braga itself was represented by *Leudigisus cognomento Iulianus*. At VI Toledo Antonius of Segorbe (Segobria) was represented by his deputy, the deacon Wamba, who according to some versions of the text signed himself *Wamba diaconus qui et Petrus*, and so he certainly appears in the *Iudicium* of Marcianus and Aventius.[2] Taio, who succeeded St. Braulio in the see of Saragossa in 651, was *cognomento Samuel*.[3] There is some reason for thinking that the famous monastic founder, St. Fructuosus of Braga, was a German in spite of his name.[4] And, among laymen, Hermenegild, when converted to Catholicism, took on the name Iohannes (p. 65 above).

---

[1] With a few changes I accept as Germanic the names listed as such by Grosse at the relevant parts of his book, but have counted as Roman those of which I am in doubt, so as not to overstate my case. Bishops who are known by name from other sources than the conciliar signatory lists are taken into account.

[2] But I do not understand *Iohannes diaconus cognomento Imbolatus* (=Involatus) who represented Valencia at XIV Toledo.

[3] Taio, *Sentent.*, *init.* (PL 80. 727). On this Taio see Lynch, pp. 60 ff., with references.

[4] *Hermathena*, xc (1957), pp. 54 f.

The figures are as follows, the fractions being rounded to the nearest quarter:

Province	Germanic bishops	Roman bishops	Gothic % of the total
Tarraconensis	23	53	30·25
Carthaginiensis	43	97	30·75
Lusitania	32	41	43·75
Baetica	17	44	27·25
Gallaecia	30	43	41·0
Gallia	10	25	28·5

The first conclusion to which these figures point is that the Goths were far more highly represented in the episcopate than was warranted by their numbers in Spain as a whole. True, we do not know what percentage they formed of the total Spanish population, but it is hard to believe that they formed much more than ten per cent of it; and it is impossible to believe that they made up anything like one-third of the total. Yet they occupied one-third of the bishoprics, taking the centuary as a whole. An ambitious cleric's chance of becoming a bishop was three or four times brighter if he were a Goth than if he were a Roman. The figures are so remarkable that they seem to be the outcome of a deliberate policy. But whose policy?

Again, the figures for Galicia and Lusitania are striking. Even before the conquest of Galicia by the Visigoths in 585 the percentage of Sueves who signed at the Second Council of Braga in 572 was high. Of the twelve bishops who attended that synod no fewer than five bore Germanic names, and one (Mailoc from the British settlement) was Celtic. This local custom continued in Galicia in the seventh century; and at the Third Council of Braga in 675 half the bishops were Germanic. But Lusitania is a greater surprise. Indeed, if we omit from our figures the metropolitan see of Merida (see below) and the remote bishopric of Ossonoba, the percentage of Gothic bishops rises to nearly fifty per cent. Yet there is no reason for thinking that this province was densely settled by Goths, and the reason for their occupying so high a percentage of the bishoprics there is unknown. Although the Goths are thought on archaeological grounds to have settled mainly in the triangle between Toledo, Palencia, and Calatayud (p. 132 above), the sees occupied by Goths do not imply any such restriction. There are only a dozen out of eighty-two sees where a Goth is not known to have been bishop at some time or other.[1] But that Goths did not settle in Baetica in large numbers is confirmed by the comparatively low figure for Gothic bishops there—the lowest of all the provinces. And although Cabra, alone of the Baetican sees, never had a Gothic bishop, so far as we know, four others (Medina Sidonia, Ecija, Seville, Ilipla/Niebla) did not have one until 681.

On the other hand, Goths were seldom appointed to the metropolitan sees. Only one Goth—the famous Ildefonsus (657–67)—is known to have occupied the see of Toledo before the unsuccessful rebel Sisebert; but in the early years of the eighth century Sisebert was followed not only by the Roman Felix but also by the Goths Gunderic and Sindered. As against two seventh-century Gothic metropolitans of Toledo we know the names of thirteen Romans who filled the royal see. At Merida no Goth except Renovatus[2] is known to have succeeded Masona, though the names of seven Romans are known who did so. The only Goth appointed to Seville was the Floresind who signed at XIII, XIV, and XV Toledo. At Tarraco not a single Goth became metropolitan. But three of the five metropolitans of Narbonensis, and three of the eight known metropolitans of Galicia, were Germans. The figures for Visigothic Spain itself are hard to explain, for we might have expected that the kings, if they took any interest at all in the matter of nationality, would have been particularly anxious to have Germans in the metropolitan sees.

If we look at the figures chronologically, we find that the Fourth and Fifth Councils of Toledo mark an innovation. At the first session of Gundemar's council in 610 not a single one of the fifteen bishops who attended bore a Germanic name; and, although four of the twenty-six who were present at the second session were Germanic, three of the four were Sueves and only one was a Goth. At Egara in 614 only one bishop out of fourteen was a Goth, and one out of eight at Seville in 619. But at the Fourth Council of Toledo in 633 a wholly new situation is revealed. Of the sixty-nine bishops who signed its acts one quarter were

---

[1] The exceptions are *Tarraconensis*: Egara, Tarraco, Tirassona; *Carthaginiensis*: Basti, Castulo, Dianium, Urci, Valeria; *Lusitania*: Ossonoba; *Baetica*: Egabra; *Gallaecia*: Asturica; *Gallia*: Carcassona.

[2] *VPE* v. 14. 4.

Germanic. Within a generation of the conversion the Goths had risen in large numbers to high office in the Catholic Church. Now, since a man could not be appointed as bishop before he was 40 years of age, the Germanic bishops at the Fourth Council had presumably been born before 593, and most of them perhaps before the general conversion of 589. It would be interesting, therefore, to know what arguments were advanced for and against the decision to forbid all those 'born in heresy' to be consecrated as bishops. At any rate, at the Fifth Council one-third of the bishops were Germanic; and from then until the last council from thirty-four to forty-two per cent of the bishops were Goths. The policy of promoting Goths to the sees in large numbers, then, began in the years that preceded the Fourth Council. And, if this policy can be ascribed to the kings, it looks as though the pious Sisebut and the less pious Suinthila had initiated it. But it was never abandoned by their successors.

The deputies who were sent to the councils by bishops unable to attend in person consisted (from 589 to 693 inclusive) of twenty-nine priests, twenty-eight deacons, six archdeacons, and six archpriests.[1] In 646 came the first case of a bishop who was represented by the abbot of a monastery; for at Chindasuinth's council Neufred of Lisbon sent the abbot Crispinus as his delegate. His example was followed in 653 by Riccimir of Dumium, who was represented by the abbot Osdulg, and again in 656, when the abbots Martin and Argefred deputized for Waldefred of Mentesa and Egila of Osma respectively. The practice then lapsed until the Councils of 683 and 684, when no fewer than eighteen abbots attended as delegates. Two abbots did so in 688, but the practice is not otherwise known. A majority of the eighteen who attended in 683–4 came from Narbonensis and Tarraconensis; and the suggestion has been made that this may have been due to the disturbed state of those provinces, which had not yet settled down after Paul's revolt ten years earlier.[2]

---

[1] On the position of the archdeacon at this time see Lynch, pp. 27 f. The term *archipresbyter* is used for the first time in Spain of Galanus, archpriest of Ampurias, who represented his bishop, Fructuosus, at the Third Council in 589, and of Hildimir, who represented Lopatus of Orense (Auria) at the same council. In 666 it was made obligatory for all the cathedral churches of Lusitania to have an archpriest and an archdeacon as well as a *primicerius*: Conc. Emerit. 10.

[2] So Bishko, art. cit. (p. 97 n. 4 above), p. 144. I am not wholly convinced by the suggestion but can think of nothing better. Bishko's paper is important, and I regret that his other works have been inaccessible to me.

Differences of nationality appear to have had no influence on the choice of delegates. A Roman or a Gothic bishop would appoint a Gothic or a Roman deputy indiscriminately. In 666 the bishops of Lusitania ruled that if bishops were unable to attend councils in person they must send archpriests or priests as deputies, but not deacons; for a deacon, 'since he is junior to priests, is in no wise permitted to take his seat with the bishops in the council' (p. 282 above). They said nothing of abbots.[1] But other provinces did not feel themselves bound by this ruling; and in fact the majority of bishops who could not attend in person did not trouble to send a deputy at all. Thus only thirty bishops were present in person at Chindasuinth's council in 646. There ought, therefore, to have been over fifty delegates in attendance; but in fact there were only eleven.

Sometimes we catch a glimpse of part of the career of these deputies. Domarius represented Carterius of Arcavica in 633 and 638, on the first occasion as an archdeacon and on the second as a priest. Citronius deputized for Gavinius of Calahorra as a priest in 638 and for Euphrasius as an abbot in 683; and so on. Sometimes a man who first appears as a deputy at the councils reappears as a bishop later on. Thus, the archpriest Galanus represented Fructuosus of Ampurias in 589 but was himself Bishop of Ampurias ten years later; and the archpriest Renatus represented Ermulf of Conimbrica in 633 but was bishop of that see in 638. The archdeacon Genesius represented Voetius of Maguelonne in 589 and himself as bishop sent a delegate to the Fourth Council in 633. The abbot Audebert represented Gudisclus of Huesca in 683 and was himself bishop there ten years later. At Osma the priest Gudiscalc deputized for Bishop Egila in 653 but not in 656 (when Egila's deputy was called Argefred) and reappears as Bishop of Osma in 675.[2] But these cases are few; and to be appointed as episcopal delegate by no means brought with it the probability of promotion in due course to the bishopric.

The metropolitans rarely attended by proxy. The metropolitans of Toledo never did so, and before 683 none of the others did so either (except Merida in 638). Omitting the Fourteenth Council,

[1] Conc. Emerit. 5.
[2] See the relevant signatory lists. The abbot Maximus who represented Stephanus of Merida in 684 may be the Maximus who was metropolitan there in 688 and 693; but the name is so common that this is not quite certain.

where the circumstances were exceptional (p. 240 above), Narbonne sent a deputy in 683, and Tarragona in 688; but no other examples are known. The practice of sending not one but two deputies is found only at the councils of 683 and 684. In all cases of double representation, at least one deputy is an abbot; and in all cases except one, one deputy is a Roman and the other a Goth. Is this a coincidence?

But at the Eighth Council, which met in 653, a new practice began: abbots started to attend the councils, not as deputies for bishops who were unable to attend in person, but in their own right. In 653 a dozen abbots thus signed the minutes; and others did so at the councils that met from 655 to 693. Several of these men attended two, three, or even four councils; and the interesting point has been made that they were all heads of monasteries in or near the diocese of Toledo.[1] The great majority of abbots throughout Spain never won the right to attend the councils. In their introductory addresses to the councils the kings never referred to the presence of the abbots; but these clearly were entitled to take a full part in the discussions, for they signed the minutes. Of the thirty-two individual abbots whose names are known, eight or nine had Germanic names. The proportion of Gothic to Roman abbots is not very different from that of Gothic to Roman bishops.

But a second innovation at the Eighth Council may have been of far greater importance. This was the appearance of a number of court officials (*illustres aulae regiae viri* or *palatii nostri seniores*) who were directed by the king to attend the sessions. They had the right to take part in the discussions (p. 257 n. 2 above), and they signed the minutes at the end. At the Third Council an unknown number of Gothic noblemen had signed the renunciation of Arianism. At the Second Council of Seville in 619 two high officials had been present. These were both of them Goths and *viri illustres*, Sisisclus, who is described as *rector rerum publicarum*, which seems to mean that he was either *dux* of the province of Baetica or Count of Seville, and Suanila, *rector rerum fiscalium*, a financial officer of whose office nothing is known. Again, according to the chronicle of 754, the *seniores* of the palace attended the Fourth Council in 633; but, if so, they did not sign the minutes, and so there is no reason to think that they had the right to speak

[1] Bishko, art. cit. 146 ff.

or vote.[1] At the Eighth Council itself Reccesuinth remarked that
it was an ancient custom for *viri illustres* of the palatine *officium* to
attend the councils;[2] and in this, no doubt, he was right. The
mere presence at the councils of members of the palatine *officium*
was, therefore, no novelty. But beginning with the Eighth
Council it became the regular practice for a varying number of
Gothic officials to sign the minutes of the plenary councils. The
clear implication is that before 653 they had been present as
observers, but in and after 653 they took a more formal and
active part in framing the resolutions than they had done at the
earlier meetings. (In fact, no officials attended the Tenth Council,
which had little of public interest to discuss and which met at a
time when relations between Church and State were strained; and
none attended the Fourteenth Council, which was concerned only
with matters of doctrine.) The questions arise: Why did Reccesuinth initiate this practice? And why did a *varying* number of
officials attend?

Hitherto the Roman bishops had been in a decided majority at
the councils, but with the appearance of the palace officials in 653
the position changed. It is true that a handful of these officials
bear Roman names and may have been Romans; but the officials
would all certainly vote for any policy that the king favoured, and
for the purpose of the argument we may regard them as Goths.
The following table shows in the first two columns not only those
bishops who attended in person but also those who sent delegates; and the nationality of the delegates is disregarded. The
'others' who are included with the abbots are the archpriests,
archdeacons, and *primicerii*, whose function at the councils is
unknown. But they had the right to sign the minutes and were
therefore presumably full members of the councils:

Council of Toledo	Bishops		Abbots and others		Officials	Total	
	Gothic	Roman	Gothic	Roman		Gothic	Roman
VIII	24	36	4	12	18	46	48
XII	13	25	1	3	15	29	28
XIII	32	45	2	7	26	60	52
XV	28	38	2	9	17	47	47
XVI	25	35	1	4	16	42	39

[1] Contin. Isid. Hisp. 20 (ii. 340).   [2] Zeumer, p. 474. 12 f.

Since Roman names sometimes conceal Goths, whereas Romans never bore Gothic names, it is scarcely open to doubt that at all these plenary councils the Goths were in the majority. Before 653 they had always been outnumbered by about two to one. Is it a coincidence that Reccesuinth introduced this change precisely at the time when he was in process of abolishing Roman law and the Roman civil administration? Did he aim to have not only the State but also the Church securely in the hands of Goths? The figures are so remarkable that it is tempting to suppose that he did. But, if so, two further facts are difficult to account for. One is the curious absence of Goths from the metropolitan sees until long after Reccesuinth's death (p. 291 above), though they seem to be in possession of the metropolitan sees somewhat more frequently after 653 than before that date. The other is the total absence of any indication in any of our documents of tensions between Gothic and Roman prelates as such. To be sure, the form in which the canons as a whole are drafted does not throw light on the various points of view that were put forward at each discussion; and in their final and published form it is not out of the question that they may hide differences of opinion between Goth and Roman. But throughout the entire corpus of conciliar documents the bishops never once in any context contrast Roman and Gothic policies, nor do they show any sign of ever having divided on national lines.

Our wisest course, then, might be to leave this important question open.

3. *The Clergy*

The procedure for appointing bishops in Tarraconensis had been clearly laid down at the Council of Barcelona in Reccared's time (p. 43 above); but by 633 abuses were widespread throughout the kingdom. Some men had canvassed for the office, others were guilty of simony, some criminals had been consecrated, and men had been transferred directly from public to ecclesiastical office, like Agapius of Cordoba (p. 110 above). The Fourth Council left these men in office but legislated for the future. Henceforth, no one could be consecrated who had been found guilty of a crime, who had lapsed into heresy or had been baptized in heresy or rebaptized, who suffered from any natural or self-inflicted blemish, or who was twice married or had married a widow or kept a mistress; no slave, no one in the civil or military service, no curial, no illiterate, no man under the age of 40. Every candidate must have gone through the ecclesiastical grades, must not have canvassed for the office, or have paid for it, or have been nominated by his predecessor. The clergy and people of his city must have selected him, and the metropolitan and his suffragans must have agreed to the appointment. He must be consecrated by at least three comprovincial bishops on a Sunday in a city chosen by the metropolitan of his province. Those comprovincials who could not attend the consecration must signify their consent in writing. The metropolitan must be present or must at any rate agree to the appointment.[1]

Three undated documents, preserved at the end of the minutes of the Twelfth Council, contain the pleas of three Goths called Sesuld, Sunila, and Ermigild, in favour of a fourth Goth, Emila. The pleas, which are addressed to 'John and his servants', respectfully ask that Emila should be appointed Bishop of Mentesa. No man can be found in the diocese who is as good as he, and 'all your priests and all the sons of the Church' had met together and asked Sunila to put forward Emila's claim to the see. We appear to have here the announcement to the Metropolitan of Toledo of the unanimous choice of the clergy and people of Mentesa.[2]

But only five years after the Fourth Council had ended the bishops were once again fulminating against simony, which was still extensive. Any bishop who had acquired his see by bribery was now condemned to lose all his goods and to be barred from Holy Communion.[3] In 653 the bishops described simony as being like the Hydra: the more it was cut back, the more it flourished; and at present it was thriving vigorously. Guilty bishops were now declared anathema, excommunicated, and liable to undergo perpetual penance in a monastery. Those who accepted payment were unfrocked, if they were clergy, and were anathema for ever, if they were laymen.[4] The Eleventh Council was more worried

---

[1] IV Tolet. 19. Note Isidore, *De Eccles. Offic.* ii. 5. 13.

[2] No Metropolitan of Toledo called John is otherwise known, nor does Emila ever appear among the signatories at the councils, so that the date of the documents cannot be recovered. It is not even certain that Emila was appointed. The Church in Mentesa was *in desolatione* at the time.

[3] VI Tolet. 4. [4] VIII Tolet. 3.

than ever by simony. It now became the rule that when a bishop was about to be consecrated before the altar of the Lord he was obliged to bind himself by an oath that he had neither paid nor promised to pay for his office. If he would not swear, he was not consecrated. But then, surprisingly, the Council lightened the penalty for those found guilty: after two years of exile and excommunication the guilty bishop was restored to his see.[1]

On none of these occasions did the bishops refer to a fact that everyone knew—that the king often appointed metropolitans and bishops at his own pleasure without consulting anyone, as Chindasuinth had appointed Eugenius II to Toledo in 646. This right of the Crown was never disputed in the seventh century. But at the Twelfth Council in 681, when Toledo was raised to the primacy of all Spain, the bishops were more candid. They then spoke explicitly of the need to notify the king promptly of the death of a bishop so that he might freely nominate a successor if he so wished.[2]

The bishops' incomes and their illegitimate methods of supplementing them continued to be of lively interest to the councils. St. Isidore observed with regret that many men wished to become bishops, not in order that they might do good, but so as to become rich and honoured.[3] Many succeeded. The Fourth Council found that bishops were apt to pocket the endowments of churches which had been constructed in their dioceses by private benefactors, so that the local priests received no salaries and the buildings fell into ruin. Bishops, therefore, were instructed to take nothing from their parishes over and above one-third of the offerings, the rents, and the income in kind (p. 45 above). If in fact they took more, the founders or their relatives might appeal to the provincial synod, which would restore what the bishop had filched.[4] The Ninth Council empowered the bishop to pay the third that he received from one church into the funds of another if he wished to do so.[5] The Lusitanian bishops declared in 666 that the money that the faithful offered in the city church must be collected carefully and delivered safely to the bishop,

---

[1] XI Tolet. 9.   [2] XII Tolet. 6.

[3] Isidore, *Sentent.* iii. 34. 5 (PL 83. 706), 'sed magis ut divites fiant et honorentur'.

[4] IV Tolet. 33. We rarely learn the name of founders; but Eugenius, *carm.* 12, tells us that a Church of St. Felix in Tatanesium (perhaps near Saragossa) was founded by Aetherius and his wife Teudesuintha (a mixed marriage).

[5] IX Tolet. 6.

who would divide it into three equal parts. The bishop himself took one of these, the priests and deacons of the church in question took the second and divided it among themselves according to the rank and dignity of each, while the *primicerius*[1] distributed the third part to the subdeacons and lesser clergy according to the diligence and application that he had observed in each of them. A similar formula was to be employed by the parish priests.[2] At the same council the Lusitanian bishops defined the position of the parish churches in this respect. One-third of the offerings was to go to the bishop; but the bishop was not allowed to remove it from the local church. He was to devote the whole of it to the repair of the church building and to see that the parish priest used it for that purpose. Churches which had no earthly goods were to be repaired at the bishops' own expense. The reason why the bishops were not allowed now to take away their third of the parish income was that the revenues of the cathedral churches were fully adequate for them.[3]

But in 693 it came to the King's ears that a large number of churches were neglected, roofless, and half-ruined. The cause was the exactions or the neglect of the bishops.[4] Egica therefore directed the Sixteenth Council to enact that parish churches, even when very poor, must (if they possessed ten slaves) have a priest of their own; and, if they owned fewer than ten slaves, they must be attached to the priest of another parish. As for repairing the buildings, each bishop must see that they were repaired at the expense of his own third of the parish revenues. The Sixteenth Council, said the King, must lay down penalties for bishops who neglected to see that the appropriate repairs were carried out, and no bishop might touch the parish revenues in order to pay the stipend of other clergy or so as to meet the royal taxes. (This

---

[1] On the *primicerius* see Mullins, p. 167, and add a reference to Conc. Emerit. 10, 14. Church property was managed by the 'steward' (*oeconomus*), and it was found necessary to prohibit the appointment of laymen to this office: II Hispal. 9; IV Tolet. 48. The Council of Seville forbade bishops to undertake the task themselves. See further Fontaine, i. 334 f.

[2] Conc. Emerit. 14.

[3] Ibid. 16, where note 'episcopus . . . cui sua plenissime sufficere possunt'.

[4] XVI Tolet. 5, 'quorumdam consuetudo inordinata sacerdotum qui parrochias ultra modum diversis exactionibus vel angariis conprimunt', etc.; IX Tolet. 2, 'quia ergo fieri plerumque cognoscitur ut ecclesiae parrochiales vel sacra monasteria ita quorundam episcoporum vel insolentia vel incuria horrendam decidant in ruinam', etc. But churches were still being built in Egica's reign: Vives, 312 (14 May 691), and perhaps 157.

phrase is the only direct evidence from the seventh century that Church lands and property were taxed.) Taxes must be paid exclusively out of the revenues of the estates of the cathedral church.[1] Accordingly, the Council dutifully decreed once again that if a bishop took his third of the revenues of a parish church he must use it to repair the church. If he did not take it, he must see that the parish priest used it for this purpose. The Council added, however, that if all churches were in good repair the bishop might freely pocket his third. The rest of the King's proposals were also accepted; and at Egica's suggestion a penalty of two months' excommunication was prescribed for disobedience, though after the expiry of the two months the guilty bishop was free to return to his duties.[2]

The bishops' extortion was no new thing in Egica's day. It had been condemned by the Third Council in 589, when the clergy were encouraged to lay their complaints before the metropolitan.[3] In Chindasuinth's reign the Seventh Council discussed the exceptional rapacity of the bishops of Galicia. In that province they had reduced some churches to extremes of poverty. It was accordingly decreed (as the Second Council of Braga had long ago ruled) that in Galicia the bishops should not be allowed to take more than 2 solidi per annum from each parish church and that monastic churches should be exempt from payment. On his annual visitation the bishop must not have more than fifty persons in his train and must not stay for more than one day in each parish.[4]

All this incessant legislation of the councils, extending throughout the whole of the century, leaves a peculiarly strong impression of the bishops' rapacity and extortion.

A canon of the Eleventh Council illuminates the personal behaviour of some bishops of Carthaginiensis. The Council had heard of bishops who, in a furious temper, would anticipate hearings in the public law courts and would take the law into their own hands. They were guilty sometimes of offences against fiscal as well as private property and occasionally would even commit murder. Sometimes, if not guilty of such crimes them-

---

[1] Zeumer, p. 482. 23.   [2] XVI Tolet. 5.   [3] III Tolet. 20.
[4] VII Tolet. 4; II Bracar. 2. The purpose of the annual visitation was to examine the state of repair of each church and to inquire into the church's income and the manner of life of the local clergy: IV Tolet. 36.

selves, they would incite their subordinates to commit them. The Council laid down two penalties. Bishops who possessed private means would have to make amends to their victims in accordance with the secular law and would in addition undergo excommunication for two weeks. But bishops who owned no property of their own presented a problem. If these were directed to indemnify their victims, they would be likely to do so by making over to them an appropriate amount of their church's property. In law the criminal who could not pay the fines imposed by the courts became the slave of the person whom he had wronged (p. 137 above). But the Eleventh Council explicitly ruled this out in the case of the bishops whom they were discussing. Instead, they laid down a tariff of penances: for a wrong involving a sum of 10 solidi the penalty was twenty days of penance, and proportionately more or less where greater or smaller sums were concerned. Church slaves who committed these crimes were simply handed over to the public courts.[1]

Wamba was obliged to publish on 23 December 675 a law on the improper use of Church funds by the bishops; and he went so far as to do away with the rule of thirty years prescription, a rule that had been recognized in Euric's code and that Reccesuinth described as not so much a law of men as a principle of nature. Indeed, Wamba made it obligatory for a bishop, when he installed a priest in a church, to supply him with an inventory of all the property of that church, including those articles that the bishop himself had removed for safekeeping.[2]

The Eleventh Council also considered cases where bishops had seduced the wives, daughters, nieces, or other relatives of the grandees (*magnates*). Such bishops were dismissed from their office, sent into exile, and excommunicated until they lay on their death-bed. This was also the penalty of those bishops who with malice aforethought murdered or wounded nobles of the court (*primates palatii*) or high-class women or girls. They would also have to submit to the *talio* in cases of wounding, as the secular law demanded, or be handed over as slaves. The canon is explicit in referring only to the nobles and their womenfolk. Nothing was said of bishops who murdered *inferiores* or seduced their wives.[3] This is one of the least edifying of all the canons.

---

[1] XI Tolet. 5.   [2] *LV* iv. 5. 6. For Reccesuinth see ibid. x. 2. 4.
[3] XI Tolet. 5.

The same council heard of bishops who so envied and hated members of their flock that under a pretence of imposing spiritual correction upon them they would try them in 'secret courts' and would impose a penance of such severity as to cause their death. The position was so bad that bishops who wished to punish one of their congregation in future must either discipline him in public or examine the offence and pronounce the penance in the presence of two or three of his brethren.[1]

Not all the bishops of Gothic Spain were as black-hearted as these canons and laws might suggest. At the Tenth Council, which met in 656, a complaint was made by the clergy of the church of Dumium concerning the last will and testament of their late bishop, Riccimir. (He had signed the minutes of the Seventh Council in 646 and was still alive in 653, though apparently too old to attend the Eighth Council in person.) His will was simple, if somewhat extreme: all the rents of his church and its income in kind should be distributed every year in their entirety to the poor; and some of the church slaves were to be freed. These, together with others belonging to himself, amounted to more than fifty persons. It was reported to the Tenth Council that the church now had no income at all, and, moreover, Riccimir had not compensated the church (as he was bound to do) for the slaves whom he had set free. The will, therefore, was declared null and void; and the new bishop, St. Fructuosus, was to decide what was to be done about the freed slaves and the property that had been given to them. He was directed to show moderation in dealing with the matter; and the whole arrangement was ratified by Reccesuinth himself.[2]

There is no need to list the comparatively minor offences of the bishops. The practices of consecrating churches on weekdays and of banqueting in private off the church plate[3] were small affairs in comparison with seduction, robbery, and murder. The last canon in the entire collection which deals with the bishops reports that they would sometimes say a Requiem Mass for a man who was still alive in the hope of bringing him into danger of death and perdition.[4]

---

[1] XI Tolet. 7.
[2] See the *Decretum* appended to the acts of the X Toletanum.
[3] III Caesaraug. 1; III Bracar. praef.; XVII Tolet. 4.
[4] XVII Tolet. 5.

It would be tedious and depressing to list the offences of which priests were found guilty. In Lusitania and Carthaginiensis they would charge a fee for baptizing the faithful, for conferring chrism, and for promotions.[1] (Those who brought the chrism from the bishop to the priest also tried to earn something by making the priest pay for it.)[2] Some priests through ignorance or audacity would offer upon the altar of God bread that was not clean and that had been cut from the loaf which they used at home.[3] Simony was not unknown among them.[4] Any delay in making a new appointment to a see where the bishop had died was still regarded as likely to lead to pilfering of Church property.[5] Priests in Galicia were criticized for compelling the Church slaves to work upon their private fields to the neglect of the lands of the Church.[6] Some priests did not know the Psalter, canticles, hymns, or the baptismal service.[7] Indeed, it was only when priests were being inducted into their parishes that they were given a Book of Offices by the bishop so that they might take up their duties with some instruction and might not offend in the holy sacraments through ignorance.[8] Some priests had taken up arms riotously. Subdeacons had gone so far as to marry. Although priests were as tightly bound to the diocese where they had been ordained as a *colonus* was tied to the place where he had been born, yet they would sometimes flee to another diocese, as Spassandus of Italica had fled to Cordoba shortly before 619. A letter of Braulio of Saragossa contains a graceful apology to a Bishop Wiligild for offering asylum to a monk of his who had fled from his diocese and for ordaining him subdeacon and deacon.[9] Some priests 'erected altars', that is, established parishes, and consecrated churches, though admittedly they did so on the orders of the egregious Agapius, Bishop of Cordoba.[10] Deacons were sometimes so presumptuous as to wear not one stole (*orarium*) but two; and

---

[1] XI Tolet. 8; Conc. Emerit. 9. On promotions cf. II Barcin. 1.

[2] Conc. Emerit. 9; cf. II Barcin. 2, with Séjourné, pp. 101 f. Some priests made their own chrism: see Montanus's letters appended to the acts of II Tolet., and Braulio, *Ep.* 35, in Vollmer's edn. of Eugenius of Toledo, p. 285.

[3] XVI Tolet. 6.   [4] Eugenius, Appendix, *carm.* 23.

[5] XII Tolet. 6, 'ecclesiasticarum rerum nocitura perditio'.

[6] III Bracar. 8.   [7] VIII Tolet. 8.

[8] IV Tolet. 26.

[9] Ibid. 45; VIII Tolet. 6, cf. 7; II Hispal. 3; Braulio, *Ep.* 17 (*PL* 80. 663 f.), with Lynch, pp. 63 f.

[10] II Hispal. 7.

the Fourth Council pointed out that the stole must be white, not multicoloured or gold-embroidered.[1]

The problem of the sexual morality of the clergy, which had been discussed so often in the sixth century, continued to be of absorbing interest to the bishops.[2] But the scandal with which the Tenth Council ended in 656 concerned not a priest but no less a dignitary than the Metropolitan of Braga, Potamius, who confessed at a private meeting of the bishops that he had been guilty of carnal sin.[3] In 655 the bishops of Carthaginiensis passed a peculiarly harsh ruling whereby if any cleric from the bishop to the subdeacon had a child by a free or a slave woman that child became for ever the slave of the church in which his father praised and worshipped God.[4] In 653 the secular power had stepped in, and Reccesuinth ordered the bishop or judge to separate the guilty couple if the male partner was a priest, deacon, or subdeacon: he was to be handed over to the bishop to be punished according to canon law, while the woman was to receive 100 lashes from the judge and be sold into slavery. If the bishop could not terminate the sinful situation, he must inform the synod or the king.[5]

But, like the bishops, the priests and lesser clergy of Spain were probably neither better nor worse than their fellows in Italy and elsewhere. The councils did not discuss honourable and conscientious priests and deacons: they were concerned with the abuses practised by the less honourable. The picture of the clergy which emerges from the conciliar documents is accordingly more sordid than the facts probably warranted. Thus, nothing is said about the parish priest who performed his duties with diligence and sympathy. He is a figure who does not find any place in our sources of information; while an honourable bishop, like Conantius of Palencia (p. 287 above) appears but rarely. It must also be said for the priests, not only that they were set an atrocious example by some of their bishops, but also that they were treated by them with a savage brutality. The Suevic bishops of Galicia were in this respect, as in others, perhaps worse than their Gothic brethren. In 675 the Council of Braga remarked that bishops

---

[1] IV Tolet. 40.   [2] Ibid. 23 f., 42; III Bracar. 4; VIII Tolet. 5.

[3] See the *Decretum pro Potamio Episcopo* at the end of the acts of X Toletanum. The Bishop of Cordoba had been found guilty of a similar sin in Isidore's day: *Epist. Wisig.* 1.

[4] IX Tolet. 10.   [5] *LV* iii. 4. 18.

treated their underlings as cruelly as they would treat brigands. In future, therefore, priests, abbots, and deacons, except when they were found guilty of mortal sins, must not be lashed with the whip, though the reason which the Council gave for its ruling was an unexpected one: if these men had to submit their 'honourable limbs' to the lash, the bishop would lose the respect that was due to him![1] The power of unfrocking priests and deacons had to be removed from the bishops of Baetica in 619. The Second Council of Seville heard that Fragitanus, a priest of Cordoba, had been unjustly unfrocked and exiled at the whim of his bishop, doubtless the Agapius who was now dead and whom the synod condemned in other connections, too. But this was only one case out of many where bishops had exercised 'tyrannical power' in hatred and envy. In future, therefore, only a synod could unfrock a priest or deacon; and in 633 this was assumed to be the national custom.[2]

Whether such bishops and priests as these propagated a high moral tone among the faithful of Spain may perhaps remain open to doubt.

4. *The Church and Slavery*

The Spanish Church as a whole seems to have owned a very large number of slaves. If a parish church possessed fewer than ten slaves it was regarded as 'very poor' and was not entitled to have a priest of its own (p. 299 above). When Riccimir of Dumium freed some of his church's slaves together with some of his own, the total amounted to more than fifty persons, male and female (p. 302 above). But these were not all the slaves owned by Dumium, for Riccimir was able to give other slaves as a gift to his new freedmen; and even then his church is not said to have been left wholly without slaves. Some of the slaves of Dumium were craftsmen (*artifices*), and others were presumably agricultural workers and house-servants.

Yet other slaves were clerics. At the Third Council Reccared directed the bishops to rule that no one should dare to ask the king to give him as a gift clergy from the *familia* of the Treasury: these men must pay their poll-tax and serve the church to which they were tied for the whole of their lives.[3] The same council

[1] III Bracar. 6. [2] II Hispal. 6; IV Tolet. 28, with Séjourné, pp. 106 f.
[3] III Tolet. 8.

remarked that such slaves sometimes had the means to build and endow churches, and it instructed the local bishop in such cases to petition the king to confirm their foundations.[1] Freed slaves of private persons might be admitted to the clergy provided that the owner surrendered all his rights of patronage over them.[2] As for slaves of the Church itself, these might become parish priests and deacons if they were morally suitable; but in 633 the bishop was required to free them before admitting them to orders, a ruling that had to be re-enacted at the Ninth Council in 655. Their property belonged after their death to the church from which they had been freed.[3] In 666 the Lusitanian bishops directed parish priests to select suitable slaves of their churches and to make them their curates.[4] No reason is given for this order.

But the councils of the seventh century were particularly concerned with two matters relating to slavery. These were the maltreatment of slaves by the clergy, and above all the manumission of Church slaves, for the bishops aimed to keep this within narrow limits.

In 666 the Lusitanian synod declared that every bishop 'must put a limit to his anger'. For no fault whatever must a bishop tear off a limb from any slave of the Church. If a major crime were commited by a slave of the Church, the local count (*iudex civitatis*, as he is called here) must be summoned and the slave punished (short of decalvation). The bishop might then give him to one of the faithful or might offer him for sale on the market. Again, when priests fell ill they would sometimes blame their illness upon the slaves of their church, alleging that they had caused it by magic; and they would proceed to torture them. If a priest thought himself to be the victim of such practices in future, he must notify his bishop, who would employ some reliable men from his staff and direct them and the judge to inquire into the matter. If a slave were then found guilty, the bishop would sentence him.[5] The Eleventh Council repeated what had more than once been enacted before: priests and bishops must not shed blood. Accordingly, they must not put anyone to death or cut off his limbs or direct another to do so. Apparently, the clergy did not confine these activities to Church slaves, for the Council also forbade them to treat freemen thus.[6]

---

[1] III Tolet. 15. [2] IV Tolet. 73. [3] Ibid. 74; IX Tolet. 11.
[4] Conc. Emerit. 18. [5] Ibid. 15. [6] XI Tolet. 6.

The bishops devoted much time and thought to the problems raised by freed slaves of the Church. The Third Council had ruled that the Church was to remain for ever the patron of such freedmen and of their descendants;[1] and strenuous efforts were made to enforce this decision. According to the Fourth Council a bishop who freed a slave without retaining his church's patronage over him must compensate the church by presenting it with two slaves of the same merit and property (*peculium*), and the proceedings must be ratified by the provincial synod.[2] Freed slaves and their descendants must inform the bishop of their status so that the church's patronage might not be forgotten through lapse of time.[3] The Sixth Council made this ruling more precise. Whenever a bishop died, all the freedmen of his church along with their descendants should publicly present their charters of manumission to the new bishop as soon as he arrived in the diocese and should renew before the clergy their recognition of their status as freedmen. If they did not do so within a year of the new bishop's consecration, their charters were annulled and they were re-enslaved.[4] But this regulation led to abuses that the Third Council of Saragossa tried to remedy in 691. Avaricious bishops, of whom there appears to have been no shortage in Spain, had taken full advantage of the letter of the law. They instantly enslaved freedmen who had not presented their charters within exactly one year of the late bishop's death; but, instead of declaring such men to be once more the slaves of the Church, they took them as their own private property. In fact, however, the freedmen had been unaware of the existence of the canon of the Sixth Council under which they now found themselves re-enslaved. Accordingly, the Council of Saragossa declared that each new bishop must in future inquire through his clergy and domestics which slaves of the Church his predecessor had manumitted and must invite these freedmen to produce their charters. If they then delayed for more than a year to do so, they were re-enslaved.[5]

Not all slaves showed a due and proper gratitude to the Church that freed them, and a sad case was discussed at the Second Council of Seville in 619. A certain Elisha, a slave of the church of Cabra (Egabra), had been freed by his bishop; and his gratitude

---

[1] III Tolet. 6.   [2] IV Tolet. 68.   [3] Ibid. 70.
[4] VI Tolet. 9.   [5] III Caesaraug. 4.

took the form of an attempt to poison the bishop—he also damaged the church that was his patron. The bishops lost no time in re-enslaving him.[1]

The Ninth Council harshly ruled that no freedman or freedwoman of the Church or their offspring should ever marry a free Roman or a free Goth: the children of such marriages, if they took place, would be the slaves of the Church. The kings did not issue Edicts in Confirmation of the decisions of the provincial synods, and Reccesuinth did not confirm this canon. But twenty years later, on 23 December 675, Wamba published a special law which ratified it.[2]

On no single subject did the bishops spend more time than on the safeguarding of their churches' property; and there is no reason to think that the Gothic bishops were any more backward in this respect than their Roman brethren.

5. *Paganism*

The Fourth Council condemned clergy, including bishops, who consulted soothsayers of various kinds, and harshly sentenced them to live out their lives in penance in a monastery. The Fifth Council banned all attempts to foretell the fate of the reigning sovereign.[3] Chindasuinth followed this up with legislation directed against persons who consulted soothsayers on the life and death, not only of the king, but of anyone else: they and the soothsayers were to be whipped and along with their possessions were to become the property of the Treasury. Guilty slaves were to be tortured and sold overseas (the only example in the seventh-century laws of such a punishment). He also re-enacted the legislation of Alaric II against magic, and thereby made Alaric's penalties applicable to Goths as well as to Romans; but, like the bishops at the Third Council (p. 100 above), he removed the death penalty which Alaric had imposed. Those convicted of the magical practices listed by Alaric were punishable with 200 lashes, suffered decalvation, and were then exhibited in public so as to deter others.[4] Persons who had recourse to *sortilegi* and diviners, and those who practised magic, were prohibited by Chindasuinth from testifying in the courts, like persons convicted of homicide,

---

[1] II Hispal. 8.   [2] IX Tolet. 13 f.; *LV* iv. 5. 7. Note Conc. Emerit. 20.
[3] IV Tolet. 29; V Tolet. 4.   [4] *LV* vi. 2. 1; 4; cf. 5.

theft, poison, rape, or perjury.[1] We have seen, too, that the bishops of Lusitania ascribed magical practices to their priests' slaves (p. 306 above). Erwig found later on that his own judges believed that they could not discover the truth unless they first consulted diviners. In future, they and anyone else who consulted soothsayers were to be subject to the penalties laid down in Chindasuinth's law, while the soothsayers themselves would receive no fewer than 500 lashes, the highest number ever mentioned in the codes.[2]

All this legislation of the first half of the century dealt only with magic and divination. Only one pagan festival was mentioned. The Church ruled that the Kalends of January was to be a day of fasting so as to counteract the pagan ceremonies associated with that day.[3] The 1st of January was celebrated among pagans with mimes and feasts. Even Christians would sometimes join them in dressing up in the skins of wild animals or in women's clothing. They consulted augurs. They danced. They sang in mixed choirs of men and women (the worst offence of all, according to St. Isidore), and they got drunk.[3] But the Twelfth Council considered other matters than augury, magic, or New Year celebrations. The worshippers of idols, those who venerated stones or lit torches and worshipped sacred trees or fountains, were to be hunted out by the local bishop and judge—ever since 589 the two had been obliged to combine in exterminating paganism—and their idolatries stopped. Evidently the guilty were often slaves, for they were to be whipped and brought in chains before their masters, who would be required to undertake on oath that they would prevent such practices in future. If the masters refused to do this, the guilty pagan was to be handed over to the king, who would present him to whomsoever he pleased, while the masters were excommunicated and lost their guilty slave without compensation. If free persons were involved in this crime, they were excommunicated for ever and exiled; but the bishops explicitly ruled out the death penalty.[4] A specific case—but only one—of

---

[1] Ibid. ii. 4. 1. *Sortilegi* were apparently soothsayers who opened the Bible at random and inferred a good or a bad omen from the first words that they chanced to read: McKenna, p. 113.

[2] *LV* vi. 2. 2.

[3] IV Tolet. 11; Isidore, *De Eccles. Offic.* i. 41 (*PL* 83. 774 f.); M. Nilssen, *Opuscula Selecta*, i (Lund, 1951), 214 ff., 234 ff.

[4] XII Tolet. 11.

pagan worship has been recorded. According to Valerius of Bierzo (Bergidum, north-west of Astorga in Carthaginiensis),[1] some of the local people worshipped at pagan shrines on the top of a high mountain near Astorga. Christians destroyed these shrines and built in their place a church dedicated to St. Felix the Martyr. Valerius gives no hint that the authorities intervened: the destruction of the shrine was the result of a spontaneous outbreak of the Christian laity.

But paganism is attested later still, and once again bishops and judges were directed to co-operate in eradicating it. In 693 Egica ordered his bishops to enact that all offerings given to idols by 'rustics' or others were to be made over to the neighbouring church. Any bishop who neglected to exterminate such practices in his see was to be driven from office and to spend a year in penance, after which he might return to his duties. During the year when he was away, another person would be installed by the king to enforce the law. The bishops accordingly dealt with worshippers of stones, fountains, and trees, together with augurs, *praecantatores*, and others. All bishops, priests, and judges were to hunt them down and punish them, no matter to what class they belonged; and all their offerings were to go to the local churches. The Sixteenth Council then confirmed the penalties proposed by the King. If anyone opposed the bishops and judges he would pay 216 solidi to the Treasury if he were a *maior persona*; while if he were an *inferior* he would be lashed 100 times, would suffer decalvation, and forfeit one half of his goods to the Treasury.[2]

It is clear that pagan practices could be found, not only in the countryside and not only among the slaves, on the eve of that day on which another religion established itself in Spain.

[1] Valerius, *Replicatio*, p. 115 in Sister C. M. Aherne, *Valerio of Bierzo, An Ascetic of the Late Visigothic Period*, The Catholic University of America, Studies in Mediaeval History, vol. xi, Washington, 1949. On the site of Bergidum see Sister F. C. Nock, *The Vita S. Fructuosi*, vol. vii in the same series, Washington, 1946, p. 132 n. 9.

[2] XVI Tolet. 2. This is the only passage in the acts of the seventh-century councils where the distinction, which is so common in the laws, is drawn between *maiores personae* and *inferiores*.

XIII · CONCLUSION

THERE are vast areas of sixth-century Spanish history where our ignorance is total. We know nothing of the conditions in which the Visigoths settled in the Roman cities. In which cities did they settle? Did they live intermingled with the Romans or did they keep to themselves in separate streets and quarters? Did they serve on the city councils? Were they socially acceptable at Roman dinner-tables, or were the Romans in their eyes at once dangerous and contemptible? Cases of intermarriage are known: were they welcomed by the relatives on either side, or was one or other party an outcast from the people of his or her nationality? Or did such a marriage, although illegal, pass without comment? The piety of a Catholic Visigothic bishop might seem something of an oddity (p. 25 above): but how did he come to be appointed at all? Was there prejudice against him simply because he was a Goth? What was the reaction of his fellow Goths to his joining the Roman Church? Again, what interest did a Visigothic landowner show in his estate? What knowledge had he of the agricultural techniques that were applied on it, or of the social organization that obtained on it? Did Roman landowners visit him and (as happened in the seventh century) write him their elaborately vapid letters? Were the rank and file of the Gothic population enriched or impoverished by the settlement in Spain, and did their fortunes increase or decline as the century progressed?

We cannot even begin to answer these and countless other questions, not least questions relating to the composition and function of the king's immediate entourage, the *aula regia*. But for all that, we can answer some of the questions with which we set out (p.v above). What we know is enough to suggest how the Visigoths solved the problems raised by the necessity to govern an almost wholly alien people, a people who had reached a decidedly higher level of material development than themselves. The basic principle of government was that of complete separation—or as nearly complete as could possibly be attained—of the two nationalities. The idea was not devised by some Visigothic political genius: it was the natural outcome of the system whereby the Romans had settled their federates in the provinces. Each nationality was served freely by its own priests in its own churches. It took its lawsuits to its own courts to be decided by its own judges under its own laws. Two civil services functioned side by side, the one manned by Goths, the other by Romans. Inter-marriage was banned by law, though not very effectively. Within wide limits, until the conversion to Catholicism, Goths and Romans alike were free to believe and to publish as they pleased. The system was maintained unswervingly by the Gothic kings until the death of Leovigild in 586. No Gothic legislation earlier than the time of Reccared bears any trace of thinking in terms of a state that is neither Roman nor Gothic but a fusion of the two.

But in no sense could this system of separation be called a form of apartheid or segregation designed to enable one nationality to exploit and humiliate the other. They lived on equal terms. True, the highest officials surrounding the king were probably Goths almost to a man (though the chief financial offices required the experience and knowledge which only a Roman could possess in the sixth century). But the work of assessing and collecting the taxes locally was in the hands of Romans; and it was exclusively Romans who assessed the Goths and, if necessary, forced them to pay their taxes. It is hard to resist the impression that throughout Western Europe it was only in Ostrogothic Italy, and perhaps in the Burgundian kingdom in the Rhone valley, that the old Roman population were left to live their old form of life so unrestrictedly as under the Visigothic kings. But the Franks absorbed the Burgundian kingdom in 534, and the Byzantines overthrew the Ostrogoths in 552. In Spain alone of the western provinces did Roman life continue with the minimum of change and inter-ference throughout the sixth century and half of the seventh.

In fact, it might be said that throughout its history until Reccesuinth's time the kingdom was under the joint administration and control of the barbarian and the Roman nobility. The Gothic nobility governed the Gothic population, and the Roman nobility the Roman population, while the Gothic king and his highest officials decided policy for them all. And it can hardly be said that the position of the Roman landowners was in general very much inferior to that of their Gothic counterparts. Not a single case is recorded with certainty from the sixth century of a revolt of the Roman nobility against Gothic rule. In the middle of the seventh century some Romans may have aimed to reach the throne; but, if so, their efforts failed, and none but Gothic kings governed Spain throughout the period of the kingdom. It is true that the reforms of Chindasuinth and Reccesuinth may have been caused by tension between Goths and Romans; but we have seen something of the difficulties and obscurities that surround those reforms.

The fact is that after the original Gothic settlement in Spain, which took place in the main immediately before and after the year 500, no Gothic king before Reccesuinth is known to have legislated against his Roman subjects. There is not the slightest indication in any of our sources that any king tried to depress the position of the Romans relatively to that of the Goths. On the contrary, we have seen that with the conversion to Catholicism Reccared gave much power, or at any rate influence, in secular matters to the plenary Church councils; and these councils were overwhelmingly Roman until the middle of the seventh century. Roman noblemen may have regretted that the highest official positions in the kingdom were for the most part closed to them; but otherwise they had little to complain of under the barbarian regime.

Between 507 and 711 there were two periods of rapid transition in Visigothic history. The first was the reign of Reccared (586–601), which brought the conversion of the Goths to Catholicism: never again were Goths and Romans to be divided by religious differences. These years also saw for the first time the enactment of laws that bound the whole population of Spain, Goths and Romans alike; though the complete unification of the legal system was not completed for over half a century. And Reccared's reign also saw the disappearance of the Gothic style of dress and of Gothic forms of art, and their replacement by Roman ones.

The second great crisis of our period came about in the reigns of Chindasuinth and Reccesuinth (642–72), when the Roman system of provincial government was abolished, and the Roman city councils lost all, or nearly all, their importance. This was the period when the Goths appear to have almost completely ousted the Romans from the government of the country, and they may even have interfered drastically, though this is far from certain, with the government of the Church. At first glance these innovations would seem to indicate antagonism, even extreme hostility, between the Goths and the Romans of the kingdom; but we have seen that it is hardly possible to discover in our sources any confirmation of such an hypothesis.

Now, these changes give rise to a question of equal importance and obscurity. What now distinguished a Goth from a Roman? What made a Goth aware of his Gothicism? If after Reccared's reign he did not differ from his Roman neighbour in his religion, his art, or even his dress, in what sense was he not himself a Roman? We know that he did not feel himself to be a Roman: he was, if anything, increasingly conscious of being non-Roman. The very basis of Reccesuinth's reforms was precisely this distinction: the reforms look as though their purpose was to elevate the Goths at the expense of the Romans.

It does not seem possible to solve this problem, and speculation is not likely to be fruitful. But (we may ask) what was the ultimate fate of the language of Ulfila? Did all sixth-century Visigoths speak Latin, however haltingly? Gothic was not only a spoken, but also a written, language in mid-sixth-century Italy. But the Visigoths had lived in the Roman Empire for two or three generations longer than the Ostrogoths: could Leovigild and his Court still write Gothic? And if they could, on what occasions did they do so?

It is hardly possible to doubt that, if Gothic was the language of the Arian liturgy in Spain, most Goths still conversed in their own language at least until 589. And if that guess is correct perhaps we may hazard another. How did a sixth-century Spanish litigant know whether to take his case to a Gothic court or to a Roman one? Roman cases were heard in Roman courts under Alaric's code, and Gothic cases were heard in Gothic courts under the codes of Euric and Leovigild. But neither Alaric nor (in their surviving laws) Euric nor Leovigild ever defines a Goth or a Roman. The codes take it for granted that a man was obviously a Goth or obviously a Roman. But what made it obvious? How was it obvious to a judge that the litigants before him were in the right court, Goths in a Gothic court and Romans in a Roman court? Is it possible that there was in practice no problem because the distinction was a linguistic one? Goths still spoke Gothic and were therefore instantly recognizable as Goths, while the native speaker of Latin was at once shown to be a Roman. But was this still true in Reccesuinth's day? The interest of these questions is profound; but even more profound is the difficulty of answering them.

Of the kings who reigned in Spain after Athanagild, scarcely one (if we leave aside those who sat upon the throne only for a year or two—Liuva II, Reccared II, and Tulga) was lacking in vigour and initiative; and they form a remarkable contrast to the Western Roman Emperors who followed Theodosius the Great. Even Witteric fought with vigour to expel the Byzantines from Spain; and the others showed a noteworthy energy either in their legislation or in repelling the hostile neighbours of their country. Not a single foreign power was able to invade Spain throughout the seventh century, if we disregard the occasion in 631 when Sisenand bribed the Franks to help him to overthrow Suinthila. The kings were responsible, too, for the foundation of three cities within their kingdom, Recopolis and Victoriacum, which Leovigild built, and Ologicus, which was founded in Vasconia by Suinthila. No other Germanic kings of the period are known to have built new cities. The successive editions of their law code became models for more than one people living north of the Pyrenees. We know little of the kings' individual personalities; but as kings they were one and all men of administrative and military capacity. And for many years in the middle of the century (642–80) they were not afraid to keep the Church at arm's length.

But it is not always possible to admire the aims at which these kings directed their energies. How, for example, can we account for their savage legislation against the Jews, legislation that was enacted by king after king and confirmed by council after council for over a century? Chintila first formulated the policy of exterminating Judaism, and he was followed with relish by all his successors except Chindasuinth and Wamba. The first dreadful climax of the persecution was reached under Reccesuinth, who made the breach of any one of his ten frenzied laws against the Jews a capital crime, for which the 'criminal' was to be put to death in peculiarly degrading and repellent circumstances. Although this uniform penalty was modified after some thirty years, a second and even more fearful climax was reached in the hysterical speech of Egica to the Seventeenth Council, with its talk of a 'plot against Christendom' organized by 'world Jewry' and betrayed by 'confessions' of some of the 'plotters'. If the bishops' ruling was enforced in practice, there followed the physical enslavement of Spanish Jewry. But why? Jews could be found in several classes of Spanish society. Some of them traded inside Spain. Others were overseas traders. Others were farmers, whose production of wool happens to be mentioned (*LV* xii. 3. 6) and who in some cases owned vineyards and olive-groves. Other Jews were poor men, who owned no property at all (*LV* xii. 3. 17). Although they are mentioned all too often in the laws, they are not known to have been very numerous in Spain. They cannot be said to have occupied any very important position in the society of the kingdom. Moreover, there is no indication in our sources of any popular feeling against them. Indeed, stringent laws had to be passed to prevent laymen and even clergy from protecting them and from ignoring the laws. To attack the Jews seems to have been by no means a way of winning favour among the people at large. And this hideous persecution was not wholly paralleled in the other Catholic kingdoms of the period. Among the Franks and the Byzantines there was nothing that resembled a sustained, systematic, and nation-wide policy of extermination. To the Arian predecessors of the Catholic kings of Spain, we may suspect, such a policy would have seemed unthinkable. Whatever the reason for the persecution, it may have contributed to the utter destruction of those who initiated and enforced it. There is a late, but far from improbable, tradition that when the Muslims landed at Gibraltar in 711 they received valuable help from the enslaved Jews, finding in each city a group of them to welcome and assist them.

It is scarcely possible to deny that throughout the seventh century, except in Erwig's reign, the bishops of Spain were supine supporters of the kings. To be sure, there were great men among them. There was Isidore of Seville. There were Braulio, Eugenius the poet, Taio, and Julian of Toledo, who were considerable figures. Their contribution to Latin literature far surpassed anything that was produced elsewhere in the contemporary West. In the field of canon law the Spanish bishops at this date had no match. As theologians they could hold their own against the Pope himself. And once, though only once, they protested against the barbarities of the kings. Led by Isidore at the Fourth Council, they protested against Sisebut (after he was safely in his grave) and against his policy of forcible conversion of the Jews—and promptly went on to ratify what he had done. At later councils, as the kings laid before them their increasingly brutal laws against the Jews, the bishops were careful to point out without fail that they had confirmed the laws on the orders of the most serene and pious prince. Was this a protest, however feeble? They were not free agents, we might say, and they dared not oppose those grim monarchs openly. But what then of Erwig's reign? Whatever the truth about the circumstances in which he had reached the throne, he was certainly deep in the debt of the nobility and the bishops. At the first Church council of his reign, then, we may expect to find the true policies of the bishops themselves. And so we do. The penalties laid down in Erwig's laws against the Jews were to be enforced by the bishops (p. 236 above). But bishops and priests had been repeatedly warned not to shed blood or cause others to shed it. Accordingly, the death penalty for breach of the anti-Jewish laws was removed; but the persecution itself was intensified. Reccesuinth had not interfered with Jews who did not celebrate the Jewish rites, or at any rate with those who were not discovered to have done so. But this attitude was too negative for the bishops when they had a free hand under Erwig. Forgotten now was the protest of the Fourth Council. The Jews were obliged, one and all, to have themselves baptized. And at that same council, the Twelfth of Toledo, not one reform was initiated by the bishops in the public interest. Whatever may have been their contribution throughout the century to the development of the liturgy and canon law, the part which they played in public affairs was ignoble.

We cannot hope to understand the reasons for the sudden collapse of the kingdom unless we first analyse the military and moral power of the Arabs who overthrew it; and such an analysis lies outside the scope of this book. But there are at least two clear indications that, even before the Arabs appeared on the scene, the Visigothic state machine was breaking down. The more forceful of these is the late-seventh-century legislation on the army. Wamba's campaign in Gallia Narbonensis shows that in 673 the central government was still capable of putting a large and effective army in the field. But the same king's army law shows equally clearly that there was no organized frontier defence on the boundaries of Septimania and the Frankish kingdoms. When the Franks launched a raid there was no frontier army ready to repel it. The local commanders, when they heard of a foray, had to set about assembling an *ad hoc* force to deal with it; and so desperate was their need of freemen that even persons who happened by chance to be in the vicinity of the raid—or within 100 miles of it— were obliged to report to the local commander and join in the defence. The local commanders could not even be sure of calling up all those who were liable for service; and a man had to report for duty when he heard of the raid, even if no one called him up. It is not easy to imagine a state of greater unpreparedness than this. The shortage of manpower was such that even the clergy were liable for military service (though in view of their active support of Paul in 673 this may not have been unwelcome to all of them). Now, the *thiufae*, which had formed the basic units of the army in the sixth century, still existed in the seventh, for Recce-suinth and Erwig retained some of Leovigild's laws relating to them. But they did not publish a single new regulation about them, and practically all the laws that they retained from Leovi-gild's code dealt with desertion. The implication is that the *thiufae* had become ossified and had lost much of their significance. Yet these were the units in which the bulk of the free Gothic population had long ago served; and it is one of the most signifi-cant points known about the seventh-century army that those free classes who were neither nobles nor slaves have almost disappeared from it. The major part of the seventh-century army, in fact, consisted of the landowners' conscripted slaves.

The second great indication of decline is Egica's law on escaped slaves. The King himself asserts that slaves had taken to flight on a massive scale in every part of Spain, and his object in publishing the law was to recover them and to put them to work again. But his only means of achieving this aim was the establish-ment of a scale of punishment for the free population, clergy as well as lay, that is unparalleled in all the rest of the codes. The very fury of the law suggests the King's powerlessness.

It is not surprising, then, that the few documents which we possess indicate a calamitous decline of law and order in the later seventh century. At any rate, life in Galicia and north-western Carthaginiensis as depicted in the works of Valerius of Bergidum was unpleasantly violent. Some monks cut the throat of Valerius's friend John, a deacon. The hermit himself throughout his life was constantly menaced by brigands, who frequently attacked him in his first hermitage; and when they stole a horse with which he had been presented they were themselves robbed by other brigands. A second John, a companion of Valerius, was so cruelly beaten by brigands that he had to leave his friend and return home. But he recovered from his injuries, only to be ordained priest against his will. In the end a rustic decapitated him as he lay in prayer before the altar of a monastic church. These and other glimpses of life in an outlying part of Spain, which are given by the works of Valerius, suggest that conditions were more un-settled than the conciliar documents prepare us for. There is very much less violence and public disorder in the *Life* of St. Fructu-osus, which deals with an earlier part of the century and which is the only comparable document that we possess. It may be that law and order were tending to break down in north-western Spain as the century progressed.

There does not seem to be enough evidence at present to enable us to describe the factors that brought this state of affairs into being. But if in fact slaves were in flight in all the provinces and if few freemen could be found in the royal forces, where the majority of the troops were conscripted slaves, King Roderic had little hope of victory when he faced the conquerors of Persia and Syria, Alexandria and Carthage.[1]

---

[1] For evidence (which I am not competent to discuss) of currency chaos during the closing years of the kingdom see P. Grierson, 'Visigothic Metrology', *Numismatic Chronicle*, Ser. vi, vol. xiii (1953), pp. 74–87, a paper which suggests that the coins have much to tell us about Visigothic history.

APPENDIX

THE BYZANTINE PROVINCE

JUSTINIAN's conquests in the far West deserve the most careful study. This was the last and most obscure stage in his grandiose effort to restore the old Roman Empire. Yet not a single Byzantine writer speaks of the conquest. Procopius closed his incomparable historical works with the very year in which Liberius's expedition sailed; and Jordanes, who alone informs us that Liberius was the commander-in-chief, knew only that the fleet was being fitted out.[1]

1. *The Extent of the Conquest*

Which areas of the peninsula did Justinian's army occupy? There are two fixed points: Cartagena and Malaga. That the East Roman forces occupied these two cities is certain.[2] It is also certain that Medina Sidonia (Asidona)[3] was taken by them, for Leovigild recaptured it from them in 572.[4] Justinian also took Sagontia, for this city eventually fell to the generals of King Witteric (603–10).[5] It was pointed out early in the eighteenth century that Sagontia is not Siguenza among the Celtiberians, a region far beyond the reach of the Byzantines, but Gisgonza or Gigonza, the first town north of Asidona on the Roman road to Seville.[6] But, if the Byzantines held Asidona and

---

[1] On Byzantine Spain see P. Goubert, 'Byzance et l'Espagne wisigothique', *REB* ii (1944), pp. 5–78; idem, 'L'administration de l'Espagne byzantine', ibid. iii (1945), pp. 127–42; iv (1946), pp. 70–134. Unless otherwise stated my references in this Appendix are to the last of these. There is little of interest in F. Görres, *Byzantinische Zeitschrift*, xvi (1907), pp. 515–38. For what the Byzantines knew of Spain see A. Freixas, 'España en los historiadores bizantinos', *Cuadernos de Historia de España*, xi (1949), pp. 5–24.

[2] See H. Gelzer, *Georgius Cyprius* (Teubner, 1890), pp. xxxiii f. (Cartagena), xxxiv–xxxvi (Malaga); Goubert, pp. 83–5 (Cartagena), 95–8 (Malaga).

[3] This is the correct form of the name: Miles, p. 103, with literature on the site.

[4] Jo. Biclar., *s.a.* 571 (ii. 212), where the *milites* are, of course, the Byzantines, a common usage at this time: examples in Gelzer, op. cit., p. xxxiii n. 1. Despite Gelzer, p. xxxvi, and Goubert, p. 108, there is no reason to think that the Byzantines ever recovered Asidona. The absence of the city's bishop from the Council of 589 and from the First Council of Seville in 590 proves nothing in this connection.

[5] Isidore, *HG* 58 (ii. 291), 'milites quosdam Sagontia per duces obtinuit'.

[6] So J. de Ferreras, *Historia de España*, iii (Madrid, 1716), p. 289. I have not searched to see whether others had noticed this before Ferreras. On the town see K. Miller, *Itineraria Romana* (Stuttgart, 1916), p. 156, and his Map 49.

Sagontia as well as Malaga, we may infer that they had seized the whole of the province of Baetica south of a line drawn from Malaga to the mouth of the Guadalete.

They also occupied Cartagena, the capital of the province of Carthaginiensis; and evidently a column marched inland from that city and took Baza (Basti). Dealing with the first campaign of Leovigild, that of 570, John of Biclarum says that the King 'laid waste places belonging to the towns of Baza and Malaga after repelling the Byzantine soldiers'.[1] The natural meaning of his words is that Leovigild ravaged the *territorium* of the two cities but was checked by the fortifications of the cities themselves and was unable to recover either of them.[2] And yet at the Third Council of Toledo in 589 one of the bishops present was Theodorus of Baza.[3] Evidently, then, the Byzantines lost the town at some date before 589. But after Leovigild's operations at Asidona in 572 we know of no Visigothic campaign against the Byzantines before Reccared's reign; and the truth may be that the chronicler's desire for brevity has led him to write a somewhat misleading entry— Leovigild ravaged the territories of Baza and Malaga, and, while he failed to take Malaga, he did succeed in capturing Baza.[4]

Justinian's army, in fact, seized not only the south of Baetica but also a wedge of land in the province of Carthaginiensis, running westwards into the interior from Cartagena; and no doubt it follows that they held the whole coastline between Cartagena and the mouth of the Guadalete.[5] How far inland did their possessions extend?

The city of Cordoba has bedevilled discussion of the extent of Justinian's conquests. It is almost universally believed that this great city

---

[1] *s.a.* 570 (ii. 212), 'Leovegildus rex loca Bastetaniae et Malacitanae urbis repulsis militibus vastat et victor solio reddit [=redit]'.

[2] So Gelzer, op. cit., p. xxxii n. 1; cf. Görres, art. cit. 520 n. 1.

[3] Mansi, ix. 1001, 'Theodorus Bastitanae ecclesiae episcopus'.

[4] So Goubert, pp. 89, 95. There are two alternative interpretations of John's words: (*a*) the Byzantines never occupied Baza itself but only some of its *territorium*, and it was this occupied portion that Leovigild attacked; and (*b*) Athanagild had already occupied Baza itself but not the whole of its *territorium*, the part which still remained in Byzantine hands being the part which Leovigild attacked. Both these hypotheses seem rather complicated and neither affects the argument. Isidore, *HG* 49 (ii. 287), says no more than that Leovigild recaptured *quaedam castra* from the Byzantines.

[5] Other readers of Mansi's *Concilia* besides myself may have been misled by his inclusion (x. 451) of a Bishop of Adra (Abdera) among the signatories of the First Council of Seville in 590. If true, this would have important implications. But (*a*) there is no other reference to a Bishop of Abdera in Visigothic times, and (*b*) in Vives's text Peter is Bishop, not of Abdera, but of Illiberris. This, too, is impossible, since one Stephanus has already signed for Illiberris in this list. Migne's text makes Peter Bishop of Acci, which again is impossible, since Acci (Guadix) is not in Baetica. We must await the appearance of a scientific text before deciding the matter.

fell into his hands. It has even been regarded as the first capital of the Byzantine province.[1] But, if the Byzantines held the triangle Cartagena–Malaga–Cordoba, they must also have held the cities lying within the triangle—Ecija (Astigi), Cabra (Egabra), Guadix (Acci), and Granada (Illiberris); and scholars have not hesitated to believe that this was so. And yet there is no independent evidence for a Byzantine occupation of any of these places. And if Cordoba was never Byzantine there is no reason for thinking that any of these cities was at any time in the Emperor's hands.

In fact, there is no evidence that the Imperial forces ever occupied Cordoba, and there is positive evidence that they did not. Early in the reign of King Agila, Cordoba was in revolt against the central government at Toledo (p. 16 above). Our authorities mention this revolt on no fewer than three occasions, and never once do they suggest that the Byzantines were in the city. The date of the outbreak of the revolt is unknown. Agila marched against the city some considerable time before the rebellion of Athanagild broke out.[2] Now, since Agila came to the throne in December 549 and Athanagild's revolt began in 551, Agila's Cordoban expedition can be dated to the campaigning season of 550. The citizens managed to rout him, and he fled to Merida, which seems to have remained his headquarters until the end of the reign—as well it might, seeing that events in the south dominated his remaining years.

Secondly, the Chronicle of Saragossa reports that Athanagild made repeated but vain attacks on the city about the years 566–7, and that he also attacked Seville, which fell to him.[3] This information is not difficult to interpret in so far as it concerns Cordoba. The implication is that Cordoba was still in revolt in 566–7 and that Athanagild failed to crush it. But what of the capture of Seville? The city had been Athanagild's headquarters at the beginning of his rising against Agila. Did he lose it to the Byzantines or to the rebels of Cordoba? There is no hint at the presence of Byzantine soldiers in Seville at any time in this or any other period of Byzantine history; and the chronicler's coupling of Athanagild's actions against Seville and Cordoba as though they formed a single campaign suggests that the rebels of Cordoba had gained ground towards the west and that Seville momentarily joined them.[4]

[1] So Gelzer, op. cit. xli; cf. Goubert (1944), p. 8; (1946), p. 81, etc.
[2] Isidore, HG 46 (ii. 286).
[3] Chron. Caesaraug., s.a. 568 (ii. 223), 'hic Athanagildus Hispalim civitatem Hispaniae provinciae Baeticae sitam bello impetitam suam fecit, Cordubam vero frequenti incursione admodum laesit'. The date given by the chronicle, 568, cannot be right, as Athanagild died somewhat before 14 June 567.
[4] Stroheker, pp. 136, 213, has no doubt that the Byzantines occupied Seville. J. B. Bury, History of the Later Roman Empire (London, 1923), ii. 287, more wisely leaves the question open.

Finally, in 572, immediately after his two campaigns against the Byzantines, Leovigild, we are told, seized by night the city of Cordoba, which had long been in a state of rebellion against the Goths, and killed the 'enemy' in it.[1]

This narrative is consistent with the view that the citizens of Cordoba were in revolt against the government at Toledo in the reign of Athanagild and the early years of Leovigild as they had been in Agila's day. But it is not consistent with the view that the Byzantines had occupied Cordoba and were now slaughtered in it by Leovigild. Our source is a careful and accurate writer, and if he had meant that Cordoba had fallen to the Byzantines he would not have described the city as 'long in rebellion against the Goths' (*diu Gothis rebellem*). The Byzantines were invaders or 'soldiers' (*milites*) or Romans, but they were not rebels. It would be possible, of course, to suppose that there was more than one revolt at Cordoba in the years 550–72; but that would merely multiply hypotheses, and it is more likely that the city had been in a state of rebellion continuously throughout the entire period from Agila's reign to Leovigild's early years.

2. *The Conquest*

Agila ascended the throne in December 549. In 550 he was disastrously defeated at Cordoba. In 551, when he was thus weakened, Athanagild rebelled against him.[2] Justinian's army was sent from Constantinople in the spring of 552 to help the rebel, and it landed in Spain no later than June or July of that year, as Stein showed.

Now, the speed with which the Byzantines arrived in Spain throws some light on Athanagild's position. He would not have asked Justinian for aid unless the situation had been desperate; for to invite help from Byzantium was to invite disaster. He cannot have been unaware of the fact that the Byzantines had entered both Africa and Italy as a result of just such a dynastic struggle as he had himself started in Spain, or of the further fact that the consequences of Byzantine intervention had been calamitous both to the Vandals and to the Ostrogoths. Only four or five years earlier an army of the Visigoths themselves had been cut to pieces at Ceuta by the Byzantines (p. 16 above); and the fact that the Visigoths had occupied Ceuta in the first place suggests that even in Theudis's reign there were fears that Justinian might attack Spain, a possibility which the occupation of Ceuta was probably intended to prevent. Nor again can Athanagild have been unaware that, when the

---

[1] Jo. Biclar., *s.a.* 572 (ii. 213), 'Cordubam civitatem diu Gothis rebellem'; and note *caesis hostibus*, not *militibus* or *Romanis*.

[2] On the words *tertio anno* in Isidore, *HG* 46 (ii. 286), see Stein, p. 562 n. 2. We can say only that the rebellion broke out between 13 January and 13 December 551.

Byzantines landed in Africa and Italy, they were not at all interested in settling the native dynastic disputes: they were concerned solely to establish and extend their own power. All this we may take as certain—Spain was no backwater in the sixth century, out of touch with events in the rest of the Mediterranean.

With the examples of Africa and Italy before him, then, Athanagild nevertheless appealed to Justinian to intervene in Spain. It looks as though, when he decided to rebel, Athanagild had under-estimated Agila's power and that his position was critical after his first campaign against the King. On the very morrow of the outbreak of the revolt he realized that his cause was hopeless unless he could receive help from abroad. Hence, although aware of the risk that he was running, he felt obliged to take the fateful step of negotiating with Justinian in the autumn of 551 or the winter of 551–2. This argument is supported by an important event. In 552 Agila had won the initiative from him. In 552 it was not Athanagild who sent an army to attack the King in Merida: it was the King in Merida who sent an army to attack Athanagild in Seville.[1]

But might we not assume that Justinian had instigated the revolt in the first place in order to have a pretext for interfering in Spain? The speed with which his army reached the rebel might seem at first sight to suggest that he had done so. In fact, however, if the Emperor could have chosen his own time for sending an expedition to Spain, he would hardly have selected the year 552. This was the year of his last great effort against the Ostrogoths in Italy. After prolonged preparations Narses was sent to Italy, reinforced to the utmost, and there he fought the final campaign against Totila, a campaign which culminated towards the end of June in the decisive Byzantine victory at Busta Gallorum. If Justinian had had a free choice he would hardly have chosen the very moment of Narses's all-out effort at which to instigate a rebellion and divert invaluable forces to Spain. The fact that he sent a force there is, if anything, a further indication of Athanagild's weakness in 552. If the Emperor had waited for two or three years—and this would have been convenient for him—there might have been no Athanagild for him to 'assist'. In fact, our sources give not the slightest hint that the revolt was engineered from Byzantium; and it is far more likely that in 551 Athanagild decided on his own initiative, and without any prompting from abroad, to take advantage of Agila's rout at Cordoba in the previous year and to try to dethrone the defeated and disgraced King.

So far we have had our feet on the comparatively solid ground of Spain. Let us now put out to sea and watch Liberius, the Imperial

---

[1] Isidore, loc. cit., 'exercitum eius [i.e. of Agila] contra se Spalim missum'.

commander, as he approaches Spain. He presumably knows that his ally's headquarters are in Seville and that Agila and the royal forces are lying at Merida.[1] This information has reached him, perhaps from the Imperial tribune at Ceuta (p. 15 above), more probably from Athanagild himself. It follows that Liberius can scarcely fail to land in southern Baetica, either at Malaga, whence a Roman road runs to Seville,[2] or somewhere near the mouth of the Guadalete, whence the approach to Seville lies through easier country. But we may guess that he cannot land at Cartagena. To put his forces ashore at Cartagena, a vast distance away from the scene of the civil war, would be a crude strategical mistake. And to divide his small army—it is agreed on all sides that Justinian can have spared only a few men for this expedition —by landing some of them in southern Baetica and others at Cartagena would be a blunder on the Patrician's part. It looks, therefore, as though the Byzantine landing in Baetica took place earlier than the landing in Carthaginiensis. This is only a hypothesis, but we shall see that, if we accept it, we shall find it easier to answer one or two other questions.

When the Byzantines landed in Spain they found that Agila had sent an army from Merida to Seville to attack the rebel. Accordingly, without delay they marched up-country from the coast and reached Seville in time to join forces with Athanagild and to defeat the royalist army.[3] The battle at Seville may be dated to August or September 552. It by no means finished Agila's power to resist.

For two whole campaigning seasons, those of 553 and 554, neither side could make substantial headway against the other. But then in 555 the Visigoths realized that they were in process of destroying themselves by carrying on a civil war when the Byzantines were actually present in their country. Hence the followers of Agila murdered their king in his headquarters at Merida in March 555 and rallied to support Athanagild. United at last, the Goths now attacked the Imperial forces.

How are we to explain this change of front? After holding out for no less than three years, why did the King's supporters now desert him? Why did it take the Visigoths no fewer than three campaigning seasons to grasp the fact that the Byzantines might overwhelm both parties alike? The real aim of the Imperial forces, of course, was not to help Athanagild but to conquer Spain. But in three years they had achieved little more than their initial landings in the south of the peninsula. There is no certain evidence that Athanagild had even allowed them to enter Seville itself (p. 322 above). Why then did their presence in Spain suddenly alarm the Goths early in 555? Why not in

---

[1] Ibid.　　[2] Miller, op. cit., Map 19, cols. 175–6.
[3] Isidore, loc. cit., 'virtute militari'.

553 or 554? Evidently, the invaders made some forward move at the beginning of 555 which in the opinion of the Visigoths transformed the situation. But what was that move?

The failure of the Byzantine forces to advance in the early stages of the attack on Spain can hardly have surprised Justinian. He cannot have expected his tiny expeditionary force to overrun the entire Iberian peninsula at one blow. Liberius himself was an administrator and a diplomat rather than a soldier. He was no Belisarius, no Narses. His work, whatever it may have been, was completed within a year, for he had already returned to the Eastern capital by the beginning of May 553, when he attended the Fifth Council of Constantinople.[1] The original purpose of the expeditionary force, then, was presumably to prevent Athanagild from disappearing from the scene altogether, and to occupy and to hold a bridge-head from which a greater effort could be made when more forces became available.

The Imperial armies were fully committed against the Ostrogoths in 552, and the invasion of Italy by the Franks and Alamanni in the following year left them with few forces to spare in 553 and 554. But at the beginning of 555, for the first time since the landing in Spain, the tension in Italy was greatly relaxed; and this was a time when reinforcements could well have been sent to the far West. The spring of 555, then, is precisely the time when we might have expected a forward move by the Byzantines in Spain; and the action of the Visigoths in killing Agila and in closing their ranks against the invaders at precisely this moment suggests that such a forward move was in fact made. Is this a coincidence? I would suggest that at the beginning of March 555 Imperial troops from Italy or elsewhere suddenly descended from the sea upon Cartagena, captured the city, marched inland at least as far as Baza, which also fell to them, and so tried to link up with their forces in southern Baetica, which were still presumably in the neighbourhood of Seville or Merida.

This guess is not unsupported by evidence. It is a fact that the Byzantine occupation of Cartagena was not a peaceful one. If the Imperial troops had originally been admitted to the city by Athanagild as his allies, their relations with the citizens would presumably have been cordial. Citizens who had already declared for Athanagild, and who were now under his control, would welcome the arrival of his allies. And there is no reason why the Byzantines should not have been well disposed towards them. But that is not how it turned out. The evidence given by Leander of Seville, who was in Cartagena at the time, shows that the landing of the Byzantines in his city had resulted in the flight of Leander himself and his family and many other citizens

[1] Mansi ix. 197, 198. See Stroheker, p. 212.

from Cartagena. At a later date he had for some reason sent his brother Fulgentius back to the city for a while; but he regretted having done so, and as long as Fulgentius was away he constantly feared for his safety. Leander speaks with peculiar bitterness about conditions in the Byzantine province, and he strongly advised his sister never to go there. His mother, too, would never return to Cartagena: she was afraid to go.[1] The inference is that the Byzantine landing was a hostile one, and that the native population, even the Catholics among them, resented it vehemently. Leander had no doubt that freedom had been extinguished in his native city.[2]

But a hostile landing in Cartagena can hardly have taken place in 552. If it did so, it would follow that the Byzantines landed in southern Baetica to help Athanagild, but instantly filched from him one of the greatest cities in what he hoped would one day be his kingdom. They supported him with one hand and robbed him with the other. Whatever the loyalties of the citizens of Carthaginiensis, such an act would certainly have driven them into the arms of Agila. And, if Cartagena had been forcibly occupied in 552 against the wishes of both Agila and Athanagild, that would have been the moment for the Visigoths to unite, rather than the spring of 555, when on any other theory the Byzantines made no move whatever. Again, the Byzantine expeditionary force being a small one, Liberius can hardly have intended to challenge both Agila and Athanagild at the very moment of his arrival in Spain. And that he did nothing of the kind is confirmed by the alliance between the Byzantines and Athanagild which lasted for three years.

Several considerations, then, perhaps give some support to the theory of a double Byzantine landing in Spain—in southern Baetica in June or July 552 and at Cartagena early in March 555. First, the theory accounts for the decision of Agila's followers to murder the King, and to do so in March 555 rather than at any other date, even though the King had managed to hold his own against the united armies of the rebels and the invaders, in spite of his defeat at Seville. Secondly, the theory accounts for the hostility shown by the native population of

---

[1] *Regula*, 21 (PL 72. 892), 'tu quaeso, cave, soror Florentina, quod mater timuit' etc. Incidentally, the mother used to say, 'peregrinatio me Deum fecit agnoscere, peregrina moriar; et ibi sepulchrum habeam, ubi Dei cognitionem accepi'. This does not necessarily imply that she was only converted to Christianity after arriving in the Visigothic kingdom: see Arevalo in PL 81. 102, 'verba Leandri ita intelligi posse, ut mater eius maiorem pietatis quam prius habuisset sensum in exilio perceperit'. It is clear from the passage that Florentina was strongly tempted to cross the frontier.

[2] Ibid., 'ut nec liber quisquam in ea [sc. patria] supersit'. That the reference is to the Byzantine landing is in my view undeniable: for discussion of the point see Fontaine, i. 5 f.

Cartagena towards the Imperial army. Although the common Catholicism of the Byzantines and the Hispano-Romans did not form a political bond between them (pp. 28f. above), yet we should not have expected the flight of substantial citizens from Cartagena as a result of the landing, or the extreme hostility which Leander expresses, unless the occupation of this part of the coast had been an act of aggression. Finally, we can now make sense of the policy and aims of Justinian. If the Emperor's ultimate purpose was to conquer Spain—and there is no doubt that it was—how can we account for his inactivity after the initial landings? On our theory the Emperor grasped his opportunity as soon as it presented itself, established a secure bridge-head, and then, when forces were released by his victory in Italy, he set about the task of overrunning the peninsula. It was only in 555 that his plans began to go awry.

If this reconstruction of the events is near the mark, we must go on to suppose that later in 555 the united Visigoths, now headed by Athanagild, were able to prevent the two Byzantine columns from joining hands. The cities lying west of Baza—Acci, Illiberris, and Astigi—are not known ever to have fallen to the Imperial army; and if in fact any of them did so, Athanagild was able to recover them.

At all events, the ability of Agila to hold out against his internal and external enemies for so many years is noteworthy, particularly in view of the loss of the royal treasure at Cordoba a few years earlier. He was an unpopular king, according to both Gregory of Tours and Isidore. Gregory says that his rule was harsh.[1] Isidore says that in his 'contempt' for the Catholic religion—the sort of phrase that had been used of no earlier king since Euric—he profaned the tomb of the blessed martyr Acisclus in the course of his campaign against Cordoba.[2] But Agila's oppressive measures were directed against the Catholic Church (p. 36 above). The armed forces of the kingdom at this date, however, were composed for the most part of Visigoths and not of Romans. Hence, the hostility shown by Agila towards the Catholics would alienate few Goths and would have little effect on his military strength. Thus it is not difficult to reconcile Agila's stubborn resistance to Athanagild and the Byzantines with our Catholic authorities' statement that his government was oppressive. It was harsh towards the Catholics but not towards the Visigoths, who held out loyally in his support. But even so, there is no evidence that the Spanish opposition to him, which Athanagild headed, was in any sense based on the Catholic and Roman elements in the population. Sectarian differences played little part in the politics of the time, as we have repeatedly seen; and even if this had not

---

[1] HF iv. 8, 'cum populum gravissimo dominationis suae iugo adterriret'.
[2] HG 45 (ii. 285), 'in contemptu catholicae religionis'.

been the case, there was little reason why Catholic Roman Spaniards should fight to replace the Arian Agila by the Arian Athanagild.

3. Administration

The Spanish possessions of the Byzantine Empire together with the Balearic Islands were formed into a province and were known as Spania; but Ceuta (Septem) belonged to the province of Mauretania II.[1] George of Cyprus, who lists the cities of the various provinces of the Eastern Empire at the end of the century, gives only one entry for Spania, and a surprising one it is—'Mesopotamians'! The term has baffled all attempts at interpretation. The province was centred on Malaga and Cartagena, but at the time of Reccared's death, and long before it, the province did not extend north of the Sierra Nevada.

It was governed by the Master of the Soldiers of Spain (*Magister Militum Spaniae*), whose office is first heard of in 589–90 but had doubtless been created by Justinian. The Master was a Governor-General directing the civil as well as the military administration. He was on a par with the Masters of Italy and Africa, and was in no sense subordinate to either of them. Accordingly, when the Patrician Caesarius was negotiating a peace treaty with King Sisebut about 614, he communicated directly, and not through any superior, with the Emperor Heraclius.[2] Four of the known Masters bore the title of Patrician,[3] and there is no reason to doubt that the fifth, the Comitiolus mentioned by Gregory the Great, had this rank also: he certainly had the status of *gloriosus*, which indicates the highest level among the Byzantine aristocracy.[4]

Whether Cartagena or Malaga was the provincial capital is unknown. It is usually assumed that Cartagena was the metropolis because the inscription of the Master Comenciolus was found there. But the inscription, which is written in Latin, merely records that Comenciolus repaired the city gates, and throws no light on the question.[5] Nor do we know the site of the mint which Justinian established in his Spanish

[1] George of Cyprus, 672–4, ed. Honigmann.

[2] *Epist. Wisig.* 3–6 (pp. 633 ff.)

[3] Apart from Comenciolus and Caesarius, we hear of two from Isidore, *HG* 62 (ii. 292), 'auxit eo proelio virtutis eius [=Suinthila] titulum duorum patriciorum obtentus, quorum alterum prudentia suum fecit, alterum virtute sibi subiecit'. These two men were successively, not simultaneously, governors of Spain.

[4] Jones, ii. 530, 543 f.

[5] Vives, 362, which ends with the words, 'Comenciolus sic haec iussit patricius / missus a Mauricio Aug. contra hostes barbaros, / magnus virtute magister mil. Spaniae. / sic semper Hispania tali rectore laetetur, / dum poli rotantur dumq. sol circuit orbem. / ann. VIII Aug., ind. VIII'.

possessions and which continued to issue coins until the last days of the province.[1]

Pope Gregory the Great interfered in the ecclesiastical affairs of Spania with a vigour which no Pope showed towards the Visigothic Church. In 603 he had to deal with the deposition of two bishops in the province, Januarius of Malaga and Stephanus of an unknown see. The former had not only been deposed by his fellow bishops but had been forcibly removed from his church and sent into exile. Stephanus, too, had been exiled. Gregory thought it possible that the bishops who had consecrated the successors of the two exiles might have done so through fear of the Master Comitiolus.[2] Accordingly, he gave rigorous instructions that Comitiolus should make good any losses that he had wrongfully caused to the two deposed bishops; and he added that, if Comitiolus should have died in the meantime, his heirs must make good the losses. It is hard to believe that he would have dealt so overbearingly with a governor of the contemporary King Witteric.

The Pope also directed Licinianus of Cartagena not to ordain ignorant men; but Licinianus replied that in that case no one would be eligible for ordination and there would certainly be no bishops in the province.[3] No provincial synod of the Catholic Church is known to have met in the province throughout its history; and no Byzantine bishop ever attended any Church council which met across the frontier in the Visigothic kingdom. But the bishops of the province evidently followed events in the kingdom closely, for Severus, Bishop of Malaga in 580, was quick to write a pamphlet against Vincentius, Bishop of Saragossa, who had been persuaded to subscribe to King Leovigild's brand of Arianism (p. 84 above). But the frontier was not otherwise closed, and private visitors could cross it freely. When Leander of Seville writes about visits or projected visits by members of his family, he foresees objections; but these objections do not include the possibility of obstruction by Byzantine officials on the provincial frontier. He knows of no regulations that would prevent his sister Florentina from going over the border. His brother Fulgentius was able to cross it when he wished to do so. His mother could have gone had she been willing to make the journey.[4]

Byzantine artistic and architectural styles, however, did not cross this frontier into Visigothic Spain; and, although such styles did make their way even into remote parts of Gothic Spain, they did not reach

[1] P. Grierson, 'Una ceca bizantina en España', *Numario Hispanico* (1955), pp. 305–14. For another coin from this mint see Tomasini, p. 142.

[2] *Ep.* xiii. 47. It would be interesting to know what exactly is meant by the statement that Stephanus was heard 'ab episcopis alieni concilii', *Ep.* xiii. 50 (p. 416. 11). And why has Stephanus no metropolitan or patriarch, ibid. (p. 416. 23)?

[3] Idem, *Ep.* i. 60.   [4] Leander, *Regula*, 21 (PL 72. 891 f.)

it from Spania.[1] The two churches that have been excavated there—
that at Aljezares, a little to the south of Murcia[2] and that at San Pedro
de Alcantara near Malaga,[3] reproduce the architectural style, not of
Constantinople itself, but of Byzantine Africa. In the mainland part of
Spania, as distinct from the Balearic Islands, the specifically Byzantine
art is unknown.[4]

4. The End of the Province

At some stage in his career Athanagild made a treaty (*pacta*) with
Justinian in which the Visigothic frontier with Spania was delimited.
There are two possibilities for the date of this treaty;[5] and unhappily
there seems to be no evidence to enable us to decide between them.
Either (i) this was the original treaty which Athanagild signed in the
winter of 551–2 and in which he gave away Spanish territory in return
for military assistance against Agila, or (ii) it was a treaty ending the
state of war that existed between Athanagild and Byzantium after 555.
The treaty was signed before 565, for it was struck with Justinian, who
died in that year.[6] We hear of it only from a letter of Pope Gregory to
Reccared.

Between the death of Agila in 555 and the accession of Reccared in
586 the Byzantines do not appear to have been able to push their
frontier forward. Indeed, they lost ground both to Athanagild and to
Leovigild. But in the reign of Reccared the position was different. The
inscription of Comenciolus (p. 329, n. 5 above) dates from the year
beginning on 1 September 589 and tells how the Patrician rebuilt a
double gate in Cartagena with high towers, porticoes on either side,
and a vaulted chamber above; and Comenciolus prays that Spain may
rejoice in such a governor as he himself had been 'as long as the poles
rotate and as long as the sun goes round the earth'. There is no reason
to think that this was anything other than a routine repair: no Visigothic invasion of his province can have been feared at that date, but
Comenciolus does refer to the Visigoths as 'barbarian enemies'. There

[1] H. Schlunk, 'Relaciones entre la península ibérica y Bizancio durante la época
visigoda', *Archivo español de arqueología*, xviii (1945), pp. 177–204, at p. 203.

[2] C. de Mergelina, 'La iglesia bizantina de Aljezares', ibid. xiv (1940–1), pp. 5–32;
H. Schlunk, *Ars Hispaniae*, ii (Madrid, 1947), p. 230.

[3] Ibid.   [4] Schlunk, art. cit., esp. 186 ff.

[5] So Stein, p. 563 n. 1. There is a discussion of the *pacta* in Goubert (1944), pp. 55–
8. He apparently dates the treaty (ibid. 9 f.) to the first year of Athanagild's rebellion.

[6] If it was from the Byzantines that Athanagild recovered Seville shortly before
his death (p. 322 above), then it would follow that he was at war with East Rome
throughout the entire reign of Justinian and even after Justinian was dead. In that
case the *pacta* would have to be dated to 551–2. But it is not certain that Seville had
ever fallen to the Byzantines.

is a hint in Isidore of Seville that later on during this reign the Byzantines were often on the offensive against the Goths;[1] and Isidore does not claim that they were repulsed or that Reccared won substantial successes against them. The inference would seem to be that the Imperial forces gained ground at the expense of the first Catholic king.

This advance of the East Roman forces appears to form the context of the letter of Gregory that tells us about the treaty between Athanagild and Justinian. Reccared had asked the Pope to write to the Emperor Maurice for a copy of the treaty: he wanted some information about the legitimate Byzantine frontier in Spain. The Pope's answer is dated to August 599. He says that the relevant archives had been destroyed accidentally in a fire before Justinian's death in 565, but that, if the treaty were found, it would in his opinion have been unfavourable to Reccared. That is to say, if the terms of Athanagild's treaty had been strictly enforced in 599, the Byzantines would have gained more than the Goths.[2] Some Byzantine territory had been recovered for the Goths by Leovigild—Medina Sidonia, for example (p. 60 above)—and this territory would have been described as Byzantine in any treaty signed by Justinian. The Byzantines, on the other hand, had won ground from the Goths in Reccared's reign, but the Byzantine gains were slighter than those of Leovigild. Hence, if the old treaty had been enforced, the Goths would have been the losers. Accordingly, Gregory urges the King to keep the peace which was congenial to him.

Reccared was certainly on the defensive when he wrote to the Pope; and the point of Gregory's reply to the King is that he should resign himself to the losses that he had just suffered and should refrain from going to war to recover them. What is hard to understand in the Pope's letter is why he tells the King to look for his own copy of the treaty. If Reccared had been able to find his own copy, he would hardly have needed to see Maurice's copy. And, if the treaty told against Reccared, why does the Pope urge him to publish it? At all events, there is no hint at the scene of the hostilities.

There can be no question of Byzantine expansion in the reign of Witteric. On the contrary, this King attacked the province with some vigour, and his generals won some success (p. 158 above). King Gundemar, if Isidore reports his actions in chronological order, attacked the Basques in the campaigning season of 610 and the Byzantines in that of 611 (p. 160 above) with little result. The great Visigothic advance came in the reign of Sisebut, when the Empire of Heraclius could spare little energy for the remote West. About 614–15

[1] *HG* 54 (ii. 290), 'saepe etiam et lacertos contra Romanas insolentias et inruptiones Vasconum movit'. I take *insolentias* to imply some aggressive action on the part of the Imperial forces: it balances the *inruptiones* of the Basques.
[2] Gregory, *Ep.* ix. 229.

the King fought two campaigns against the Imperial forces and captured some of their cities.[1] It is certain that one of these was no less a place than Malaga, for among the bishops who attended the Second Council of Seville in 619 was Theodulf of Malaga.[2] What, then, of Cartagena? When Isidore published his *Etymologiae* Cartagena had been 'overturned' by the Goths and 'reduced to desolation'; and it was not the only town to meet with such a fate.[3] The destruction of Cartagena was so complete that the city disappears from history for the rest of the Visigothic period. So far from being re-established as a metropolitan see, it actually ceased to be a bishopric (though some texts give it a solitary appearance at the Eleventh Council of Toledo). Its place was taken by Bigastrum, which was first represented at Gundemar's Council in 610 and thereafter sent its representatives to the councils very regularly. This utter ruin of Cartagena at the hands of the Goths themselves throws a little light on the circumstances in which they captured it.

It was notorious in the ancient world that the Germanic peoples were ineffective in attacking walled cities; and the criticism was as justified in the sixth and seventh centuries as it had been in the first.[4] Accordingly, in the barbarian kingdoms the Germans sometimes made a practice of destroying the fortifications of any city that happened to fall into their hands. On occasion they would even destroy the city itself. But they did so only when there was some fear that a revolt of their Roman subjects, or an attack by an invading Byzantine army, might lead to the city's recapture by the Romans: it could then be used by them as a stronghold from which attacks might be launched on the barbarians themselves. Hence, Geiseric tore down the walls of the African cities except those of Carthage;[5] and impressive archaeological evidence for this practice has been found at Tipasa, where the city walls were systematically destroyed by the Vandals and the towers overturned.[6] In Italy during the last years of the Ostrogothic kingdom Witigis burned down Pisaurum and Fanum, and he reduced the height of the walls by one half so as to make them useless to the Romans, should the Romans ever recover them.[7] But it was Totila who applied this policy on an extensive scale. He razed the walls of Beneventum,

[1] Isidore, *HG* 61 (ii. 291); idem, *Chron.* 415 (ii. 479); Chron. Isid. Hisp. 15 (ii. 339).

[2] Mansi, x. 570.

[3] *Etym.* xv. 1. 67, which is confirmed by Fredegar, iv. 33, 'et plures civitates ab imperio Romano Sisebodus litore maris abstulit et usque fundamentum destruxit'.

[4] E. A. Thompson, *The Early Germans* (Oxford, 1965), pp. 131 ff.

[5] Procopius, *BV* iii. 5. 8; 15. 9.

[6] J. Baradez, *Tipasa: Ville antique de Maurétanie* (Algiers, 1952), p. 69, with Plate 42.

[7] Procopius, *BG* vii. 11. 32; 25. 7.

Naples, Spoletium, and Tibur.[1] At one time he even planned to level
Rome itself with the ground; and he was afterwards criticized by the
Ostrogothic nobles for not destroying the city completely.[2] Similarly,
the Lombards destroyed the walls of those Italian cities which they
feared the Byzantines might reoccupy and use as bases against them, or
they even destroyed the cities themselves.[3]

From this it would seem to follow that Cartagena fell to the Visigoths and was completely destroyed by them at a time when there was
still a powerful force of Byzantines in Spain that might one day
reoccupy the city. The Visigoths would have had no occasion otherwise for destroying so thoroughly one of the great cities of their
country, a former provincial capital. Since they are not recorded as
having treated Malaga in the same way, and since Malaga reappears as
a bishopric and (under Sisenand) as a mint, we must infer that Cartagena fell before Malaga was captured. Presumably, when Malaga was
taken, the Byzantines were now so weak that there was little possibility
of their recovering the city. And so there was no need to destroy it.

Malaga was recaptured by the Goths before 619, when its bishop
attended the Second Council of Seville, and Cartagena, we may think,
had fallen before it. But the Byzantines had not yet been completely
expelled from Spain when Suinthila ascended the throne in 621. Now,
if the Byzantines had already lost Cartagena and Malaga, what towns
did they still occupy in 621? Isidore says that they then held more than
one city;[4] but, if so, their names are unknown. At all events, in one
swift campaign Suinthila finally cleared the Byzantines from the
shores of Spain.[5] It would be more than ordinarily interesting to know
where he won his victories.

[1] Procopius, *BG* vii. 6. 1; 25. 11 (Beneventum); 8. 10 (Naples); 23. 3 (Spoletium); 24. 32 f. (Tibur); cf. 24. 29.
[2] Ibid. 22. 6 ff.; 24. 3, 9, and 27.
[3] Paul. Diac., *HL* iii. 18 (Brixellum); iv. 23 (Patavium levelled to the ground);
iv. 28 (Cremona razed); iv. 45 (Opitergium destroyed); etc.
[4] *HG* 62 (ii. 292), 'urbes residuas, quas in Hispaniis Romana manus agebat,
proelio conserto obtinuit [sc. Suinthila]'.
[5] Idem, *Chron.* 416[b] (ii. 480). 'celerique victoria'.

INDEX

b. = bishop.   m. = metropolitan.   s. = son.

PRINTED IN GREAT BRITAIN
AT THE UNIVERSITY PRESS, OXFORD
BY VIVIAN RIDLER
PRINTER TO THE UNIVERSITY